Performance Theory

"Reading *Performance Theory* by Richard Schechner again, three decades after its first edition, is like meeting an old friend and finding out how much of him/her has been with you all along this way."

Augusto Boal

"It is an indispensable text in all aspects of the new discipline of Performance Studies. It is in many ways an eye-opener particularly in its linkage of theater to other performance genres."

Ngũgĩ wa Thiong'o, University of California

"Richard Schechner has defined the parameters of contemporary performance with an originality and insight that make him indispensable to contemporary theatrical thought. For many years, both scholars and artists have been inspired by his unique and powerful perspective."

Richard Foreman

"Schechner has a place in every theater history textbook for his ground-breaking work in environmental theater in the 1960s and 1970s and for his vision in helping to found the discipline of performance studies."

Rebecca Schneider

"Richard Schechner is the master teacher and the master conversant on the transformative power of performance to both performer and spectator, at its deepest level. *Performance Theory* is the essential book which brilliantly illuminates the world as a performance space on stage and off."

Anna Deavere Smith

Routledge Classics contains the very best of Routledge publishing over the past century or so, books that have, by popular consent, become established as classics in their field. Drawing on a fantastic heritage of innovative writing published by Routledge and its associated imprints, this series makes available in attractive, affordable form some of the most important works of modern times.

For a complete list of titles visit
www.routledgeclassics.com

Richard
Schechner

Performance Theory

Revised and expanded edition, with a
new preface by the author

 London and New York

Essays on Performance Theory published 1977 by
Ralph Pine, for Drama School Specialists

Second edition first published 1988
by Routledge
270 Madison Ave, New York, NY 10016

First published in the United Kingdom 1988
by Routledge

First published in Routledge Classics 2003
by Routledge
270 Madison Ave, New York, NY 10016
2 Park Square, Milton Park, Abingdon, Oxon OX14 4RN

Reprinted 2005, 2006

Routledge is an imprint of the Taylor & Francis Group, an informa business

© 1988, 2003 Richard Schechner

Typeset in Joanna by RefineCatch Ltd, Bungay, Suffolk
Printed and bound in Great Britain by
TJ International, Padstow, Cornwall

Library of Congress Cataloging in Publication Data
A catalog record has been requested for this book

British Library Cataloguing in Publication Data
A catalogue record for this book is available from the British Library

ISBN10: 0–415–31455–0
ISBN13: 978–0–415–31455–8

To my brothers
William   Arthur   David
To my sisters
Danice   Judi   Norma

A highlands Papua New Guinea man takes a break from dancing (see chapter 4, "From ritual to theater and back: the efficacy–entertainment braid").

CONTENTS

PREFACE TO THE ROUTLEDGE CLASSICS EDITION

With two exceptions, I wrote the essays in this book between 1966 and 1976. It was a very busy decade. My interests had dramatically shifted from theater to performance and from aesthetics to the social sciences. Today I write "performance," but at the time I wasn't sure what performance was. I knew it was more than what was appearing on the stages of New York, London, or Paris. From the advent of Happenings in the early 1960s to the vibrant enactment on American streets of what Victor Turner termed "social drama" – the freedom movement led by thousands of ordinary people but iconicized in the eloquent words and enacted testimony of Martin Luther King, Jr. – I discovered that performance can take place anywhere, under a wide variety of circumstances, and in the service of an incredibly diverse panoply of objectives.

My experiences as a civil-rights and anti-Vietnam War activist, and a sometime participant-creator of Happenings, pointed me toward a whole new range of research. I "found" social and cultural anthropology extremely useful because in ethnographies and theoretical treatises anthropologists treated the actual lived behavior of people performatively. Taking a cue from Erving Goffman's 1959 breakthrough book, *The Presentation of Self in Everyday Life*, I sensed that performances in the broad sense of that word were coexistent with the human condition. Goffman did not propose that "all the world's a stage," a notion which implies a kind of falseness or put on. What Goffman meant was that people were always involved in role-playing, in constructing and staging their multiple identities. By means of roles people enacted their personal and social realities on a day-to-day basis. To do this, they deployed socio-theatrical conventions (or "routines") even as they devised personae (sometimes consciously, mostly without fully being cognizant of what was happening) adapted to particular circumstances. What Turner added was that these performances often took the form of rituals and social dramas.

Anthropology led me to a deepening interest in non-western cultures. At first, I read about these. But beginning with a six months' journey in 1971–2 to almost every nation in Asia except Laos, Cambodia, Vietnam, and China, I began to travel in earnest – and gather the notes and experiences that comprise the basis for the essays in this book and in the book that followed, *Between Theater and Anthropology* (1985). Also at that time, I read Charles Darwin's *The Expression of the Emotions in Man and Animals*. This, combined with my interest in rituals, led me to the work of ethologists such as Julian Huxley and Konrad Lorenz, then later to Irenaus Eibl-Eibesfeldt. At the same time, people were learning about "body language" and a whole range of expressive behavior outside of spoken or written words. In Asia, I saw dancing and music that was both expressive and dramatic. This helped me connect ethology to sports, play to ritual, and art to role-playing.

I became more and more interested in what links cultures and species. I looked into pre-written history, drawn to the Paleolithic "cave art" of southwestern France and northern Spain. I studied similar phenomena from Africa, the Americas, and Asia. I soon saw that this was not illustrative art; that the caves were not galleries for the exhibition of visual arts but theaters, sites of ritual enactments. I assumed that these rituals were not only efficacious, but that they also gave pleasure to the performers (and, if there were any, the spectators). Of course, I could not listen to the music or witness the dances or storytelling enactments that may have taken place in the Paleolithic sites. These were silenced centuries ago. But I believed that these sites could only be understood performatively. I wondered whether the shamans of Siberia, Korea, or Native America were not up until very recently practicing similar kinds of performances. Furthermore, I suspected that some of the utopianism of youth culture I felt around me in the America of the 1960s and 1970s was also connected to these earliest of human performances. In other words, I began thinking holistically. I shared these interests and the holistic approach with Jerzy Grotowski, whose artistic work had taken Europe and North America by storm in the 1960s. My own artistic work was influenced by Grotowski. There was a healthy flow back and forth between my artistic work and my scholarship.

At the same time, throughout the period of this book, I continued an extremely active artistic life and academic life. I founded groups, I directed plays, I wrote scripts. I taught, first at Tulane University (1962–7) and then at New York University (1967–present). I co-founded The New Orleans Group (1964–7), was a producing director of The Free Southern Theater (1964–7), and the founding director of The Performance Group (1967–80). Also, from 1962 to 1969 I edited the *Tulane Drama Review* (later, *TDR, The Drama Review*). As editor, I came in contact with, and vetted, writings and ideas from all over the world. And I was instrumental in bringing into existence first the concept of "performance studies" and later, at the end of the 1970s, the world's first university Department of Performance Studies, at New York University, officially so-designated in 1980. In other words, my education never stopped.

The journey of this book is an account and a trace of one intense phase of that education – a journey that did not abandon the performing arts but placed them in active relation to social life, ritual, play, games, sports, and other popular entertainments.

At the outset of this Preface I mentioned that two essays included here were not written in the 1966–76 time span. "Magnitudes of Performance" and "Rasaesthetics" are later works chronologically but linked conceptually to the other essays in this book. "Magnitudes" began as my contribution to the 1982 World Conference on Ritual and Theater that I co-convened with Victor Turner. "Rasaethetics," conceived and reworked throughout the 1990s, appeared in print in *TDR* in 2002. These two essays are of a piece – part of my attempt to deal with the complex relation between performance and the emotions. The essays, though of a later date than most in this book, belong in this volume because in them I wrestle with notions of expressive universality versus cultural particularity.

I confess that I believe both in universals and singularities. How can that be? In a nutshell, biology provides humans with templates, building blocks, integers (you pick your term, your metaphor), while culture and individuality determine how these are used, subverted, applied, and "made into" who each person and each social unit is. For me, there are "realities" at all levels of the human endeavor: biological–evolutionary, cultural–social, individual. These overlap and interplay. To assert a connection between the ethological, the anthropological, and the aesthetic is not to deny local and individual variation and uniqueness.

If I may be permitted a not-irrelevant analogy ... The world abounds in thousands of spoken languages. There are profound differences between, say, Swahili, Mandarin, Spanish, Bengali, and Quechua. One may go so far as to assert that specific cultural values are uniquely embedded in every language, that many "feels" cannot be translated effectively. Even in languages that are closely linked, such as English and French, the texture of a phrase can't be exactly translated: "Je t'aime" is different to "I love you." At the same time, it's true that the human species, qua species, "has" language. This ability to make and use language is not specific to any particular culture; it is the property and the ability of the species as a whole. In other words, there is no human society without language, nor is any particular language the same as any other. What is true of language, I believe, is true across the incredibly wide range of human cultural activities. In other words, individual variation, local usages, societal norms, and so on, do not cancel out the underlying species-wide need to gather into groups, develop social bonds, interact with and remake the environment (farming, housing, path-making, and so on).

How and why these interactions take place is the thread binding together the essays in this book.

RICHARD SCHECHNER
2003

ACKNOWLEDGMENTS

Performance Theory first appeared in 1977, as Essays on Performance Theory 1970–1976 published by Drama Book Specialists of New York. For the 1988 revised edition certain changes were made – see "Author's Note." The publication history of individual essays is as follows: "Approaches" appeared as "Approaches to Theory/Criticism" in the TDR, The Drama Review 10 (4) (1966). "Actuals: A Look into Performance Theory" (here "Actuals") was written for The Rarer Action: Essays in Honor of Francis Fergusson, edited by Alan Cheuse and Richard Koffler, New Brunswick, Rutgers University Press, 1970. "Drama, Script, Theater, and Performance" appeared in TDR, The Drama Review 17 (3) (1973). "From Ritual to Theater and Back" was delivered as a paper to the Rassegna Internazionale de Teatri Stabili in Florence, Italy, 1974; it was revised and printed in the Educational Theater Journal 26 (4) (1974). "Toward a Poetics of Performance" was delivered as a paper at the Ethnopoetics Symposium, sponsored by the Center for Twentieth Century Studies of the University of Wisconsin-Milwaukee in 1975; it was revised for this book. "Selective Inattention" appeared in Performing Arts Journal 1 (1) (1976) but was written for the first edition of this book. "Ethology and Theater" was also written for this book. The first version of "Magnitudes of Performance" was written for the 1982 World Conference on Ritual and Theater, sponsored principally by the Wenner-Gren

Foundation for Anthropological Research and supported in part by a grant from the National Endowment for the Humanities. It appeared in an earlier version in *The Anthropology of Experience* edited by Victor W. Turner and Edward M. Bruner, Urbana: University of Illinois Press, 1986. "Rasaesthics" first appeared in *TDR, The Drama Review*, 45(3) (2001).

AUTHOR'S NOTE

The differences between this edition of *Performance Theory* and the 1977 and 1988 editions are considerable. One essay that was in the 1977 edition was dropped for the 1988 ("Kinesics and Performance"). Two essays were added in 1988 ("Approaches" and "Magnitudes of Performance"). For the 2003 edition, "Approaches" has been edited and a new essay, "Rasaethetics" added. Overall, the book follows the trajectory of my thinking about performance from 1966 to the present, with an emphasis on the first twenty years of that span.

Writing a book is not a one-person job. I want to thank the performers and others from many different cultures who have made my work possible. I thank the members of The Performance Group, The Wooster Group, and the TDR, *The Drama Review* staff. And I thank my colleagues at the Department of Performance Studies, Tisch School of the Arts, New York University, and elsewhere, especially Carol Martin, Michael Kirby, Brooks McNamara, Barbara Kirshenblatt-Gimblett, Marcia B. Siegel, Peggy Phelan, Phillip Zarrilli, Ann Daly, Mariellen R. Sandford, Rebecca Schneider, and David Oppenheim. And plenty of thanks to my son, Samuel MacIntosh Schechner and my daughter, Sophia Martin Schechner.

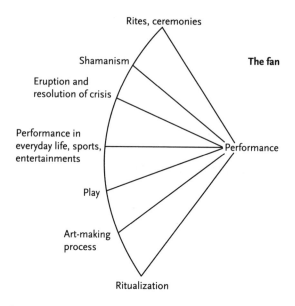

Rites, ceremonies

Shamanism

Eruption and
resolution of crisis

Performance in
everyday life, sports,
entertainments

Play

Art-making
process

Ritualization

Performance

The fan

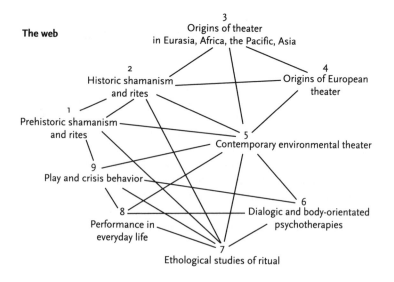

The web

3
Origins of theater
in Eurasia, Africa, the Pacific, Asia

2
Historic shamanism
and rites

4
Origins of European
theater

1
Prehistoric shamanism
and rites

5
Contemporary environmental theater

9
Play and crisis behavior

6

8
Performance in
everyday life

Dialogic and body-orientated
psychotherapies

7
Ethological studies of ritual

INTRODUCTION: THE FAN AND THE WEB

This isn't a potluck book. The essays are organized around a system that can be configured as both a fan and a web. This system has occupied me for more than twenty-five years in my practical work and in my theorizing.[1]

Performance is an inclusive term. Theater is only one node on a continuum that reaches from the ritualizations of animals (including humans) through performances in everyday life – greetings, displays of emotion, family scenes, professional roles, and so on – through to play, sports, theater, dance, ceremonies, rites, and performances of great magnitude.

The web is the same system seen more dynamically. Instead of being spread out along a continuum, each node interacts with the others. It's no accident that I put my own practical theater work – environmental theater – in the center: this position is arbitrary. An ethologist would put herself at the center of another web that includes items that don't figure in my scheme – genetics and evolutionary theory, for example. Also I put historical events side by side with speculative ideas and artistic performances. My method is similar to that of the Aborigines who credit dreams with a reality as powerful and important as events experienced while awake. Or is it the other way round? I know that analyses could be made separating out planes of reality; but sometimes – especially in the theater – it is necessary to live as if "as if" = "is."

The web isn't uniform. Connections among items 1 through 4 can be investigated historically and may be linked to performances around the world from Paleolithic times onward. Connections among items 6 through 9 reveal "deep structures" of performance – so that these items actually underlie the first five, thus activating a second plane of "reality." These deep structures include preparations for performance both by performers (training, workshop, rehearsals, preparations immediately before going on) and spectators (deciding to attend, dressing, going, settling in, waiting) and what happens after a performance. The ways people cool off and the sometimes extended aftermath of performances are less studied but very important. Cooling off includes getting performers and spectators out of, or down from, the performance; putting the performance space and implements to rest; the aftermath includes spreading the news about performances, evaluating them – even writing books about them – and in many ways determining how specific performances feed into ongoing systems of social and aesthetic life.

Also not only the narratives but the bodily actions of drama express crisis, schism, and conflict. As Eugenio Barba noted, performers specialize in putting themselves in disequilibrium and then displaying how they regain their balance, psychophysically, narratively, and socially – only to lose their balance, and regain it, again and again. Theatrical techniques center on these incompletable transformations: how people turn into other people, gods, animals, demons, trees, beings, whatever – either temporarily as in a play or permanently as in some rituals; or how beings of one order inhabit beings of another order as in trance; or how unwanted inhabitants of human beings can be exorcised; or how the sick can be healed. All these systems of performative transformations also include incomplete, unbalanced transformations of time and space: doing a specific "there and then" in this particular "here and now" in such a way that all four dimensions are kept in play.

Performances are make-believe, in play, for fun. Or, as Victor Turner said, in the subjunctive mood, the famous "as if." Or, as Sanskrit aesthetics would have it, performances are *lilas* – sports, play – and *maya*, illusory. But, the Sanskrit tradition emphasizes, so is all life *lila* and *maya*. Performance is an illusion of an illusion and, as such, might be considered more "truthful," more "real" than ordinary experience. This, too, was Aristotle's opinion in his *Poetics* where theater did not so much reflect living as essentialize it, present paradigms of it. As lilas, performances not only play out modes, they play with modes, leaving actions hanging and unfinished, so theatrical events are fundamentally experimental: provisional. Any semiotics of performance must start from, and always stand unsteadily on, these unstable slippery bases, made even more uncertain by the continually shifting receptions of various audiences. Because performances are usually subjunctive, liminal, dangerous, and duplicitous they are often hedged in with conventions and frames: ways of making the places, the participants, and the events somewhat safe. In these relatively safe make-believe precincts, actions can be carried to extremes, even for fun.

RICHARD SCHECHNER
NEW YORK, 1977, 1987

NOTE

1   Although this is not the place for an autobiography, a precis in not inappropriate: to let the reader know a little about who s/he is coming in contact with. From 1967 until 1980 I was artistic director of The Performance Group (TPG), a leading experimental theater. With TPG I directed many plays and workshops, including *Dionysus in 69, Makbeth, Commune, Mother Courage and Her Children, The Marilyn Project, The Tooth of Crime, Cops, Oedipus* (Seneca), and *The Balcony*. Since leaving TPG I have continued to direct, including *Richard's Lear, Cherry Orchard* (in Hindi with the professional Repertory Compay of the National School of Drama, New Delhi), *The Prometheus Project*, and *Don Juan* Most of these productions were developed during workshops. Before 1967 I was co-director of The New Orleans Group and a producing director of The Free Southern Theater. And in the summer of 1958 and again in 1961 I was artistic director of the East End players of Provincetown, Massachusetss. From the age of 27 I have taught fulltime, first at Tulane University and then, from 1967 to the present, at the Tisch School of the Arts, New York University. My speciality is performance theory – which for me is rooted in practice and is fundamentally interdisciplinary and intercultural.

1

APPROACHES

THE CAMBRIDGE ANTHROPOLOGISTS

For the last hundred years or more, Greek tragedy has been understood as an outgrowth of rites celebrated annually at the Festival of Dionysus. Those rites have been investigated both in their relation to the god Dionysus and in their relation to the primitive religion of the Greeks. The result is a conception of Greek tragedy which is very different from that which prevailed from the Renaissance into the eighteenth century. The Renaissance humanists and their successors saw it in "civilized" and rational terms; in our time we see that much of its form and meaning is due to its primitive source, and to the religious Festival of which it was a part. This new conception of Greek tragedy has had a very wide effect upon our understanding of the sources of poetry in our tradition, and also upon modern poetry itself, including theater and music. . . .

Unfortunately little is known directly about the rites of the Dionysian Festival, or about the poets, Aeschylus' predecessors, who gradually made the tragic form out of ritual. The scholars who devote their lives to such matters do not agree upon the evidence to be accepted, nor upon the interpretation of the evidence. But some of their theories are extremely suggestive, especially those of the Cambridge school,

Frazer (of *The Golden Bough*), Cornford, Harrison, Murray, and their colleagues and followers. It is this school which has had the deepest influence upon modern poetry and upon the whole climate of ideas in which we now read Greek tragedy. . . .

The theory expounded by Murray has been much criticized by other experts, and the whole field is full of disputes so erudite that the non-specialist can only look on in respectful silence.

(F. Fergusson, in Aristotle 1961: 36–9)

It's time to break the silence.[1] The instrumental books Fergusson alludes to are Jane Ellen Harrison's *Themis*[2] (1912), Gilbert Murray's *The Four Stages of Greek Religion* (1912a – later *Five Stages*, 1925), and Francis Cornford's *The Origin of Attic Comedy* (1914). Cornford's book is the only one entirely devoted to the theater, and thus it has been extremely popular among theater people. But the ideas espoused by the other books are just as well known. The Cambridge thesis purports to explain not only the origins of Greek tragedy and comedy, but their "essential natures" as well. Second- and third-generation critics have extended the somewhat modest proposals of the Cambridge group into "universal" systems widely used to explain the "basic form of theater" not only in the west but everywhere. Fergusson's *The Idea of a Theater* (1949) is a most distinguished American example. Fergusson applies the Cambridge thesis to a wide range of authors, from Sophocles to T. S. Eliot, Shaw, and Pirandello. His essays on *Oedipus* and *Hamlet* are classics. But these essays would be just as interesting, and a good deal less cluttered, if he did not insist on a ritual beneath the theatrical action of the plays.

The Cambridge thesis is not difficult. Studying survivials of Greek ritual, these scholars found what they thought to be traces of a "Primal Ritual" from which they felt both Attic tragedy and the surviving rituals derived. Murray began his "Excursus":

> The following note presupposes certain general views about the origin and essential nature of Greek Tragedy. It assumes that Tragedy is in origin a Ritual Dance, a *Sacer Ludus*. . . . Further, it assumes, in accord with the overwhelming weight of ancient tradition, that the Dance in question is originally or centrally that of Dionysus, performed at his feast, in his theater. . . . It regards Dionysus in this connection as an

"Eniautos-Daimon," or vegetation god, like Adonis, Osiris, etc., who represents the cyclic death and rebirth of the earth and the world, i.e., for practical purposes, of the tribe's own lands and the tribe itself. It seems clear, further, that Comedy and Tragedy represent different stages in the life of this Year Spirit.

(Murray 1912b: 341)

The rub is: the assumptions of the Cambridge group have never been proven. A tremendous amount of archeological digging has gone on in Greece over the past seventy-five years, but nothing has turned up expressing all the elements of either drama or the Primal Ritual.[3] This is crucial because Murray asserts, "If we examine the kind of myth which seems to underlie the various 'Eniautos' [death-rebirth] celebrations we shall find an Agon . . . a Pathos . . . a Messenger . . . a Threnos or lamentation . . . an Anagnorisis – discovery or recognition . . . [and a] Theophany" (1912b: 343–4). This formal sequence, propagators of the Cambridge thesis say, is the core action of the Primal Ritual, surviving fragments of the dithyramb, and Greek tragedy. Cornford's contribution was to do for comedy and phallic dances what others did for tragedy and dithyramb. His reasoning is identical. "Athenian Comedy arose out of a ritual drama essentially the same in shape as that from which Professor Murray derives Athenian Tragedy" (Cornford 1914: 190). Harrison, in *Ancient Art and Ritual*, gleefully makes the connections:

We shall find to our joy that this obscure-sounding Dithyramb, though before Aristotle's time it has taken literary form, was in origin a festival closely akin to those we have just been discussing [seasonal death-rebirth celebrations]. The Dithyramb was, to begin with, a spring ritual; and when Aristotle tells us tragedy arose out of the Dithyramb, he gives us, though perhaps half unconsciously, a clear instance of a splendid art that arose from the simplest of rites; he plants our theory of the connection of art with ritual firmly with its feet on historical ground.

(Harrison 1913: 76)

Before discussing how firmly Aristotle had his feet on the ground, let me depict the Cambridge thesis (figure 1.1). The Primal Ritual

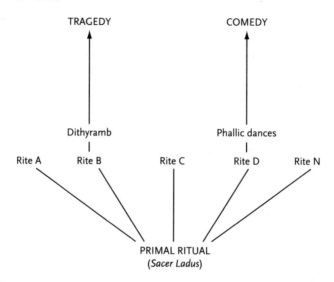

Figure 1.1

(Murray calls it a *Sacer Ludus*) gave rise to a number of rites. One of these developed into the dithyramb from which Greek tragedy arose; another became the phallic dances from which comedy evolved. The argument applies turn-of-the-century anthropological theories of cultural evolution and diffusion. It is highly speculative with several missing links.

The clearest example of the Primal Ritual's form comes from one of the last Greek tragedies to be written, Euripides' *The Bacchae* where, from line 787 to the end, Murray finds the "whole sequence" of his *Sacer Ludus*. To do this, however, he must assume that "Pentheus is only another form of Dionysus himself"[4] – thereby "explaining" why it is the young king, and not the god, who is torn to pieces. Nor is there any resurrection or apotheosis of Pentheus. It is Dionysus who appears, not to signal, as Murray says, an "extreme change of feeling from grief to joy," but to curse the whole city of Thebes. Using *The Bacchae* at all makes Murray's argument smell of tautology. But the Cambridge group must use *The Bacchae*, because other links with the Primal Ritual are even weaker. There is no Primal Ritual yet discovered;[5] the connections between what rituals can be shown to have existed and the dithyramb are doubtful; and the connections between the dithyramb and Greek theater are unprovable.[6]

Theories of cultural evolution have long been challenged by anthropologists. The methodology of J. G. Frazer, which the Cambridge group freely uses, has been almost entirely discredited. Yet Murray maintained as late as 1961 (in his Foreword to Theodor H. Gaster's *Thespis*) that "It is hardly an exaggeration to say that when we look back to the beginnings of European literature we find everywhere drama, and always drama derived from a religious ritual designed to ensure the rebirth of a dead world" (Murray 1961: 9). However true this may be about the emergence of Christian theater from medieval church ritual, it is not true of either Greek theater or European theater (and its derivatives) from the Renaissance to the present. We might even see the reverse process: a dynamic braiding of ritual and entertainment (see chapter 4).

The connection between Greek drama and the dithyramb depends largely upon Aristotle's comments in chapter 4 of *Aristotle's Poetics* (Butcher's translation, 1961):

> Tragedy – as also Comedy – was at first mere improvisation. The one originated with the authors of the Dithyramb, the other with those of the phallic songs, which are still used in many of our cities.

Even Cornford doubted Aristotle's authority as an ethnologist:

> How much he [Aristotle] knew or might have inferred about the earliest stages of Comedy we cannot tell. He may have known as little as Boileau knew of the beginnings of the modern French Theatre. . . . If Boileau could be so ignorant of two centuries of ecclesiastical drama, of which tens of thousands of lines were in existence, we need not wonder if Aristotle did not know that the plays of Chionides and Magnes retained traces of a broken-down ritual plot, and that yet fainter traces survived in Aristophanes.
>
> (Cornford 1914: 219)

Pickard-Cambridge is equally clear, but to prove the opposite point:

> as regards comedy, it is very doubtful whether he [Aristotle] is strictly correct; as regards tragedy, the difficulties of his view will shortly

become plain. We have, in short, to admit that it is impossible to accept his authority without question, and that he was probably using that liberty of theorizing which those modern scholars who ask us to accept him as infallible have certainly not abandoned.

(Pickard-Cambridge 1962: 95)

T. B. L. Webster finds that Aristotle makes "two completely distinct points: 1) tragedy was an offshoot from the Dithyramb; 2) (six lines later) it changed from satyric and was solemnized late; and there is not justification for equating them" (in Pickard-Cambridge 1962: 96). Murray deals with this slippery transformation thus:

It would suit my general purpose . . . to suppose that the Dionysus-ritual had developed into two divergent forms, the satyr-play of Pratinas and the tragedy of Thespis, which were at a certain date artificially combined by a law.

(Murray 1912b: 344)

This rescues the Cambridge thesis, but it is all speculation. The fact is we cannot depend on Aristotle; nor can we accept what he says and arrive at the Cambridge thesis.

Why then has the Cambridge idea held such sway? It can be compressed, codified, and generalized: it is teachable. It is self-repairing: where the Primal Ritual cannot be found it has simply "evolved out of recognition"; where only "fragments" exist, these are vestiges, and so forth. It seems to explain everything: origins, form, audience involvement, catharsis, and dramatic action – especially the conflicts, mutilations, and deaths that characterize Greek tragedies. In short, the thesis is elegant, brilliant, speculative criticism. But it is no more than that. The "scientific proofs" the Cambridge group sought for their ideas have not been found. And perhaps it is time to abandon the Cambridge thesis as one which is too limiting, that no longer suits current perceptions of theater.

Ritual as the Cambridge group understands it does not seem very closely related to Greek theater – or Elizabethan or modern.[7] The meaning of the word must be distorted out of usefulness if it is to apply equally to *Seven Against Thebes, Philoctetes, The Bacchae, Lear, Mother Courage,*

Waiting for Godot, The Bald Soprano, The Tooth of Crime – or any other random group of distinguished plays. Even if one restricts the selection to a single period, the difficulties are immense. To apply the Cambridge thesis is to force the plays into contexts other than their own, to read around and under them. The development of happenings, intermedia, performance art, and so on raises still further questions. As for medieval theater which had as one of its sources church ritual,[8] the players kept the biblical characters and plots while soon abandoning the form of the Mass and embroidering the stories with secular incidents.

I am not going to replace the Cambridge origin theory with my own. Origin theories are irrelevant to understanding theater. Nor do I want to exclude ritual from the study of the performative genres. Ritual is one of several activities related to theater. The others are play, games, sports, dance, and music.[9] The relation among these I will explore is not vertical or originary – from any one to any other(s) – but horizontal: what each autonomous genre shares with the others; methods of analysis that can be used intergenerically. Together these seven comprise the public performance activities of humans.[10] If one argues that theater is "later" or more "sophisticated" or "higher" on some evolutionary ladder and therefore must derive from one of the others, I reply that this makes sense only if we take fifth century BCE Greek theater (and its counterparts in other cultures) as the only legitimate theater. Anthropologists, with good reason, argue otherwise, suggesting that theater – understood as the enactment of stories by players – exists in every known culture at all times, as do the other genres.[11] These activities are primeval, there is no reason to hunt for "origins" or "derivations." There are only variations in form, the intermixing among genres, and these show no long-term evolution from "primitive" to "sophisticated" or "modern."[12] Sometimes rituals, games, sports, and the aesthetic genres (theater, dance, music) are merged so that it is impossible to call the activity by any one limiting name. That English usage urges us to do so anyway is an ethnocentric bias, not an argument.

PLAY, GAMES, SPORTS, THEATER, AND RITUAL

Several basic qualities are shared by these activities: 1) a special ordering of time; 2) a special value attached to objects; 3) non-productivity in terms of goods; 4) rules. Often special places – non-ordinary places – are set aside or constructed to perform these activities in.

Time

Clock time is a mono-directional, linear-yet-cyclical uniform measurement adapted from day–night and seasonal rhythms. In the performance activities, however, *time is adapted to the event*, and is therefore susceptible to numerous variations and creative distortions. The major varieties of performance time are:

1. *Event time*, when the activity itself has a set sequence and all the steps of that sequence must be completed no matter how long (or short) the elapsed clock time.

    Examples: baseball, racing, hopscotch; rituals where a "response" or a "state" is sought, such as rain dances, shamanic cures, revival meetings; scripted theatrical performances taken as a whole.
2. *Set time*, where an arbitrary time pattern is imposed on events – they begin and end at certain moments whether or not they have been "completed." Here there is an agonistic contest between the activity and the clock.

    Examples: football, basketball, games structured on "how many" or "how much" can you do in *x* time.
3. *Symbolic time*, when the span of the activity represents another (longer or shorter) span of clock time. Or where time is considered differently, as in Christian notions of "the end of time," the Aborigine "Dreamtime," or Zen's goal of the "ever present."

    Examples: theater, rituals that reactualize events or abolish time, make-believe play and games.

Boxing offers an unusual combination. The length of each round (3 minutes) and the fight (a certain number of rounds) is set time. But a

KO can end the fight at any moment and is event time while the measure of a KO (the 10 count) is set time.

In racing, the racers are competing against each other, either directly or indirectly (attempting to set a new record). The clock is the means by which racers are compared to each other. In football, however, the clock is very active in the game itself. Both teams, while playing against each other, are also playing with/against the clock. Time is there to be extended or used up. While stalling is a negligible strategy in baseball and a disastrous one in racing, it is crucial in football, where many games end with the leading team "running out the clock." Suspense drama takes a similar attitude toward time; frequently the hero is trying to get something done before time runs out.

Most orthodox theater uses symbolic time, but experimental performances often use event or set time. Allan Kaprow's happenings – both those he did in the late 1950s and 1960s and the more private conceptual work of the 1980s – use event time. Take, for example, Fluids (1967). As Kaprow describes the piece,

> Fluids is a single event done in many places over a three-day period. It consists simply in building huge, blank, rectangular ice structures. . . . The structures are to be built in about 20 places throughout Los Angeles. If you were crossing the city you might suddenly be confronted by these mute and meaningless blank structures which have been left to melt.
>
> (Kaprow 1968b: 154)

Fluids is over when the monoblocks melt, however long that takes. Kaprow is aware of what this piece is about.

> Obviously, what's taking place is a mystery of sorts; using common material (at considerable expense) to make quasi-architectural structures which seem out of place amid a semi-tropical city setting. . . . Fluids is in a state of continuous fluidity and there's literally nothing left but a puddle of water – and that evaporates.
>
> (Kaprow 1986b: 154–5)

Similarly, Anna Halprin's Esposizione (1963) consisted of 40 minutes of performers' carrying heavy burdens while climbing up a huge cargo net. They moved as rapidly as they could and carried as much as they were able. When the time was up, the piece was over.[13]

Ionesco's *Victims of Duty* – like so many other dramas from Sophocles' *Oedipus* onward – presents an action controlled by event time within a world defined by symbolic time. Choubert must look for Mallot, that's his "duty." The steps of that search, though unknown to Choubert, are known to the Detective who forces Choubert to re-experience his past. What is important is that Choubert do what he is asked, not how long it takes. The "chew–swallow" sequence that ends the play locks Choubert, Madeleine, Nicolas, and the Lady into a routine from which there is no escape – the activity is endless because it is looped. An even clearer use of event time within the frame of symbolic time is the first scene of Jean Genet's *The Maids*. Claire is dressed as and playing Madame while Solange plays Claire. Because these are actors, the audience is fooled – performer X could play Madame as easily as play Claire. Step by step Claire/Madame and Solange/Claire move through the routine leading to the attempted murder of Claire/Madame. This scene is actually a dress rehearsal for the crime that ends the play. Both women are careful that the other does everything "necessary," no matter how long it takes. Still, they are in a rush – they must finish before Madame arrives. An alarm clock, brought from the kitchen (the maids' domain) into Madame's bedroom, ticks off the available minutes. The scene ends when the alarm rings – too soon for the murder to be consummated. Claire complains, "It's over already. And you didn't get to the end." Solange replies, "The same thing happens every time. And it's all your fault, you're never ready. I can't finish you off." This ritual-farce opening scene, with its deus ex alarm clock, is built on the tensions aroused by the conflicting temporal rhythms of symbolic (the drama), event (the murder), and set (the alarm clock) time.

Symbolic time, seemingly absent from happenings and the like, is actually most difficult to banish. Once action is framed "as theater" spectators read meanings into whatever they witness. Orthodox acting and scenic arrangements stress mimesis with its symbolic time; happenings stress the breaks between persons and tasks, thus the thing done may be mimetic without being a "characterization."

Objects

In everyday life objects are valued for their practical use (tools), scarcity and beauty (jewels, precious metals, art), bartering power (paper, wooden, and metal money), or age. In the performance activities all objects – except certain ritual implements and relics[14] – have a market value much less than the value assigned to the objects within the context of the activity. Balls, pucks, hoops, batons, bats – even theatrical props – are mostly common objects of not much material value and cheaply replaced if lost or worn out.[15] Often theatrical props and costumes are designed to look more costly than they actually are. But during the performance these objects are of extreme importance, often the focus of the whole activity. Sometimes, as in theater and children's play, they are decisive in creating the symbolic reality. The "otherworldiness" of play, sports, games, theater, and ritual is enhanced by the extreme disparity between the value of the objects outside the activity when compared to their value as foci of the activity. From the standpoint of productive work it is silly to put so much energy into the "control of the ball" or the "defense of 10 yards of territory." It is equally silly to think that a costume can make a king out of an actor, or even help Lee J. Cobb become Willy Loman. And of what material value is a saint's bones – or the Veil of Turin?

Non-productivity

The separation of performance activities from productive work is a most interesting, and unifying, factor of play, games, sports, theater, and ritual. What J. Huizinga and Roger Caillois say about play applies to all performative genres.

> Summing up the formal characteristics of play, we might call it a free activity standing quite consciously outside "ordinary" life as being "not serious," but at the same time absorbing the player intensely and utterly.
>
> (Huizinga 1955: 13)

> A characteristic of play, in fact, is that it creates no wealth or goods.
>
> (Caillois 1961: 21)

But how can this be? On every side we see professional sports and theater (not to mention the churches and synagogues) enmeshed in big-time economics. Individual athletes earn millions, and leagues sign TV contracts worth billions. Money is exchanged for admissions, salaries, media contracts, concessions, endorsements, and so forth. Billions more exchange hands through betting. Large-scale enterprises are entirely dependent on these activities. And, as more leisure time becomes available, we may expect a steady increase in these expenditures. Are we then to believe, as Huizinga does, that modern play is "decadent" because it participates so completely in the economic arrangements of society?

The issue is complex. It can be unraveled only by appreciating the structural elements of the performative activities. In productive work the economic arrangements determine the form of the operation. Thus a man with little money may run a small automotive shop employing a few workers. A large corporation with millions to spend may operate an assembly line. In large parts of our life home industry has stopped because it is more cost-efficient to mass-produce. Even when home industry makes a modest comeback it is either because computers secure linkups forming a network, or because individual consumers can afford to buy handmade goods. In those sectors where there are both small and large manufacturers – furniture, for example – the method of work, the means of assembly, and even the final product differ according to the scale of the operation. It is not simply a case of "increased efficiency" or the production of more objects. The entire operation changes its shape, *what it is*, according to various modes of production.

Rules

But the difference between sandlot and major league baseball is one of quality, not form. The same rules apply to both games. The San Francisco Giants may have *better* players than the Sixth Street Eagles, but the Giants can't have *more* players on the field and still call their game baseball. When the rules are changed – and sometimes they are changed in response to economic pressures, TV has had an effect on sports – they are usually changed all the way down the line. And when adjustments are made at the sandlot level – because not enough players show up, or whatever – these adjustments are recognized as necessary compromises with what the game *should* be. What I've been saying about sports could be said, with some variations, about rituals, games, and theater too. No matter how much is spent, paid, bet, or in other ways implicated in these performative activities, their respective forms remain constant. When money does "corrupt" a form – a game is fixed, a star hired not for her ability to play a given role but simply because of her "name" – people are able to recognize the misalignment. Some activities, like professional wrestling, fall between sports and theater: the matches are known to be fixed but a certain willing suspension of disbelief is practiced.

Economic arrangements thus affect the players, their bosses, spectators, audiences, fans, and bettors – everyone involved in the activity – while the activity itself remains largely unaffected. The money, services, and products (clothing, sports equipment, etc.) generated by these activities are not part of them. In games, sports, theater, and ritual – play, again, is a separate case – the rules are designed not only to tell the players how to play but to *defend the activity against encroachment from the outside.* What rules are to games and sports, traditions are to ritual and conventions are to theater, dance, and music. If one is to find a "better way" to perform, this better way must conform to the rules. The avant-garde is apparently a rule-breaking activity. But actually, experimentation in the arts has its own set of rules. Think about it: the ordinary technological environments most of today's Americans live in and with – cars and planes, appliances, TV and stereo, etc. – have changed much more radically over the past seventy years than have the concerns or techniques of the avant-garde. Performance activities all along the continuum – from play through to ritual – are traditional in the most basic sense.

Special rules exist, are formulated, and persist because these activities are something *apart from everyday life*.[16] A special world is created where people can make the rules, rearrange time, assign value to things, and work for pleasure. This "special world" is not gratuitous but a vital part of human life. No society, no individual, can do without it. It is special only when compared to the "ordinary" activities of productive work. In psychoanalytic terms, the world of these performance activities is the pleasure principle institutionalized.[17] Freud believed that art was the sublimation of the conflict between the pleasure and reality principles; and he felt that artistic creation was an extension of fantasy life – he identified art with play. Indeed, the art of the individual may be as Freud described it. But these performance activities are something different. Only theater (music, dance) is art in the strict sense. Individuals engaged in ritual, games, or sports must conform to the rules which separate these activities from "real life." Although I do not wish to elaborate here, I think these activities are the social counterparts to individual fantasy. Thus their social function is to stand apart from ordinary life, both idealizing it (in these activities people play by the rules) and criticizing it (why can't *all* life be a game?).

Performance spaces

Perhaps this will be clearer if we consider for a moment where sports, theater, and ritual are performed. Great arenas, stadiums, churches, and theaters are structures often economically non-self-supporting. Situated in population centers where real estate comes high, these large spaces lie fallow during great hunks of time. Unlike office, industrial, or home spaces, they are used on an occasional rather than steady basis. During large parts of the day, and often for days on end, they are relatively unused. Then, when the games start, when services are scheduled, when the show opens, the spaces are used intensely, attracting large crowds who come for the scheduled events. The spaces are uniquely organized so that a large group can watch a small group – and become aware of itself at the same time.[18] These arrangements foster celebratory and ceremonial feelings. In Goffman's words, there is "an expressive rejuvenation and reaffirmation of the moral values of the community" in those spaces where "reality is being performed" (Goffman 1959: 35–6).[19] Certainly, more than elsewhere, these places promote social solidarity: one "has" a religion, "roots for" a team, and "goes to" the theater for essentially the same reasons.[20] What consequences flow from TV's ability to conflate all these spaces into one box multiplied millions of times, we are just beginning to discover.

It will facilitate matters if I summarize the formal relations among play, games, sports, theater, and ritual in a "performance chart" (figure 1.2).[21] Referring to it, we see that theater has more in common with games and sports than with play or ritual. However, certain key characteristics of happenings relate more to play than anything else; this is one strong indication of the real break between orthodox and "new" theater. Furthermore, play is obviously the ontogenic source of the other activities: what children do, adults organize.[22] The definitive break between games, sports, and theater on the one hand, and play and ritual on the other, is indicated by the different quality and use of the rules that govern the activities. These distinctions in the rules are the keys to more general distinctions. The five activities can be rather neatly subdivided into three groups (figure 1.3). Play is "free activity" where one makes one's own rules. In Freudian terms play expresses the pleasure principle, the *private* fantasy world. Ritual is strictly programmed, expressing the individual's submission to forces "larger" or at least "other" than oneself. Ritual epitomizes the reality principle, the agreement to obey rules that are *given*.[23] Games, sports, and theater (dance, music) mediate between these extremes. It is in these activities that people express their *social* behavior. These three groupings constitute a continuum, a sliding scale with many overlaps and interplays. However, differences in degree become differences in kind. Ritual and play are alike in many ways – periods of playful license are often followed by or interdigitated with periods of ritual control, as in Mardi Gras–Lent or in the activities of ritual clowns. The performance chart, to be read accurately, might be folded into a cylinder so that play and ritual are close together, the "opposites" of games, sports, and theater.

In figure 1.3 games, sports, and theater are "middle terms," balancing and in some sense mediating and combining, play (+) and ritual (−). In the middle terms rules exist as frames. Some rules say what must be done and others what must not be done. Between the frames there is freedom. In fact, the better the player, the more able s/he will be to exploit this freedom. This is clear for sports and games, but what about theater? For the actress playing Hedda Gabler, to give an example, the situation is complex (figure 1.4). The first frame concerns the physical stage or space, the second the conventions of her epoch; the third the drama itself; and the fourth are the instructions given to

Figure 1.2 Performance chart

	Play	Games	Sports	Theater	Ritual
Special ordering of time	Usually	Yes	Yes	Yes	Yes
Special value for objects	Yes	Yes	Yes	Yes	Yes
Non-productive	Yes	Yes	Yes	Yes	Yes
Rules	Inner	Frame	Frame	Frame	Outer
Special place	No	Often	Yes	Yes	Usually
Appeal to other	No	Often	Yes	Yes	Yes
Audience	Not necessarily	Not necessarily	Usually	Yes	Usually
Self-assertive	Yes	Not totally	Not totally	Not totally	No
Self-transcendent	No	Not totally	Not totally	Not totally	Yes
Completed	Not necessarily	Yes	Yes	Yes	Yes
Performed by group	Not necessarily	Usually	Usually	Yes	Usually
Symbolic reality	Often	No	No	Yes	Often
Scripted	Sometimes/No	No	No	Yes	Usually

Note: Happenings and related activities are *not* included as theater in this chart. Happenings would not necessarily have an audience, they would not necessarily be scripted, there would be no necessary symbolic reality. Formally, they would be very close to play.

Figure 1.3

Self-assertive "I": +	Social "We": ±	Self-transcendent "Other": −
Play	Games Sports Theater	Ritual
Rules established by player	Rules establish frames: "Do" (freedom), "Don't Do"	Rules given by authority
Pleasure principle, Eros, id, private world, assimilation	Balance between pleasure and reality principles, ego, accommodation	Reality principle, Thanatos, superego

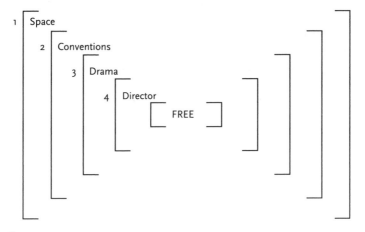

Figure 1.4

the actress by her director. She need not worry about any except this last, for each inner frame contains within it the rules established by frames further out.

There is an "axiom of frames" which generally applies in the theater: the looser an outer frame, the tighter the inner, and conversely, the looser the inner, the more important the outer. Thus the improvisational actor is freed from both director and drama, but s/he will therefore have to make fuller use of conventions (stock situations and characters, audience's expectations, etc.) and the physical space. The actor will also find himself directly confronting his own limitations: there will be little mediating between him and his audience. Even the wildest avant-garde work will be framed by space, sometimes literally interstellar space.[24] I know of no production where conventions are completely disregarded. However, the frames are not static, even within a single production. Kaprow's *Calling* (1965) took place in several locations, some of them outdoors. Because there were so few spatial or conventional limitations, Kaprow gave his performers very specific tasks: the inner frame was tight, the outer ones very loose.

This kind of analysis doesn't say much about the particular role of the actor, director, playwright, or architect-designer. But it does outline their relationships to each other and suggest that each function is meaningful only in terms of the whole set. One cannot discuss a single frame without referring to the others, because it is only within a pattern of relationships that a specific phenomenon takes place.

The indication that theater has more in common with sports and games than with ritual or play should be the cue to explore work in mathematical and transactional game analysis as methodologies for the study of theater. These studies could range from a close look at the ancient Olympic Games (rather than the Primal Ritual) and bearbaiting and cock-fighting as models for Greek and Elizabethan theater to the application of contemporary game theory. Philip McCoy, who undertook such an application, observes:

> If one looks at a play as the crystallized interweave of conflicting interests, some of the structural tangles may be resolved into graphic patterns by the use of game theory principles. Martin Shubik in the introductory essay to his collection, *Game Theory and Related Approaches to Social Behavior* (1964) defines game theory in general terms: "Game Theory is a method for the study of decision making in situations of conflict. . . . The essence of a 'game' in this context is that it involves decision makers with different goals or objectives whose fates are intertwined." A tentative analysis of the first scene of

King Lear according to the techniques of game theory reveals four separate "games" woven into a complex total texture which might be called the Lear-game. The shifting combination of players, the rhythmic occurrences of moves, and the directions of players' choices give in the graphic form of a "game tree" a structural picture of the scene more elemental than a mere design of the physical action or of the psychological motivation could ever be. This kind of analysis would be of practical use in determining broad patterns of movement and specific stage groupings; its advantage over a purely intuitive interpretation of a scene based upon character psychology is that it assumes an integral dramatic structure which supports characterization while transcending individual action.

(McCoy 1965)

It would seem that mathematical game theory and transactional analysis have rich futures in the theater. This is so because dramas are completed actions involving interpersonal relationships usually pivoting on a conflict situation. Thus there is a nice fit between what drama encodes to what these theories are attempting to analyze. Further work needs to be done in the entire area relating theater to plays, games, sports, and ritual. What I have tried to do here is to outline some of the relationships and suggest possibilities for future work. [. . .]

These new approaches may be productive because they urge explorations of *horizontal* relationships among related forms rather than a searching vertically for unprovable origins. They also situate theater where it belongs: among performance genres, not literature. The text, where it exists, is understood as a key to action, not its replacement. Where there is no text, action is treated directly. The possibility exists that a unified set of approaches will be developed that can handle *all* performance phenomena, classical and modern, textual and non-textual, dramatic, theatrical, playful, ritual. Could it be that the historical rifts separating theorists, critics, and practitioners may be ending?

NOTES

1 William Arrowsmith on several occasions attacked the Cambridge thesis. For example, "It seems to me that nothing but chaos can come from the

fashionable notion that because Greek tragedy begins in ritual, its structure is therefore ritual dramatized, its hero a ritual scapegoat, and its action a shadow-play of the death of the *Eniautos-daimon*" (1959: 37). My tack, as I hope will become clear, though in no way opposed to Arrowsmith's, is in a different direction. And whatever my quarrels are with the Cambridge thesis, a number of productions of Greek tragedies have exploited it, including my own *Dionysus in 69*.

2   It was in *Themis* that Murray placed his "Excursus on the Ritual Forms Preserved in Greek Tragedy" (1912b), the kernel of much thinking connecting theater and ritual.

3   The earliest mention of the dithyramb is found in a fragment of Archilochus of Paros (fr. 77 D) dating from the first half of the seventh century BCE. Most of our evidence comes from the fifth century: the epoch of Aeschylus, Sophocles, Euripides, and Aristophanes. As A. W. Pickard-Cambridge notes (and my facts are taken from his *Dithyramb, Tragedy, and Comedy*, 1962): "The attempts to throw light upon the original character of the dithyramb by references to the derivation of the name have so far led to no certain results" (p. 7). This observation regarding philology is crucial because Pickard-Cambridge also states: "The dithyramb may be very old *if the philological indications are to be trusted*" (p. 31, italics mine). The point is that we don't know the original form – or even date – of these dances. Certainly we know nothing of a Primal Ritual that came *before* them. What is exercised is a version of the myth of origins: older is truer.

4   Murray associates Pentheus with Zagreus, Orpheus, and Osiris "who are torn in pieces and put together again." Pentheus' body is reassembled, but not as a prelude to a celebration. And we may ask why the "whole sequence" is contained in only the later part of the play – what are we to make of the first part? Murray's observations may be ingenious literary criticism, but they are neither convincing anthropology nor helpful dramaturgy.

5   T. B. L. Webster, editor of the second edition of Pickard-Cambridge, notes that he attacked Murray's Primal Ritual theory and in 1943 Murray responded: "I was wrong, as Mr. Pickard-Cambridge pointed out, in attributing too exclusive and original an importance to this type of play [the Primal Ritual], but its existence is clear." Webster adds:

> With our extended knowledge of the history of the Dionysus cult the theory can be re-stated in a form which is both tenable and valuable. But briefly, it is this: ritual of the *eniautos daimon* type in the Mycenaean age very early (and certainly before Homer) gave rise to myths which were dramatized very early and so established a rhythm which was so satisfying that stories from other mythological cycles were approximated to it.
>
> (in Pickard-Cambridge 1962: 128)

Murray, however, did not abandon his thesis; certainly those theater scholars who draw on it have not been as shy as Webster suggests they ought to be. And even Webster admits his thesis is unproven.

6 Webster, who *supports* the dithyramb theory, says:

> Our evidence for the early history of tragedy is so slight that any account is unsatisfactory. If *The Persians* must now be accepted as the earliest surviving play of Aeschylus, more than sixty years separate it from the beginning of the competition. *The Persians* already has all the solemnity and grandeur of Aeschylean tragedy.
>
> It is difficult to see a thread leading back from here to a performance of fat men and satyrs.
>
> (in Pickard-Cambridge 1962: 130–1)

Webster asserts that the

> worship of Dionysus goes back to Mycenaean times and before that to Minoan times. The ecstatic dances of the maenads and the dances of the satyrs and fat men can be traced back to these sources. Much of the mythology . . . was already formed before Homer. The Dionysus cult of the seventh and sixth centuries are revivals, not new creations.
>
> (p. 129)

7 Artaud has muddied the waters by introducing in such a powerful way his notion of ritual. But by "ritual" I understand him to mean nothing other than the transcendence of the actor's personality by outside forces – codified systems of performance such as those used by the Balinese, or trance possession. Artaud does not say that theater *comes from* this or that ritual. He argues that theater *is* – or ought to be – ritual. The ritual process – as worked out by Victor Turner and others – applies more to the workshop-rehearsal process than to dramatic literature. See "Restoration of Behavior" and "Playing with Genet's *The Balcony*" in my *Between Theater and Anthropology* (1985).

8 There are two theories concerning the links between Church and theater in the Middle Ages. The traditional view locating theater's origins in Church ritual has been eloquently put by O. B. Hardison, Jr, in *Christian Rite and Christian Drama in the Middle Ages* (1965). Benjamin Hunningher in the second part of *The Origin of the Theater* (1961) argues that the Church took in and then spit out the folk theater which had persisted from Roman times. Allardyce Nicoll's *Masks, Mimes, and Miracles* (1963) traces the history and remarkable persistence of the genres and characters of popular theater from the ancient Greeks, through Rome, into the Middle Ages and on to the *commedia dell'arte*. Turkish scholar Metin And traces cultural exchange in terms of dancing, puppetry, and popular entertainment across the Islamic belt from Indonesia to North Africa and Spain. Many of these exchanges began well before the advent of Islam (And 1976, 1979, 1987).

9 I do not deal in any detail with dance and music, though obviously these are "performance activities" as important as theater, play, games, and sports. In terms of the discussion to follow, dance and music can be considered varieties of theater. In the performances of many cultures, including some of the

west, there is no separating music–dance–theater. I am not only referring to opera or musical comedies, but religious services, parades, festival celebrations, and even sports. Also, experimental movements in the arts have emphasized intermedia.

10   Performance is an extremely difficult concept to define. From one point of view – clearly stated by Erving Goffman in *The Presentation of Self in Everyday Life* (1959) – performing is a mode of behavior that may characterize *any* activity. Thus performance is a "quality" that can occur in any situation rather than a fenced-off genre. Various kinds of psychotherapy develop both practical and theoretical consequences from this. Or, as John Cage has argued, simply framing an activity "as" performance – viewing it as such – makes it into a performance. Documentary film and the splicing in of documentary footage into "fiction" films transforms ordinary behavior into performances. So do shows like *Candid Camera*. However, in this writing I mean something much more limited: a performance is an activity done by an individual or group in the presence of and for another individual or group. I recognize that some activities legitimately called play, games, sports, and ritual would be excluded from my definition. My definition is further complicated by the fact that game theory applies both to performance and non-performance activities. However, in trying to manage the relationship between a general theory and its possible applications to various art forms, I thought it best to center my definition of performance on certain acknowledged qualities of live theater, the most stable being the audience–performer interaction. Even where audiences do not exist as such – some happenings, rituals, and play – the function of the audience persists: part of the performing group watches – is meant to watch – other parts of the performing group; or, as in some rituals, the implied audience is God, or some transcendent Other(s).

11   See, for example, Herskovits (1950: 427 ff.), Bohannan (1963: 48 ff.), or Pfeiffer (1982). The point is that these activities are so ancient and universal that discussion of origins are metaphysics, not anthropology.

12   Technology is cumulative and in many cases the result of diffusion. Therefore one can speak of technological evolution. But even here a strictly Darwinian model does not apply. Cultural evolution – in which the discussion of the "development of art forms" was a part – flourished in the heyday of social Darwinism, the late nineteenth and early twentieth centuries. No one denies the Darwinian theory as it applies to genetically linked species (no one but creationists, that is); but, as Claude Lévi-Strauss has said, axes do not *beget* axes. There are no genetic links between or within cultures that explain the diffusion or coincidence of cultural traits. Influences occur and cultural development follows patterns not yet clearly understood. In artistic matters – where technology as such is usually not so important – there is no such thing as accumulation. Artists, when they know the past, pick and choose what materials they want to use. They often do not build according to generally agreed-upon rules. The twentieth century has seen in the west an awakened

interest in "primitive" art forms. And, more recently, artists in many cultures – Asian, African, native American, etc. – have begun to explore, and use "root" materials from their own and other cultures. But the term "primitive" – even in its literal meaning of "first" – is misleading. Early art forms, or fragments ripped from them, often repeat themselves; that is all anyone can say with certainty.

13   For a more complete account of *Esposizione*, see Halprin 1965. For a historical account and theoretical discussion of happenings and related activities, see Michael Kirby (1965a, 1965b, 1972).

14   Gold, silver, and precious jewels are part of many rituals; and some ritual events – potlatches, for example – depend on the display and dispersal of wealth. In the first instance, the market value of these objects – were they offered for sale by weight or size – would be far less than the value society assigns to them as "holy objects." In the days when relics were sold the fraud was that people thought they were buying objects with a specific history while the priests knew the bones, or whatever, had only a fictive salable history. Priceless paintings bring high prices, but for what would the Vatican, or the Metropolitan Museum of Art, sell its collection? And where paintings have entered the market place as such their value has no relation to the raw materials – paints, canvas, etc. – of which they are made. As for potlatches, what is being displayed and enhanced by means of the distribution of wealth is the prestige of the giver.

15   Musical instruments are an exception. Maybe this is because the quality of sound – the essence of music – depends on the relation between the quality of the instruments and the skills of the performer. But even here great folk performers have made extraordinary sounds come from such common objects as washboards or steel pots. In most performance activities the human manipulation of simple objects is the determining factor; beyond a certain minimum standard, greatness is entirely in the hands of the performers. Whatever quality linen Desdemona's handkerchief is woven of, it takes first-rate actors to play *Othello*.

16   Even in non-industrial societies, where the means of production are not mechanized, play, games, sports, theater, and ritual are considered different than ordinary work. Ritual especially is thought to be a *necessary* prelude to, adjunct of, or thank-you for production: rituals must be performed or crops won't grow, etc. But this necessary link is not a confusion between the two kinds of activity; rather it is an acting out of the belief that both productive and non-productive activities are essential for human life. Furthermore, these rituals often include dances, dramas, games, sports, and playful activities.

17   In play and individual fantasy this world has not been institutionalized but remains the private privilege of each. It is in fantasy that people break the rules – even the most rigorous rules of sports, decorum, law, etc. – and get away with it. There is a tangent running from this leading to theories of myth and the "creative impulses" of artists and scientists. See, for example, Lévi-Strauss (1963: 206–31) and Ehrenzweig (1970).

18 This self-awareness, and the awareness of the awareness, reflexivity, is a function of both the activities and the spaces where the activities take place. Audience self-awareness is both informal and formal. Formal self-awareness is inculcated by applause, responsive reading, singing, organized cheering, etc. In orthodox proscenium theaters – where there is less opportunity for the audience to become aware of itself – there are lobbies and intermissions. See chapters 5 and 6.

19 I know I'm quoting Goffman out of context. He meant that any place where something is done that "highlights the official values of the society" – such as a "party," or "where the practitioner attends his client" – is a celebratory place. I have specified what Goffman intended to keep general.

20 Going to the theater is consciously motivated only weakly by celebratory solidarity. If we include movie attendance with theater-going, we can perhaps say that people go because witnessing mimetic events relates them to their fellow human beings ("catharsis" in tragic theory). However, there is no denying that this function of theater-going has decreased compared to fifth century BCE Greece or Elizabethan England. At one point theater-going was a civic event; later, during the seventeenth and eighteenth centuries, it became a social event and people sat according to their class. Although it still expresses elements of this today – the better seats cost more money – I suspect that theater, and certainly movies, like watching TV, is more and more a simple pastime. That is why the theater audience is so slight: movies and TV are much cheaper pastimes. Still, theater and movies retain some qualities of social occasions – relatively few people go, or like to go, alone, while TV is acceptably solitary. Experimental performances are more expressive of social solidarity than orthodox theater. Spectators at avant-garde shows often know one another; people know what kind of audience to expect and whom to identify with. Arriving in clusters of two or more, larger groups are soon formed during intermissions and the impromptu socializing frequently continues after the performances.

21 I am indebted to Arthur Koestler (1961) for the way in which I use the terms "self-assertive" and "self-transcendent" in figures 1.2 and 1.3.

22 The relation between child play and adult fantasy needs more exploration. Freud's suggestion linking the operation of the pleasure principle in infancy with our adult artistic creations is extremely interesting. See Freud's "The Relation of the Poet to Day-Dreaming," first published in 1908 and reprinted in *On Creativity and the Unconscious* (1958: 44–54). Also see Ehrenzweig 1970 and Winnicott 1971. A great student of child play is Jean Piaget whose *Play, Dreams, and Imitation in Childhood* (1962) I recommend. Adults also play, and the relation between adult play and productive activity has not been given sufficient attention. I separate play from games in the following way: play is an activity in which the participant(s) set her/his own rules, while a game has generally acknowledged rules. Many of the activities transactional analysts would call games I call play.

23 Eric Berne (1964: 36 ff.) defines ritual this way:

a ritual is a stereotyped series of simple complementary transactions programmed by external social forces. . . . The form of a ritual is parentally determined by tradition. . . . Some formal rituals of special historical or anthropological interest have two phases: 1) a phase in which transactions are carried on under rigid parental strictures, 2) a phase of parental license in which the child is allowed more or less complete transactional freedom, resulting in an orgy.

This fits neatly with my contention that ritual and play join in crucial ways.

24 Kaprow's works often extend in time and space, but still there are boundaries. Lowry Burgess is working on a piece, *Quiet Axis*, that extends from Earth to the far side of the Moon and on to the Large Cloud of Magellan. As of 2002, Burgess – by then sixty-two years old and a Professor of Art at Carnegie-Mellon University – was still working on his decades-long piece.

2

ACTUALS

Tiwi society is established on what a non-Tiwi might consider an absurdity. These north Australian Aborigines make no connection between intercourse and pregnancy. The mother is the sole biological source of the child. The mother's husband controls his wives and his children and of these he particularly values his daughters. Women, like money with us, are the main means of exchange. It is not necessary to detail the system. The result is that old men have young wives and young men marry crones.

Where there are old men with young wives and young men without sex mates there will be adultery. A Tiwi elder accuses a young man of adultery by coming to the center of the village, preferably on a feast day so he can be sure of a large crowd, and calling the offender out. The old man is painted from head to toe in white. In one hand he carries some ceremonial spears and in the other hunting spears. A crowd arranges itself in an ellipse with the old man at one elongated end and the young man at the other. Everyone in the village, and often outsiders too, are present – men, women, children, dogs. They sit, stand, move about, according to their excitement. The young man is naked, except for a few strokes of white coloring applied to his flanks. The more white he wears the more defiant he declares himself to be. Perhaps he carries a spear or two or only a throwing stick. The old man begins a harangue of about 20 minutes duration. He details the young man's worthlessness and ingratitude – talking not only of the offence at hand but the whole life of the young man. The old man stamps his feet and chews his beard: he puts on a good show. The young man shows his good form by taking in this verbal assault in silence. When the harangue is over the old man throws a hunting spear at the young man. The young man dodges – which is not hard to do because the old man is old and he is throwing from 40 to 50 feet away. But if the young man moves too far away at his end of the ellipse the crowd jeers at him. If the old man is wild in his throws, he is jeered. The trial/duel continues until the young man has dodged enough spears to prove his prowess, but not too many to appear insolent. Allowing himself to be hit takes great skill and the crowd enjoys a young man who takes a spear in the fleshy part of the thigh or the upper arm. There is much blood but no permanent harm. The young man's bravery and humility have been demonstrated while the old man's authority and dignity have been repaired. The crowd, entertained, happily applauds both parties to the dispute.

Such is the Tiwi ritual combat according to the rules. But sometimes a young man is extremely defiant. He dodges too many of the old man's spears, or he answers the harangue, or he returns the old man's fire. In such cases the old man is joined by more and more old men, while still others restrain the relatives of the young man. Spears are thrown in volleys and the young man is driven from the village permanently, seriously wounded, or killed.

The Tiwi trial does not determine "right" or "wrong." It doesn't matter whether in fact the young man is guilty of adultery, or if there are extenuating circumstances. The trial is a test of the young man's willingness to confirm the authority of the old man. Whenever that authority offers itself for confirmation, Tiwi custom demands submission. Tiwi society rests on the authority of the old, and the only capital offence is defiance of that authority. The crowd enjoys the spectacle which makes the law tangible. If the ceremony were a true trial with a doubtful outcome, Tiwi society would collapse.

In 1967, Alan Kaprow composed *Fluids*,

> a single event done in many places over a three-day period. It consists simply in building huge, blank, rectangular ice structures 30 feet long,

> 10 feet wide, and 8 feet high. The structures are built by people who decide to meet a truck carrying 650 ice blocks per structure. They set this thing up using rock salt as a binder – which hastens melting and fuses the block together. The structures are to be built (and were) in about 20 places throughout Los Angeles. If you were crossing the city you might suddenly be confronted by these mute and meaningless blank structures which have been left to melt. Obviously, what's taken place is a mystery of sorts.
>
> (Kaprow 1968b)[1]

I could multiply examples of similar "mysteries." The avant-garde from the Italian Futurists through the Dadaists, surrealists, and on to practitioners of earth art[2] and happenings introduces us to the idea that art is not a way of imitating reality or expressing states of mind. At the heart of what Kaprow calls a mystery is the simple but altogether upsetting idea of art as an event – an "actual."

Plato in Book X of The Republic attacks the arts. "The tragic poet, too, is an artist who represents things; so this will apply to him: he and all other artists are, as it were, third in succession from the throne of truth" (Plato 1945: 327). Art is an imitation of life and life merely a shadow of the ideal forms. Thus "the work of the artist is a third remove from the essential nature of the thing" (ibid.). Plato's translator, Francis Cornford, comments that "the view that a work of art is an image of likeness (eikon) of some original, or holds up a mirror to nature, became prominent towards the end of the fifth century together with the realistic drama of Euripides and the illusionist painting of Zeuxis. Plato's attack adopts this theory" (Plato 1945: 323–4).

Plato's student Aristotle agrees that art is mimetic but asks precisely what does art imitate and how? Art does not imitate things or even experience, but "action." Action is a problematical idea and, at best, I can only sketch an interpretation of what Aristotle might have meant. Art imitates patterns, rhythms, and developments. In art, as in nature, things are born, they grow, they flourish, they decline, they die. Form, which is crystalline in Plato, is fluid in Aristotle. Each organism (animate, natural, artistic[3]) conceals a determining pattern-factor that governs its development. This DNA-like factor determines the growth rate, shape, rhythm and life-span of every organism. Everything has its own life-plan, its own "indwelling form." It is this form which art imitates.

Aristotle's idea is sublime. It imparts to everything – from thought to the slow unwinding of a galaxy to the lives of people to the grain of sand – a living, intrinsic, and dynamic participation in creating, being, becoming, and ceasing. From the Aristotelian perspective "individuality" is seen in its original meaning: not divisible. Things are integral both inherently and in their relationships to their environments. Destiny is the interplay between what is inborn and what is met. Every acorn is an oak-in-process. But between acorn and oak is sun, rain, wind, lightning, and men with axes. "Count no man happy until the day of his death," intones the chorus at the conclusion of *Oedipus*. That tragedy is fulfilled, and ended, but not so Oedipus the character – he goes on to other adventures. As Aristotle said, "Tragedy, then, is the imitation of an action that is serious, complete and of a certain magnitude" (Aristotle 1961: 61). Of an action, not of a person's life. Oedipus' life offered to Sophocles two complete actions – *Oedipus* and *Colonus*. Another author might have found more, or less.

From a naive biographical vantage, tragedies are about broken lives, early death, unfulfilled promises, remorse, maimed ambitions and tricks of fate. What has a "beginning, middle, and end" is the artwork. At the deepest level a play is about itself. Aristotle suggests that the playwright takes from life an impulse – a story, an idea, an image, a sense of person. This impulse is the kernel of the artwork whose process is a twisting and transformation of the impulse until, at a decisive moment, the artwork breaks off and becomes itself. From then on, the artwork makes its own demands in accord with its indwelling form or action. These, as artists know, may be stubbornly unlike those of the original impulse or conscious plan.

Thus an Aristotelian artwork lives a double life. It is mimetic in the Platonic sense, but it is also itself. As Fergusson points out, the relationship between artwork and experience is one of "analogy." The root idea of mimesis is sophisticated by Aristotle, but not transmuted. Art always "comes after" experience; the separation between art and life is built into the idea of mimesis. It is this coming after and separation that has been so decisive in the development of western theater.

An analogy will make clear exactly what I mean by "coming after."

Cooked food "comes after" raw food. Cooking is something that is done to raw stuff to change it into food and, perhaps, to purify it. All cooked food was once raw; all raw food is cookable. Some fruits and vegetables are "food" raw or cooked, but most meats need to be cooked before they are considered to be food. The process of cooking is irreversible. There is no way for raw food to "come after" cooked food. So it is with art and life. Art is cooked and life is raw. Making art is the process of transforming raw experience into palatable forms. This transformation is a mimetic, a representation. Such, at any rate, is the heart of the mimetic theory. In non-mimetic art the boundaries between "life" and "art" – raw and cooked – are blurry and permeable.

The hot interest in anthropology over the past generation or so has not been all good. Artists and theorists alike have, in their yearnings, constructed neo-Rousseauian fantasies of "primitive" peoples. As Charles Leslie wrote:

> There is . . . a fashionable modern conception of "primitive man" as inhabiting a "mystical" world of "timeless," "cosmological," "metaphorical" and "magical" presences. Costumed in the "archetypal" masks of tribal art, and possessed of a special "primitive mentality," this phantasmagoria is said to perform "ritual dramas" of "mythic reality." This particular conception of primitive man enjoys greatest currency in artistic and literary circles [where] primitive cultures are to modern thought what classical antiquity was to the Renaissance.
>
> (Leslie 1960: xi)

Although anthropologists have mostly cured themselves of such illusions, soft-headed artists continue to look afield, hoping to find in the Other a finer version of what their own self might be.

But it is no better to think of the Tiwi as the guys next door. Leslie thinks the counter-current attributing an urban pragmatism to people like the Tiwi an apologia for a kind of rationality which many anthropologists feel is in jeopardy. What makes *The Savage Mind* so satisfying is Claude Lévi-Strauss's ability to uphold the claim of what is special in "primitive" peoples while not denying what is common to all. Aristotle's particular brand of logic is not universal, but, Lévi-Strauss says, an appetite for classification is. Peoples think differently, but every people thinks systematically in its own terms. Lévi-Strauss does not resurrect the noble savage or blur differences with an archetypal smear.

We live under terrible stress. Politically, intellectually, artistically, personally, and epistemologically we are at breaking points. It is a cliché to say that a society is in crisis. But ours, particularly here on the North American continent,* seems gripped by total crisis and faced with either disintegration or brutal, sanctioned repression. The yearnings of the young may be a combination of infantile wishes for the wholeness of Mama's breast and a thrashing toward an impossible Utopian socialism. Or these yearnings may indicate a genuine alternative to our horrific destiny. I cannot distinguish between the true and the false. But I can identify yearnings which have triggered not only an interest in primitive peoples but artistic movements that concretize that interest and start to satisfy those yearnings.

Wholeness. Participatory democracy, self-determination on the local, national, and international levels. Therapies which start from the oneness of mind/body/feelings. "Getting it together." Total theater, intermedia, integrated electronic systems, McLuhanism. An end to dichotomies, so that:

a whole person	not mind/body
families	not fragmented individuals
communities	not government vs. governed
jobs like play	not alienated work
art where we are	not in museums far away
one world in peace	not wars and international rivalries
human one with nature	not ecological warfare

Process and organic growth. An end to the assembly-line approach to the production of goods and the conformism of people. Animosity toward the police, the military-industrial complex. "Process, not product." "Do your own thing." "Turn people into artists, not on to art." Turbulence and discontinuity, not artificial smoothness. Organic foods. Kicking out your feelings. Ritual art, all-night dances.

Concreteness. Down with theories, abstractions, generalizations, the

* In 1970, when this essay first appeared.

"biggies" of art, industry, education, government, etc. Make your demands known, act them out and get an answer now. Radicalize the students. Street and guerrilla theater, Provo action, marches on Washington, demonstrations on campus. Arm the blacks, urban warfare in the ghettoes. Dig the physicality of experience. Sensory awareness, involvement, and expression. Happenings, earth art, concrete poetry and music, pornography.

Religious transcendental experience. Mysticism, shamanism, messianism, psychedelics, epiphanies. Zen, yoga, and other ways to truth through participation or formulation, as in macrobiotics, yoga, and mantra-chanting. Eschatological yearnings: what is the meaning of life? Make all experience meaningful. Sacralize everyday living. Sung poetry, encounter groups, experimental theater, marathons, T-groups, performances made in and by communities, tribalism, rock festivals, drugs, trips, freak-outs, ecstasies.

Wholeness, process and organic growth, concreteness, and religious transcendental experience are fundamental to many oral-based tribal cultures. The terms differ from culture to culture, and differ radically between any tribal culture and our own. But there are links joining us and them. These links, or metaphors, are strongest and clearest between what we call art, particularly new theater, and what they call by names ranging from play to dancing to doing.

The four categories are inseparable. They overlap, interpenetrate, feed from each other, exchange, transform into one another. Any separation is artificial. In many cultures the very separations that make this essay possible would be impossible.

A try at explaining actuals involves a survey of anthropological, sociological, psychological, and historical materials. But these are not organized to promote the search. And the scope of this essay prohibits me from taking anything but a quick glance at the sources. There I find an incipient theory for a special kind of behaving, thinking, relating, and doing. This special way of handling experience and jumping the gaps between past and present, individual and group, inner and outer, I call "actualizing" (perhaps no better than Eliade's "reactualizing," but at least shorter). Actualizing is plain among rural, tribal peoples and it is becoming plainer among our own young and in their avant-garde art. The questions are not polemical, but structural: not whether the new theater (and life-style) is good, but how is it built and what, precisely, are its bases? Then, what are its functions and how do these relate to the life we live individually and collectively? I think we will find that the new theater is very old, and that our localized urban avant-garde belongs next to worldwide, rural-tribal tradition.

What might we make of the possible etymological link between the word "drama" – from the Greek *dran*: to do, to act, to make – and the word "dream" – from the Old English and the Old Frisian *dram*: a dream, a shout of joy? Somewhere in that pretty connection is the feel of actualizing. "According to the [Australian] aborigines," says Lommel (1967: 146), "in the dream state man has a share in the creativity of nature, and if he were to be creatively active in this state he would really, as the painter Baumeister expressed it, 'not create after nature, but like nature.' "

Understanding actualizing means understanding both the creative condition and the artwork, the actual. Among primitive peoples the creative condition is identical with trances, dances, ecstasies; in short, shamanism.[4] Shamanism is "a method, a psychic technique" (Lommel 1967: 148)[5] of which the "fundamental characteristic . . . is ecstasy, interpreted as the soul foresaking the body." This technique is very ancient, with roots among Central Asian peoples during the Alpine Paleolithic period, some 30,000 to 50,000 years ago. "No one has yet shown that the ecstatic experience is the creation of a particular historical civilization or a particular culture cycle. In all probability the ecstatic experience, in its many aspects, is coexistent with the human condition" (Eliade 1965: 100–1). What is an ecstatic experience? Eliade and Lommel quote examples. And Rothenberg cites Isaac Tens' own account of how he became a shaman:

> Then my heart started to beat fast, & I began to tremble, just as has happened before. . . . My flesh seemed to be boiling. . . . My body was quivering. While I remained in this state, I began to sing. A chant was coming out of me without my being able to do anything to stop it. Many things appeared to me presently: huge birds & other animals. . . . These were visible only to me, not to the others in my house. Such visions happen when a man is about to become a *shaman*; they occur of their own accord. The songs force themselves out complete without

any attempt to compose them. But I learned & memorized those
songs by repeating them.

(Rothenberg 1968: 51–2)[6]

Rothenberg (1968: 424) thinks that Tens' experience is "typical of
1) the psychology of shamanism; 2) the shaman's 'initiation' through
dream and vision, 3) transformation of vision into song." Eliade and
Lommel cite similar examples. Eliade (1965: 87) says there are three
ways of becoming a shaman: as Tens did through the "call"; by inherit-
ance; and by personal ambition or the will of the tribe. A shaman is
authenticated only after having received two kinds of instruction. The
first is ecstatic (for example, dreams, visions, trances); the second is
traditional (for example, shamanic techniques, names and functions of
the spirits, mythology and genealogy of the clan, secret language). The
instruction of the fledgling shaman first by older shamans and then by
the spirits is a universal aspect of shamanism. Its structure is much like
Dante's travels with Virgil through the Christian other worlds. Lommel
describes an Australian shamanic instruction.

At sunset the shaman's soul meets somewhere the shadow of a dead
ancestor. The shadow asks the soul whether it shall go with it. The
shaman's soul answers yes. . . . Then they go on together, either at
once into the kingdom of the dead or to a place in this world at which
the spirits of the dead have gathered. . . . The spirits begin to sing and
dance. . . . When the dance is over the spirits release the shaman's
soul and his helping spirit brings it back to his body. When the
shaman wakes, his experiences with the spirits seem to him like a
dream. From now on he thinks of nothing but the dances which he has
seen and his soul keeps on going back to the spirits to learn more
and more about the dances. . . . Then he will first explain the dances to
his wife and sing them to her, and after that he will teach them to
everyone else.

(Lommel 1967: 138–9)

The shaman's journeys are neither gratuitous nor for private use. He
goes to get something and he must deliver what he gets back to his
people – he must teach them what he learns. His work is social work.

The shaman is prized by his people. He is "the exemplar and model for all those who seek to acquire power; [he] is the man who knows and remembers" (Eliade 1965: 102). But sometimes his powers fail him, his link with the other world breaks. This is a crisis for the entire community. (I am reminded forcefully of the plague which starts the search for Laius' murderer. King Oedipus is a shaman. His sacrifice cures Thebes, and his search, assisted by the townsfolk, is a paradigm of shamanic quest. The story is overlaid with other things, but its roots go deep into pre-Aristotelian patterns of feeling and doing.) Lommel says that in Australia when a shaman loses touch with the other world "his poetic gift for creating songs and dances vanishes." All the men of the community sit in a circle around the shaman. They sing for hours a "regularly rising and falling note" and rub his body. The shaman goes into trance. He seeks a spirit of a dead ancestor whom he tells that he "cannot 'find' any more songs." The spirit promises help and the shaman comes out of trance. Several days later the shaman "hears a distant call. It is his helping spirit calling him. He goes off by himself and converses for a while with the spirit." A few days later his soul leaves his body. "Many spirits now come up from the underworld [and] tear the [shaman's] soul to pieces and each spirit carries a piece into the underworld. There, deep under the earth they put the shaman's soul together again. They show him the dances again and sing songs to him" (Lommel 1967: 139).[7] The shaman is whole; his link is repaired. Everyone helped him get it together.

What are we to make of these experiences? It has been customary to "interpret" reports like these – to find in our way of thinking analogues making such experiences rationally acceptable. Thus Lommel (1967: 139) says that the quest for the missing ceremonial link is "an authentic account of the nature of artistic creativity [which shows vividly] the connection of an artist's creative potency with tradition – with the ancestors." Eliade never tires of showing that shamanic experiences are prototypes of our own religious beliefs. Psychoanalysts interpret in the direction of instinctual needs and unconscious processes. I accept these interpretations. But they are not complete. Shamanic experiences are real and whole. Our interpretations diminish and fragment them – we want to make the experiences "otherworldly," "transcendental," or "fantasies." But these experiences are the result of something which Cassirer notes about the thinking of oral peoples. "By a sudden metamorphosis everything may be turned into everything. [There is] the deep conviction of a fundamental and indelible *solidarity of life* that bridges over the multiplicity and variety of its single forms."[8] Everywhere there are overlaps, exchanges, and transformations (like those, for example, in figure 2.1). Experience is not segregated onto hierarchical planes. It is not that everything is the same, but that all things are part of one wholeness, and that among things unlimited exchanges and transformations are possible.

Some artists among us experience the way the Australians do. Artists treat experience as something indivisible but exchangeable; as endlessly varied but on the same plane; as here and now but other-worldly. It is this hard-to-talk-about-in-our-language thing that Lévi-Strauss means when he says that

> there are still zones in which savage thought, like savage species, is relatively protected. This is the case of art. . . . Savage thought is definable both by a consuming symbolic ambition such as humanity has never again seen rivaled, and by scrupulous attention directed entirely towards the concrete, and finally by the implicit conviction that these two attitudes are but one.
>
> (Lévi-Strauss 1966: 219–20)

From here it is just a short step to understanding actualizing.

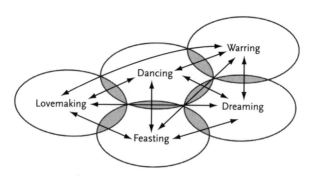

Figure 2.1

Eliade does not define reactualization. Instead he gives examples of it. An initiation is a ceremony in which "a new generation is instructed, is made fit to be integrated into the community of adults. And on this occasion, through the repetition, the *reactualization*, of the traditional rites, the entire community is regenerated" (Eliade 1965: 40). The actualization is the making present of a past time or event. Eliade describes a puberty initiation of eastern Australia called a Bora. The initiates are surprised at home and "kidnapped," held at the place of initiation. There, secluded, they are instructed in the lore, dances, and songs of their tribe. This schooling lasts for months. During it, the initiates are kept under strict discipline. The ceremonial area is a "sacred space" within which ordinary time has been abolished and dreamtime is. Dreamtime is the time of the first initiation rite performed by Baiamai, the supreme being. Finally, amid dancing and singing, the initiates are circumcised: their bodies irrevocably marked with a sign of their belonging to the tribe. The Bora ground is Baiamai's first camp and the initiators are those who were with Baiamai when he inaugurated these ceremonies. This reintegration of time and place is not peculiar to the Australians. It is true

> for the entire primitive world. For what is involved here is a fundamental concept in archaic religions – the repetition of a ritual founded by Divine Beings implies the reactualization of the original Time when the rite was first performed. This is why a rite has efficacy – it participates in the completeness of the sacred primordial Time. The rite makes the myth present. Everything that the myth tells of the Time of beginning, the "*bugari* times" [Dreamtime], the rite reactualizes shows it as happening, *here and now*.
>
> (Eliade 1965: 6)[9]

This is true not only of compact rites but of those which are narrative and of long duration. The Elema of New Guinea celebrate a cycle called the *Hevehe*, after the majestic 30-foot-high mask-spirits whose appearance and dances are the climax of a process that takes from 6 to 20 years or more to complete. The masks are built in the men's ceremonial house, the *eravo*, which is lengthened and heightened to accommodate the painstaking work. A number of ceremonies mark the

Hevehe over the years – there is a close-knitting of the eravo, the masks being built in it, the political and economic life of the people, the life-cycle of individual and social life meaning and continuity. Some cycles which Williams observed were started in 1914 but not finished by 1937 when he gathered his data. Others, begun at about the same time, were completed in 1920, 1932, and 1934.

> It may be thought that this dragging out of the cycle is the result of modern influences, as if the Hevehe were drawing a series of long, dying gasps. [But] there is ample evidence to show that formerly, as well as now, the Hevehe cycles occupied very long periods.
>
> (Williams 1940: 118)[10]

A man with a full life might participate in three, possibly four, Hevehe.

In a cycle that takes as long to complete as the Hevehe, things are not so strict moment to moment as they are in the Bora. The cycle develops in bursts, with intensive activities surrounding particular ceremonies, and long periods of inactivity between. The ceremonies all take place in and around the village, and many involve the women and children. In one, people from neighbouring villages wearing small dancing masks, *eharo*, invade the host village. Bunched around the eharo are enthusiastic women and children, and resisting the invaders are hundreds of people who shower the invaders with coconut flakes. A mock battle is fought on the beach and then the invaders sweep into the village. Erotic pantomimes vie with more staid dancing and children run about the village armed with toy bows and arrows which they shoot at bunches of bananas, or sago. Throughout all this some of the village elders lounge on the veranda of the eravo, seemingly disinterested and certainly unperturbed. This carnival mock-war dance seems altogether different from the Bora. There the ceremony was formal, far from the village, in total seclusion, and no women or children were permitted to watch or even know of the rituals. The elders were the most important participants. Here, everything is the opposite; but the differences are not of an essential kind.

The climax of the cycle is the month-long dancing of the hevehe masks. Months of hard preparation have laid away stores of food, and inside the eravo the last touches have been completed on the masks.

The night before the emergence of the Hevehe drumming begins from the upper level of the eravo. Before dawn a large crowd of women and children gather before the eravo's 30-foot double doors. The drumming suddenly stops and the pushing and shoving of the crowd reaches a "perfect fury of joy and excitement."

> There are many dramatic situations in the cycle, but none can compare with this supreme moment which the hevehe, after wellnigh twenty years of confinement, issue forth to commence the brief fulfillment of their existence. In the grey light of early morning the first of them, "Koraia," stood framed against the blackness of the open door – a tall, fantastic figure, silvery white, its colored patterns in the atmosphere of dawn appearing pale and very delicate. . . . For a brief moment "Koraia" stood there, the great crown of spectators gazing in silence. Then, with a thump of the drum and a prodigious rattling of *harau*, it started down the gangway. Immediately behind it came "Pekeaupe"; and after that, in crowded succession, 120 others.
>
> (Williams 1940: 356–7)

As each mask starts dancing, groups of women and children detach themselves from the large crowd and dance around masks worn by fathers, husbands, brothers, and sons. The women carry green twigs and they flick the legs of the mask-dancers.

> In the center are the portentous figures of the hevehe, with their staring eyes and their fierce jaws abristle with teeth, their mantles rising and falling and their human arms vigorously belaboring the drums and kicking up the dust. Though they are 20 feet high and more they dance, not lightly (that would be a sheer impossibility) but with amazing animation.
>
> (Williams 1940: 361)

The hevehe dance throughout the village and on the beach. They dance all day and part of the night for a month. It is hot, and a man dances with his mask on for from 15 minutes to an hour. Then he returns to the eravo and attaches his mask to its hooks.

Streaming with perspiration, the last wearer sits down to cool off; but presently he will be seen fitting some other mask over his head, shuffling a little to get it balanced to his satisfaction and then making his way towards the door, fully prepared for a further tour. Any man, in fact, may wear any mask with its owner's permission; nor is the owner likely to refuse it, since he is flattered to see his hevehe in frequent use.

(Williams: 1940: 360)

The dancing is a performance, but of a special kind. It is thought that when a man wears a mask he is "animated by the spirits which are derived from the myths." Each hevehe has a name because each is a spirit. The spirit moves only when a man is in the mask. Conversely, a man dances well only when he is moved by the spirit. Two autonomous, symbiotic existences support each other. The women and children know who is in the masks – they accompany their close relatives and tease them into more vigorous dancing. Men freely exchange masks, animating and being animated by many spirits in one day. Here is a clear example of the exchange between two realities which the Elema put on one plane: 1) the masks which are living things; 2) the men who wear the masks. The masks do not represent the spirits or contain the spirits; the masks are the spirits.

At the end of the month of dancing the hevehe make their way to the beach for the last time. The women "rush to the giant masks and embrace their projecting jaws and kiss their faces, while not a few were shedding tears" (Williams 1940: 365). Some beat their breasts and others try to stop the hevehe from reaching the beach. But the masks get there and dance. Then one by one, in no set order, each gives up its drum and slowly they from into two lines. These lines start a solemn procession back from the beach to the eravo. Soon all but 8 of the 122 hevehe have gone into the eravo. The last eight masks are intercepted by some young women and a ritual combat begins. The men have arranged that the last eight masks should be small and light and the men in them strong.

Next moment they were circled about by a score of robust females clasping one another's hands. Almost immediately the circle broke up into two, one for either *eravo*-side and each imprisoning four hevehe. ... The hevehe try again and again to burst through the circle. They turn side on and hurl themselves on the out-stretched arms of the women. But the women are strong, and they are reinforced by others, standing outside the ring, who clamp their hands together. They easily hold their own and send the hevehe staggering back into the center; but after repeated charges the wall begins to break and one after another the prisoners escape.

(Williams 1940: 367)

When the last hevehe enters the eravo the 200 women turn toward the eravo, raise their arms over their heads, and chant. Some hours later, after a feast, four of the masks re-emerge. A shaman arms his bow and says, "I, Aku-akore, stand here and am about to kill you. I am taking all you possess." He shoots through the face of a mask. "Very realistically, as if mortally wounded, the hevehe staggered and fell" (Williams 1940: 373). The women cry out in grief and flee from the village. The other three masks are shot.

With the fall of the four hevehe and the exodus of the women there began a scene of deliberate destruction. Masks, no longer worn but carried, came pouring out of the door to be propped against the house-walls or thrown carelessly on the ground. Without the slightest trace of reverence or regret their owners proceeded to strip them of their *mae* mantles and their feathers.

(Williams 1940: 375)

Parts of the masks are kept for the next cycle; parts are loaned to neighbouring villages. The dead hulks are taken to the stream and thrown into three piles. "It seemed as if the masks were to be disposed of without any touch of ceremony whatever, so keen was everyone on the practical side of the business." But, before the masks are burned, the shaman says,

"Now I am going to burn you. Look kindly on the men of my *eravo*. When they hunt let not the arrow stick in the ground, but in the eye of the pig. I do no harm to you. Constantly, from long ago I have fed and fostered you. Do not be angry with us."

Or,

> "I have called you up because of my pigs and sago. I have fed you
> constantly. In the future some other strong men will call you. Do not
> be angry." "The man of pigs, the man of dogs, calls you. But now I
> burn you. Ivo and Leravae, our women, girls and little boys – let no
> centipede sting them, no thorns pierce them, no snakes or sharks bite
> them. Guard them well."
>
> (Williams 1940: 376–7)

There is personal variation and style in the invocations. The masks have
life and must be killed. When they are burned, the hevehe spirits go back
to the bush. "Why the hevehe should be killed at all is a question which
no native was ever able to answer" (Williams 1940: 373). The spirits
are immortal and they will be recreated in the next cycle. The eravo
is empty.

> Gradually the great grey building falls into decay; the floor-boards rot;
> thatching, ripped off by the wind, goes unrepaired; and rain falls mis-
> erably upon deserted hearthsides. One by one the members seek
> other sleeping quarters, and at last the *eravo* is a ruin. Then, when it
> threatens to collapse, . . . the community will make a strenuous effort
> and demolish it. For some years, perhaps, they will content them-
> selves with humbler lodgings; but at last, if spirit is willing and flesh is
> strong, they will set to and build themselves another *eravo*, and with
> that the long Hevehe cycle will start all over again.
>
> (Williams 1940: 390–1)

The cycle is majestic. Its duration, the harmony among its many parts,
and the close-fitting almost symbiotic ties between it and other aspects
of the life of the Elema make it one of mankind's great creations. But
along with its solemnity and grandeur is a joviality and irreverence that
at first glance jars.

The women are not supposed to see parts of the cycle, or the masks
hanging dead inside the eravo. Eliade says that when men swinging
bullroarers enter the village "they have the right to kill any woman or
non-initiate who tries to discover their identity" (Eliade 1965: 33). But

Williams tells of many times when concealment is treated casually. The doors of the eravo are often left open and the women see "quite enough to dispel their curiosity" (Williams 1940: 365). If a woman dances with the hevehe of a son rather than a husband, the offended man may get very angry. During the "cutting off" combat the women are strong enough to keep the eight masks trapped indefinitely. But Williams heard one young man brag how he told his sister, "Isn't it time you let me go?" and at the next charge he was free (p. 367).

The Hevehe cycle mixes the ceremonial and the personal without diluting or blending either. A mask dances because it is alive. A man dances because he is animated by the mask. A mask dies when its face is shot through by an arrow. Parts of its hulk can be used again. The spirits may suffer as they are killed. Yet they do not die but go to the bush and wait to be recalled. After the audience of weeping women leave the village, the masks are killed simply by being thrown down. Both the dancing and the dying are performances – and all performances are vis-à-vis someone. There is an absolute separation between the performance and the performer. A separation that encourages exchange and transformation. Bravado, joking, rehearsing, and special backstage behavior are possible because the Elema know when they are on stage and when they are off. Their performances are not impersonations, but possessions and exchanges; the spirit and the man interpenetrate each other without either losing his identity. The dancing of the hevehe lifts the whole community to a month of exaltation. When the hevehe are killed and the spirits gone, the eravo falls to shambles.

What is the relationship between the mask and the masker? At every moment during each ceremony during the long Hevehe cycle the people know two independent but reciprocating realities.

1) The reality of the hevehe masks and the autonomously unfolding cycle. These spirits are not abstract or generalized. They move in space, can be touched and seen, and are known *personally* by the men building them. Slowly they are built in the eravo, and each phase of building is marked by celebration. The masks are never half-alive, but like embryos they are not ready for independent dancing life outside the eravo until they are complete and whole. When they emerge they dance among all the people for a month. The spirits can be heard in the roar of the bull-roarers and the clamor of the gongs. They do not die, but they must be

killed anyway, and not mysteriously but by bow and arrow, and then burned by fire.

2) The reality of the villagers' everyday lives – of hunting and farming, feasting, sharing, exchanging, marrying, child-rearing, politicking, fighting, ageing, sickening, dying. In theatrical terms neither the performed (masks) nor the performers (villagers) is absorbed into each other; one does not "play the role" of the other. They stand whole and yet autonomous. Their relationship is what Grotowski called a "confrontation." It is not that one reality reflects, represents, or distills the other. Both move freely through the same time/space. The realities confront, overlap, interpenetrate each other in a relationship that is extraordinarily dynamic and fluid.

The burning of the hevehe masks and the circumcising of the initiates at the Bora are culminating irrevocable acts proclaiming that there can be no turning back. The Australians mark off a special place where the men bring the boys into the whole community. The initiation is relatively swift and certainly intense, convulsive, and isolated. Contrarily, the Elema cycle unfolds among the villagers' homes, meeting places, and playgrounds. After the masks are burned, the village is only half-alive until the start of the next cycle. But the apparently opposite actuals of Australia and New Guinea are founded on the same belief in multiple, valid, equivalent, and reciprocating realities. The actuals are here and now, efficacious and irrevocable.

William Finley, playing Dionysus in *Dionysus in 69*, had to start his performance each night by emerging naked amid an audience of 200 and saying, "Good evening, my name is William Finley, and I am a god." Only by finding, releasing, and showing his deepest impulses of fear, hilarity, fraud, and humiliation could he begin to cope with the actuality of his preposterous situation. His claim to divinity is thinkable only in the terms of the trapped hevehe who said to his sister, "Isn't it time you let me go?"

When a performer does not "play a character" what is s/he doing? Stand-up comics play aspects of themselves. Disclosure is the heart of the comic's art. S/he carefully keeps to the edge – just a little too much and the act is embarrassing and painful. The audience teeters between knowing it is being put on and glimpsing brief, but deep, looks into the "real person." Like a Malibu Beach muscleman, the comic overdevelops part of his/her personality and displays these shamelessly.

The movie star wears a different story and costume in each film. But s/he is groomed for one limited set of traits and these vivify all his/her roles. The cynical, easy violence of Bogart; the sharp-as-a-whip worldliness of Hepburn; the austere integrity of Cooper; the slurred, rough goodness of Wayne; the slut-who-is-good of Monroe. The star has his/her own thing that organizes the filmic "vehicle" around it. One is never sure how much of the "star personality" is genuine, and how much put on. The star is usually not sure either. A stereotyped mask thickens and freezes – this mask is worn publicly and privately throughout life.

Circus performers are like performers of actuals – except that at the circus everything is made to look more glamorous and dangerous than it is. The motive of the circus is "I dare you" and this is blatantly stimulated in the audience by the performers and ringmaster. The great circus performers are those who go to the utmost limit, seem about to fail, recover, and succeed brilliantly. Hokum and skill – coming out of a near fall with a perfect landing capped by a superbly graceful bow to the cheering house: that's the essential circus.

Athletes, like circus performers, display their skills. The rules of games are designed to show prowess, quick judgement, finesse and grace, speed, endurance, strength, and teamwork. Also the rules encourage spectators to measure performance against some objective standard. American athletics are embellished by the ballyhoo and excitement natural to large crowds and focused by the intense competitiveness of our way of sporting. But among Mexico's Tarahumaras racing is participatory – men, women, and children, old and young race together. It doesn't matter who finishes first – to arrive last is as honorable as to arrive first. The whole race is of interest to all spectators who measure individual performance against individual ability. What counts is that everyone who participates does their best. To be a laggard brings shame on you and your family.

The idea of danger is exploited by the circus; that of excellence is the kernel of athletics. This combination of risk and mastery is asked of the performer of actuals. S/he is not a shaman or an acrobat or an athlete – but he shares the quality of these.

An actual has five basic qualities, and each is found both in our own actuals and those of tribal people: 1) *process*, something happens *here and now*; 2) *consequential, irremediable,* and *irrevocable* acts, exchanges, or situations; 3) *contest*, something is *at stake* for the performers and often for the spectators; 4) *initiation, a change in status* for participants; 5) space is used *concretely* and *organically*. Each of these basic qualities deserves extensive explication. I shall only be able to skim what is available.

Process, something happens here and now. This is largely a matter of emphasis. Even naturalistic actors affirm that something happens to them psychologically and physiologically during a performance. But training and rehearsals are designed to hide most of this process or to bring it entirely in line with the playwright's intentions as envisioned by the director so that the performance reveals not the actors but the characters they are playing. The goal of orthodox acting and the basis of Stanislavsky's great work is to enable actors to "really live" their characters. Nature ought to be so skillfully imitated that it seems to be re-presented on stage. The tendency of an actual is the opposite. Instead of the smooth "professionalism" of the "good actor," there are rough and unexpected turbulences, troubled interruptions. These are not stylistic, but the genuine meeting between performer and problem.

Two processes unfold simultaneously. The first is the one shaped by author and director, the play and the *mise-en-scène*. But just as important is the more evanescent process of the performer. The play and *mise-en-scène* have a quality of having-been-lived, while the performance has the quality of living-now. The play will be completed only if the performers are able to carry through the process they start afresh each night. That process cannot be rehearsed.

Perhaps this will be clearer if I relate what Ryszard Cieslak of the Polish Laboratory Theater told me. I did not understand what Cieslak meant by "score" and I asked him to explain.

> We work in rehearsals to find an objective set of actions and relationships that, understood apart from anything we the performers might feel, communicate to the audience the images, actions, and meanings we want to communicate. This process takes months and it is a *via negativa* – that is, we reject more than we accept and we search so that we can remove obstacles to our creativity. We play out the actions at

hand, the associations that offer themselves to us. Grotowski watches. He helps us remove blocks, things that prevent us from fully confronting and experiencing the actions at hand.

Finally we construct a coherent score. This score, which grows minutely day by day, includes all the objective things a spectator sees from night to night. For example, in *Akropolis* my score includes how my body lies in the wheelbarrow, what tone my voice has, how I breathe, how my fingers move. The score even includes the associations I have, what I think about from moment to moment. These associations I change from time to time, as they get stale. And as it is for me, so it is for everyone else. Ideally the score is whole and does not need completion or revision. In practice, it is never that way. Only a percentage of each production is scored when we begin performing it for audiences. After four years of performing *Akropolis* about 80 per cent of it is scored for me.

The score is like the glass inside which a candle is burning. The glass is solid, it is there, you can depend on it. It contains and guides the flame. But it is not the flame. The flame is my inner process each night. The flame is what illuminates the score, what the spectators see through the score. The flame is alive. Just as the flame in the candle-glass moves, flutters, rises, fall, almost goes out, suddenly glows brightly, responds to each breath of wind – so my inner life varies from night to night, from moment to moment. The way I feel an association, the interior sense of my voice or a movement of my finger, I begin each night without anticipations. This is the hardest thing to learn. I do not prepare myself to feel anything. I do not say, "Last night, this scene was extraordinary, I will try to do that again." I want only to be receptive to what will happen. And I am ready to take what happens if I am secure in my score, knowing that, even if I feel a minimum, the glass will not break, the objective structure worked out over the months will help me through. But when a night comes that I can glow, shine, live, reveal – I am ready for it by not anticipating it. The score remains the same, but everything is different because I am different.

(Personal conversation, 1970)

Grotowski describes the score as the "two banks of a river" and the performer's process as the "water flowing between those banks."[11]

We conventionally think of "process" as the sequence of events in the script – if these were "really happening" the story would be "inevitable." Thus the "death" of Hamlet or the "blinding" of Oedipus. When I think of process, I think of something that occurs in fact here and now: the melting of the ice-liths in *Fluids*, the dodging and ultimate taking of spears in the Tiwi trial, the dancing of the *Hevehe*. These processes are not gimmicks, but fundamental elements of the performance structure.

The whole of the Living Theater's *Paradise Now* is a process. The audience is given a program which is a chart of the event in phases. The performance passes through eight phases from "The Rite of Guerrilla Theater" to "The Street." There is no time limit, and many performances take 6 hours or more. All eight steps have never been genuinely accomplished – that is, the permanent revolution has not happened. (It is, of course, an error to think that it could. The Australians are more modest and successful with their ceremonies. And in so far as *Paradise Now* is a "demonstration," it is mimetic.) *Paradise Now* is pushed and pulled this way and that, seemingly in total disarray, until you realize that the performers are like tour guides – they want to move the thing along, but only after most of the audience is ready to move on. If anyone wants to stop off here or there, to examine a detail, to "put on a show," to shout, protest, or in any way detour the performance, that is fine. *Paradise Now* develops through random movement towards goals and through phases. It distends and collapses, intensifies and slackens, coheres and fragments. But still it does move: the performers decide when one phase has been sufficiently explored and then initiate another. Many spectators cannot adapt themselves to a structure that feels so disorderly. But *Paradise Now* is very well-organized if one recognizes diversion, disruption, and side-tripping as part of its organization. It is much briefer than most tribal ceremonies – many of which also include side-trips in the guise of new dances and stories, and disruptions when the community runs out of wealth or is threatened by hostile outgroups. Our sense of smooth time is jolted by *Paradise Now* which treats time as lumpy, malleable, and turbulent.

The performers in *Paradise Now* have two tasks. They act things and they nudge the audience along. Like shamans they are the principal performers and the masters of ceremony. Throughout the performance spectators wisecrack and taunt the performers. This is not irrelevant – each phase must pass through ordeals to achieve the next stop. Taunts and mockery are also part of many tribal ceremonies. Even the not-paying-attention is part of some solemn occasions – like the Yom Kippur service of Hassidic Jews, from which the Living Theater took elements of *Paradise Now*. Eventually *Paradise Now* arrives at the eighth phase and the performers, accompanied by many spectators, confront the police outside the theater. I am reminded of Irma's little speech at the end of *The Balcony*. "You must now go home, where everything – you can be quite sure – will be even falser than here." The Living Theater turns Genet on his head.

Consequential, irremediable, and irrevocable acts. There are almost none of these in our theater. Among some tribal peoples irrevocability is finely expressed in the circumcision of initiates. But it could also be taken from the exchanges of goods and people that vivify tribal life. Mauss calls these each "a total social fact." Lévi-Strauss interprets them as events which have "significance that is at once social and religious, magic and economic, utilitarian and sentimenal, jural and moral" (Lévi-Strauss 1969a: 52). Even at Christmas and on birthdays or anniversaries we are not likely to involve ourselves in such whole exchanges. To demonstrate this I devised a classroom exercise. I asked everyone to choose a partner and to exchange something for fun. Men gave their wallets, shoes, pens; women their rings, cosmetics, handbags. Then I said, "Now exchange something for real." People gave each other empty cigarette packages, blank paper, matches.

Ralph Ortiz's *The Sky is Falling* includes elements that are irrevocable. In it mice and chickens are killed, a piano axed to bits, and participants doused with blood. Participants are divided into a small number of Initiators and a large number of Initiates. The scenario is written in the terminology of ceremony, freely using words like "ritual" and "shaman." Initiates are interrogated by the Initiators and verbally abused when they refuse to participate in any detail of the piece. Violence is combined with sexuality and scatology. The violence increases through a series of overlapping and simultaneous "rituals" culminating in the "Piano Destruction Rite" and the "Birth of Henny Penny Rite." Preparatory events include breaking eggs, killing mice, cutting paper screens on which images of human dissections are projected, burning clothes, burning food, ripping and kicking apart overstuffed furniture, dismembering dead chickens, tearing clothes off participants, and throwing blood at each other. The piano destruction is carefully orchestrated and precisely performed by Ortiz. He is exact about how the demolition should be done. "One hundred live mice in a wire screen and two gallons of blood in plastic bags are to be placed inside the piano behind the panel above the keys." The axe must be "brand new," the piano "pushed on its back to the floor – the keyboard and hammer sections smashed away so that the harp is completely exposed," and so on. The "Birth of Henny Penny" has two "men Initiators wearing maternity full-length dresses . . . under spotlights ten feet apart. Each has a live chicken tied between his legs under the dress. There is also fifteen feet of tubing connected to a balloon tied low on their waists under the dresses which extends to an upright tire pump." Initiates are "harangued into pumping the pumps." The dresses inflate, all participants "join in the sighing moaning groaning and sexual motions" which continue until the balloons explode and the chickens are "delivered." Two initiators (now called Shamans) raise the birds "victoriously . . ., then waving the chickens like flags they race through the Ritual Room shouting irrational violent sounds" which convert into a "Henny Penny" chant. The other Initiators pick up the chant and then attack the Shamans, grabbing the chickens and bringing them to the demolished piano. The chickens are spread-eagled over the piano harp. The Initiators form a tight circle. The Shamans, outside the circle, start chanting "The sky is falling." They take the axe, the circle admits them, and each Shaman decapitates the other's chicken. As this happens, everyone cries like children, "Mommy!" The decapitated heads are worn in small plastic sandwich bags "taped inside the fly" of each Shaman's pants. The cry changes to "Mousie" as the tight circle opens and the Initiators go to "zones" where the Initiates have watched the sacrifice. The Initiators shout at the Initates, "You're just a bunch of fucking voyeurs!" Then the Shamans give each Initiator a live mouse. The Initiators surround the mouse trap area and throw the live mice in. Led by one of the Shamans, the Initiators begin to leave the room, "seeking out Initiates and seductively and lovingly telling them 'You love me, you love me.' "[12] The room after the performance was strewn with guts, living, dead, and half-dead mice. The floor was about an inch deep in blood. Bits of furniture, tatters of clothes, mashed food, a student vomiting – and on a platform to one side and 15 feet high were ten observers, some with cameras. The room stank of guts and blood. The effect was hideous.

Eliade comments that modern "so-called initiation rites frequently betoken a deplorable spiritual poverty. . . . But the success of these enterprises likewise proves man's profound need for initiation, that is, for regeneration, for participation in the life of the spirit" (Eliade 1965: 134–5). The Sky is Falling is a moralizing piece founded on a belief in Artaud's dictum that violence will purge violent feelings. This, in turn, is Aristotelian catharsis escalated toward the Roman reality games of gladiatorial combatants locked in deadly embrace for fun. The fun, that is, of the spectators in the Coliseum. There is, however, another frame of Ortiz's piece. Those who did not choose to participate or watch from the platform saw everything on close-circuit TV. During a discussion which followed the performance a woman berated Ortiz for "promoting such things. How can you kill animals?" she asked. Ortiz answered, "You were watching on TV, you knew where it was happening, why didn't you stop it?" This converted The Sky is Falling into a political parable: the room was Vietnam, the TV viewers were American citizens, the Initiates were draftees, the Initiators were the regular army, the Shamans were the brass and top government officials. But I don't think we can leave it at that. The Sky is Falling raises the question of what kind of irrevocable acts?

Roman reality games and mimes are the ultimate mimetic spectacles. Ortiz's work shares that mimetic ambition. His mirror is distorted and the stakes are not so high – animals, not people. Unlike the Maori of New Zealand who press earth on an initiate's chest to make him understand death, Ortiz slings animal blood and chops the heads off chickens. The "symbolic ambition" Lévi-Strauss detects as the motor of savage thinking is converted into reductive imitation. Irrevocability is understood as something which happens to the objects of the drama – the chicken and mice, the pianos and furniture – not to the subjects of the piece, the Initiates and spectators. At best these are put through a harrowing hour and left with scalding memories. Or, perhaps, like soldiers they grow war-weary, blunted to bloodshed. When violence, cruelty, sacrifice, even ritual murder and combat (as among the Dani of

West Irian[13]) are incorporated into authentic ceremonies, they are always part of a known system. Violence without the system is meaningless. Ortiz tries to invent a system through mini-violent homeopathic demonstration. His scenario is rich with the terminology of holistic religion, but without a link to a system. Irrevocable acts are rare in our theater. They can't be made by magic. When they happen they usually manifest themselves as metaphors. And they act on the people, not the props.

Contest, something is at stake for the performers and often for the spectators. In *Dionysus in 69* there is a scene about halfway through that starts when Dionysus offers Pentheus "any woman in this room." Pentheus says he can have his pick without Dionysus' help. "Okay," says Dionysus, "try it yourself." Pentheus is left alone in the center of the room. Almost every night some woman comes to him and offers help. The scene plays privately between them, and ends with the woman rejecting Pentheus (or the actor playing Pentheus?) and going back to her place. The performance resumes and Pentheus, defeated, is sacrificed. Once it did not happen that way. In the words of William Shephard who played Pentheus,

> The one time the sequence was completed was when Katherine Turner came out into the room. ... The confrontation between us was irrational. Her concern for me was not based on the play, my playing a role, whether or not I was going to die, or any of that. What happened was that I recognized in one moment that the emotional energy Katherine was spending on me literally lifted me out of the play, as though someone had grabbed me by the hair and pulled me up to the ceiling. I looked around and I saw the Garage and the other actors and I said, "It finally happened." The play fell away, like shackles being struck from my hands. The way the play is set up Pentheus is trapped inside its structure. But on that night it all seemed to fall away and I walked out of the door.
>
> (The Performance Group 1970: n.p.)

Joan MacIntosh was playing Dionysus that night. Her reactions were different.

> Bill got up and left the theater with the woman. I announced that the play was over. "Ladies and gentlemen, tonight for the first time since

the play has been running, Pentheus, a man, has won over Dionysus, the god. The play is over." Cheers and cries and celebrations. . . . I felt betrayed. I was hurt and angry at Shephard. . . . I learned something corny but true: that if you invest all of yourself in the work, the risks are very great.

(The Performance Group 1970: n.p.)

On only one other occasion was the performance similarly torn from its rehearsed path. But many times people came into the play challenging performers, participating in the "death ritual" (where Pentheus is "killed"). Some of this participation was naive, but much of it came from people who had seen *Dionysus in 69* more than once. In June, 1968, Shephard was "kidnapped" by five students from Queens' College who planned to stop the "killing" of Pentheus and spent an afternoon working out their strategy. Many of the performers felt that the play should not stop because Pentheus was not "genuinely" rescued. I agreed and asked for a substitute Pentheus from the audience. A young man of 17 volunteered – he did very well: he had seen the play five times and knew what was expected of him.

Contest, something is at stake. It is hard to build into a performance both narrative power and the tensions of a sporting match. The two ambitions cross each other. The tensions of sports come not so much from the spectators being in doubt about the outcome as from the doubt and resulting struggle among the players. There is some doubt like this in all performances because actors seek the unknown in their partners. In conventional theater an actor's creativity is most powerfully engaged in the narrow band between the details of the *mise-en-scène* and the obligation not to throw your partner off by doing something wholly unexpected.

The band is much wider in *Dionysus in 69* and theater like it. Those in the audience who know the performance can enter it at any of several places and change the flow of the action. In the scene cited the play can end abruptly. Mostly, however, the changes are modular – in tone, speed, intensity. Even those who are at the performance for the first time can participate if they stick to the rules. These are implicit: you can do anything that will not prevent the performers from performing. What varies wildly from night to night is not the text or the story but the quality of the action. If we expand Cieslak's analogy, the gestures and text are the candle-glass and the action is the flame.

Grotowski thinks that Artaud's proclamation that "actors should be like martyrs burnt alive, still signaling through the flames" contains the "whole problem of spontaneity and discipline, the conjunction of opposites which gives birth to the total act ... [which is] the very crux of the actor's art" (Grotowski 1967: 125, 123). Both spontaneity and discipline are risks for the performer. His entire effort is in making his body-voice-mind-spirit whole. Then he risks this wholeness here and now in front of others. Like the tightrope walker on the high wire, each move is absolutely spontaneous and part of an endless discipline. The kind of performer I am talking about − like the shaman, Artaud's martyr, and Grotowski's Cieslak − discards the buffer of "character." Cieslak does not "play" the Constant Prince; MacIntosh does not "play" Dionysus. Neither "are" they the characters. During rehearsals the performer searches his personal experiences and associations, selects those elements which reveal him and also make an autonomous narrative and/or action structure, strips away irrelevancies and cop-outs, hones what remains until everything is necessary and sufficient. What results is a double structure, not unlike that of the Hevehe. The first is the narrative and/or action structure of The Constant Prince or Dionysus in 69. The second is the vulnerability and openness of the performer. Each performance he risks freshly not only his dignity and craft, but his life-in-process. Decisions made and actions done during performance may change the performer's life. The performance is a set of exchanges between the performer and the action. And of course among all the performers and between them and the audience. "The theatrical reality is instantaneous, not an illustration of life but something linked to life only by analogy" (Grotowski 1968a: 118).

Initiation, a change in status for the participants. This change in who you are flows from the first three qualities. If something has happened here and now, if the actual is made of consequential, irremediable, and irrevocable acts and exchanges, and if these involve risk for the performers (and maybe for the spectators too), then there will be changes, new dimensions of integration and wholeness. Change will either be bunched, troubled, difficult − an initiation; or smooth and continuous.

Initiation can be the kernel of a performance. The structure of events will parallel the process stimulated by the events. For example, *The Constant Prince* is a set of initiations both for the Prince and for Cieslak. The performance is made of climactic bursts leading Cieslak from resistance to resignation to sacrifice. The Prince goes one step more, to apotheosis. At each of the first two crossings Cieslak is in crisis, and surrenders to it. His role is passive − to take in all that happens to him. The more he gives up the farther he progresses. When he "dies," he remains still. Other performers apotheosize the Prince, but nothing more happens to Cieslak who merely lends his body to the work of the others. Cieslak's inner movements night to night are not as rational as those proposed for the Prince; but the Prince is a fiction. The narrative of the Prince is a whole and Cieslak is a metaphor. But this does not mean that Cieslak is less whole than the Prince. Cassirer says:

> Whoever has brought any part of a whole into his power has thereby acquired power, in the magical sense, over the whole itself. . . . The very nature of this magic shows that the concept in question is not only of mere analogy, but of real identification. If, for instance, a rain-making ceremony consists of sprinkling water on the ground to attract rain, or rain-stopping magic is made by pouring water on red hot stones where it is consumed amid hissing noise, both ceremonies owe their true magical sense to the fact that the rain is not just represented, but is felt to be really present in each drop of water. . . . The rain is actually there, whole and undivided, in the sprinkled or evaporated water.
>
> (Cassirer 1946: 92–3)

Thus, and in precisely that way, Cieslak is there.

The question of efficacy goes to the very heart of theater's function. The dynamics of ritual have been nicely put by Lévi-Strauss:

> There is an asymmetry which is postulated in advance between profane and sacred, faithful and officiating, dead and living, initiated and uninitiated, etc., and the "game" consists in making all the participants pass to the winning side by means of events.
>
> (Lévi-Strauss 1966: 32)

Events are the ritual. When they are over initiates have been initiated and everyone is together. If theater could be an initiatory participatory game, it could be at once entertaining and fateful. But as Cassirer notes, "words and mythic image, which once confronted the human mind as hard realistic powers, have not cast off all reality and effectuality" (Cassirer 1946: 99). Cassirer welcomes this "liberation," hoping that now art will attain "its own self-realization." Artaud wanted to make language "spatial and significant . . . to manipulate it like a solid object" (Artaud 1958: 72). Language is the heated focus of a more general conflict. The ambition to make theater into ritual is nothing other than a wish to make performance efficacious, to use events to change people. Cassirer's analysis seems old-fashioned and Artaud's prophetic.

Space is used concretely and organically. Eliade describes an initiation of Fiji called Nanda. For this ceremony a stone enclosure 100 by 50 by 3 feet is built a long way from the village. This is the *nanda* which means "bed." Two years pass between the building of the nanda and the first ceremonies, which do not use it. Two more years pass before the second and final ceremony. For weeks before the second ceremony large quantities of food are stored in cabins built near the nanda.

> On a particular day the novices, led by a priest, proceed to the nanda in single file, with a club in one hand and a lance in the other. The old men await them in front of the walls, singing. The novices drop their weapons at the old men's feet, as symbols of gifts, and then withdraw to the cabins. On the fifth day, again led by the priest, they once more proceed to the sacred enclosure, but this time the old men are not awaiting them by the walls. They are then taken into the nanda. There "lie a row of dead men, covered with blood, their bodies apparently cut open and their entrails protruding" [Fison 1885: 22]. The priest-guide walks over the corpses and the terrified novices follow him to the other end of the enclosure. "Suddenly he blurts out a great yell, whereupon the dead men start to their feet, and run down to the river to cleanse themselves" [ibid].
>
> (Eliade 1965: 34)

Obviously the mysteries of death and rebirth animate the Nanda. But what interests me here is the building of a simple space for one ceremony. This *ad hoc* theater is built for four years before its use. Somehow the elapsed time "prepares" the space. The space is designed by the event performed in it. The walls are high enough to conceal the corpses until the last minute; the nanda is large enough to engulf the initiates in the bloody field of death. When the dead rise and race to the river, the initiates are alone in a large fenced-in space.

The eravo of the Elema is another *ad hoc* space. Made for the hevehe masks, it grows over the years from rear to front as the masks grow taller. At the culminating moment of the cycle the huge eravo doors open and the masks dance out to fulfill their lives. The eravo is a vagina-womb, whose doors are the masks' passageway to life. The doors open just once. When the eravo is empty of masks, it is left to deteriorate. But, while the masks are growing in the eravo, the building is also the men's living quarters and the village meeting house.

When the hevehe dance through the village and on the beaches, tight circles of women and children numbering around twenty-five weave around them so that the whole scene is made of as many as fifty dancing groups, each orbiting around a gigantic dancing mask. The space and feel of the Hevehe cycle is dynamic and expansive. It moves freely through the village and in spaces around the village. Other elements of the cycle include scaling walls, mock battles fought with lighted torches at night and coconut flakes and sticks during the day. The burning of the hevehe takes place near the tidal river. High tide washed the remains of the masks out to sea. Thus throughout the cycle there is an interplay between the village, the beach, the river, the sea, and the bush. Unlike the nanda there is no special stage. The eravo is backstage, shop, office, and dormitory. Bateson describes how

> the ceremonial house [of the Iatmul] serves as a Green Room for the preparation of the show. The men put on their masks and their ornaments in its privacy and thence sally forth to dance and perform before the women, who are assembled on the banks at the side of the dancing ground. Even such purely male affairs as initiations are so staged that parts of the ceremony are visible to the women who form an audience and who can hear issuing from the ceremonial house the mysterious and beautiful sounds made by the various secret musical instruments – flutes, gongs, bullroarers, etc. Inside, behind screens or

in the upper story of the ceremonial house, the men who are producing these sounds are exceedingly conscious of that unseen audience of women. They think of the women as admiring their music, and
if they make a technical blunder in the performance, it is the laughter
of the women that they fear.

(Bateson 1958: 128)

Wherever we turn in the tribal world we find theater – the interplay
among space, time, performers, action, and audience. Space is used
concretely, as something to be molded, changed, dealt with. The simplest arrangement is, of course, an open area with a performance in the
center and the audience on all sides. That is the shape of the Tiwi trial.
Or a musical performance from inside to a gathering outside randomly
standing, sitting, or moving. Or the multiple simultaneous performances of the Hevehe which cohere into a whole that no one person can
see all of. Or the construction of special places as in the Nanda. Or the
building of an entire camp away from the village as in the Bora. Often
space is articulated by the deployment of props or elements, such as a
large fire or a hollow log on which the initiates to be circumcised are
put, or a throne, or an animal pen where a sacrificial feast-beast is kept.
Examples of different spaces can be multiplied at will. Each is made for
and is part of a particular ceremony, event, or ritual.

Nowhere do we find a permanent theater or ceremonial place – a
single structure whose shape is "neutral" and "adaptable" to all uses.
The closest we come to that is an open space for dancing, debating,
trading, duelling, trying. Or the whole village which is a stage for
everything that goes on in and around it. Throughout the tribal world
events make shapes. In many ceremonies the principal architectural
element is people – how many there are, how and where they move,
what their interactions are, whether they participate or watch or do
both. Mead's and Bateson's film *Dance and Trance in Bali* (1938) shows
some people keenly watching the show, others lounging disinteres-
tedly, and several walking through the performance on their way to
other business. Our culture is almost alone in demanding uniform
behavior from audiences while clearly segregating audience from performers and audience from others in the area who are neither audience
nor performers.

We are almost unique in using ready-made spaces for theaters. Possibly the development of a theater as a special place which can accommodate many different kinds of performance is tied to urban cultures where space is expensive and must be clearly marked out for uses. Surely the need for scene design in our theater is an attempt to overcome the limitations of ready-made space as well as an outlet for mimetic impulses. A strong current of the new theater is to allow the event to flow freely through space and to design whole spaces entirely for specific performances. Grotowski is a master of this, using very simple elements and combining these with meaningful deployment of the audiences and precise movement of the performers so that the spatial dynamics of the production metaphorize the drama. Thus the audience peeps down at the sacrificial planks on which the constant Prince is immolated, or sits amid the proliferating crematorium pipes of *Akropolis*, or only slightly fills the large open volume of *Apocalypsis*. *Paradise Now* stumbled through the Brooklyn Academy of Music because that large proscenium theater blocked the flow of the performance.

In The Performance Group's *Makbeth* (1969) I experimented with audience movement through a complicated space. The environment, designed by Jerry Rojo (see McNamara, Rojo, and Schechner 1975), is not easy to describe. It is an interlocked arrangement of cubic spaces, ladders, a stairway, and a long curved ramp. The whole space is 50 by 40 by 20 feet. The lowest level is a trench 6 feet deep and 35 feet long cut below floor level on one side of the space's 50-foot axis. Over it a vertical grandstand of five stories rises from floor to ceiling. On floor level is a table 25 by 12 feet around which audiences can sit and on which scenes are played (plate 2.1). In three corners of the room are similar but not identical two-and three-story cubes rising to the ceiling. Along the wall opposite the grandstand is a long ramp rising from the head of the stairs to the top of a corner structure. All the space is open – there are no interior walls, doors, or hangings. At the edge of most of the platforms are narrow strips of carpet on which the audience sits. The floor is concrete and the walls of the room white.

The performance occurs throughout the space, often with three or four scenes playing simultaneously. There is no place a spectator can see everything from. On several occasions I met with audience of

Plate 2.1 Makbeth environment, designed by Jerry Rojo. (Photograph by Frederick Eberstadt)

around seventy-five before the show and told them they could move during the performance.

> If you are noisy or block the performers' movements, you can bust this thing up. If you take off your shoes so that you are absolutely silent and move from carpeted area to carpeted area, you can intensify your own and our experience. Try to understand the action and go with it. Think of yourselves as witnesses, or people in the street. Something happens – you go to see what. But you can't interfere or change what's happening.

The audiences were beautifully cooperative and some impressive things occurred. During the banquet scene the empty table swiftly filled with people who became guests at Dunsinane. The murder of Banquo under a platform was witnessed by a few. During the prophecy scene in the trench where Makbeth learns of Macduff and Birnam Wood, fifty spectators stood or crouched, as around a bear-pit, while Makbeth talked to the Dark Powers who dangled upside down from pipes. Duncan's funeral cortege and Makbeth's coronation parade were augmented by people linking the ramp and joining in the processions. The soldiers advancing through Birnam Wood found allies. In many ways the performance found focus as crowds condensed and dispersed; as a few people showed up here and there; as many silently and swiftly tiptoed stocking-footed through this open but secretive castle. The audience became the soldiers, the guests, the witnesses, the crowds – the powerless but present and compliant public.

Elements exchange, interpenetrate, and transform – but there is no hierarchy that permanently or a priori puts any life-process "above" any other. To dream is as "real" and as "vital" as to eat or dance or make love or war. Different contexts will of course make one activity more important within a given circumstance and time. The model is not ethical or personal – that is, it does not distinguish between right and wrong, good and bad, your taste and mine. Ethics, values, and tastes are always making hierarchies – but these are contingent, not fundamental. It has been customary to view theater hierarchically. For the writer the text is first and most important; to the performer his/her own presence on stage is the center of the event; the director knows that the theater would be impossible without him/her; and every technician will tell you that lights, sets, and costumes can make or break a show. Production has been thought of as a blend of many arts and as the "realization" of a text. But it really is a system of equal independent elements (figure 2.2).

Figure 2.2 makes a complicated picture, one that gets more so the more elements there are. Perhaps an absurd model – for how can the director "transform" or "interpenetrate" or "exchange" with time or space; how can the audience do likewise, and so on? And if I do not mean these operations literally, what do I mean? First, I mean that all elements of the theater are (like experience generally) on the same plane – there is no a priori hierarchy, no way of determining before rehearsal what will be the dominating element, if any. Secondly, all elements need rehearsal – which means that all elements are capable of radical, total change. Thirdly, in a way that is difficult to explain but which I have experienced, by a sudden metamorphosis anything may be turned into anything. That is, the director may become deeply and personally enmeshed with the performers and their life problems; the environmentalist recognizes that action shapes space and space shapes action; the writer sees her/his text signify things s/he never intended; the audience is plunged into the difficulties of the performance so completely that its reactions regulate the tone and flow of the action; the amount of time spent in rehearsals and the immediate time span of

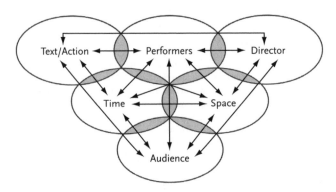

Figure 2.2

a performance condition the performers' way of working and inter-actions with each other. These are only a few of the many combinations and outcomes possible.

Mimetic theater has given us great masterpieces. Mimetic acting is a major tradition. There are other kinds of performances, however. Of these, actuals relate practices among tribal "whole-seeking" peoples and parts of our own population. Parallels can be misleadingly over-drawn. But I think people in the west are whole-seeking in ways and on a scale not experienced in our culture for hundreds of years. What we are undergoing is not a neo-primitive movement, but a post-modern one.

NOTES

1 Kaprow's work, more than any other I know, has the simple quality of "happen-ing" – of something that is. By ever so slight a change or heightening he converts everyday actions into "mysteries." See his *Assemblages, Environments and Happenings* (1966b), also his "poster-scenarios" which are both announcements of his pieces and their scenarios.

2 For a popular explanation of earth art, see Bongartz (1970: 166 ff.). Earth art develops from some very old impulses and is based on two principles: 1) art includes the arrangement of natural objects or the confrontation between a natural object and a man-made object – for example, draping a cliff for 1 mile with cloth; 2) art is autonomous and can therefore be "displayed" anywhere, even where it is not likely to be seen by human beings such as under water or deep in a desert.

3 Aristotle's view of the world is organic – he sees all growth and development modeled on what he observed in plants and animals. He believed that every event contained at the beginning the virtuality of its entire career. He believed in "fulfillment" rather than "transformation."

4 Shamanism has both a technical and a broad meaning. Its technical meaning is that of a certain kind of magico-religious system originating with hunter peoples in Central Asia. The word is of Siberian origin. The techniques of shamanism spread westward across the northern tier of Europe and to the north shores of the Mediterranean and eastward across Siberia into Alaska and down into both North and South America. Shamanism in its more general meaning includes all kinds of ceremonial systems combining curing by means of spirit-journey and exorcism with techniques drawn from the performing arts. It is in this wider sense that I use the word.

5 Shamanism is not "magic" in our debased sense of the word. It is religious technique that assumes communication and transformation among several

kinds of experience including the reintegration of the past and present, conscious and unconscious, dead and living, dream and waking, individual and group. There are specific techniques to be learned. See Eliade (1970).

6 Rothenberg's (1968) is an extraordinary anthology of "sacred poetries" from Africa, America, Asia, and Oceania. It includes scenarios and events and a very concise and informative set of commentaries. Rothenberg is a poet and his view of the material is particularly stimulating for artists.

7 The techniques of repairing the broken link are not improvised. An identification is made between words and body power and the spirits. Rothenberg comments (in regard to another but similar ceremony):

> What's of interest here isn't the matter of myth but the power of repetition and naming (monotony too) to establish the presence of a situation-in-its-entirety. This involves the acceptance (by poet and hearers) of an indefinite extension of narrative time, and the belief that language (i.e. poetry) can make-things-present by naming them.
>
> (Rothenberg 1968: 385)

This is a fundamental part of actualizing.

8 Quoted by Rothenberg (1968: 417). It is very hard to explain this way of thinking to those who have not thought this way. It is a very fluid way of thinking. All experiences are virtually equal in their claim for attention, combination, transformation, overlap, and interpenetration. The distinctions which we make automatically and absolutely between a mental event (say, a dream) and a physical event (say, snow falling) are not made. Each situation possibly can equate *any* two (or more) events. This is the "concrete" thinking Lévi-Strauss admires and the "poetic" thinking Rothenberg admires.

9 The implications of an event happening here and now that is an actualization of a situation which occurred "there and then" are widespread and complicated. There is no doubt that such phenomena are universal. In our own culture, psychoanalysts call these things "acting out" and "abreaction." There is a very rich literature from that point of view – see especially the special issue on acting out of the *Journal of the American Psychoanalytic Association* 5 (4) (1957). What is involved is treating time concretely and being able to manipulate it so that any time may be any other time. This takes two forms: 1) the living of time A at time B; 2) making time T omnipresent. In both cases an integration of time is accomplished and linear unidirectional time is abolished. This ability to manipulate time is essential for performing. We may also have a metaphorical actualizing – that is, the event actualized is not the "original" event, but a substitute (a displacement or a *pars pro toto*). Or there may be no "original" event but rather a series none of which "came first" and all of which are "available," given the right techniques to evoke them.

10 Williams (1940) details the whole Hevehe cycle.

11 Grotowski in a lecture at the Brooklyn Academy of Music, 1969.

12 All quotations and descriptions of *The Sky is Falling* are taken from the

manuscript scenario which Ortiz distributed about two weeks before the event which took place at the Middle Atlantic States regional meeting of the American Educational Theater Association held at Temple University in January, 1970. The event itself was modified the night before performance and some changes were made improvisationally during the performance. I arrived too late to see the performance. I walked through the aftermath in the Ritual Destruction Room and took part in a discussion of the performance. Ortiz told me of the changes made from scenario to performance. Most important of these were: 1) Song – my atrocity posters were distributed on the campus and the piece took on a definite anti-Vietnam war tone. Interrogations focused on killing and atrocities; the eggs were called "enemy foetuses"; each preliminary act of destruction was identified with killing Vietnamese; initiates were treated as draftees and their participation in the event called "a tour of duty"; the destruction of the piano was identified with the destruction of a Vietnamese village – and the Indian goddess of destruction Kali was identified with Lieutenant Calley; 2) When the chickens/babies were delivered the participants divided into two groups, one shouting "Kill the enemy!" and the other, "Let them live!" The chickens were identified as Vietcong babies. The Shamans left the theater and ran through the campus pursued by the two groups. The goal was to run through the city streets and then back into the Ritual Destruction Room – this goal was achieved and the chickens were not killed; 3) The audience sat in the large Temple University theater and watched the event over TV – the "six o'clock news," Ortiz calls it. The pursuit of the Shamans with the chicken/babies included climbing over and through the audience watching on TV. Just prior to this a man was brought out and dumped on the stage. He was bloody and his role was to create empathy for his plight as a victim of brutalization. He dragged himself to the edge of the stage. He vomited, drooled, writhed. Brutalizers returned from time to time to lift this man's face, spit in it, throw blood on him. People in the audience thought the man had freaked out. Several demanded that a doctor be called. But no one acted. And when the man tried to crawl off the stage and sit with the audience he was pushed back by people from the audience, who said, "There's something wrong with this man – don't let him get off the stage."

Since writing my impressions of *The Sky is Falling* I have spoken at length to Ortiz. He is interested in provoking "skizoid" reactions in participants in his events – he believes that the "paleologic" of schizoid ritual-making is basic to "visceral acting." He feels that the individual is capable of producing his own private systems; he makes distinctions between societies that are whole and have social ritual systems and societies, like ours, that are alienating and force people to make their own ritual systems.

13 The Dani engage in ritual warfare. See Gardner and Heider (1968) and Gardner's movie, *Dead Birds* (1963).

3

DRAMA, SCRIPT, THEATER, AND PERFORMANCE

The phenomena called either/all "drama," "theater," "performance" occur among all the world's peoples and date back as far as historians, archeologists, and anthropologists can go.[1] Evidence indicates that dancing, singing, wearing masks and/or costumes, impersonating other humans, animals, or supernaturals, acting out stories, presenting time 1 at time 2, isolating and preparing special places and/or times for these presentations, and individual or group preparations or rehearsals are coexistent with the human condition. Of countless examples from Paleolithic times none is more interesting than the cave at Tuc d'Audoubert:

> A sunken river guards the fearsome Tuc d'Audoubert, two hundred long underground feet of which one breasts or boats upon before the first land; then comes a precarious thirty-foot steep shaft up ladders placed there and slippery pegs; and next a crawl through claustrophobic low passages, to reach the startling footprints of ancient dancers in bare feet and the models of copulating bisons, in clay on the floor beyond.
>
> (La Barre 1972: 397)

This cave is not the only one to make difficult, if not altogether inaccessible, its performance space. These earliest theaters – or shall I call them temples? – are hidden in the earth, lit by torch, and the ceremonies enacted therein apparently concerned hunting–fertility. It is clear why the two are associated: Even today, among the hunters of the Kalahari Desert, for example, when large game is taken a brief ceremony entreats the gods for replenishment of "so large a life" converted into meat by the thrusting of spears.[2] Hunters do not breed cattle – they depend on what game is available; the more prolific the species hunted the better the hunting.

But it was not only animal fertility that Stone Age humans celebrated. Figures, carvings, paintings, and symbols depict human fertility as well. The most ancient are of enlarged vulvas and/or huge thighs and buttocks (not unlike what females of some non-human primates display during estrus), or of pendant, milkful breasts. Then come the ubiquitous phallic symbols, many of them exaggerated replications of the original, others more far-fetched. Associated with these human fertility figures are dances, some of them persisting into historical times. One has to think only of the erotic sculptings at Konarak (Orissa,

Plate 3.1 A Paleolithic cave performance space at Lascaux. (Photograph by C. Pécha. Courtesy of Commissariat Général au Tourisme)

thirteenth century) to recall how the association among fertility, dancing, and music has continued over the millennia. The sheer fecundity of the Konarak figures is overwhelming; and many of the copulatory and fondling poses are also dance positions. This is also true of Paleolithic cave art. Take, for example, the succinct association in the mind/behavior of humans between fertility–sexuality, fertility–hunting, and performance depicted in the second vestibule of the cave at El Castillo. There one sees.

> five bell-shaped signs. They have long been recognized as representing the vulva. They are red and very large (ca. 45 cm.) and are divided by a short vertical stroke. Between them is an (80 cm.) upright black line, feathered at the end. . . . The red female symbols and the single black male symbol are spectaclarly situated within a slightly raised part of the so-called second vestibule of the cavern of El Castillo. Below the smoothened surface of the niche which they occupy is a small table-like projection of the rock, beside which fall the folds of a curtain-like rock formation. . . . Parts of this rock curtain show signs of having been rubbed smooth by long usage.
>
> (Giedion 1962: 190–2)

In India and elsewhere it is common practice to rub the representations of both phallus and vulva when one passes by them in a temple. I've seen people reach out in museums, making the same life-taking touch. Everywhere cult items are fondled; curing and blessing is commonly practiced by the "laying-on" of hands.

We know nothing of the scripts used by the dancer–shamans of the Paleolithic temple-theaters. I don't say "texts," by which I mean written documents. I say "scripts," by which I mean something that pre-exists any given enactment, which persists from enactment to enactment.[3] Extrapolating from the prehistorical and historical evidence, as well as modern experience, I assume that the dancing took a persistent (or "traditional") shape which was kept from one event to another; that this shape was known by the dancers and by the spectators (if there were any), and that the shape was taught by one group of dancers to another.[4] Furthermore, the script was important: maintaining it intact contributed to the efficacy of the rite; abandoning it endangered that efficacy. Even more: the efficacy was not "a result of" dancing the script but "contained in" dancing the script. In other words, in prehistoric ritual theater, as in contemporary ritual, the doing is a manifestation more than a communication.

However, the manifestation is merely implicit, or potential, in the script; it is not until much later that power is associated with the written word. To conceive of these very ancient performances – some as far back as 25,000 years ago – one has to imagine absolutely non-literate cultures: "aliterate" is probably a better word. Drawings and sculptings, which in the modern world are associated with "signs" and "symbols" (word-likeness), are in Paleolithic times associated with doings. Thus, the "scripts" I am talking about are patterns of doing, not modes of thinking. Talking does not appear first as configuration (words-as-written) but as sound (breath-noise). Ultimately, long after writing was invented, drama arose as a specialized form of scripting. Potential manifestations previously encoded in patterns of doings were later encoded in patterns of written words. The dramas of the Greeks, as Aristotle pointed out, continued to be codes for the transmission of action; but action no longer meant a specific, concrete way of moving/ singing – it was understood "abstractly," a movement in the lives of people. At that point, in the west, drama detached itself from doing. Communication replaced manifestation.

From the Renaissance until very recently, concomitant with the rapid extension of literacy, the ancient relationship between doing and script was inverted. In the great tradition of the west the active sense of script was forgotten, almost entirely displaced by drama; and the doings of a particular production became the way to present a drama in a new way. The active sense of script was preserved in popular enter-tainments persisting from Greco-Roman times (and probably before) to our own epoch. But in the great tradition the script no longer functioned as a code for transmitting action through time; instead the doings of each dramatic "production" became a way of re-presenting and interpreting the words-of-the-drama. Maintaining the words intact grew in importance; how they were said, and what gestures accompanied them, was a matter of individual choice, and of lesser importance.

Thus, we in the west are accustomed to concentrating our attention on a specialized kind of script called drama. But the avant-garde in the west, and traditional theaters elsewhere, refocused attention on the doing aspects of script, and beyond script altogether to "theater" and "performance." Before attempting a concrete, taxonomical delineation of these words I must acknowledge the difficulty of using them. Words like "script," "drama," "theater," and "performance" are loaded, and none has neutral synonyms. My choice is either to invent new words, which no one will pay attention to, or to use the old words in as precise a manner as I can, hoping to define regions of restrictive meaning into the more general areas covered by these words. To help in this task I offer a model (figure 3.1) of concentric, overlapping circles; a set of four discs with the largest, and least strictly defined, "performance," on the bottom, each of the others resting on the one immediately larger than itself. The larger the size the more time and space covered and the broader the "idea area" occupied. Generally speaking, though not in every case, the larger disc contains all those smaller than itself.

The drama is the domain of the author, the composer, scenarist, shaman; the script is the domain of the teacher, guru, master; the theater is the domain of the performers; the performance is the domain of the audience.

Clearly, in many situations, the author is also both guru and performer; in some situations the performer is also the audience. Also, the boundary between the performance and everyday life is shifting and arbitrary, varying greatly from culture to culture and situation to situation. Different cultures mark the boundaries differently. Preparations may begin anywhere from minutes before a performance (an improvised guerrilla theater action) to years before (the Hevehe cycle play of the Orokolo, see chapter 2). However, wherever the boundaries are set, it is within the broad region of performance that theater takes place, and at the center of the theater is the script, sometimes the drama. And just as drama may be thought of as a specialized kind of script, so theater can be considered a specialized kind of performance. Thus, another model can be generated, one of oppositional pairs (figure 3.2).

Those cultures which emphasize the dyad drama–script de-emphasize theater–performance; and vice versa. Generally, among the world's cultures an emphasis on drama–script has occurred only

Drama: the smallest, most intense (heated up) circle. A written text, score, scenario, instruction, plan, or map. The drama can be taken from place to place or time to time independent of the person or people who carry it. These people may be just "messengers," even unable to read the drama, no less comprehend or enact it.

Script: all that can be transmitted from time to time and place to place; the basic code of the events. The script is transmitted person to person, the transmitter is not a mere messenger. The transmitter of the script must know the script and be able to teach it to others. This teaching may be conscious or through empathetic, emphatic means.

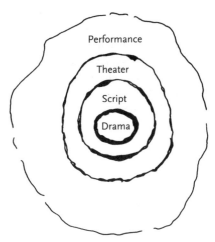

Theater: the event enacted by a specific group of performers; what the performers actually do during production. The theater is concrete and immediate. Usually, the theater is the manifestation or representation of the drama and/or script.

Performance: the broadest, most ill-defined disc. The whole constellation of events, most of them passing unnoticed, that take place in/among both performers and audience from the time the first spectator enters the field of the performance – the precinct where the theater takes place – to the time the last spectator leaves.

Figure 3.1

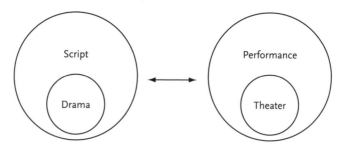

Figure 3.2

occasionally: ancient Greek drama, the Sanskrit drama of India, various Chinese and Japanese traditions, the modern drama of Europe and its cultural extensions from the Renaissance on. Even among these, only "modern drama" since the late nineteenth century has so privileged the written text as to almost exclude theater–performance altogether. And since the early twentieth century a strong non-western influence has worked its way through western theater from the avant-garde to the mainstream.

But however strong the counter-emphasis on theater–performance, drama–script still dominates western performances, even in the avant-garde. What is happening is an increasing attention to the *seams* that apparently weld one disc to the others. Illusionistic mimetic theater is based on hiding the seams joining drama to script to theater to performance. Stanislavsky went so far as to deny the existence of the performance altogether; that is the import of his famous assertion that going to see Chekhov's *The Three Sisters* ought to be like visiting the Prozorof household, with the fourth wall removed. Many years, and much theatrical activity, has intervened between Stanislavsky's assertion and now; at least since Meyerhold and Vakhtangov, performance has been readmitted to western theaters. Brecht, influenced both by documentary films and Chinese acting, exposed the seam between the theater and the script: his *V-effekt* is a device revealing the script as of a different conceptual order than the theater event containing it. Artists like Richard Foreman and Robert Wilson explore the disjunctions between script and drama.

Why are the seams, which traditionally held the four elements together, now being explored in ways that break them apart? The attention of the spectators is redirected to those structural welds where the presumed unified event is broken open. Instead of being absorbed into the event the spectator is invited (or forced) to experience where the event is "weak" and disjunctive. This breaking apart is analogous to the process of defiguration and abstraction that happened earlier in painting, and which has left a permanent mark on all the arts.

In rehearsing Sam Shepard's The Tooth of Crime, The Performance Group (TPG) opened the seam between performance and theater. Ultimately these were experienced by performers and spectators alike as *separate systems*. This opening of the performance–theater seam was facilitated by an environment that not only was dominated by a central construction that made it impossible for a spectator to see everything from a single vantage, but which also required the scenes to move from place to place, audience following; as this movement became orchestrated during months of rehearsal and performance, the Garage environment clearly developed two sides, a public side and a private side (figure 3.3). This division into spatial-emotional areas strongly contributed to opening the performance–theater seam. In a condensed and reduced way, TPG's Tooth was like a medieval pageant play; the actual progression of events in space matched the awakening of consciousness on the part of the drama's protagonist, Hoss.

Our contract with Shepard did not allow us to restructure his text, as TPG had done with Euripides' The Bacchae in making Dionysus in 69. Furthermore, what attracted us to Tooth was its wholeness, and Shepard's rich, allusive language. We didn't want to deconstruct his text. But as we worked on the play, and the seam between performance and theater opened wider, definite changes occurred in the script, if not in the actual words of the drama.

1. The cast of seven males and one female became four males and two females. Four roles were condensed into two, and these became the Keepers, a kind of chorus of one man and one woman.
2. A song written to be sung by Hoss at the start of the play became the production's theme song: "So here's another illusion to add to your confusion / Of the way things are." The song was sung at the start, and three other times, but never by Hoss.

The performing garage

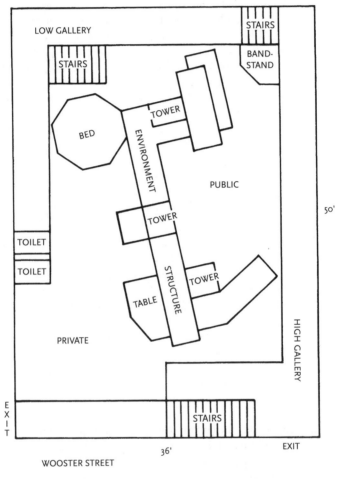

Figure 3.3

Plot summary

A brief plot summary of *The Tooth of Crime* may help those readers unfamiliar with the play. Hoss is a famous rock singer. He lives in a mansion, is surrounded by his woman, Becky, his driver, Cheyenne, his private doctor, his astrologer, and other members of his staff. He complains that he is "insulated from what's really happening by our own fame". (In this, Hoss is very like modern politicians.) Although he is on top, Hoss is insecure. He feels threatened by the "gypsy movement" – young stars who move up the ratings not in the traditional ways but on their own. Throughout the play, the worlds of big music, organized crime, and sports are intermixed. Hoss is a singer, a killer, an athlete: a superstar in all realms. As the first act proceeds, Hoss is told of a gypsy killer coming to challenge him; and he prepares for the contest. The gypsy, Crow, finally arrives – in Shepard's text at the start of Act II, in the TPG's production at the end of Act I. Crow is very cool, he speaks a new language that Hoss can't keep up with. When the two of them meet, Hoss is confused, asks Crow to "back the language up, man, I'm too old to follow the flash." Finally they engage in a word-duel, a combat of styles, a battle of the bands. Hoss brings in his own referee, but loses anyway. Dejected, Hoss asks Crow to teach him how to be a gypsy. Crow shows Hoss gypsy moves, but is in fact leading Hoss towards death. Ultimately, Hoss commits suicide, and Crow comments: "It took you long enough, but you slid right home." Then Crow sings a triumphant song, tinged with doubt: "Keep me in my state of grace." There Shepard's text ends. The TPG production added a final touch: just before the final blackout, Crow looks at Becky, who makes the first gesture challenging him – the cycle, much more accelerated, starts once more.

3. Crow appeared at the end of Act I instead of at the start of Act II.
4. The rock band which Shepard wanted to play backup music was not used. The performers played music they composed during workshops; being musicians – part of Hoss's band, or allies of Crow – became an integral part of their roles.

This last is very important because it built into TPG's *Tooth* a definite

pop performance aspect: in American society musicians are performers, not actors; their "role playing" is life-style role playing not
"characterization" as in drama. By making the characters in *Tooth* pop
musicians, we threw into doubt the nature of "characterization" in the
play, and moved the entire production toward a mode of performance
more identified with rock music life-style than with conventional
drama. In this way, although our production lacked actual rock music,
it was fundamentally an examination of rock-music style.

The concentration on the seam between performance and theater,
the inclusion of the audience in the performance as the major collective architect of the action, stemmed partly from my lack of interest as a
director in character work. I make little attempt to harmonize the feelings of the performers with the alleged feelings of the characters; I try
not to question performers about what they are feeling. I am more
interested in patterns of movement, arrangements of bodies, "iconography," sonics, and the flow of the audience throughout the
environment. The criteria I use for evoking, guiding, and selecting
patterns are complicated: but the "demands" of the drama are of low
priority.

It is this that Shepard doubtlessly sensed. He never saw TPG's *Tooth*.
He saw one rehearsal in Vancouver and helped us considerably then by
giving a rendition of the speaking style he wanted in the Hoss–Crow
fight. It is to his credit, and a testimony to the faith he has in his drama,
that he never interfered with our work. He and I had a correspondence
about *Tooth*; most of it is about basic tones, and very little about specific
staging. In May, 1973, Shepard wrote me:

> I can see from the reviews, eyewitness accounts from some of my
> friends, and your public writings . . . that the production is far from
> what I had in mind. But I never expected it to be any different and I
> don't see why you should expect my vision of the play to change. . . .
> I've laid myself open to every kind of production for my plays in the
> hope of finding a situation where they'll come to life in the way I vision
> them. Out of all these hundreds of productions, I've seen maybe five
> that worked. . . . For me, the reason a play is written is because a writer
> receives a vision which can't be translated in any other way but a play.
> It's not a novel or a poem or a short story or a movie but a play. It

seems to me that the reason someone wants to put that play together in a production is because they are pulled to its vision. If that's true then it seems they should respect the form that vision takes place in and not merely extrapolate its language and invent another form which isn't the play. It may be interesting theater but it's not the play and it can never be the play. . . . I'm sure that if you attempt other plays by living writers you're going to run into the same situation. It's a question you should really look into rather than sweep it aside as being old-fashioned or even unimportant.

TPG's production resulted in a dissociation between drama–script and theater–performance, as well as a further dissociation between theater and performance. The model can be redrawn into utterly discrete units, each of which may be in opposition to one or more of the others (figure 3.4). It is this process of dissociation, and its consequent tensions, ambivalences, and novel combinations that characterizes the contemporary avant-garde, including postmodern dance.

An issue of importance raised by Shepard in his letter is what to do with the author's "vision." To what degree ought the drama determine the script, theater, and performance? The issue has too often been avoided since the mid-1960s because those most deeply into dissociating elements have written their own dramas (Foreman, Wilson), brought dramatists into the theaters and controlled their visions (Chaikin–van Itallie, Brook–Hughes), or worked from existing

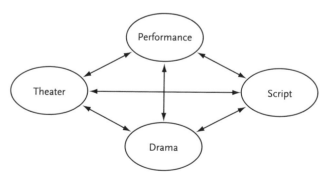

Figure 3.4

public-domain material that has been restructured according to need (TPG, Polish Laboratory Theater). But I, for one, want to work with writers, and must therefore find a way of dealing with their "vision."

I assume that plays "present" themselves to their authors as scenes, that this scening is coexistent with playwriting. (Beckett, with his ear for music and sense of wordness, may be an exception; he may not "see" his plays but "hear" them.) The act of playwriting is a translation of this internal scening into dialog + stage directions. The stage directions are vestiges and/or amplifications of the internal scening. The whole scening process is, in my view, a scaffold that is best dismantled once the play takes shape as dialog. In this way was the Classical and Elizabethan drama passed on: as sheer dialog unencumbered by didiscalia. I think the survival of many of those plays is due to the fact that later generations have been spared stage directions and character descriptions.

The work of those doing the production is to re-scene the play not as the writer might have envisioned it but as immediate circumstances reveal it. Generally, it is not possible to do the play in the author's vision anyway. That vision may be unknown, as with most premodern writers; or the play is produced in a culture outside that of origin; or the conventions and architecture of the theater make it impossible. Re-scening is inevitable because the sociocultural matrix of the play-as-visioned soon changes. The drama is, by definition, that which can be passed on through successive sociocultural transformations. The original vision is tied to the original matrix, and decays with it. I don't think that even the first production of a drama is privileged in this regard – unless the author stages the play himself, and that privilege dies with the author.

The Garage environment for *Tooth* facilitated the division into public and private sides. An 11-foot-high gallery overlooked the public half on three sides framing the fight arena; Cheyenne's bandstand, and a narrow bridge 7 feet high, further defined the arena. The centerpiece limited the depth of the public side to about 15 feet. Two rectangular archways connected the public to the private side, with additional flow spaces at either end of the centerpiece. The private side had an 8-foot gallery continuing around two short sides and one-half of the longest side of the theater. The playing area was much narrower – never more

Plate 3.2 The Performance Group's production of Sam Shepard's *The Tooth of Crime*, showing from the private side the large structure dividing the performing space into "public" and "private" sides. (Photograph by Frederick Eberstadt)

Plate 3.3 The Performance Group's *Tooth of Crime* from the public side.
(Photograph by Frederick Eberstadt)

than 9 feet – than on the public side. The private side really had two playing areas: the large, octagonal bed near the backstairs, and the breakfast table on a foot-high platform near the front stairs. Also the Garage toilets, the entrance–exit to the theater, and extensive wall postering were on the private side.

During the first months of using the environment, scenes were staged randomly – I just wanted to keep the audience moving. But as time went on this movement got simpler and more tied into thematics; ultimately most scenes found their "right place." I use quotation marks because the division between "public" and "private" emerged slowly as separations occurred between spectators/performance and performers/theater. As I sensed a seam opening – and most of my work was intuitive, not analytic as it is presented here – I adjusted staging and environment to further advance what was already becoming explicit. By June, 1973, the following pattern was set:

Private side

Act I: Hoss's first dressing scene, during which he meets with his astrologer; the breakfast table scene between Hoss and Becky; the second dressing scene during which Becky helps Hoss on with his fighting glove; the Grandpa monologue; the first confrontation between Hoss and Crow when Crow emerges from the audience to sing his song; the end of the act when Hoss and Becky sleep on the bed, while Cheyenne guards them and Crow watches.

Act II: The second confrontation between Hoss and Crow, which ends with Hoss sending Crow into the public side to wait; the after fight scenes with Crow: first on the bed when Hoss offers Crow everything if Crow will teach him how to be a gypsy, then near the breakfast table as Crow teaches Hoss; the car scene where Becky acts out an incident from her past with Hoss and definitely signals that their relationship is over.

Public side

Act I: Hoss's first scene with Cheyenne; the scene where Doc gives Hoss a shot of heroin; the scene where Becky explains to Hoss that power is all that counts – and then tries to escape by literally climbing the wall; Hoss's recollection of a fight he and two buddies won while in high school.

Act II: The third confrontation between Hoss and Crow; the duel between them; Hoss's suicide and funeral; Crow's last song and his brief confrontation with Becky.

There was relatively little use of the centerpiece. It was mostly occupied by the Keepers; the scene between Hoss and Galactic Max ("Jack" in Shepard's script) was played on the corner of the centerpiece overlooking the bed and was a private scene because, although it could have been viewed from both sides of the environment, more than 90 per cent of the audience crowded around the bed to look up at it. The Ref officiated the third round of the fight from a director's chair atop the highest point of the centerpiece. Generally, the centerpiece was used by the Keepers, occasionally by Becky and Cheyenne, once by Hoss, and never by Crow. And although it could accommodate on its upper levels 25 to 30 spectators there were rarely more than 15. The galleries were not used for any scene, except when during the first act Crow, participating as one of Hoss's musicians, cheered Hoss on so that it was as if Crow emerged almost secretly from Hoss's entourage. Interestingly, although Timothy Shelton played a saxophone on the gallery, and engaged in several other obviously theatrical deeds, spectators were generally surprised when he emerged at the end of Act I as Crow.

The long pit on the public side of the environment was covered with one trap door opened at the end of the play as Hoss's grave. For the funeral, after brief orations, Hoss's body was roughly pulled down into the pit by the Keepers, and the trap door slammed shut on him and them. Several scenes, which in terms of the drama were "private," were played on the "public" side of the environment. For example, the first scene between Hoss and Cheyenne (the sidekick) became a public confrontation with and rejection of Hoss – a big blow because it was played on the public side followed by the play's theme song. Were this scene played on the private side without the song it would simply be a disagreement between old comrades. It would not reverberate with overtones of doom. Why is that? The public side of the Garage was performance-oriented, rather than theater-drama-oriented. On the private side people were peering in at intimate encounters in more or less familiar settings, a kitchen table, a bed. A TV-soap-opera mood was evoked, a version of the fourth-wall convention. This mood was undercut with irony, created by the asides given by performers to spectators, and by ironic gestures – the laughter shattered what otherwise would be sentimental. But on the public side the feeling was of a gathering: an athletic event, a party, a contest of some kind. The public was *meant to be there, judging what happens.* What happened on the private side was rehearsal for what happened on the public side. In moving from one side to the other, spectators and performers shifted their mode of experiencing.

The audience quickly learned the conventions of the production. A full house of 120 was evenly distributed awaiting the play's start. By the time of the third scene – around the breakfast table – spectators were sitting in a close semi-circle on the floor around the table; others were crowded onto the galleries or peering down from the centerpiece. Only a few people hung back in bad viewing places. Generally, people pressed in closer on the private side. Almost always a few spectators actually remained sitting on the bed during scenes that were played there. The bed scenes gathered four groups of people: a close circle on the bed; a slightly more distant group watching from a right angle on the low gallery over the bed; a few people peering straight down from the centerpiece; a distant group on the high gallery along the east wall. For the bed scenes, more than 90 per cent of the audience came over to the private side, crowding in, jostling, although much of the action on the bed could have been seen through windows and archways cut into the centerpiece. Not only the tone of the scenes – naturalism charged with irony – but the intensely focused lighting drew people in close. They wanted to be close – the mood was of participating in a private scene. When asides broke that mood, surprised laughter came; sometimes embarrassment.

Special techniques helped the audience to learn the conventions. Each of these techniques dissociated the drama–theater complex from the performance. When spectators assembled in the Garage lobby over the theater, I was selling tickets, Stephen Borst (Keeper) was selling refreshments. About 10 minutes before letting people into the theater James Griffiths (Cheyenne) relieved me. Borst and Griffiths were in costume but not in character. No attempt was made to reconcile the contradiction. Just before sending the audience downstairs I explained the "ground rules." I told people they could move around, that hooks were provided so they could hang up their coats, and where the toilets were. Sometimes I said that they should think of the play as a movie they were filming, and that it was more fun if they frequently changed their positions to gain new perspectives on the action. Upon entering the theater, spectators were greeted by performers who acted as hosts, explaining the ground rules. Then, just before the play began, Griffiths explained the conventions again, this time in a loud voice addressed to everyone. Then, at the beginning of the breakfast-table scene, Spalding Gray (Hoss) invited everyone to "come in close," to "sit around the table."

Up through mid-June I thought all these reinforcements were necessary. Then, as an experiment, we decided to say nothing for several performances. The audience moved just about the same as when they were supplied with information. There were differences, however. Older people moved less. Pockets of people remained on the "wrong" side of the environment and watched through the centerpiece. It was much more likely that people would stay on the public-side gallery and watch private scenes than the other way around. When people gathered, they did so more irregularly, and their bodies were much "freer." When told to move, spectators arranged themselves in rows, and in neat semi-circles. When moving on their own, they arranged themselves in irregular patterns, with clumps of standees among the sitters. At the same time, there was some grumbling from spectators and confusion. Some people didn't know they could move – even though they saw many others do so. Finally, the only encouragement to movement was a brief announcement by Griffiths before the play started.

Performers-to-spectator interaction (as opposed to character-to-spectator interaction) was not limited to before the play. During intermission the performers remained in the playing space. A crowd usually gathered around the bed talking to Gray and Joan MacIntosh (Becky), who were often joined by Elizabeth LeCompte (Keeper). Shelton put on his Crow costume near the bed. Griffiths and Borst sold refreshments. The conversations ranged over many topics, but the themes and style of production were not avoided. There was no attempt to maintain a fictional reality concerning the play. The performers were *telling a story by means of theater.* In earlier TPG productions many spectators closely identified the performers with their roles. So much so in *Dionysus in 69* and *Commune* that we were hard-pressed to explain that some of the actions of the plays were not identical to what we did in "real life." There is a tendency in orthodox theater to segregate actors from audiences in order to maintain an illusion of, paradoxically, fictional actuality. The need to foster such an illusion is diminishing. Environmental theater certainly fosters fantasies, but these are of a different order than illusionistic make-believe.

The curtain call for *Tooth* (and some subsequent TPG productions) ended when the house lights were switched on and the performers applauded the audience; usually the mutual applause was vigorous, but sometimes both performers and spectators walked away in disgust. Most of the time the play ended but the performance went on in the form of conversations, even arguments. On one occasion a man disrupted the performance several times by making inappropriate remarks, finally taking hold of the prop gun just before Hoss's suicide.

The play stopped. Shelton talked to the man, inviting him to stick around after the play ended. About fifteen spectators remained after the play and the argument almost became a fist-fight. I don't recommend resolving a performance by fisticuffs, but I do say that this event was definitely part of the performance called *The Tooth of Crime* for that night.

In TPG's *Tooth*, the environment developed into two interrelated spaces, each of which sponsored a special kind of interaction between performers and spectators. The private side featured intimacy, one-to-one scenes, sharply focused and defined, lighting areas, *sotto voce* delivery of lines, and direct contact between performers and spectators (ad-libs and asides). The public side featured big numbers, agonistic stances, intense rhetoric, bright, general lighting, formal inclusion of the audience in a contest. The kinetic activity of the audience encouraged a detachment, a critical attitude. Each spectator was self-conscious enough to move to where the action was, station herself in an advantageous position to see, and decide what her relationship to the theater was to be. Often enough people changed places in mid-scene. This is not participation in the *Dionysus* sense. It is each audience educating itself concerning the difference between performance and theater. The theater event people saw remained the same regardless of what perspective spectators adapted, but how that event was received changed. Instead of being in a predetermined relationship to the theater event each spectator was able to modify this relationship scene by scene. These modifications were usually not thought out. In moving, the spectator discovered his attitude regarding the play. He learned that he can *control the performance*, even if the performers *control the theater*. As every member of TPG from that time can testify, performances of *Tooth* varied widely, much more so than performances of *Commune*. This is so because the performance-control aspect of the audience is activated in *Tooth*. The mood of the audience – as directly conveyed in how its members moved, positioned themselves, and reacted to scenes (sometimes these signals were communicated very subtly) – firmly controlled the feel of each night's rendition of *Tooth*.

This control occasionally ran against what I wanted to do, but I had to yield to the audience. For example, I wanted the second round of the fight to break the frame of the arena, travel around the space in a wide circle, and return to the arena. When the second round is over, the Ref comments, "something's funny, something's out of whack," and I felt that moving from the arena would incarnate the weirdness of the round. For several months, the round was staged according to my wishes. But spectators followed grudgingly, if at all, making a lot of noise. The performers found it difficult to concentrate, and most of the round was lost both to seeing and hearing. I compromised, staging most of the round in the north-east corner of the Garage, just on the other side of the narrow bridge that delineates one side of the arena. Still, it didn't work. Spectators were loath to move even a few feet; they simply dropped out of the scene and waited for round 3. The fight was simply "public," no matter what niceties of interpretation I wanted to emphasize. As the round finally was played, Crow leaves the arena for only a few seconds as Hoss drives him around the supporting post of the narrow bridge. Crow immediately re-enters through the arch. The audience stays put; the scene has focus, intensity, rhythm, completeness.

Most of the seam-breaking in TPG's *Tooth* was between the realms of performance and theater; the audience was, as it were, enfranchised. For about ten performances we experimented with breaking the drama away from the script and the theater. During May–June, 1973, two scenes were repeated with no change whatsoever except for the repetition. After Hoss got a shot of heroin from Doc, Gray stopped the drama by saying: "That's one of my favorite scenes, I'm going to do it again." Usually there was a big laugh from the audience, some readjustment of bodies, and an appreciative delight in re-viewing the scene, and the make-believe high Hoss–Gray got. After committing suicide, Gray again stopped the drama and said: "I'm going to take the suicide again. Anyone who wants to watch it from a different perspective, just move around." Most everyone made an adjustment. The reaction to repeating the suicide was closer to shock. The second time through the house was extremely quiet. We discontinued repeating scenes because the performers felt the repetitions were becoming routine. As part of the script they were not exciting to perform. But, however much part of the script the repetitions were, they were always breaks in the drama.

Pirandello's plays are an attempt to integrate into the drama breaks between drama and script. Genet's *The Maids* is a deeper elaboration of this theme. The action of *The Maids* is the drama, and the fantasy life of the characters is the script. Claire/Madame and Solange/Claire ultimately convert their script into the drama, playing out once and for all the murder of Madame. Genet turns the screw an extra time in Solange's epilogue where she confesses that the whole enterprise has been a drama – but is it Solange's or Genet's?

In Bali, theater and drama are fixed while the script floats in relation to them. The minute gestures of a dance – the movement of fingers and hands, the way a torso is held and bent, the facial expression (or lack of it, the famous Balinese "away" look) – are fixed; so is the traditional story or story fragment: often a contest between good and bad demons or a fragment from the *Ramayana*. But how long the theatrical gestures will be performed, how many repetitions of movement, what permutations or new combinations occur – these things are unknown beforehand, depending on the "power" of the trance and/or the creativity of the performers. In Indian classical music, the progression of every *raga* is known; this progression is the "drama" of the music. But how a specific performer or group will proceed from one phase or note of a raga to the next, and how the progressions will be organized (how many repetitions, sequences, speed, volume), are not known in advance, not even by the performers: the script evolves on the spot out of a relationship between the drama (raga) and the theater (particular skills of specific performers). In both the Balinese and Indian examples, the western distinction between "author" and "performer" does not apply. Dancer and musician did not author the trance dance or the raga; nor are they conforming to the exact prior script or drama. Most western improvisatory theater is not like Asian theater but a means by which the performers function as dramatists, ultimately arriving at a very orthodox form that is repeated night after night with little or no immediate invention or permutation.

To summarize thus far: the drama is what the writer writes; the script is the interior map of a particular production; the theater is the specific set of gestures performed by the performers in any given performance; the performance is the whole event, including audience and performers (technicians, too, anyone who is there).

It is hard to define "performance" because the boundaries separating it on the one side from the theater and on the other side from everyday life are arbitrary. For example, in Vancouver TPG did two "real time" performances of Commune in which audiences were invited to come to the theater at the same time the performers did. About twelve people showed up at 6 p.m., watched the Group clean up, set props, get into costume, do warm-ups, establish the box office, admit the regular audience, do the play with spectators, remove costumes, clean up, and shut the theater. Two different performances occurred simultaneously: one for the "real time" audience and one for the "regular" audience. For the "real time" audience the "regular" audience was part of the theater, as were a number of events not normally included in the production of Commune.

As a theater director I am attempting to make both performers and audiences aware of the overlapping but conceptually distinct realities of drama, script, theater, and performance. Also to make myself more aware. Others have gone further than I in the process of breaking one realm from another, but often at the expense of one part or another. I want to find ways of keeping three or all four in living tension. I believe that none has a priori precedence over the others.

In many rural areas, especially in Asia and Africa, the performance is the most important thing: the whole panoply of events at the center of which is theater or a script. (I distinguish a "performance" from a simple "gathering," such as for a party, by the presence in a performance of a theatrical event guided by a script – something planned, designed for presentation, following a prescribed order. Parties are prototheatrical events, performances that sometimes may contain theater or even drama. For example, the dancing of a kathakali sequence by a professional troupe at an Indian wedding is a theatrical dance-drama included within a wedding-performance.)

I know these distinctions are somewhat arbitrary. Taxonomy in a social science is based on structures that tend to blend into each other on a continuum rather than exist as compartmented "species" of events. Thus, the exact points to set boundary markers distinguishing performance, theater, script and drama from each other are somewhat arbitrary, but the center of each is very different from that of any of the others.

In 1972 I attended a pig-kill, dance, and meat-exchange at Kuru-mugl in the Highlands of Eastern New Guinea (see chapter 4). Although the dancers exhibited considerable skills, and the music was vigorous, no one was much interested in appreciating these as such. At one time or another everyone was dancing/singing; the move from being a spectator to being a performer was easy. This ease of movement between these two realms is one of the characteristics of performance as distinct from theater or drama where displaying particular techniques in an exact sequence/context makes movement between realms difficult. The climactic event of the two-day celebration at Kurumugl was the invasion of the "council grounds"[5] by one group in order to get meat being given to them by another group. This invasion took four hours during which armed dancers from both groups confronted each other. The men charged at each other, raising their spears and arrows as if to throw or shoot. Then, they began a rapid kicking-from-the-knee dancing; a running in place accompanied by fierce shouting and whooping. With each charge by the invading (guest) group, the resisting (host) group retreated a few yards. Ultimately the invaders arrived at the center of the council grounds where the women and some men had assembled a huge, tangled pile of meat 75 feet in diameter, 3 feet deep. After a half-hour of running in a big circle around the meat, while shouting in high-pitched tones, guests and hosts fused into one unit of about 500 men watched by a more than equal number of women and children. Then the orations began. Men climbed into the pile of heads, torsos, flanks, legs, foreparts of pig and cow and tugged at specific morsels, declaiming and exhibiting the meat. In the Highlands meat is a valuable item of wealth representing years' husbanding precious pigs. So much meat in one place is a collection of terrific wealth, a focus of ecstatic energy. To one side were three white goats, still living, tethered to a small tree. These were not slaughtered, I don't know what happened to them. Slowly the pigs-meat was distributed; small groups departed for their home villages singing and carrying meat shoulder high on stretchers made from bamboo, vines, and leaves.

A celebration like that at Kurumugl privileges performance over script, drama, and theater. The script is not very tight, though it does determine the overall flow of events. There is no drama. No one cares much about the quality of the theatrical presentation. But there are definite dance steps and shouts, a known style of singing, an overall pattern consisting of accepted sequences of events. And much care is taken in costuming. The dancing, mock-battling, orating, distributing of meat, and recessional constitute, in Erving Goffman's rich phrase, the way in which and the place where the Highlanders' "reality is being performed" (1959: 36).

On January 15–16, 1972, Joan MacIntosh and I attended, and to some degree participated in, a thovil ceremony in Koratota, a Sri Lankan village about an hour's drive from Colombo. A. J. Gunawardana took us there. The occasion was the fulfillment of an oath made six months before when an outbreak of chickenpox passed harmlessly. The performance took more than 30 hours and we saw about 14 hours of it. It consisted of dances, songs, chants, ritual observances, partying, gambling, clowning, and story-telling. These occurred sequentially rather than simultaneously. The main performing area was an oval about 80 feet by 60 feet, rising slightly to a 15-foot-high roofed shed enclosed on three sides containing an altar; five other altars scattered around the oval; a chair with ritual implements (flowers, incense, cup); and other decorations. The audience varied from less than 50 to more than 400 during the late-night trance-fire dance. Some of the performers – such as the trance dancer, the musicians, and some of the other dancers – were professionals; others were local people. Appeals for money were interspersed with the performance. As westerners and outsiders we were given a special place to view the performance, inside the oval, almost part of the show. (As indeed we were, openly for the village children, and more discreetly for the adults.)

The portion of the thovil[6] we saw had five parts: (1) arrival and set-up, (2) events before supper, (3) main dances and events until midnight, (4) intermission, side events, slow-down until 4.25 a.m., (5) an hour-long trance dance. Gunawardana told me that the events of the following day would include more singing and dancing, and closing ceremonies. Each part of the thovil had theatrical elements embedded in a performance matrix. There was no drama, and the script was very loose, adjusting itself to our arrival, for example. Many of the early dances were danced to us, directly in front of the mat on which we sat. The main priest took time to explain to us what he was doing. These were alterations of the script. The crowd's appreciation was divided between simply enjoying each other, a good-time-at-the-party feeling, and evaluating the quality of the dancers. At one point a local, obviously amateur, dancer began to perform. No one stopped him or derided him, but he was studiously ignored, which in Sri Lankan society is a distinct put-down. He was drunk or I'm sure he would have ended his dance even more abruptly than he did. On the other hand, a very old man who, I was told, was the village's chief "devil dancer" executed a few steps and sang a chant to the full appreciation of a very quiet crowd. The old man had no skills in the usual theatrical sense, but he was thought to have "power," and was deeply respected, even feared, for this. His presence rather than his theatrical ability got attention.

Preparations for the trance-fire dance began a little before 4 a.m. The thovil had come almost to a complete halt before then. The musicians were drunk, most of the village was asleep except for about a dozen men who were gambling in a shelter about 50 feet from the oval. The trance dancer was a young medical technician from Colombo. We had driven to Koratota with him. On our way out I questioned him:

"How did you become a trance dancer?"

"My teacher taught me."

"Why do you do it?"

"I like it. I earn extra money."

"Does your dancing conflict with the 'scientific ideas' of your work?"

"No. Why should it?"

The preparations for the trance-fire dance were very simple. The man sat in a chair behind the shelter containing the main altar. He looked at himself in a hand-mirror. Two assistants wrapped his torso with a bandage like cloth, very stiffly. (This is very much how young trance-dancing girls are wrapped in Bali.) When he was firmly wrapped, incense was lit, and he took very deep drafts of it, holding the incense tray directly below his nose. Finally, he put on his turban-like head-dress. After about 20 minutes his assistants lifted him from the chair and placed him at the end of the oval.

A large crowd of about 400 had gathered, and they were very quiet. The musicians – two drummers, a flute player, and several singers – were sitting expectantly on their mats. Very suddenly the drums began a very loud, very fast beat and the dancer leaped to the center of the oval. I say *leaped* – the dance was incredibly athletic. Some of it was sheer

Plate 3.4 A thovil in Sri Lanka. An exorcist dances with fire. (Photograph by Richard Schechner)

running up and down and around the oval. At another time the dancer lifted his knees very high, almost to his chest. The most spectacular part of the dance involved "fire-throwing." One of the dancer's assistants pursued him carrying a large pot of "fire dust," some kind of highly inflammable powder. The dancer was carrying one, sometimes two, kerosene-soaked burning torches. Without looking at the assistant, the dancer reached into the pot, took a fistful of fire dust, hurled it into the air, and ignited it. The flash explosion, and whooshing noise generated exciting heat, light, sound.

For more than an hour – until 5.35 a.m. – the trance dancer never broke rhythm; he never rested. The trance dances of Bali are sometimes quiet, meditative affairs, but this thovil was fierce. Finally, his two assistants entered the oval, the drumming stopped, and they wrestled the dancer to the ground, unclenching his fists to pry the torches from him. It was an actual fight to get him to stop dancing. Then, as suddenly as he started, he relaxed. He was not even breathing heavily, not even sweating. He knelt, said a prayer. He was absolutely relaxed, alert, not tired. As soon as the dance ended people dispersed. The next morning we drove back to Colombo.

The thovil trance-fire dance is theater nested in performance. There is no drama, and the script is very loose. There are certain steps to be done but these may be varied according to the strength of the possession. The thing the crowd loves most is the fire-throwing. They appreciate it with ooh's and ahh's; they are thrilled by the dancer's stamina and energy. The spectators do not participate in the event, they watch; the dancer is totally oblivious to them. He is even, apparently, oblivious to his own assistants – though he has enough presence of mind to reach into the fire dust pot. But when the time comes to end the dance he must be wrestled out of trance. This is not a gradual process, as going into trance seems to be; but a sudden re-emergence, a letting go of the trance and a falling directly into full, relaxed, ordinary consciousness. It is my belief that western culture is generally unable to enjoy trance dancing because of our insistence on drama and scripts. However, in black and Pentecostal churches – revivals, healings, chants and responses, talking in tongues, snake-handling, and the like – there is ample evidence that trance is a viable mode for theater in the west, if we so choose.

Structurally, the thovil presents a complicated picture. Entertainment, ritual, athletics, partying, gambling, and spirit possession are all mixed. Apparently informal, yet with a special building toward the trance dance that joins the darkest, stillest hour of night to dawn. What holds the thovil together is a sequence of punctuations – ritual chants, further decoration of the performance oval, expected dances and farce – that keep up the people's interest. Between these punctuations the space/time is open, and a variety of events transpire. Men move from gambling to watching dances to sleep. Alcohol is dispersed; children play games to the side of the oval and then return for the farces; women watch, go away to prepare meals or nurse infants, then return. Even the musicians wander in and out so that sometimes the full orchestra is playing and sometimes only a single drummer. Only with the fire-trance dance is everyone focused on a single event.

Drama is tight, verbal narrative; it allows for little improvisation; it exists as a code independent of any individual transmitter; it is, or can easily be made into, a written text. A script – which can be either tight or loose – is either a plan for a traditional event such as the Koratotan thovil or the Kurumugl pig-kill, or it is developed during rehearsals to suit a specific text as in orthodox western theater. The theater is the visible/sonic set of events consisting either of well-known components, as in Bali, or of a score invented during rehearsal, as in the west. To some degree the theater is the visible aspect of the script, the exterior topography of an interior map. Performance is the widest possible circle of events condensing around theater. The audience is the dominant element of any performance. Drama, script, theater, and performance need not all exist for any given event. But when they do, they enclose one another, overlap, interpenetrate, simultaneously and redundantly arousing and using every channel of communication. This kind of behavior characterizes many human activities, from ritual to art.

I began this essay by describing some Paleolithic caves; I indicated that ancient humans associated themselves with animals, connecting hunting with the need to replenish the hunted species. A parallel connection apparently was made between human and animal fertility; and initiation rites, which are closely associated with human fertility, were also often totemistic/animist. I now want to return to those themes and elaborate on them in a direction that will link up with what has thus far been the main subject of my essay.

More than in the first part of this essay I caution now against accepting my remarks as definite. About performing I know something, having made many careful observations; about playing in man and some other primates I know very little, and hardly anything from systematic observations. I present my speculations in the spirit of those sixteenth-century cartographers who drew hilarious maps of the New World. But all succeeding maps were revisions, not rejections, of those first shapes drawn on vellum: the New World existed, it had a definite shape, it remained to measure it accurately.

One can only speculate, and many have, about the origins, structure, and functions of totemism and animism. What is very clear is that people identify themselves with animals, dress in animal skins and heads, and develop specific ceremonies and observations to keep intact links connecting animal species to humans. Such phenomena are not new. In the Hall of Hieroglyphs at Pech-Merle "is the earliest known presentation of the fusion of a human being with an animal" – a bird-headed woman apparently in some dancing attitude (Giedion 1962: 284). Also "the celebrated 'Dancing Sorcerer' or 'Reindeer Shaman' of Trois Frères wears the antlers of a stag, an owl mask, wolf ears, bear paws and a horse-tail, but is otherwise a nude human male dancing, perhaps wearing streaks of body paint" (La Barre 1972: 410). La Barre emphasizes that shamanistic animal cults can be traced from contemporary subarctic cultures back to the Stone Age:

> Similarities in European Paleolithic and Asiatic Paleosiberian shamanism, indeed, are present even down to arbitrary details. For example, the Old Stone Age had both bird and reindeer shamans quite like those of Paleosiberian tribes. ... The reindeer shaman shows an extraordinary continuity in Europe down to proto-historic and modern ethnic times; the bird shaman can be traced from Magdalenian to modern Siberian times.
>
> (La Barre 1972: 410)

There is some hard evidence pointing to dancing ceremonies accompanying the visual representations in the Paleolithic caves. "Near the final chamber [of the cavern of Tuc d'Audoubert], which contains the high relief of two bison, footprints of the Magdalenian age have been preserved beneath a layer of crystalline lime deposit" (Giedion 1962: 284). These are interpreted as footprints of dancers.

If ancient humans drew and carved beings who combine the physical attributes of humans and animals can we not assume that actual costumes were created; and can we not further assume that the paintings on the cave walls are either of dances, or at least in their own way "accompany" dancing? We don't know the structure of these dances, except as we may extrapolate from historic times. The dances were probably both evocations of animal spirits and emulations/transformations of animal movements. The ancient hunters who felt such a dependency on the animal world knew also of similarities between that world and their own. Generally those similarities extended animal nature into the realm of human life. Always it is the human who is adorned, who shows how he is like an animal. No animal dances wearing human skin, or puts over its head the face of a human. But there are connections I believe we can make without falling into the error of anthropomorphism.

Jane Goodall described this scene in her masterful study of chimpanzee life in the wild:

> At about noon the first heavy drops of rain began to fall. The chimpanzees climbed out of the tree and one after the other plodded up the steep grassy slope toward the open ridge at the top. There were seven adult males in the group . . . several females, and a few youngsters. As they reached the ridge the chimpanzees paused. At that moment the storm broke. The rain was torrential, and the sudden clap of thunder, right overhead, made me jump. As if this were a signal, one of the big males stood upright and as he swayed and swaggered rhythmically from foot to foot I could just hear the rising crescendo of his pant-hoots above the beating of the rain. Then he charged flat-out down the slope toward the trees he had just left. He ran some thirty yards, and then, swinging round the trunk of a small tree to break his headlong rush, leaped into the low branches and sat motionless.
>
> Almost at once two other males charged after him. One broke off a low branch from a tree as he ran and brandished it in the air

before hurling it ahead of him. The other, as he reached the end of his run, stood upright and rhythmically swayed the branches of a tree back and forth before seizing a huge branch and dragging it farther down the slope. A fourth male, as he too charged, leaped into a tree and, almost without breaking his speed, tore off a large branch, leaped with it to the ground, and continued down the slope. As the last two males called and charged down, so the one who had started the whole performance climbed from his tree and began plodding up the slope again. The others, who had also climbed the bottom of the slope, followed suit. When they reached the ridge, they started charging down all over again, one after the other, with equal vigor.

The females and youngsters had climbed into trees near the top of the ridge as soon as the displays had begun, and there they remained watching throughout the whole performance. As the males charged down and plodded back up, so the rain fell harder, jagged forks or brilliant flares of lightning lit the leaden sky, and the crashing of the thunder seemed to shake the very mountains.

My enthusiasm was not merely scientific as I watched, enthralled, from my grandstand seat on the opposite side of the narrow ravine, sheltering under a plastic sheet. . . . I could only watch, and marvel at the magnificence of those splendid creatures. With a display of strength and vigor such as this, primitive man himself might have challenged the elements.

(Goodall 1972: 66–7)

But don't confuse "primitive man" with chimps. The chimps are not forerunners of Homo sapiens – chimps have been around as long or longer than humans. Probably both humans and chimps have a common ancestor, the evolutionary tree branching some millions of years ago; since then Homo sapiens developed in one way, Pan troglodytes in another. Thus, chimp performance is not a prototype of human performance, but a parallel. As such it is even more interesting than as a prototype. A prototype tells us nothing more than that human performing has antecedents; a parallel means that another species, developing in its own track, is engaged in deliberate, conscious, chosen activity that can best be described as "performing." If this is true, so-called "aesthetics" is not the monopoly of humans; and theories about aesthetics that talk about art as a "luxury," or a function of "leisure," are wrong. Instead one ought to seek the *survival value* of performance; what purpose does it serve in the behavior scheme of chimps and humans, and possibly other species too? I am using words like "deliberate," "conscious," "chosen," and "survival value" in their strict senses.

Examples abound of "animal rituals" or "playing," which, viewed from a human perspective, appear to be performances. But these patterns of instinctive behavior are automatic and cannot be thought of as performance in the sense that human and chimpanzee displays are. However, even events as regulated by instinct as the "triumph dance of geese," or the offering of the throat by a vanquished wolf to the victor, can indicate the bio-antiquity of behaviors where status, territory, mates, and social hierarchy are mediated by rituals rather than by direct combat which would severely deplete at least the male population of many species. In the opinion of Lorenz (1967), Tinbergen (1965), and other ethologists, an instinctive animal ritual is an alternative to violent behavior; the rituals developed – were "selected" evolutionarily speaking – because those individuals within a species with the rituals bred-in survived. In time, entire species instinctively responded to stimuli that evoked the rituals.

For me, performance is something else, more consciously "chosen" on a case-by-case basis and transmitted culturally not genetically. Performance probably belongs only to a few primates, including humans. But the rituals of lower animals are indeed prototypes for primate performances. Humans do consciously, by choice, lower animals do automatically; the displaying peacock is not "self-conscious" in the way an adolescent male human is on Saturday night. The behavior of peacock and boy may be structurally identical; but self-consciousness and the ability to change behavior according to self-consciousness (and not just "objective" stimulation) sets most animal ritual off from non-human primate and human performance.

However, before examining some of the conscious behavior I call performance, I think it is necessary to scan the more ancient patterns of ritual behavior. These patterns involve display, fight–flight, turf, and mating (connections between ethology and performance are also discussed in chapter 7). Many animals put on shows in order to demonstrate status, or to claim and defend territory, or to prepare for mating. These displays are aggressive. When challenged, the animal will either continue the display, transform it into a submissive gesture, flee, or fight. According to Lorenz, it was Julian Huxley who first called this kind of behavior "ritual."

> [Huxley] discovered the remarkable fact that certain movement patterns lose, in the course of phylogeny, their original specific function and become purely "symbolic" ceremonies. He called this process ritualization and used this term without quotation marks; in other words, he equated the cultural processes leading to the development of human rites with the phylogenetic processes giving rise to such remarkable "ceremonies" in animals. From a purely functional point of view this equation is justified, even bearing in mind the difference between the cultural and phylogenetic processes . . .
>
> . . . The triple function of suppressing fighting within the group, of holding the group together, and of setting it off, as an independent entity, against other, similar units, is performed by culturally developed ritual in so strictly analogous a manner as to merit deep consideration.
>
> (Lorenz 1967: 54–5, 74)

Ritualized behavior extends across the entire range of human action, but performance is a particular heated arena of ritual, and theater, script, and drama are heated and compact areas of performance.

However, something else is involved in performance, and that is *play*. Play also occurs in many species, but nowhere is it so extensive, nowhere does it permeate so many activities, as in human beings. This is only relatively less true of chimpanzees, and so on down the primate ladder. A tentative definition of performance may be: *Ritualized behavior conditioned/permeated by play*. The more "freely" a species plays, the more likely performance, theater, scripts, and drama are to emerge in connection with ritualized behavior. Some animals, such as bees and ants, are rich in ritualized behavior but absolutely bereft of play. No species that I know of plays without also having a wide repertory of ritual behavior. But it is only in the primates that play and ritual coincide, mix, combine; it is only in humans and closely related species that the aesthetic sense is consciously developed. Art may be considered a specific coordination of play and ritual.

What is play? What are its characteristics, functions, and structure? Huizinga defined play as

> a free activity standing quite consciously outside "ordinary" life as being "not serious," but at the same time absorbing the player intensely and utterly. It is an activity connected with no material interest, and no profit can be gained by it. It proceeds within its own proper boundaries of time and space according to fixed rules and in an orderly manner. It promotes the formation of social groupings that tend to surround themselves with secrecy and to stress their difference from the common world by disguise or other means.
>
> (Huizinga 1955: 13)

Just as the 1908 publication of Van Gennep's *Les Rites de passage* introduced a way of classifying and therefore understanding rituals, so the 1938 publication of Huizinga's *Homo Ludens* made it possible to speak of play in a full variety of cultural contexts. Huizinga connects playing to ritual, and stresses the importance of sacred time/place and of contest (*agon*). But, unfortunately, he rejects function, believing that to discuss what purposes play serves is to deny its unique nature, its "in-itselfness." I think an examination of play's biological function – its survival value – will add to our understanding of its structure and process, pointing the way to relating primate play behavior to human performances.

In her review of the theories concerning the functions of play, Loizos (1969: 236 ff.) identifies the following:

1. As schooling or practice for the young.
2. As an escape from or alternative to stress.
3. As a source of "vital information" about the environment.
4. As an exercise for muscles involved in agonistic and reproductive behavior.

Loizos rejects these functions as being neither sufficient nor necessary;

but she maintains nevertheless that play has survival value. Instead of suggesting more functions she extrapolates from observations of primate behavior certain characteristics of play:

> One of [play's] immediately noticeable characteristics is that it is behavior that borrows or adopts patterns that appear in other contexts where they achieve immediate and obvious ends. When these patterns appear in play they seem to be divorced from their original motivation and are qualitatively distinct from the same patterns appearing in their originally motivated contexts. . . . The [similarity between human and other primate play] lies in the exaggerated and uneconomical quality of the motor patterns involved. Regardless of its motivation or its end-product, this is what all playful activity has in common; and it is possible that it is all that it has in common, since causation and function could vary from species to species.
>
> (Loizos 1969: 228–9)

Loizos recounts the ontogeny of play in chimps. At a very early age the animals begin "exploration and manipulation"; later comes "organized play, or play behavior that has a logical sequence to it"; then comes "bodily activity" in which things like acrobatics are practiced; and finally there is "social play," such as threatening and swaggering, requiring playmates to be effective. The addition of new ways of playing does not eliminate old ways; playing is additive and all kinds can be combined, forming very complex activities.

What is particularly significant about Loizos's observations is that she says that play apparently derives from "behavior that appeared earlier phylogenetically and for purposes other than play." In other words, in her view, play is not rehearsal for life situations but a derivation from life situations, a ritualization and elaboration of "patterns of fight, flight, sexual and eating behavior." And in so far as these patterns are specific to each species so will play be species-specific.

An interesting sidelight that most probably applies to human behavior as well as to other animals' is that experiments show that a reduction of sensory input, particularly deprivation in the mother–infant relationship, "increases the likelihood of repetitive, stereotyped behavior." And that the "most damaging and least reversible of sources of stereotyping occurs in primates raised in restricted and, in particular, socially restricted circumstances" (Loizos 1969: 252). The smaller the cage, the less interaction, the more the stereotyping. Also, by and large, laboratory-reared chimps are more stereotyped in their behavior, less given to creative play, than chimps in the wild. There are even cases of autism developing in chimps reared in isolation.

Primate studies disclose more interesting aspects of play. According to Carpenter (1964), social play is a main means by which young monkeys find their place in the group. The agonistic nature of play itself establishes a dominance scale; and the practice of play prepares the young animal for similar kinds of ranking as an adult. Also, sexual elements make their appearance early in the play of primates. However, as animals approach adulthood many kinds of play seen in childhood give way to other activities like social grooming, actual mating, or hunting. But isn't the swaggering and displays characteristic of adults in a troop of chimps play? Whatever the function and consequences of these displays – ethologists say that this is a key way the chimps maintain and change hierarchical order – they are not actual combats. Leaving such swaggering and displays aside, "play between fully grown adults is rare" (Loizos 1969: 269). Here humans are the spectacular exception.

Loizos speculates that "the more rigid the social hierarchy in a primate species, the less likely it is that play will occur among the *adults* of that species" (1969: 270). What about humans? I see no evidence that people in democratic, flexible human societies play more than those in rigid societies. Often enough, the function of play as manifested in ritual clowning or large-scale blowouts like Carnival is to introduce flexibility into otherwise rigid social structures. Many rigid societies sponsor great ritual displays of play. And it is not possible to measure accurately what play is going on privately or underground. In the so-called democratic societies play may occur on a more individual or small-group basis, while in so-called rigid societies people may play privately, out of the sight of repressive authorities.

What might also be said is that rigid social systems tend to generate events that concentrate on theater and performance, on spectacular confirmations of the existing social order within which brackets of play are allowed, while flexible social systems tend toward drama and small-scale play, the expression of individual opinions and tastes. The impulse toward collectivity, groupness, identification with others leads toward theater and performance; the impulse toward individuality, personal assertiveness, and confrontation between individuals leads toward drama. In certain periods – such as the heydays of Greek and Elizabethan theater drama – a palpable tension was felt between two contradictory modes. In the Greek, the tension was between the shamanistic and collective modes of celebration represented directly in the satyr plays, the Eleusinian mysteries, and other Orphic ceremonies and a newly emerging rationalism and individuality. In the Elizabethan era, the tension arose between the variety of medieval collectives (guilds, feudalism, Catholicism) and a surging Renaissance spirit of rationalism and individuality (self, cities, Protestantism). I won't elaborate these theories here. But studies of non-human primate behavior is not incidental to understanding patterns of human culture.

I want to say a few words in favor of another theory of the function of play. It is not a new theory, and my contribution to it is to connect it to the whole field of performance. I believe play is what organizes performance, makes it comprehensible. If the distinction I made earlier between play and ritualized behavior is kept in mind, then clearly play belongs mainly to carnivorous and omnivorous species: hunters. It belongs to species that depend on other species for life, who stalk, attack, and kill prey. Furthermore, not only among lions, but also with chimps and certainly with humans, hunting is group activity. Goodall says of chimp hunting that

> sometimes it appears that the capture of a prey is almost accidental. . . . On other occasions the hunting seems to be a much more deliberate, purposeful activity, and often at such times the different individuals of a chimpanzee group show quite remarkable cooperation – as when different chimpanzees station themselves at the bases of trees offering escape routes to a cornered victim.
>
> (Goodall 1972: 205)

Hunting demands not only cooperation but sudden bursts (climaxes) of energy balanced against extended periods of stealth. That, and a great deal of practice. This is where play comes in – especially creative or "free" play. One of the qualities of play in higher primates in the wild is the balance between its improvisational quality and its orderliness: in fact, play is the improvisational imposition of order, a way of making order out of disorder. And where play is not autistic it is outer-directed, involving playmates. Although play prepares a young primate for more than hunting, hunting is a particularly full use of play. The most difficult hunts are those where the prey is intelligent and strong. To hunt baboons effectively chimps must develop strategies that take into account the formidable qualities of the resourceful baboon. Such strategy is actively futurist; the present moment is conditioned by what is presumed to be coming next. The hunter must know what the prey is going to do, or the hunt will fail. What develops is a game in the true sense. This game involves the hunter, or hunting group, the prey, and the environment.

Hunting is inherently, not metaphorically, theatrical/dramatic. A script is necessary in order to develop strategies that culminate in a climactic attack-event; agonistic and cooperative behaviors combine in a complicated way so that a "we and them" mentality is heightened; signals are given that not only express feelings but direct actions; there usually is a leader of the hunt and a single, identifiable prey so that activity focuses and climaxes in a swift, violent confrontation during which the issue is settled; the activity that builds to a climax is itself active (this is the difference between hunting and trapping). After the kill there is a feast with meat being shared according to strict rules (a hierarchical communion); and after the feast, total relaxation.

This aspect of the functional theory of play needs, I think, special elaboration because of its relationship to theater. Species that play most also engage in activities that call for sudden expenditures of kinetic energy: crises. This energy is spent on fighting, fleeing, hunting, mating, maintaining dominance, and defining and/or protecting turf. In the energy economy of any animal these crises arise relatively infrequently; but when a crisis arises an animal that cannot swiftly mobilize and direct high energy is doomed. An energy "bank" is necessary for survival. This bank has two primary "accounts," erotic and combative; and several secondary (displacement) accounts: display, dominance–submission gestures, marking (depositing urine or feces, scratches on trees, etc.). But I use the word "bank" only metaphorically. The metabolisms of higher animals are ill-equipped for long-term storage. Instead, play keeps in practice, on call, a regular, crisis-oriented expenditure of kinetic energy. In play, energy is spent in behavior that is not only harmless but fun. Decisively, play allows kinetic potential to be maintained not by being stored but by being spent. Playing is also adaptive in the "creative" ways mentioned earlier. When a crisis arises, the animal is able to meet it by switching play energy into fight energy, for example.

Crisis – the sudden and unstinting spending of kinetic energy – is the link among performance, hunting, ritual, and play. Each gives rise to the others; together they comprise a system through which the animal maintains its ability to spend kinetic energy irregularly, according to immediate, even unexpected, needs (figure 3.5).

The problem remains: How do animals (and persons) tell the difference between play and "for real"? Ritualized behavior, including performances, are a means of continually testing the boundaries between play and "for real." The "special ordering of time and place" – Bateson's (1972: 177–93) "play frame" – which most observers note in both human and animal play are signals that the behavior taking place within the brackets is "only play." Even so, mistakes and confusions happen, so placating gestures, or the presence of a referee, are necessary to keep play in hand.

What might the relationship be between hunting and play, hunting and ritual, ritual and play, play and theater? Earlier I suggested some connections between Paleolithic cave art and hunting/fertility rituals;

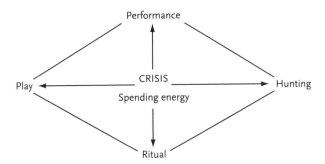

Figure 3.5

also between these rituals and theater. Now I want to argue from a structural basis what I previously adduced from prehistory. To do so I assume a homology between the behavior of the higher primates and humans.

Recall that Loizos (1969) argued that "playful patterns owe their origin to behavior that appeared earlier phylogenetically and for purposes other than play." She described "some of the ways in which motor patterns may be altered and elaborated upon when transferred to a playful context." In her review of the theories concerning the functions of play, Loizos (1969: 236 ff.) identifies the following:

1. The sequence may be re-ordered.
2. The individual movements making up the sequence may become exaggerated.
3. Certain movements within the sequence may be repeated more than they would normally be.
4. The sequence may be broken off altogether by the introduction of irrelevant activities, and resumed later. This could be called fragmentation.
5. Movements may be both exaggerated and repeated.
6. Individual movements within the sequence may never be completed, and this incomplete element may be repeated many times. This applies equally to both the beginning of a movement (the intention element) and to its ending (the completion element).

These qualities are characteristic of "creative" or "free" play. In such play the animal is not bound by circumstances to stick to a pattern that will yield results. A cat playing with a crumpled-up paper ball may "hunt" it for a few moments and then stop; a chimp may chase a playmate through the tree tops and stop before making contact; humans involve themselves in dozens of momentary, incomplete play activities each hour. In fact, the more advanced the animal, the more likely that each of the six play elements will be used. Behavior is recombined in new ways, exaggerated, repeated, fragmented, short-circuited. In lower animals, the flow of behavior is mostly one-directional; it is clear whether or not the animal is playing. But, as organisms grow more complicated, the flow becomes two-way. A cat with a captured mouse is "playing" with its prey; it is also completing the hunting process. Chimps will convert play behavior into serious behavior and back again, so that a play chase suddenly erupts into a fight, the fight is resolved by gestures of dominance and submission, this "contract" is "ratified" by mutual grooming, and soon enough there is another playful chase.

In humans, the situation is the most complicated. First off, people hunt other people with the same diligence that most other species reserve for interspecies warfare. But if human aggression is non-specific, so is human inventiveness. So-called "serious" work in humans is treated playfully; and so-called play can become very serious. Humans can speak truthfully of "war games" and "theaters of war," and great issues can be carried on the shoulders of athletes or actors who become important politicians. I will not elaborate these ideas here except to insist that Huizinga was wrong when he decried the "deterioration" of play because serious issues get involved in it. Serious issues are always involved in play; just as, in humans, play is inextricably involved in all "serious" work. When through industrial or other means the play elements are taken out of work, work becomes drudgery and less efficient, not more; and when the seriousness is taken away from play, then playing grows sloppy and dull, not fun.

But what is "fun"? Everyone agrees that play is often fun. Certainly this is so for humans, and it appears to be so for animals too. But I think it is wrong to say that play is "free," if Loizos was correct in saying that play is the restructuring of other behavior. Also, we know that the "rules of the game," which order an otherwise chaotic situation, add to the fun while taking away from freedom. Playful activity constantly generates rules, and although these may change swiftly, there is no play without them. In other words, to use terms developed earlier, all play is "scripted." Thus, "having fun" does not mean being "free from rules." Fun is something else.

Let me again return to the hunt. Real hunting – going for the kill – can be fun. Watch a cat "playing with" a mouse or other small animal. The cat lets the prey go, chases after it, catches it, lets it go again, and so on. Finally, the kill is made and the prey is either eaten or carried around triumphantly. Humans have even more fun hunting, including hunting other humans. It's not nice to think of war as a kind of hunt-and-destroy sport but that's how war colleges teach it and one way recruiters sell it. On the other hand, hunting for food is no longer a major human occupation. And in human play – other than war and hunting – the actual kill is avoided. (Most murders are something else, not the result of detailed planning, and not much fun, no matter what the movies show us.) But there still is fun in playing – and I think this "fun" is a playing at killing.

Not all playing maybe, but the kind that is related to dramatic theatrical performance. Drama, as distinct from script, performance, and theater, is not universal. That is, drama occurs at certain times and among certain peoples who have consciously made a connection among hunting, warfare, human and/or animal sacrifice, and play.[7] The dynamics of the relationships between hunting, playing, ritual, and drama might be modeled as in figure 3.6.

My thesis is that much play behavior is adapted from hunting, that hunting is a kind of playing. This kind of playing is strategic, future-and-crisis-oriented, violent and/or combative; it has winners and losers, leaders and followers; it employs costumes and/or disguises (often as animals); it has a beginning, middle, and end; and its underlying themes are fertility, prowess, and animism/totemism. This kind of playing at killing emphasizes individual or small-group action and teamwork. It is scripted behavior. In time, playing/hunting may generate the symbolic activities of ritual and drama. This transformation may be a function of what Lorenz calls "displacement activity": when two conflicting impulses prevent each other from being activated a third

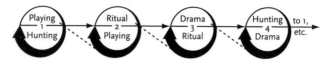

Figure 3.6
Note
The bottom half of each circle is the "source" of the top half, although there is a significant amount of feedback from the top. The bottom is, in psychological terms, "unconscious" and the top "conscious." The top half of each transaction becomes the bottom half in another transaction. Ecological and social circumstances determine which transaction is dominant in a given culture.

action results. In animals, displacement activity is often ritualized behavior. In humans, the conflicting impulses may be the wish to hunt people versus love bonds for members of one's own species, culture, or kin group. The displacement activity is a ritual or drama in which humans kill humans – but only "in play." Or instead of hunting them, loved ones are scarred, circumcised, or marked: some refiguration or signal written on the body. Through the ordeal of being (temporarily and in play) prey, the initiated gains the status of hunter.

Like the behavior they derive from and elaborate, rituals and dramas are violent and crisis-oriented; they test individual courage, stamina, and ingenuity; participation in them is in itself status-raising; they occur within special times/places; they operate according to rules, traditions, strategies. Agricultural societies develop spectacles organized around ceremonies whose function it is to entreat the regularity of the seasons, the falling of rain, the warming of sun. Agricultural ceremonies emphasize what I have been calling performance and theater; hunting rites emphasize script and drama.

I think drama as it developed in China, Japan, Korea, India, America, and Greece derived from circumpolar hunting cultures (the remnants of which still exist in Siberia and in pockets throughout the Americas) that also developed shamanism. These cultures very early associated hunting-killing, fertility, animality, curing, spirit possession, and crisis initiation through man-made ordeals. Most significantly, they translated strategic, future-oriented hunting behavior into strategic language: story-telling. This story-telling was done not merely through words but through songs, chants, dances, drumming, and "setting" (such as the caves). Ultimately, drama arose as a playful combination of these strategic behaviors.

I don't speak of Africa because I know little about Africa. But if I'm right, then African drama will also be associated with hunting. As for Australian, Melanesian, and Polynesian cultures, these deserve special discussion but from what I know, and what I've observed in Papua New Guinea, I think my thesis will hold up. Performance and theater are universal, but drama is not. Drama develops in cultures for whom hunting is especially important.

A difficulty with my thesis is that warfare is universal. And if war is a specialized kind of hunting – especially war as practiced in traditional societies during premodern times – then drama ought to be universal. Maybe it was once. Remember that drama does not depend on *written* texts, but on carefully *scripted* actions.

Another difficulty arises in modern times. The world, which used to be made up of thousands of distinct cultures, is fast becoming global. The consequences of this emerging global megaculture are barely known. In industrialized societies – east and west – "workshop" has developed as one way of re-creating, at least temporarily, some of the security and intimacy of small, autonomous cultural groups. The workshop is a way of playing around with reality, a means of examining behavior by reordering, exaggerating, fragmenting, recombining, and adumbrating it. The workshop is a protected time/space where intragroup relationships may thrive without being threatened by intergroup aggression. In the workshop special gestures arise, definite sub-cultures emerge. The workshop is not restricted to theater, it is ubiquitous. In science, it is the "experimental method," the laboratory team, the research center, the fieldwork outpost. In psychotherapy, it is the "group," the rehabilitation center, the "therapeutic community." In living styles, it is the neighborhood, the commune, the collective. (When the workshop is repressive rather than facilitating, as in many "total institutions" such as asylums, prisons, hospitals, and schools, it is a most violently abusive way of treating human beings.) The aim of the workshop is to construct an environment where rational, arational, and irrational behavior exist in balance. Or, to put it biologically, where cortical, brain-stem, motor, and instinctive operations exist in balance, leading to expressive, symbolic, playful, ritualized, "scripted" behavior. It is my opinion that workshops are more important than most people dream of.

And if I may end on a somewhat fanciful note: I associate the workshop environment with those ancient, decorated caves that give evidence of singing and dancing, people celebrating fertility in risky, sexy, violent, collective, playful ways.

NOTES

1   See La Barre (1972: 387–432), Giedion (1962), and Pfeiffer (1982). These, in turn, are copiously documented.

2   The John Marshall–Robert Gardner film *The Hunters* (1958) depicts the giraffe hunt of a small group of Kalahari tribesmen.

3   From a 1986 perspective, I might differently gloss the distinctions between "text" and "script." Someone with a Derridean turn of mind might say that what in 1973 I called a "script" a deconstructionist would now call a "text." There are many different kinds of text – performance texts, dramatic texts, musical texts, movement texts, painterly texts, etc. A text is a way of inscribing – encoding – information. Such inscriptions may be on stone, vellum, or paper – or they may be charges on a silicon chip, memory traces in a dancer's body, or what have you. Various notation systems exist: alphabetical, digital, analogical, graphic, etc. New languages can be constructed. Information can easily be translated from one of these inscriptive/storage systems (languages) into another. That's why I can so easily write this text on my computer: the machine almost instantaneously inscribes and translates the several languages it uses – while what comes up on my screen is the one language I know fairly well, English. This translatability promotes discourse across disciplines and genres that might otherwise be mute in relation to each other: talk of dance and drama, of prose fiction and athletic contests, of audience participation in the theater and solitary reading.

4   Most probably this teaching was not formal, but through imitation. However, a case could be made that the inaccessibility of the caves indicates an esoteric cult, and that the "secrets" of the cult would be definitely and formally transmitted.

5   Council grounds are a temporary village established by the Australian authorities (in 1972, Papua New Guinea was not yet an independent nation) to facilitate cooperation and exchange rather than combat which had been the principal means of contact among many Highlands groups. After independence, these grounds were kept in use. Several forms of Asian drama and meditation have been derived from martial training. The dancing at Kurumugl was a direct adaptation of fighting modes; a conscious inhibition of combat which led to a transfer of energy from thrusting shoulders (shooting arrows or throwing spears) to the thighs and legs: the unique rapid kicking-from-the-knee dancing.

6   See Kapferer (1983) for an in-depth study of Sri Lankan performative exorcism.

7   I know that many scholars identify sacrifice with agriculture, particularly in ancient Egypt and the Middle East. But I think it could also be connected to hunting and warfare. I believe warfare is mainly an adaptation and elaboration of hunting behavior, and in this sense all human societies are hunting societies, since all make war. For discussions of the relationship between violence and sacrifice, see Girard (1977) and chapter 7 of this book.

4

FROM RITUAL TO THEATER AND BACK: THE EFFICACY– ENTERTAINMENT BRAID

PERFORMANCE RHYTHMS

The kaiko celebration of the Tsembaga of Highlands Papua New Guinea is a year-long festival culminating in the konj kaiko – pig kaiko.[1] Kaiko means dancing, and the chief entertainments of the celebrations are dances. During 1962–3 the Tsembaga entertained thirteen other local groups on fifteen occasions, not counting the grand finale, the konj kaiko.[2] To make sure that a kaiko was successful, young Tsembaga men were dispatched to neighboring areas to announce the shows – and to send back messages of delay should a visiting group be late; in that case the entertainments were postponed. A kaiko day began with the dancers, all men, bathing; then they took several hours putting on costumes and facial and body makeup. Self-adornment is an exacting, precise, and delicate process. When dressed the dancers assembled on the flattened, stamped-down grounds where they danced both for their own pleasure and as rehearsal in advance of the arrival of their guests. The visitors announced their arrival by singing – they could be heard well before they were seen. By this time many spectators were gathered, including men, women, and children from neighboring villages. These spectators came to watch, and to exchange goods. Finally,

> the local dancers retire to a vantage point just above the dance ground, where their view of the visitors is unimpeded and where they continue singing. The visitors approach the gate silently, led by men carrying fight packages,[3] swinging their axes as they run back and forth in front of their procession in the peculiar crouched fighting prance. Just before they reach the gate they are met by one or two of those locals who have invited them and who now escort them over the gate. Visiting women and children follow behind the dancers and join the other spectators on the sidelines. There is much embracing as the local women and children greet visiting kinfolk. The dancing procession charges to the center of the dance ground shouting the long, low battle cry and stamping their feet, magically treated before their arrival . . . to enable them to dance strongly. After they charge back and forth across the dance ground several times, repeating the stamping in several locations while the crowd cheers in admiration of their numbers, their style, and the richness of their finery, they begin to sing.
> (Rappaport 1968: 187)

The performance transformed combat techniques into entertainment. All the basic moves and sounds – even the charge into the central space – were adaptations or direct lifts from battle. But the Tsembaga dance was a dance, and clearly so to everyone present at it. The dancing was not an isolated phenomenon – as theater-going in America usually is – but a behavior nested in supportive actions. The entry described took place late in the afternoon, and just before dusk the dancing stopped and the food which had been piled in the center of the dancing ground was distributed and eaten. It might be said, literally, that the dancing is *about* the food, for the whole kaiko cycle pivots on acquiring enough pigs for meat to afford the festival.

> The visitors are asked to stop dancing and gather around while a presentation speech is made by one of the men responsible for the invitation. As he slowly walks around and around the food that has been laid out in a number of piles, the speechmaker recounts the

> relations of the two groups: their mutual assistance in fighting, their exchange of women and wealth, their hospitality to each other in times of defeat. . . . When the speech of presentation is finished they gather their portions and distribute them to those men who came to help them dance, and to their women.
>
> (Rappaport 1968: 188)

After supper the dancing resumes and goes on all night. By dawn almost everyone has danced with everyone else: and this communality is a sign of a strong alliance.

With dawn the dancing ground is converted into a market. Ornaments, pigs, furs, axes, knives, shells, pigments, tobacco are all traded or sold (money has come into Tsembaga economy).

> The transactions that take place on the dance ground are completed on the spot: a man both gives and receives at the same time. . . . At the men's house, however, a different kind of exchange takes place. Here men from other places give to their kinsmen or trading partners in the local group valuables for which they do not receive immediate return.
>
> (Rappaport 1968: 189)

This orchestrated indebtedness is at the heart of the kaiko. At the start of the celebration the hosts owed meat to the guests and the guests owed items of trade to the hosts. In the first part of the kaiko the hosts paid meat to their guests; in the second part of the kaiko the guests paid trade items to their hosts. But neither payment results in a balance. When the kaiko is over the guests owed their hosts meat, and the hosts owed their guests trade items. They had exchanged roles while perpetuating a necessary imbalance of payments. This symmetrical imbalance guaranteed further kaikos – continued exchanges between groups. Guaranteed for as long as the whole socio-economic-aesthetic-ritual system of which the kaiko is a part is not ripped to shreds. Following the public trading and the more private gift giving was some more dancing. Then everyone went home.

The kaiko entertainments are a ritual display – not simply a doing but a showing of a doing. Furthermore, this showing is both actual (= the trading and giving of goods resulting in new imbalances) and symbolic (= the reaffirmination of alliances concretized in debtor–creditor relationships). The entertainment itself is a vehicle for debtors and creditors to exchange places; it is also the occasion for a market; and it is fun. The kaiko depends on the accumulation of pigs and goods, a necessity for trade, and a willingness to visit, dress up, and dance. No part of the kaiko is enough by itself. The dancing is a performance – and enjoyed as such, with spectators serving frequently as acerbic critics – but it's also a way of facilitating trade, finding mates, cementing military alliances, and reaffirming (or reordering) tribal hierarchies.

> The Tsembaga say that "those who come to our kaiko will also come to our fights." This native interpretation of kaiko attendance is also given expression by an invited group. Preparations for departure to a kaiko at another place include ritual performances similar to those that precede a fight. Fight packages are applied to the heads and hearts of the dancers and *gir* to their feet so that they will dance strongly, just as, during warfare, they are applied so that they will fight strongly. . . . Dancing is like fighting. The visitors' procession is led by men carrying fight packages, and their entrance upon the dance ground of their hosts is martial. To join a group in dancing is the symbolic expression of willingness to join them in fighting.
>
> (Rappaport 1968: 195–6)

The kaiko dance display is a cultural version of territorial and status displays in animals. The rituals of the Tsembaga are ethological as well as cultural. They are also ecological: the kaiko is a means of organizing the Tsembaga's relationships to their neighbors, to their lands and goods, to their gardens and hunting ranges.

A kaiko culminates in a konj kaiko. The kaiko lasts a year, the konj kaiko a few days, usually two. Kaiko years are rare. During the 50 to 60 years ending in 1963 the Tsembaga staged four kaikos, with an average of 12 to 15 years between festivals. The whole cycle is tied to the war/peace rhythm which, in turn, is tied to the fortunes of the pig population. After a konj kaiko – whose major event is a mass slaughter of pigs and distribution of meat – a short peace is followed by war, which continues until another kaiko cycle begins. The cycle itself lasts for enough years to allow the raising of sufficient pigs to stage a konj kaiko. The konj kaiko of November 7–8, 1963, saw the slaughter of 96 pigs with a total live weight of 15,000 pounds, yielding around 7,500 pounds of meat. Eventually about 3,000 people got shares of the kill.

What starts in dancing ends in eating. Or, to put it in aesthetic-religious terms, what starts as theater ends as Communion. Not since the Athenian festivals of ancient Greece or the cycle plays of medieval Christian Europe, have we in the west used performances this way, as pivots of systems involving economic, social, political, and religious transactions. With the re-advent of holism in contemporary society at least a discussion of such performances seems practicable. It is clear that the kaiko dances are not ornaments or pastimes or even "part of the means" effecting the transactions among the Tsembaga. The dances both symbolize and activate the process of exchange.

The dances are pivots in a system transforming destructive behavior into constructive alliances. It is no accident that every move, chant, and costume of the kaiko dances are adapted from combat. A new, or additional, use is found for this behavior. Quite unconsciously a positive feedback begins: the more splendid the displays of dancing, the stronger the alliances; the stronger the alliances, the more splendid the dancing. Between kaikos – but only between them – war is waged. During the kaiko cycles there is peace. The transformation of combat behavior into performance is the theatrical heart of the kaiko. This transformation is identical to the action at the heart of Greek theater, and from the Greeks down through western theater history. Namely, characterization and the presentation of real or possible events – the story, plot, or dramatic action worked out by people, gods, or demons – is a transformation of real behavior into symbolic behavior. Theatrical transformation appears to be of only two kinds: 1) the displacement of antisocial, injurious, disruptive behavior by ritualized gestures and displays, and 2) the invention of characters who act out fictional events or real events fictionalized by virtue of their being acted out (as in documentary theater or film or Roman-type gladiatorial games). These two kinds of transformation may occur together, but in the mix usually one is dominant. Western theater emphasizes characterization and the enactment of fictions; Melanesian theater emphasizes the displacement of hostile behavior. Theaters that balance the two tendencies –

examples can be found in Asia, native America, medieval Europe, Africa, and some western experimental performances – offer, I think, the best model for the future of the theater.

Much performing among tribal peoples is, like the kaiko, part of the society's overall ecology. The *engwura* cycle of the Arunta as described by Spencer and Gillen (1899, repr. 1968) in the late nineteenth century[4] is an elegant example of how a complicated series of performances both expressed and participated in a people's ecology. The fact that the engwura is no longer performed – that the Arunta, culturally speaking, have been exterminated – indicates the incompatibility of the wholeness I am talking about and western culture as it is presently constituted. In so far as performing groups adapt techniques from the kaiko or engwura they are bound to remain outside the western "mainstream." But the chief function of the avant-grade is to propose models for change: to be "in advance." The engwura was an initiation cycle that spanned several years; the last phase consisted of performances staged sporadically over a 3–4-month period. Each phase of the engwura took place only when several conditions meshed: enough young men of a certain age gathered in one place ready to be initiated; enough older men willing to lead the ceremonies (particularly decisive in an oral culture); enough food to support the celebration. Then the sacred implements and grounds were prepared painstakingly according to tradition. Finally, there had to be peace among neighboring tribes – sometimes the announcement of an impending engwura was enough to settle a peace.

The engwura's daily rhythm recapitulated its monthly rhythm: performance spaces were cleared, implements repaired and laid out, body decorations applied, food cooked and eaten. Each performance day saw not one but several performances, with rest and preparations between each. Each performance lasted an average of ten minutes, and was characteristically a dance accompanied by drumming and chanting. After finishing a performance, the performers rested for about two hours; then preparations for the next performance began, and these preparations took about two hours. The day followed a rising and falling rhythm (figure 4.1).[5] The whole performance cycle constituted and recapitulated the major events in the life-cycle of Arunta males. Individual events were nested within, even as they as a series

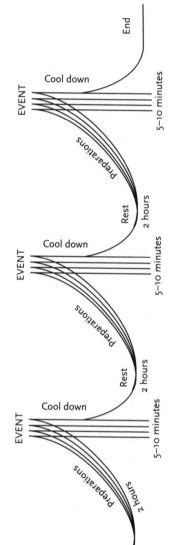

Figure 4.1

comprised, the small cycle of performances. And the big cycle, a completed series of small cycles, coincided with Arunta ecology, in Rappaport's sense (figure 4.2).

Each Arunta male, during his life, could expect to play roles in the performance cycles coexistent with his status in society: initiate, participant, leader, or onlooker. On each day the performers enacted condensed and concentrated versions of their lives as they played and displayed their emergent relationships with their fellow Aruntans: the dances, stories, songs, and actions that constituted the core of their "Aruntaness." And the 3–4-month series of performances comprising the small cycle also replicated the rhythms of the Arunta life-cycle. Each phase of the cycle, from individual events lasting only minutes, to the big cycle lasting years, was a replication (an extension, concentration, and repetition) of every other phase. The whole performance

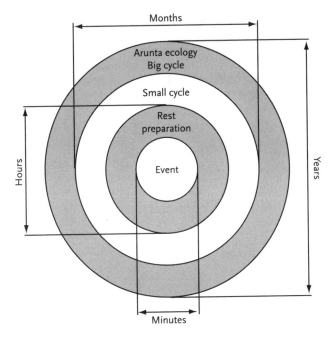

Figure 4.2

cycle was, in fact, an important – probably the most important – set of events in an Arunta male's life.[6]

The subject matter of each brief dance-drama was events of Dreamtime beings who populated the Aborigine world "in the beginning."[7] These events were very important to the Arunta and constituted for them a history and, since each Dreamtime event was connected to specific places and landmarks, a geography.[8] To some extent the eng-wura is familiar to us because it resembles western dramas and religious rituals. But while we grant reactualizations only symbolic status, the Arunta experienced the Dreamtime enactments as actual presences, as an orthodox Catholic might regard the Eucharist.

The overall structure of the engwura is analogic, while its interior structure is dramatic. The two structures are integrated because the Arunta believed concretely in the Dreamtime and felt their own lives moving from "ordinary" to "super-ordinary" reality. They experienced the interaction between these realities: the engwura performances were the navel, or link, or point of time and place where the two realities intersected and meshed.

THE PIG-KILL AT KURUMUGL

I saw an ecological ritual similar to the konj kaiko (but much less inclusive than the engwura) in March, 1972 in the Eastern Highlands of Papua New Guinea.[9] Surrounding the performance of the kaiko is no special self-consciousness. That is, the ritual is performed without the Tsembaga being explicitly aware of its functions; and aside from praising or critical comments on the dancing offered by anyone who cares to, no aesthetic judgements are passed. In other words, there are neither performance theorists nor critics in the western sense among the Tsembaga. But at Kurumugl the people knew what the ritual does and why it was established – to inhibit warfare among feuding groups. The ritual at Kurumugl is already traveling along the continuum from ritual toward theater.

It's my purpose to outline a process through which theater develops from ritual and, conversely, ritual develops from theater. My evidence will not come from archeology or anthropological reconstructions.[10] I will document this process by referring to contemporary or near contemporary sources. As I said, the process runs in two directions – from ritual to theater and back.

Unlike the kaiko dancing grounds, the "council grounds" (as they are called) at Kurumugl are near no regular village. The colonial Australian government – Papua New Guinea became independent in 1976 – set up the grounds as a place where former enemies assemble to sing-sing (pidgin for dance–music–theater). The difference between the Tsembaga and the people at Kurumugl is that the kaiko brought together traditional allies while at the Kurumugl sing-sing traditional enemies met. The performance at Kurumugl was in danger of tipping over into actual combat, even though the performing looked very much like that of the konj kaiko: dance movements adapted from combat, war chants, the arrival of a guest group at a dance ground piled high with freshly slaughtered, cooked pork. The celebration I saw at Kurumugl took two days. The first day consisted of arriving, setting up temporary house inside long rectangular huts, and digging cooking ovens. All of the about 350 people assembled on the first day were of one tribal group. They awaited the arrival of their guests, a group comparable in size, and recently the enemy. The second day began with the slaughter by the hosts of about 200 pigs. These were clubbed on the snouts, their heads smashed. As each owner kills his animal he recites – sings – a speech telling how difficult it was to raise the pig, who it is promised to, what a fine animal it is, etc. These pro forma recitatives are applauded with laughs and roars, as they often contain jokes and obscene invective. The orations are accompanied and punctuated by the death squeals of the pigs. Then the animals are gutted, butchered, and lowered in halves and quarters into earth ovens where they cook over hot rocks. Their guts are hung in nets over the ovens and steamed. Their bladders are blown into balloons and given to the children who rush around the grounds shouting and playing. The sight and smell of so much meat and blood excites the people, including me. No special clothes are worn for the killing. The only visible ritual element I detected was the careful display of pig jawbones on a circular altar-like structure in the middle of the dance grounds. From each jaw flowers were hung.

As the cooking starts, the men retire to the huts to begin adorning themselves. From time to time a man emerges to try on a towering head-dress of cassowary and peacock feathers. The women cook and tend to the children. About four hours later the meat, still nearly raw, is taken from the ovens and displayed in long rows. Each family lays out its own meat – the women doing most of this work – like so much money in the bank. Pork is wealth in the Highlands. As more and more men finish dressing they emerge from the huts to show off and admire each other in a grudging way – the adorning is very competitive. Some women also adorned themselves, dressing much like the men. I couldn't tell if this was traditional or an innovation or why some women did it and not others. A man invited Joan MacIntosh[11] and me into his hut to watch him put on his makeup. He set out a mirror and some tins of pigment (bought from a trading store run by Japanese). Then he applied blue, red, and black to his torso, shoulders, arms, and face. He painted half his nose red and the other half blue. I asked him what the patterns meant. He said he chose them because he liked the way they looked. The Australian Aborigines, by contrast, adorn their bodies with patterns each detail of which is linked to ancestral or Dreamtime beings, sexual magic, or recent events. Aborigine body painting is map-making and story-telling.

Our performer-host showed us his head-dress of four-foot-long feathers. Then he stepped out from the darkness of the hut into the brilliant glare of the sunshine to try it on. As he emerged his casual air vanished and he literally thrust his chest forward and up, gave a long whooping call, put on his head-dress, and displayed himself. He was costumed for a social not a dramatic role – that is, not to present a fictional character whose life was separable from his own, but to show himself in a special way: to display his feathers, his strength, his authority, his power, his wealth, his position among the people. It is not easy to distinguish between these kinds of roles. They are not binary opposites. In drama the script is already fixed in its details, the precise gestures of the role are rehearsed for a particular occasion (and other occasions, other "productions," might eventuate in different gestures), while "in life" the script is "replaced by an ongoing process, this process is set in motion by the objective demands of the role, and the subjective motives and goals of the actor."[12] An awareness that social and dramatic roles are indeed closely related to each other, and locating their points of convergence in the mise-en-scène rather than in the mind of a playwright, has been one of the major developments in its contemporary theater theory and practice. This development has been helped by movies and television – by film because it presents dramatic actions on location, as if in "real life," and by TV because it brings the allegedly "real life" of news into the living-room. TV news is staged not only by the obvious editing of raw footage to suit the video format, especially the need to sell time in prescribed short units (based on how long an average viewer's attention can be held), but also because "media events" and "camera opportunities" are classes of events created for TV. Many guerrilla theater events, terrorist acts, kidnappings, assassinations, and street demonstrations – not to mention more banal happenings such as press conferences, dedications of public buildings, parades – are theatricalized in order to catch the TV eye. The idea is to "get to" large masses of people via TV. The powerful have always had access to if not control of the media. But TV, being so much more flexible and instantaneous than print, democratizes by celebrating its appetite for "news." Otherwise silent and invisible groups can be seen and heard if they do something "newsworthy." Thus these groups gain in power. In response the authorities make statements, stage reprisals, and in other ways attempt to terrorize the terrorists. The ordinary viewer, too often paralyzed by these displays and counter-displays of force, is called on to choose "right" from "wrong." Apparently two-person exchanges between activist and authority are actually three-person interactions, with the invisible spectator being the addressee of last resort. So are we continually being educated to the histrionics of communication.[13]

At Kurumugl a very similar histrionic sense is present. The men displaying themselves are out to impress their friends and then later in the day their enemies. As these people become "technified" (they already have planes before cars, TV before newspapers), they will leap not into the twentieth century but beyond, going directly from pre-industrial tribalism to postmodern tribalism. The big difference between the two is that pre-industrial tribalism scatters power among large numbers of competing local leaders; postmodern tribalism can easily become collective, mass, megapolitical. I mean by tribalism the shaping of social roles not through individual choice but by collective formation; the substitution of histrionic-ritualized events for ordinary events; the sacralization or increasingly codified parameters of experience; and the disappearance of solitude and one-to-one intimacy as these have developed in the west since the Renaissance. Postmodern tribalism is medievalism under the auspices of technology.

Such tribalism is good for the theater – if by good one means that most social situations will be governed by conventional, external gestures loaded with metaphoric/symbolic significance. The theater in the theater will probably continue to decline; but the theater "in life" will permeate more and more activities, both ordinary and special. Anomie and identity crisis diminish, while in their place are fixed roles and rites of passage transporting persons not only from one status to another but from one identity to another. These transformations are achieved by means of performance.

When the performer at Kurumugl stepped outside his hut he joined a group of envious males whose costumes were, like his, peculiar amalgams of traditional and imported stuff; sunglasses and bones stuck through the spectrum; cigarette holders and home-made tobacco pipes; khaki shorts and grass skirts. But despite the breakdown of traditional costuming, at the level of discrete items an old pattern was being worked out. An ecological ritual where the pig meat was a "payback" (pidgin for fulfilling a ritual obligation) from the hosts to the guests. As among the Tsembaga every adult male at Kurumugl was in a debtor relationship to persons arriving in the afternoon of the second day. The nature of the payback is such that what is given back must appear to exceed what is owed.[14] The payback ceremony involves an exchange of roles in which creditors become debtors and debtors become creditors. This insures that more ceremonies will follow when the new debtors accumulate enough pigs. The circle of reciprocating imbalanced obligations may involve a number of groups linked in a complicated network. Never is a balance struck, because balance would threaten an end to the obligations, and this would lead either to war or a stale peace. As long as the obligations are intact the social web transmits continuous waves of paybacks throughout the system.

The visitors approaching Kurumugl came not as friends to a party but as invaders demanding what was theirs to claim. The afternoon's performance was a ritual combat with the guests assaulting Kurumugl in a modified war dance, armed with fighting spears, as the campers at

Kurumugl defended their ground and the immense stack of meat piled in the center of it. Instead of a secret raiding party there were dancers; instead of taking human victims, they took meat. And instead of doubt about the outcome everyone knew what was going to happen. Thus a ritualized social drama (as war in the Highlands often was) moved toward becoming an aesthetic drama/celebration guided by a script of actions – a script known in advance, carefully prepared for, and strictly carried out.

Again, differences between social and aesthetic drama are not easy to specify. Social drama has more variables, the outcome is in doubt – it is more like a game or sporting contest. Aesthetic drama is almost entirely prearranged, and the participants can concentrate not on strategies for achieving their goals – at Kurumugl, to penetrate to where the meat is, or to defend the meat pile – but on displays. Aesthetic drama is less instrumental and more ornamental than social drama. Also, it can use symbolic time and place and in doing so become entirely fictionalized.

Early in the afternoon of the second day I heard from outside the camp the chanting and shouting of the invaders. The people in camp, excited by what they heard, returned these shouts so that an antiphonal chorus arose. Then the men in camp – and a contingent of about twenty women who were fully armed – rushed to the edges of Kurumugl to begin the ritual combat. Both sides were armed with bows and arrows, spears, sticks, and axes. They chanted in a rhythm common to the Highlands – a leader sings a phrase and is overlapped by the unison response of many followers. This call-and-response round is sounded in loud nasal tones, with an ascending pitch progression of quarter and half notes. Such chants alternate with *ketchak*-like[15] staccato grunts– pants–shouts. From about 1 to 5 in the afternoon the two groups engaged in fierce ritual combats. Each cycle of singing and dancing climaxed when parties of warriors rushed forward from both sides, spears ready for throwing then, at apparently the last second, they substituted a rapid kick-from-the-knee step for hurling their weapons. At Kurumugl the weapons became props in a performance of aggression displaced if not into friendship at least into a non-deadly confrontation.

The assaults of the invaders were repeated dozens of times. A lush and valuable peanut field was trampled to muck. Each assault was met by a determined counter-attack. But foot by foot the invaders pene-trated to the heart of the camp ground – to the pile of meat, the altar of jaw bones and flowers. All the meat previously laid out in rows was now piled 3 feet deep – a huge heap of legs, snouts, ribs, and flanks all tangled together. Three live white goats were tethered to a pole at the edge of the meat pile. Once the invaders reached the meat they merged with their hosts, forming one large, whooping, chanting, dancing doughnut of warriors. Around and around the meat they whirled, for nearly an hour. I was pinned up against a tree, between the armed dancers and the meat. The blur of warriors rushing round and round made me dizzy. Then, suddenly, the dancing stopped and orators plunged into the meat, pulling a leg, or a flank, or a side of ribs, and shouted–sung–declaimed things like (in translation):

> This pig I give you in payment for your pig you gave my father three years ago! Your pig was scrawny, no fat on it at all, but my pig is huge, with lots of fat, much good meat – see! see! – much better than the one my father got! And my whole family, especially my brothers, will remember that we are giving you today better than what we got, so that you owe us, and must help us if we need you to stand with us in a fight!

Sometimes the speechifying rose to song. Sometimes insults were hurled back and forth. The fun in orating, and the joking, stood on a very serious foundation: the participants did not forget that not so long ago they were blood enemies. After more than an hour of orating the meat is distributed. Sleds were made to carry it shoulder-high and whole families, with much singing, departed with their share of meat. This meat found its way by means of the network of obligations to places far from Kurumugl and among people who were not present that afternoon.

TRANSFORMANCES

The performance at Kurumugl consisted of displaying the meat, ritual combat, the merging of the two opposing groups into a collaborative group, orating, and carrying the meat away. Preparations for this performance were both immediate, the day before at the camp (and at the visitor's residence) and long-range: raising the pigs, acquiring costumes and ornaments, setting the precise date for the kill and distribution of meat. After the performance came the clean-up, the travel home, the distribution of meat, feasting, and the telling and retelling of stories about the sing-sing. By means of the performance the basic relationship – one might say the fundamental relationship – between the invading and the host group was reversed.

ACTUALITY 1   ⟶   TRANSFORMANCE ⟶ ACTUALITY 2
Hosts are in debt   Invaders are in
to invaders   debt to hosts

As in all rites of passage something had happened during the performance. The performance both symbolized and actualized the change in status. The meeting at Kurumugl – killing pigs, dancing, giving–taking the meat – was the process of changing the valence of the relationship between hosts and invaders. This process was the only one other than war recognized by all the parties assembled at Kurumugl. Dancing and giving–taking the meat more than symbolized the changed relationship between hosts and invaders, it was the change itself.

This conflation of symbolic and actual events is missing from most aesthetic theater. In aesthetic theater and dance the symbolic alone exists. However, even in aesthetic theater something approaching actuality has been sought for by making the performer the "author" of his/her own actions or "visible" side by side with the character in a Brechtian way. The incorporation of psychodramatic techniques reflects the preoccupation with the individual that marks modern western societies. Where "distancing" is used a definite social or political consciousness is engaged and the appeal of the performance is not to people as individuals but as participants in larger social units.

In the 1960s a new move began that climaxed in the 1970s and 1980s. Performance artists created "actuals" (see chapter 2), homemade rituals where changes like those achieved at Kurumugl are sought. But a contradiction undermines these efforts. At Kurumugl enough actual wealth and people could be assembled in one place so that what was done by means of performance effected definite economic, political, and social power. In contemporary western societies only a charade of power can be displayed at theatrical performances; or the actual changes played through by performance artists affect very few people. When artists, or their audiences, recognize that these staged "rituals" are mostly symbolic activities masquerading as effective acts, a feeling of helplessness overcomes them. So-called "real events" are revealed as metaphors. Governments can organize large-scale displays – parades of military hardware, for example – but far from effecting change these rituals are designed to forestall change.

At Kurumugl the transformation of debtors into creditors was not simply the occasion for a celebratory performance (as a birthday party celebrates but does not effect a change in age). The performance at Kurumugl makes happen what it celebrates. It opens up enough time in the right place for the exchange to take, be made: it is liminal, a fluid mid-point between two fixed structures. This mid-point occurs when for a brief time the two groups merge into one dancing circle. During this liminal time/place *communitas* is possible – that leveling of all differences in an ecstasy that so often characterizes performing (see Victor Turner 1969, 1974, 1982, and 1985). Then and only then can the exchange take place (figure 4.3). The transformations above the line convert dangerous encounters into less dangerous aesthetic and social enactments. Those below the line effect changes from one actuality into another. It is only because the transformations above the line happen that those below the line can take place in peace. All the transformations – aesthetic and social as well as actual – are temporary. The meat will be eaten, the costumes doffed, the dance ended. The single group will divide again according to known divisions; today's debtors

Figure 4.3

war parties	. . .	transformed into	. . .	dancing groups
human victims				pig meat
battledress				costumes
combat				dancing

two groups				one group
debtors				creditors
creditors				debtors

are next year's creditors, etc. The pig-kill and dance at Kurumugl managed a complicated and potentially dangerous exchange of goods and status with a minimum of danger and a maximum of pleasure. Performing was the mode of achieving "real results" – paying debts, incurring new obligations. The dancing does not celebrate or mark the results, it does not precede or follow the exchange – it is the means of making the transformations below the line, it is part of the exchange: more than meat is being traded. The performance at Kurumugl was effective.

The Tsembaga, Arunta, and Kurumugl performances are ecological rituals. Whatever enjoyment participants take in the dancing, and however carefully they prepare themselves for dancing, the dances are danced to achieve results. If the dance fails – if instead of two groups merging into one, fights break out – then the exchange of meat will not take place; the transformation of debtors into creditors and vice versa will not happen. In religious rituals results are achieved by appealing to a transcendent Other (who puts in an appearance either in person or by surrogate). In ecological rituals the other group, or the status to be achieved, or some clearly defined human arrangement is the object of the performance. An ecological ritual with no results to show "below the line" soon ceases to be performed. At Kurumugl, the "above the line" transformations changed aggressive behavior into harmless, pleasure-giving performances. I am struck by the analogy to certain biological adaptations among animals.[16]

THE EFFICACY–ENTERTAINMENT BRAID

In the Papua New Guinea Highlands, first under the pressure of the colonial police, later under its own momentum, warfare has been transformed into dancing. As above-line activities grow in importance, entertainment as such takes over from efficacy as the reason for the performances. It might be that at first people assembled at Kurumugl to dance so that they might exchange pigs/social obligations. But later it became that they would exchange pigs etc., so that they might dance. It is not only that creditors and debtors need to exchange roles, but also that people want to show off, want to dance, want to have a good time. It is not only to get results that the dances are staged, but also because people like sing-sing for its own sake. Efficacy and entertainment are not so much opposed to each other; rather they form the poles of a continuum (figure 4.4). The basic polarity is between efficacy and entertainment, not between ritual and theater. Whether one calls a specific performance "ritual" or "theater" depends mostly on context and function. A performance is called theater or ritual because of where it is performed, by whom, and under what circumstances. If the performance's purpose is to effect transformations – to be efficacious – then the other qualities listed under the heading "efficacy" will most probably also be present, and the performance is a ritual. And vice versa regarding the qualities listed under "entertainment." No performance is pure efficacy or pure entertainment. The matter is complicated because one can look at specific performances from several vantages; changing perspectives changes classification. For example, a Broadway musical is entertainment if one concentrates on what happens onstage and in the house. But if one expands the point of view to include rehearsals, backstage life before, during, and after the show, the function of the roles in the lives of each performer, the money invested by the backers, the arrival of the audience, the reason spectators are attending, how they paid for their tickets (as individuals, on expense accounts, as members of a theater party, etc.), and how all this information indicates the use they're making of the performance (as entertainment, as a means to advance careers, as charity, etc.) – then

Figure 4.4

EFFICACY Ritual	⟷	ENTERTAINMENT Theater
results		fun
link to an absent Other		Only for those here
symbolic time		emphasis now
performer possessed, in trance		performer knows what s/he's doing
audience participates		audience watches
audience believes		audience appreciates
criticism discouraged		criticism flourishes
collective creativity		individual creativity

even the Broadway musical is more than entertainment, it's also ritual, economics, and a microcosm of social structure.

In the 1960s and 1970s artists emphasized and displayed rehearsal and backstage procedures. At first this was as simple as showing the lighting instruments and using a half-curtain, as Brecht did – or using no curtain at all. (Brecht got the idea from Asian theater where the half-curtain is an important and dynamic device.) But since around 1965 what has been shown to the spectators is the very process of developing and staging the performance – the workshops that lead up to the performance, the various means of theatrical production, the ways the audience is brought into and led from the space, and many other previously conventional and/or hidden procedures. These all became problematic, that is, manipulable, subjects of theatrical inquiry. These procedures have to do with the theater-in-itself and they are, as regards the theater, efficacious: that is, they are what makes theater into theater regardless of themes, plot, or the usual "elements of drama." Theater directors and choreographers discovered reflexivity even as they were discarding (temporarily) narrativity. The story of "how this performance is being made" replaced the story the performance more ordinarily would tell. This self-referencing, reflexive mode of performing is an example of what Gregory Bateson called "metacommunication" – signals whose "subject of discourse is the relationship between the speakers" (Bateson 1972: 178). As such theater's reflexive phase signaled loudly that the spectators were now to be included as "speakers" in the theatrical event. Thus it was natural that reflexivity in theater went hand in hand with audience participation.

Furthermore, all this attention paid to the procedures of making theater was, I think, an attempt to ritualize performance, to make theater yield efficacious acts. "This is who we really are and what we really do," and "We can do this together with you" were the key messages sent. In a period when authenticity was, and is, increasingly difficult to define, when public life is theatricalized, the performer was asked to take off her traditional masks – to be an agent not of "playing" or "fooling," or "lying" (kinds of public masquerade), but to "tell the truth" in some absolute sense. If not this, then at least to show how the masks are put on and taken off – perhaps in that way to educate the public to the theatricalized deceptions daily practiced on them by political leaders and media bosses. Instead of mirroring the age, performers were asked to remedy it. The professions taken as models for theater included medicine and the Church. But no wonder shamanism is so popular among theater people: shamanism is the branch of doctoring that is religious and the kind of religion, full of tricks, that is theatrical.[17]

In the 1960s and 1970s efficacy ascended to a dominant position over entertainment. Although the 1980s have seen an apparent return to the dominance of entertainment, a little thinking shows this not to be so. First, certain procedures advanced in the 1960s have become commonplace: performance events are routinely staged in many "untheaters," the preparation and "process" phases of performance are displayed, very personal stuff is integrated into or shown side by side with public/fictional materials, etc. Secondly, many performance artists as well as practitioners of "third" or "alternative" theater draw directly on shamanistic techniques while involving themselves in, or creating, community celebrations or other ritual/efficacious events.[18] Paratheatrical events dissolve the audience–performer opposition,[19] while a whole branch of performance art is aimed at eliminating the "art–life" distinction.[20] Finally, there has been a sea-shift in the perception of what is "theatrical" – so that political action, conflictual or aharmonic behavior on both the personal and the "social drama" levels, role playing in everyday life, emotional training using acting exercises to help professionals (police, airline personnel, etc.) to deal with crisis (see Hochschild 1983) are all evidence to the increasingly complicated interactions between, and continuing convergence of, theater and ritual.

Figure 4.5 shows how theater history can be given an overall shape as a development of a braided structure continuously interrelating efficacy (ritual) and entertainment (theater). At each period in every culture one or the other is dominant – one is ascending while the other is descending. Naturally, these changes are part of changes in the overall social structure of the culture. But performance is not a passive mirror of these social changes but a part of the complicated feedback process that creates change. Nor is there an evolutionary "progression" making today's theater better than yesterday's or tomorrow's better than today's. "Better" and "worse" are wholly conventional terms anyway.

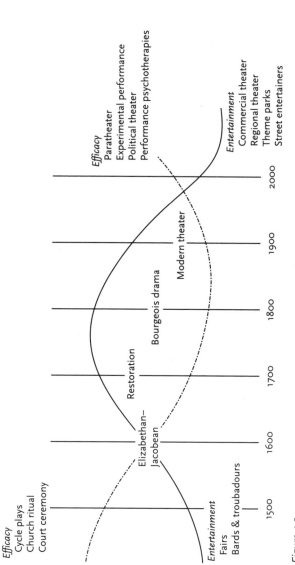

Efficacy
Cycle plays
Church ritual
Court ceremony

Efficacy
Paratheater
Experimental performance
Political theater
Performance psychotherapies

Elizabethan–
Jacobean

Restoration

Bourgeois drama

Modern theater

Entertainment
Fairs
Bards & troubadours

Entertainment
Commercial theater
Regional theater
Theme parks
Street entertainers

1500   1600   1700   1800   1900   2000

Figure 4.5

What the braided model depicts is a dynamic system yielding change, not necessary improvement or decay. At all times a dialectical tension exists between the efficacious and the entertainment tendencies. For western theater, at least, I think it can be shown that when the braid is tight – that is, when efficacy and entertainment are both present in nearly equal degrees – theater flourishes. During these relatively brief historical moments the theater answers needs that are both ritualistic and pleasure-giving. Fifth-century-BCE Athenian theater, Elizabethan theater, and possibly the theater from the late nineteenth century to our own times show the kind of convergence I'm talking about.

When efficacy dominates, performances are universalistic, allegorical, ritualized, tied to a stable established order; this kind of theater persists for a relatively long time. When entertainment dominates, performances are class-oriented, individualized, show business, constantly adjusting to the tastes of fickle audiences. The two most recent convergencies in western theater – the rise of entertainment before the Elizabethan period and the rise of efficacy during the modern period – are necessarily structural opposites of each other, though the kind of theater of each period may appear strikingly similar, reflecting the balance–tension between efficacy and entertainment.

Figure 4.5 is of course a simplification of the historical process of western theater. I present the figure as a help in conceptualizing the process. The late medieval period was dominated by efficacious performances: church services, court ceremonies, moralities, cycle plays, carnivals, fairs, pageants. As the Renaissance took hold in England these began to decline and popular entertainments, always present, became predominant in the form of the Elizabethen public theaters. The private and court theaters developed alongside the public theaters. The private theaters and masques were for the upper classes. Although some professionals worked in both public and private theaters, and some spectators attended both, these entertainments were fundamentally different from each other. The conflicts between the public and private theaters never worked themselves out because all theaters were closed in 1642 by the Puritans. When the theaters reopened after the Restoration of 1660 the Elizabethan public theater was gone. All the theaters resembled the private theaters and masques, the property of the upper classes. The behavior inside Restoration theaters combined the acting of plays with the play of rakes, libertines, and prostitutes. During the eighteenth and nineteenth centuries this aristocratic theater developed into the bourgeois theater still dominant today. Parallel developments took place on the Continent and in America. The dominant efficacious mode of medieval performance went underground to re-emerge in the guise of social and political drama during the last third of the nineteenth century.[21] This new naturalistic theater opposed the commercialism and pomposity of the boulevards and allied itself to scientific positivism. The resurgent efficacious spirit also spawned an avant-garde whose mission it was to reconstruct theatrical styles and techniques while puncturing the pretensions of the bourgeoisie. Members of the avant-garde were "bohemians" (outcastes from and enemies of the middle class) yet frequently enamored of science, identifying themselves with this new source of power, the rival to and replacement of the Church. Avant-garde artists freely used terms like "experimental" and "research" to characterize their work which took place in "laboratories." Efficacy is the ideological heart of these theaters – but what efficacy refers to changes over time. From the late-nineteenth to mid-twentieth centuries efficacy was positivistic and scientific, after that it becomes increasingly religious.

In twentieth-century America, the entertainment theater, threatened by extinction, broke into two parts: an increasingly outmoded commercial theater typified by Broadway and a subsidized community museum-type theater typified by the regional theaters. The 1974 First American Congress of Theater (and, as it turned out, the last) was an attempt by New York commercial producers to ally themselves with the regional theaters.[22] Although such an alliance is inevitable – many Broadway plays now originate at regional theaters – it's most likely ultimately that the regional theaters will absorb Broadway. Whether or not this comes about, the entertainment theaters remain fundamentally opposed by the avant-garde – which, by the last third of the twentieth century, had expanded to include direct political action, performance in everyday life (breaking down the art–life dichotomy), psychotherapy, and other manifestly efficacious kinds of performance. It is my opinion that efficacious performances are on the upswing. In the early 1970s I thought efficacious theater would dominate by 1990. That probably won't happen, but certainly a whole range of art–life, personal testimony, and ritual performances have emerged and are multiplying.

THEATER FOR TOURISTS

Up to here I've said: 1) in some social settings ritual performances are part of ecosystems and mediate political relations, group hierarchy, and economics; 2) in other settings ritual performances begin to take on qualities of show business; 3) there is a dialectical-dyadic continuum linking efficacy to entertainment – both are present in all performances, but in each performance one or the other is dominant; 4) in different cultures, at different times, either efficacy or entertainment dominates, the two being in a dynamic braided relationship to each other.

O. B. Hardison quotes Honorius of Autun's twelfth-century view of the Mass as evidence that people at the time saw this ceremony as drama:

> It is known that those who recited tragedies in theaters presented the actions of opponents by gestures before the people. In the same way our tragic author [i.e., the celebrant] represents by his gestures in the theater of the Church before the Christian people the struggle of Christ and teaches to them the victory of his redemption. [Honorius then compares each movement of the Mass to an equivalent movement of tragic drama.] When the sacrifice has been completed, peace and Communion are given by the celebrant to the people. . . . Then by the *Ite, missa est*, they are ordered to return to their homes with rejoicing. They shout *Deo gratias* and return home rejoicing.
>
> (Honorius of Autun, in Hardison 1965: 39–40)

What's extraordinary about Honorius' description is that it is a medieval view, not a backward glance by a modern. Honorius' Mass is more familiar to those who have attended avant-garde performances than to those whose experience is limited to orthodox mainstream theater. The medieval Mass employed many avant-garde techniques. It was allegorical, it encouraged – no, forced – audience participation, it treated time teleologically, it integrated dance, music, and drama, it extended the spatial field of the performance from the church to the roadways to the homes of the participants. Yet for all this I still would call the Mass a ritual rather than theater. Why? Because it was efficacious. As Hardison says, "The service . . . has a very important aesthetic dimension, but it is essentially not a matter of appreciation but of passionate affirmation" (Hardison 1965: 77). The Mass was a closed circle which included only the congregation and those officiating. There was literally and figuratively no room for appreciators. The Mass was an obligatory action, entered into either joyfully or sullenly, by means of which members of the congregation signaled to each other and to the hierarchy their continued participation in the Holy Roman Church. What I say of the medieval Mass, Rappaport, drawing on Durkheim, says of the Tsembaga:

> While the scope of the social unity is frequently not made explicit, it would seem that in some studies it is what Durkheim called a "church," that is, "a society whose members are united by the fact that they think in the same way in regard to the sacred world and its relations with the profane world, and by the fact that they translate these common ideas into common practices." . . . Such units, composed of aggregates of individuals who regard their collective well-being to be dependent upon a common body of ritual performances, might be called "congregations".
>
> (Rappaport 1968: 1)

Because of its all-inclusive hold on its congregation and its guarantee of efficacy, the Mass was not theater in the classical or modern sense. It used theater but did not become theater. Theater comes into existence when a separation occurs between spectators and performance. The paradigmatic theatrical situation is a group of performers soliciting an audience who may or may not respond by attending. The audience is free to come or stay away – and if they stay away it is the theater that suffers, not its would-be audience. In ritual, staying away means rejecting the congregation, or being rejected by it, as in schism, excommunication, or exile. If only a few stay away, it is they who suffer; if many stay away, the congregation is in danger of schism or dissolution. To put it another way: ritual is an event upon which its participants depend; theater is an event which depends on its participants. In no case is it cut and dried. But the evidence of the transformational steps by which theater emerges from ritual – by which an efficacious event upon which the participants depend is transformed into an entertainment where the entertainers depend on their audience – is not locked in ancient or medieval documents. Transformations of rituals into theater occur today. And so does the opposite: the transformation of theater into ritual.

Makehuku is a village about 70 miles east of Kurumugl in the Asaro River valley of Papua New Guinea. There the famous dance of the "mudmen" is performed as a tourist entertainment three times a week. It was not always so. The villagers originally performed only when they felt threatened by attack. Before dawn village men went to a local creek, rubbed their bodies with white mud (the color of death), and constructed grotesque masks of wood frames covered by mud and vegetation. Emerging from the creek at dawn, possessed by the spirits of the dead, the dancers moved in an eery, slow, crouching step. Sometimes they went to the village of their enemies and frightened them, thus preventing attack. Sometimes they danced in their own village. The dances took less than ten minutes, but preparations took most of the previous night. (This ratio of preparation to performance is not unusual; it is so even in modern western theater in the rehearsal-to-performance ratio.) The dance of the mudmen was performed occasionally, when needed.[23]

After pacification by Australian colonial authorities, the villagers of Makehuku had less need for the mudmen's traditional functions. However, in the mid-1960s a photographer from the *National Geographic* paid the villagers to stage their dance for him. These photos became world famous. It was not long before tourists demanded to see the performance of the mudmen. (Even the name "mudmen" is an invention for tourists. I don't know the original name of these dancers.) Because Makehuku is near the Mount Hagan-Goroka road – the Highlands' major highway – it was easy to arrange for minibuses to bring spectators to the village. Tourists pay up to $20 each to see the short dances. Of this sum the Makehuku villagers get 10 per cent. Because the ten-minute dance is not a long enough show by western standards, the dancing has been augmented by a display of bow-and-arrow

Plate 4.1 The mudmen of Asaro. (Photograph by Joan MacIntosh)

marksmanship, a photo session, and a "market" (see plate 4.1). But Makehuku is not (yet) a craft village, and the few necklaces and string bags I saw for sale were pathetic. The day I was there no one bought anything.

These days the people of Makehuku don't know what their dance is. It doesn't frighten enemies, or anyone else. On the contrary, the mudmen attract tourists who attend in order to be amused. The dance has no relationship to the spirits of the dead who appear only before dawn while the mudmen now dance when the tourists arrive a little after midday. The social-ritual fabric of Makehuku has been torn to shreds, and the changes wrought in the mudmen's dance are part of deeper disruptions in Highlands life. Because of these disruptions, and despite the exploitation of the village by the tourist agencies who take 90 per cent of the income for themselves, the meagre sums paid the villagers are needed desperately during a period when the barter economy has fallen apart and money jobs are not available. I expect future changes in the dance will make it longer, more visually complicated, possibly adding musical accompaniment. The craft skills of the villagers will improve, or they will import goods to sell. Their percentage of the take will rise. In short, the dance will approach western standards of entertainment, represented by the tastes of the audience. Monetary benefits will rise accordingly. Presently, the Makehukans perform a traditional ritual emptied of its efficacy but not yet wholly regarded as a theatrical entertainment.

One day in March, 1972, Joan MacIntosh and I arrived in Makehuku before the tourists and stayed after they left. The villagers looked at us curiously. We were taking pictures of the tourists as well as of the dancers. After the other outsiders left, a man came up to us and in pidgin asked us to come with him. We walked 4 miles along a ridge until we got to Kenetisarobe. There we met Asuwe Yamuruhu, the headman. He wanted us to go to Goroka and tell the tourists about his dancers. He wanted tourists to come to his village and watch a show which, he assured us, was much better than what the mudmen did. It began to rain very hard as we squatted in the entrance to a round hut. Around us in the rain a few villagers watched. We agreed on a price – $4 a person – and a time, the next afternoon. Not only would we see dances but we could tape-record songs too.

The next afternoon we arrived with two friends, paid our $16, and saw a dance consisting of very slow steps, as if the dancers were moving through deep mud, their fingers splayed, and their faces masked or tied into grotesque shapes. Peter Thoady, headmaster of the Goroka Teachers' College, told us that the distortion of the faces probably was an imitation of yaws, a disfiguring disease common in the area. The dancers moved in a half-crouch and occasionally shouted phrases and expletives. The dancing of the grassmen of Kenetisarobe was very like that of the mudmen of Makehuku. After the dancing we spent about an hour recording music, talking, and smoking.

The Kenetisarobe dance was adapted from ceremonial farces of the region. Asuwe Yamaruhu staged them for us. He knew that Makehuku was making money from its dance, and the Kenetisarobe show was modeled on the Makehuku formula: a slow dance, grotesque masks (to western eyes), plenty of photo opportunities, and a follow-up after the dance. What the people of Makehuku did with a minimum of

Plate 4.2 Dancers at the village of Kenetisarobe. (Photograph by Richard
    Schechner)

self-awareness or reflexivity, Asuwe Yamuruhu did with a keen sense of
theater business.

Examples of the same kind of thing abound. In Bali tourist versions
of *barong* and ketchak are everywhere. Along the Denpasar-to-Ubud
road signs advertising these performances are as frequent as movie
marquees in America. Signs, often in English, say such things as:
"Traditional Ketchak – Holy Monkey Dance Theater – Tonight at 8,"
or "Barong – Each Wednesday at 8 on the Temple Steps." The Balinese, with characteristic sophistication, make separate shows for
tourists while keeping "for Balinese only" shows more or less secret
– or, more importantly, far from the main road. Tourists want to
drive to their entertainments; they want a dependable schedule; they
want a way to leave early conveniently if they are bored. Most
authentic performances – of ketchak or of "for Balinese only" – are
accessible by foot through somewhat thick jungle. Often foreigners

can attend only with the permission of the village giving the performance.

During two weeks in Bali in 1972 I saw two such performances. MacIntosh and I stumbled on a ketchak while walking through the monkey forest near Ubud – we followed some women carrying offerings of food. Once in Tigal we stayed there for ten hours before the ketchak began a little after 9 p.m. Years later, around 1980, I discovered that the ketchak which I thought was traditional, that is, very old and part of the Balinese ceremonial cycle, was a rather recent addition to the island's repertory. According to Bandem and de Boer:

> This composite genre was first created by dancers in Bedulu village, Gianyar Province, who were commissioned by Walter Spies [in the 1920s or 30s?]. The group was requested to devise a new kind of Ramayana performance, accompanied solely by the Cak chorus found in Sang Hyang Dedari [a form of trance dancing]. Today fourteen professional groups perform [ketchak] regularly.
>
> (Bandem and de Boer 1981: 146)

Of course it remains to be seen when, or if, even an invented genre is organically grafted onto an indigenous tradition. Were my field notes wrong – or did the Balinese by 1972 already have two kinds of ketchak, one for tourists, one for themselves?

At Tenganan, a "Bali aga" village – a place where descendants of the presumed original inhabitants of the island live – we saw, and to some degree participated in, what all authorities agree is an old, traditional ritual dance, the annual *abuang Kalah*. Some of the ceremony was public and about fifty tourists joined the villagers to enjoy the afternoon dancing. These people were asked to leave by 5 p.m. We were quietly told to remain in the town office. Then, after dark, we were taken to different compounds in the village for different aspects of the ceremony. We were also allowed to listen to special gamelan music played before dawn. We weren't allowed to photograph and only a limited amount of tape-recording was permitted. The daytime ceremonies definitely had the feel of an entertainment – outsiders came in, shops were open and doing a brisk business, the dances were carefully choreographed to the gamelan music. At night the scene was different. Each aspect of the ceremony was privatized and done not with an eye to its prettiness but to its correctness. Time gaps between elements were longer and more irregular; many long discussions centered on how to do certain things – these conferences delayed the ceremonies. The subject matter of the Abuang – if I can use that phrase – is the presentation of all the unmarried females to all the unmarried males. The daytime dances showed everyone off; the night-time ceremonies concerned actual betrothal.

Surely the tourist trade has influenced so-called "authentic" performances in Bali and elsewhere. I don't have contempt for these changes. Changes in conventions, themes, methods, and styles occur because of opportunism, audience pressures, professionalism (itself often a new concept), new technology, and other fallout from culture contact. Tourism has been really important and worldwide only since the advent of cheap air travel. Before that for centuries mass migrations have taken place due to economic circumstances, war, and colonialism. And from the start of the human species people have been on the move. But tourism on a mass scale is unique because the people moving are seeking pleasure, including entertainment; and their travels are temporary excursions. This means that the entertainments set up for tourists often amalgamate the qualities of "away" with those of "home." The job of the tour manager is to make the strange familiar, a kind of reverse *Verfremdung*. Theater historians will regard tourism as of as much importance as the exchange between England and the Continent was in the sixteenth and seventeenth centuries. Theater people imitate popular imported modes, and the local respond to the demands of rich visitors – or local audiences demanded changes because they've adopted the tastes of alien cultures. From one point of view these changes are corruptions – a clamor is raised to establish culture zoos in which the "original" versions of "age-old" rituals can be preserved. But even traditional performances vary greatly from generation to generation – an oral tradition is flexible, able to absorb many personal variations within set parameters. And the culture-zoo approach is itself a variant of colonial aesthetics. I hate the genocide that has eradicated cultures such as the Tasmanian, but I see nothing wrong with what's happening today in Bali and New Guinea, where two systems of theater coexist. The relationship between these is not a simple division between the tourist and the "authentic." More studies are needed on the exchanges between what's left of traditional performances and the emerging tourist shows. And at what moment does a tourist show become an authentic theatrical art?

Tourism is a two-way street. Travelers bring back experiences, expectations, and, if the tourists are practitioners, techniques, scenes, and even entire forms. The birth ritual of *Dionysus in 69* was adapted by me from photographs I saw in a book about the Asmat of West Irian. Several sequences in the Living Theater's *Mysteries and Smaller Pieces* and *Paradise Now* were taken from yoga and Indian theater. Mabou Mines used *bunraku* in the *Shaggy Dog Animation*. Philip Glass's music draws both on gamelan and Indian raga. Imamu Baraka's writing is deeply influenced by African modes of story-telling and drama. A whole movement in American theater and dance influenced by Asian forms is called "fusion." The list of cross-referencing among the arts of various cultures could be extended without limit. Many innovators since World War II (a great war for travel) have been decisively influenced by work from cultures other than their own. This means, for western artists, Asia, Africa, and Oceania. The impact of communal-collective forms on contemporary western theater is like the impact of classical forms on the Renaissance. The differences, however, are also important. In the Renaissance all that remained of classical culture were architectural ruins, old texts, and relics of the plastic arts. This material was frequently fragmented and corrupt. Also, Renaissance scholars looked with respect, even awe, at what they found of classical Greece and Rome. Today's intercultural feed is mainly in the area of performances; the shows imported have been seen more or less intact; the originators of the performances are often former colonial peoples, or peoples who were considered inferior by populations living around the north Atlantic basin. In other words, it is logical that today's influences should be felt first in the avant-garde. Furthermore, there's lots of traffic running back to the Third World. Western performing arts are practiced everywhere, and, frequently enough, persons who want to preserve indigenous traditions have traveled to or been educated in the west.

A very clear and provable Asian influence on contemporary western theater is seen in Grotowski's work. In 1956, three years prior to the establishment of his Theatre Laboratory, Grotowski made a two-month trip to central Asia and China. According to Jennifer Kumiega (1985: 6), "between December 1957 and June 1958 Grotowski organized and led a series of regular, weekly talks on Oriental philosophy in the Student Club in Cracow. The subjects covered included Buddhism, Yoga, the Upanishads, Confucius, Taoism, and Zen-Buddhism." Soon after, during his poor theater phase (1959–68), Grotowski began to create with the Laboratory such notable productions as *Dr Faustus, Kordian, Akropolis, The Constant Prince*, and various editions of *Apocalypsis cum Figuris*. These works were based on the psychophysical exercises Grotowski and actor Ryszard Cieslak taught in many of their workshops, including one I attended at New York University in 1967. The exercises were influenced not only by yoga, which Grotowski acknowledges, but by kathakali, the south Indian dance–theater form.

In 1972, while visiting the Kathakali Kalamandalam in Kerala, the principal kathakali school, I asked if Grotowski had visited. No one remembered him, but Eugenio Barba was recalled, and in the Kalamandalam's visitors' book I found the following entry:

The Secretary   29 September 1963
Kalamandalam
Cheruthuruthy

Dear Sir:

I had not the occasion, last night at the performance, to thank you for all the kind help you have given me during my stay here. To you, and to the Superintendent, and to all the boys who were so willing to be of service, I would like to express my gratutide and sincerest thanks.

My visit to Kalamandalam has greatly helped me in my studies and the research material I have collected will surely be of the greatest assistance to those people working at the Theatre Laboratory in Poland. Many thanks again,

Yours sincerely,

Eugenio Barba [signed]

Barba brought kathakali exercises to Grotowski in Poland where they formed the core of the "plastique" and psychophysical exercises. When

Barba founded his Odin Teatret in 1965, he used these same exercises – as codified by the Polish Lab and Barba's own work. Barba's intense research project of the 1980s – the International School of Theatre Anthropology (ISTA) – focuses on techniques of Asian performing (see Barba 1986).

Western directors looked not only to Asia but to Africa, the Caribbean, and native America as well. In 1972–3 Peter Brook led a group of thirty theater artists on a three-month trip through Algeria, Mali, Niger, Dahomey, and Nigeria. Their experience is much like what Barba calls "barter" – where performers from different cultures exchange techniques, songs, stories, whatever. In Brook's words:

> Once we sat in Agades in a small hut all afternoon, singing. We and the African group sang, and suddenly we found that we were hitting exactly the same language of sound. Well, we understood theirs and they understood ours, and something quite electrifying happened because, out of all sorts of different songs, one suddenly came upon this common area.
>
> Another experience of that same sort occurred one night when we were camping in a forest. We thought there was no one around for miles, but as always, suddenly, children appeared from nowhere and beckoned. We were just sitting and doing some improvised song, and the children asked us to come down to their village, only a couple of miles away, because there was going to be some singing and dancing later in the night and everyone would be very pleased if we could come.
>
> So we said "sure." We walked down through the forest, found this village, and found that, indeed, there was a ceremony going on. Somebody had just died and it was a funeral ceremony. We were made very welcome and we sat there, in total darkness under the trees, just seeing these moving shadows dancing and singing. And after a couple of hours they suddenly said to us: the boys say that this is what you do, too. Now you must sing for us.
>
> So we had to improvise a song for them. And this was perhaps one of the best works of the entire journey. Because the song that was produced for the occasion was extraordinarily moving, right, and satisfying, and made a real coming together of the people and ourselves. It is

impossible to say what produced it, because it was produced as much by the group that was working together in a certain way, with all the work that has gone into that, and as much by all the conditions of the moment that bore their influence: the place, the night, the feeling for the other people, so that we were actually making something for them in exchange for what they had offered us.

(Brook 1973: 45–6)[24]

Throughout Asia I found this same "exchange policy" in force. MacIntosh and I were invited to stay at Tenganan in Bali because the people there knew we performed, and at the main public performance the chief insisted that I do a dance(!).[25] At Karamui in Papua New Guinea – far from any road (we flew there) – we were shown funeral ceremonies. A villager, amidst much laughter, played the role of the corpse. We were expected to sing songs in exchange. In the Sepik River village of Kamanabit the headman insisted that MacIntosh be awakened and brought to his house to sing even though she was exhausted from a day's travel. Her request concert came after I'd been listening to and recording village women singing.

But things don't always turn up roses, especially when the story is told by the "others." Brook and members of his troupe arrived in India in 1983 to conduct research for their upcoming production of the *Mahabharata*. Probir Guha, director of the Living Theatre of West Bengal, said this about Brook's visit:

He saw all the Chhau [masked dance–theater] performances I arranged, made many notes, tried to ask many questions about the performances, and we answered. Later he came a second time with three of his artists to see Chhau. We conducted a three-day workshop with his people and Chhau artists. The first night I organized a show for him of Chhau dances of the *Mahabharata*. . . . He wanted his actors to learn some of the steps. . . . Then he told me, "I'd like to take one Purulia Chhau dancer from here for my *Mahabharata*. . . . He will be with me for at least two years. . . . He will receive money and I will look after him." – So he went back to Paris.

Later several of Brook's company members came and worked with me, and then went back. After a long period, I had no contact with them. I was still expecting to go to Paris, and so had told everyone that I was going to assist Brook in the *Mahabharata*.

The young Chhau dancer, Dohonda, was also expecting to go . . .

Then suddenly, Brook wrote me to come to Paris. I didn't know what to do about the boy because he was not mentioned. . . . As the time got near [to go] I wondered what to do. So I wrote personally to Peter about the situation and asked him to inform me what to do about the boy. He wrote back personally and said everything had completely changed. He had previously thought the production would be very much a physical thing. . . . But now it had become a hard speaking French text, and so they would not need us.

(Zarrilli 1986: 93–5)

Brook unintentionally created problems for Guha and Dohonda. Among the villagers where they worked, great excitement turned sour. The Bengalis did not understand that production plans change – that change is the essence of the western experimental theater. As Guha commented, "It's not a personal thing with Peter Brook and I don't take it personally. But people have to consider how to accept the culture into which they are coming" (Zarrilli 1986: 95). Guha's bitterness, in fact, is palpable:

If Brook brings this *Mahabharata* to India and goes to the villages where he worked and shows people what he has done with their materials, then he is really being honest. And if he doesn't do it, then I would call it cultural piracy. We don't want to be exploited culturally, we don't want to be guinea pigs for experiments.

(Zarrilli 1986: 98)

Barba served his apprenticeship with Grotowski and then went on in 1964 to found what has become the Odin Teatret/Teaterlaboratorium of Holstebro, Denmark. Among the several important operations of Barba's lab are the journeys called "barter" which members of the Odin have made in Europe, Africa, and Latin America. Barba defines barter thus:

Imagine two very different tribes, each on their own side of the river.

Each tribe can live for itself, talk about the other, praise or slander it. But every time one of them rows over to the other shore it is to exchange something. One does not row over to teach, to enlighten, to entertain, but rather to give and take: a handful of salt for a scrap of cloth, a bow for a fistful of beads. The goods we barter are cultural. . . .

In May 1976 Odin Teatret accepted a proposition from the Kurare Film Cooperative (Caracas): a barter with the Yanomami, a meeting between origins (rituals and dances) and historical development (theater). In the middle of the *shabono* – the great house – the dances presented by the Yanomami and the tales of their shaman alternate with the Odin's *Book of Dances* and *Come! And the day will be ours*, the talk of how the white men destroyed the shaman. This barter took place in the Kahori *shabono*, where the anthropologist Jacques Lizot had been living for six years. They introduced Odin Teatret to the Yanomami, showing them a new face of the *nape*, the white stranger.

(Barba 1986: 161, 166)

Barba's method of barter systematizes what Brook did in Africa. What is disingenuous about barter is that thus far at least the traffic is all one-way. Residents of the First World travel to the Third World for the purpose of barter. One wonders how well-received in New York, Paris, or even Holstebro a Yanomami shaman in search of Odin-style barter would be. That is, if the shaman arrived paying his own way, setting his own agenda and calendar. The whole system of intercultural exchange cannot escape history: it occurs in the aftermath of colonialism.

The analysis of that aftermath is the subject of another essay. For now let it be noted that the kind of influencing through observation and trading reflected in Barba's letter and his later experiments with barter, Brook's trips, and my experiences is different from Artaud's reactions in the 1930s to Balinese theater. Artaud was influenced, but the Balinese didn't care. There was no exchange. In the more recent examples work is being consciously traded as professionals seek to expand their knowledge.

Whatever the ritual functions of kathakali in village life, the training Barba saw at the Kalamandalam was to a certain degree professional in the western sense (see Schechner 1985: 213–60 and Zarrilli 1984). The Kalamandalam troupe performs for pay in India and overseas.

Foreigners come to study at the Kalamandalam – there is even a teacher who specializes in teaching these visitors. While I was there in 1976 about five westerners were studying. This training has not led to the establishment of kathakali troupes outside India (though that may yet happen) but rather the work is integrated into existing styles. It remains to be seen how the presence of outsiders at the Kalamandalam, and the frequent tours of the troupe, affect the work in Kerala.

The situation with Brook in Africa is different. The villagers were in the midst of a religious ritual, a funeral, but they were also apparently eager to trade songs and share their entertainments. That the exchange was mutually moving is no surprise, ritual and entertainment coexist easily; Barba's barter work shows how willing people are to exchange. Brook's expeditions to India preparatory to his *Mahabharata* resulted in a more ambivalent aftermath.

Touring ritual performances around the world – and thereby converting them into entertainments – is nothing new. The Romans were fond of importing exotics; and the records of many courts – non-western as well as western – show the same imperial curiosity. Colonial and/or conquering powers everywhere have done the same. Modern times – from the period of the great international expositions and circuses to our own day – transform this artiscratic privilege into a commercial venture. The enterprise is often cloaked in the rhetoric of respect. In 1972 at the Brooklyn Academy of Music the following show took place (I quote from the program):

THE BROOKLYN ACADEMY OF MUSIC

in association with
Mel Howard Productions, Inc.
And
Ninon Tallon-Karlweis
in cooperation with
The Turkish Ministry of Tourism and Information
Present

THE WHIRLING DERVISHES OF TURKEY

(THE PROGRAM IS A RELIGIOUS CEREMONY.
YOU ARE KINDLY REQUESTED TO REFRAIN FROM APPLAUSE.)

The BAM audience had to be told that what they paid money to see as an entertainment retained enough of its ritual basis to require a change in conventional theatrical behaviour. Or was BAM's announcement a P. T. Barnum ploy? Telling the audience why they were not to applaud was signaling the importance and rarity of what they were about to see. The fact that "dervishes" is an imposed but recognizable name, not what the dancers call themselves, provides part of the answer. The performance itself was simple and moving – I suppose a fairly accurate presentation of the Sufi Mevlevi ritual. I know that several groups in New York were influenced by it. At the Byrd Hoffman space run by Robert Wilson and in The Performance Group which I led people experimented with whirling. Laura Dean developed many dances based on whirling.

In October, 1973 Shingon Buddhist monks came to BAM with "ceremonies, music, and epics of ancient Japan." The dervishes whirled on a stage facing the 2,000-seat opera house. The monks performed in the Lepercq Space, an open room about 75 feet by 40 feet with a height of about 30 feet. The night I was there the audience numbered around 200, seated on cushions scattered on the floor and on bleachers. As at Makehuku and Kenetisarobe the Buddhist rituals were not long enough to constitute an entertainment by western standards. So the program was augmented by performances of Japanese contemporary music and a recitation of Japanese war tales from the twelfth to the fourteenth centuries. Only after the intermission did the monks perform their temple service. The program distributed to the spectators described in detail what the monks were doing, what it meant, and how the ceremony is used in Japan. Thus the audience was treated as if it were attending Grand Opera where the libretto is summarized – or maybe a new sport where the rules, equipment, and structure need to be explained. It seemed to me that the monks, like the dervishes, were deeply into what they were doing. They were "in character" – and it was impossible to distinguish what they were doing from what Stanislavsky required of actors. I was convinced: these dervishes were Dervishes, these monks were Monks. A defined interface between spectators and performers existed: on one side was authenticity, efficacy, and ritual, on the other side was entertainment and theater.

Any ritual can be lifted from its original setting and performed as theater – just as any everyday life event can be.[26] This is possible because context and function, and fundamental structure or process, distinguish ritual, entertainment, and ordinary life from each other. The differences among them arise from the agreement (conscious or unexpressed) between performers and spectators. Entertainment/theater emerges from ritual out of a complex consisting of an audience separate from the performers, the development of professional performers and economic needs imposing a situation in which performances are made to please the audience rather than according to a fixed code or dogma. It is also possible for a ritual to arise out of theater by reversing the process just described. This move from theater to ritual marks Grotowski's work and that of the Living Theater. But the rituals created were unstable because they were not attached to, or integrated into, ongoing social structures outside theater. Also, the differences among ritual, theater, and ordinary life depend on the degree spectators and performers attend to efficacy, pleasure, or routine; and how symbolic meaning and effect are infused and attached to performed events. In all entertainment there is some efficacy and in all ritual there is some theater.[27]

FROM THEATER TO RITUAL

When in 1973 The Performance Group was working on Brecht's *Mother Courage* most of our rehearsals were open. When the weather permitted the big overhead front door of the Performing Garage was raised so that people off the street, students, and friends could drop in to watch us work. Every rehearsal had from 5 to 40 people attending. The rehearsals had a feeling of stop and go, with nothing special planned to accommodate the spectators. Yet their presence made a deep difference: work on the play began to include a public social core; and the work became about showing a way of working. This theme was knitted into the after-opening performances of *Courage*. The space designed by Jery Rojo and Jim Clayburgh, collaborating with other members of the Group, expressed the interplay between Brecht's drama and the larger performance in which this drama takes place. Part of the theater was made into a "green room" wholly visible to the audience. When a performer was not in a scene she or he went to the green room for some coffee, to read, and to relax. A little more shielded, but still in sight, were places for performers to change costumes and apply makeup (most performers played two or more roles). The theater was divided into three main spaces: a central empty cube 30 feet by 20 feet by 15 feet (including an open pit 20 feet by 8 feet by 7 feet); a frame filled with irregular scaffolding, platforms, and ropes surrounding the central cube – this frame was anchored at one end by a structure made of aluminium scaffolding that served as Courage's home base, as close to a "wagon" as this production had; and around the frame galleries and walkways. A 14-foot-long bridge rising about 9 feet off the ground jutted into the central empty cube. I intended spectators to move freely through the entire space continually changing perspective and mood. It was possible to see everything from a single vantage, but only if one looked through other structures. But as the 10 to 20 in attendance at rehearsals became the 150 to 200 buying customers of the run, people settled into fixed positions.

There were a few scenes where spectators had to shift perspective. Scenes 9 and 10 – where Courage, Kattrin, and the Cook beg food and sing for their supper – were played outside the theater in Wooster Street. The Garage door was open forming a small proscenium arch through which the spectators inside the Garage looked. To see at all most people had to come down from the galleries and sit on the Garage floor or stand around the edges. The door stayed open for the rest of the show. In the winter, when the temperature plunged, spectators reached for their coats. After scene 10 people didn't return to their former places but watched the last half-hour from where they were. Certain aspects of the cruel experience of Courage and her family were convincingly shared with the chilly audience.

The TPG production had one intermission, after scene 3. During scene 3 Courage, Kattrin, and the Chaplain are preparing food to be sold to the soldiers. This preparation actually went on during the production. The scene ends when Courage pretends she does not recognize the corpse of her son Swiss Cheese. Immediately a meal is offered for sale to the spectators. The drama is mixed with the actual life going on in the theater. Spectators eat and mix with each other and with the performers some of whom are serving, some simply socializing.

Toward the end of supper the "Song of the Great Capitulation" is sung cabaret-style by Courage. This is all TPG played of scene 4, and there was no insistence that everyone in the theater pay close attention. When the drama resumed with scene 5 after supper I think it was experienced differently by both spectators and performers because of the hour of mingling, talking, and sharing of food and drink.[28]

By having open rehearsals, by opening the Garage door, by serving supper as part of the performance, Mother Courage was treated as a drama nested in a larger performance event. The ideas behind TPG's production of Courage are common in ritual performances: to control, arrange, or manipulate the whole world of the performance, not just present the drama at its center. In this way a theatrical event in SoHo, New York City, was nudged a little way from the entertainment end of the continuum toward efficacy. Without diminishing its theatricality, The Performance Group worked to enhance Courage's ritual aspects.

Orthodox theories say that ritual precedes theater, just as efficacy and monism ("primitive oneness") precede entertainment. It is a cliché of interpretations of Paleolithic cave art that some kind of "ritual" generated the art – and by ritual is meant a serious, efficacious, result-oriented performance whether to insure fertility, to placate the powers who control the hunt, to maintain a balance between male and female, to initiate, or something. These things, or some of them, may be true; but they are not the whole truth. Entertainment, the passing of time in play and fun (not the passive and cut-off feeling of "art for art's sake," but an active involvement with the process of making art), is interwoven with and inseparable from any efficacious aspects of the earliest art.

The idea of primitive oneness combines Edenic fantasy with the Protestant work ethic. This combination was supported by the projections of early ethnographers too many of whom were missionaries. Accumulating evidence from Paleolithic, early historical, classical, Asian, African and contemporary communal peoples suggests that a complex social life and rich, symbolic art are coexistent with the human condition. There is no "simple primitive," either noble or savage. Shamans are artists and performers and doctors and trance-possessed ecstatics and priests and entertainers. To argue that because several roles are played simultaneously by one person or that because a single performance expresses many contradictory impulses means that the art of such people (and their cultures) is "simple" is to look at things upside down.

Industrial cultures separate and standardize functions and expressions; communal societies combine many functions and expressions in extended, complicated events. Industrial cultures specialize in sequencing univocal actions while communal cultures generalize by means of events that are multivocal. The industrial line itself is a strong example of a sequence of single-function actions that add up to a final complicated product. An extended ritual such as the Arunta engwura cycle is an example of a multivocal event. Urban life is more like the production line than the engwura cycle. In a city people move from one more or less "pure" event to another, eating here, doing business there, coming home to the family at still another time and place. Only over time and by means of a synthesis managed by each individual (and many people can't manage it) does a sense of overall unity emerge. I personally enjoy urban pluralism and freedom of choice, but it can go too far, leading to extreme fragmentation, cutting people off, even cutting them up. Communal life, on the other hand, includes in each event – even a ceremony as short as a ten-minute Arunta dance – a bundle of meanings–functions–expressions. These are explicit: each initiated participant knows the connections. The leader of the dance is also the leader of his band, is also a skilled hunter, is also related to the boys being initiated, etc. And, as I've shown, the dance is nested in a complex of ceremonies where each part is a synecdoche.

Much of the post-World-War-II avant-garde has been an attempt to overcome fragmentation by approaching performances as part of rather than apart from the community. Sometimes this community is of artists making similar works. This has been the pattern in New York, London, Paris, Tokyo, and other cities where artists form a distinct group. Sometimes, as in the general uprisings of 1968, art is joined to larger political movements. Sometimes, as in black, Chicano, women's, and gay-movement theaters, artists identify with – and even help form – ethnic, racial, gender, sexual, or political unity. The community-related avant-garde is not only a phenomenon of the industrialized west and Japan, but also of countries that are undergoing great changes in social organization by means of modernization. In Eastern Europe,

Latin America, Asia, and Africa pockets of avant-garde work like that in the First World can be identified. Names and groups like the Gardzien-ice Theater Association, Augusto Boal's Theater of the Oppressed, Indonesia's Rendra, Badal Sircar and Habib Tanvir in India, and Wole Soyinka of Nigeria can be added to a growing list.

This work is not atavistic, not a wild attempt to dismantle industrial-ism, or halt its spread. It is an active seeking to find places within industrial societies – even within the industrial process itself – for small-scale communities to exist. And to demand a restructuring of the social order to meet the needs of communities for person-to-person interactions or "meetings," as Grotowski says. The problems of ali-enation, reification, and anomie are clearly not problems of capitalism alone. Experiments of the kind I've been talking about are taking place in socialist states too. These experiments, still relatively scattered and tentative, and always being pressed back by a hostile establishment, are showing signs of taking root. They address themselves to the audience not as sticks of money-paying individual strangers, or as forced parti-cipants in a show of solidarity (as in mass rallies, parades, or coercive church-going), but as a community, even a congregation. The goal of such performances is to entertain, to have fun, and to create what Victor Turner calls "spontaneous communitas," the dissolution of boundaries shutting people off from each other. The resulting experience is of collective celebration. This contemporary tendency originated in the experimental theater as a movement toward ritual.

Performance doesn't originate in ritual any more than it originates in entertainment. It originates in the binary system efficacy–enter-tainment which includes the sub-set ritual–theater. From the begin-ning, logically as well as historically, both terms of the binary are required. At any historical moment there is movement from one pole toward the other as the efficacy–entertainment braid tightens and loosens. This oscillation is continuous – performance is always in an active state.

The whole binary continuum efficacy/ritual–entertainment/theater is what I call "performance." Performance originates in impulses to make things happen and to entertain; to get results and to fool around; to collect meanings and to pass the time; to be transformed into another and to celebrate being oneself; to disappear and to show off; to bring into a special place a transcendent Other who exists then-and-now and later-and-now; to be in a trance and to be conscious; to focus on a select group sharing a secret language and to broadcast to the largest possible audience of strangers; to play in order to satisfy a felt obligation and to play only under an Equity contract for cash. These oppositions, and others generated by them, comprise performance: an active situation, a continuous turbulent process of transformation. The move from ritual to theater happens when a participating audience fragments into a collection of people who attend because the show is advertised, who pay admission, who evaluate what they are going to see before, during, and after seeing it. The move from theater to ritual happens when the audience is transformed from a collection of separate individuals into a group or congregation of participants.

These polar tendencies are present in all performances. Brecht, and Meyerhold before him, worked to keep alive the tensions between these extremes. They wanted to move audiences back and forth moment to moment. The way Brecht's *Verfremdung* works is to unexpectedly shift mode, style, rhythm, perspective so that at the moment and place of change, when an emotional scene is abruptly halted, or a "cold" scene suddenly becomes moving, the dramatist, director, or performer (whoever is "authoring" the moment) can insert her or his own "statement," an ironic or telling comment that encourages the spectator to think about what's been seen and/or felt. The performance structure is broken open by its anti-structure and in that liminal space a direct communication, a potentially deep contact, connects author to audience. Of all the experiments with theatrical structure over the past century this one is most likely to stick. In it are resonances of medieval theater as well as of many folk theaters existing now.

CONCLUSIONS

I can best summarize by drawing four simple models, explaining each in turn.

Actuality 1 ⟶ ENCOUNTER/EXCHANGE ⟶ Actuality 2

A meeting takes place at a market or on a battlefield. Goods are traded, money earned, territory taken, an enemy routed. The encounter is intended to be entirely efficacious, even though sometimes nothing is traded or the battle ends in a stand-off. The rituals of this kind of activity are ethological and/or sociological. That is, they are based on "fixed action patterns," and they are intended to regulate human interaction so that what is supposed to happen, or be determined by the meeting of individuals and/or groups actually happens. The entertainment/theatrical elements in these kinds of meetings are at a minimum, though they are present. The job is to get through the encounter/exchange as efficiently as possible and to arrive at Actuality 2. But even this model doesn't show all that really happens. Markets are places of display, joking, gossiping, singing, and often outright theatrical performing. Markets attract every kind of popular street entertainer. So too battlefields are arenas for the display of colors, parades of strength. At least in the premodern period, the idea was to stiffen the courage of your own troops while scaring the shit out of the enemy. Mass combat, war at a distance (via the air or missiles), and guerrilla warfare work against combat's theatricality on the battlefield, while enhancing it during the "rehearsal" phase where war games and simulated action rise in importance.

Even at the level of marketplace and battlefield, ethological and sociological rituals are embroidered with entertainment. There is a tendency toward:

Actuality 1 <———— BY MEANS OF PERFORMANCE ————> Actuality 2

This is the case with ecological rituals such as those of the Arunta and Tsembaga. Their performances effect changes both in the status of some people participating (through initiation, marriage, and other rites of passage) and in economic matters (pigs, sago, trade items). In fact, how good a performance is can be an important element in determining social status. The Greeks offered prizes to their tragedians; our society offers wealth and fame. Among the Aborigines and New Guinea peoples effective performers are treated with respect, even fear.

A shaman among native Americans, Siberians, or Koreans is honored for her or his tricks, style, and ability to heal. But this honor is ambivalent because the shaman's normative status or caste is often very low.

But the process doesn't always effect a transformation. It can be very open:

Ritual ⟨————— BY MEANS OF THEATER ————— Entertainment

This is what happened when the Mevlevi Sufis whirled or the Shingon monks chanted at the Brooklyn Academy. Rituals which have efficacy in one context become entertainments in another. At *The Yoshi Show*, presented at the Public Theater in New York in 1975, a Buddhist monk, a shinto priest, a martial arts expert, and a Tibetan monk performed with Yoshi Oida, a Japanese actor and member of Peter Brook's company. The show combined elements of different religious ceremonies with martial arts and theatrical performing. Yoshi had used these disciplines in his own training; they are visibly present in his acting. *The Yoshi Show* was excitingly confusing because it was between theater and ritual. This ambiguity gave it a special almost sacrilegious power. The different forms of worship clashed/harmonized with each other and with the martial arts and Yoshi's own skills. Performances like *The Yoshi Show* evidence the transformation from "the liminal to the liminoid." As Victor Turner says:

> In tribal societies, liminality is often functional, in the sense of being a special duty or performance, *required* in the course of work or activity; its very reversals and inversions tend to compensate for rigidities or unfairnesses of normative structure. But in industrial society, the *rite de passage* form, built into the calendar and/or modeled on organic processes of maturation and decay, no longer suffices for total societies. Leisure provides the opportunity for a multiplicity of optional, liminoid genres of literature, drama, and sport, which . . . are to be seen as Sutton-Smith envisages "play," as "experimentation with variable repertoires," consistent with the manifold variation made possible by developed technology and an advanced stage of the division

of labor. . . . In the so-called "high-culture" of complex societies, liminoid is not only removed from a *rite de passage* context, it is also "individualized." The solitary artist *creates* the liminoid phenomena, the collectivity *experiences* collective liminal symbols.

(Victor Turner 1982: 52)

In shows like Yoshi's money is exchanged for a peek at theatricalized esoteric ceremonies. And "new rituals" are manufactured as entertainment or art.

This same process can be reversed:

Entertainment ⟵⟶ BY MEANS OF THEATER ⟶ Ritual

This is what Grotowski tried to do during his paratheater phase.[29] The tendency to transform entertainment into ritual by means of theater has been present in Grotowski almost from the beginning. His works have been played in churches, their themes are religious, the details of the performances are full of Polish Catholicism and Hassidic practices as well as materials drawn from Asian ritual traditions. On a more immediate level, Grotowski carefully selects his audiences by limiting their numbers, allowing a relatively high price to be charged for tickets, and by staging his shows and paratheatrical events in faraway venues. Much of the paratheatrical work involved invited participants working intensively, bringing about an intimacy and quasi-religious solidarity – "spontaneous communitas" – by means of exercises, group-encounter techniques, and the submission to the will of strong leaders. Grotowski's paratheatrical work has close analogies both to American encounter-group therapy and self-help weekends as well as to traditional initiation rites where neophytes are separated from familiar surroundings, removed into liminal (or liminoid) space and time where by means of ordeals they are "broken down." What the paratheatrical experiments lack is the final phase of reintegration. Too often the newly initiated person is left hanging, betwixt and between, disoriented. Only the strongest personalities can effect a successful reintegration on their own.

The 1973 performances in Philadelphia of the Polish Laboratory Theater's *Apocalypsis cum Figuris* were only the first step in a more elaborate ceremony. During each of the shows Grotowski literally "tapped" 5 to 10 persons and asked them to remain after the performance. These people were then invited, after the run of *Apocalypsis* was over, to go with Grotowski and his company to a retreat in the hills not far from Philadelphia. There they and the performers would "meet" on a one-to-one basis. Clearly the performances of *Apocalypsis* were a first-step entry into some other kind of experience, one which can't be called theater in the usual sense.

In *Paradise Now* the Living Theater attempted a similar transformation of entertainment into ritual – in the Living's case a political rather than a religious ritual. By challenging audiences directly, by inviting them to come onto the stage, by not presenting a drama or even a set of incidents but rather a plan and a series of provocations designed to infuriate and then illuminate spectators, the Living undercut orthodox theater, even avant-gardism. Then, after many spectators left – often the majority, a winnowing similar to Grotowski's but carried out publicly in a way that gave individual spectators more liberty to choose themselves – the performers led some of the remaining spectators into the streets. An actual political event arose out of the entertainment by means of a theatrical confrontation. In the streets, performers and spectators-turned-performers were often met by the police. Some performers joined the Living for a few hours, days, or longer periods of time. The group's numbers expanded and contracted over the months. While Grotowski's work eventuated in religions "meetings" the Living's eventuated in public acts and a traveling, extended theater-cum-family.

The origins of theater – thought since Aristotle's day to be ritual – look different when seen from the perspective of popular entertainment. E. T. Kirby (1975) sees theater as starting in shamanism, a system of spiritual journeying, symbolic combat, and healing. But shamanism itself – as Kirby notes – is closely connected to magic acts, acrobatics, ventriloquism, puppetry, and other popular entertainments. La Barre points out that the Asiatic-American trickster – a figure who can be traced back to Paleolithic times – is a "mixture of clown, culture hero, and demigod." La Barre reminds us of the connections between the trickster and Greek theater:

> The great antiquity of the trickster should be suggested first of all by his being much the same in both Paleosiberian and American hunting tribes; and again by the fact that the more a tribe has been influenced by agriculture in America, the less important he becomes in the total tribal mythology as compared with his pre-eminence among both Siberian and American hunters. . . . We must not forget the element of *entertainment* in Old World shamanism: were tales of the erotic escapades of eagle-Zeus once told in the same tone of voice as those of Sibero-American Raven? And did not shamanistic rivalry develop into both the Dionysian bard-contests of Greek drama in the Old World and into *midewewin* medicine-shows in the New? As for that, have modern medicine-men entirely lost the old shamanic self-dramatization?
>
> (La Barre 1972: 195–6)

So wherever we look, and no matter how far back, theater is a mixture, a braid, of entertainment and ritual. At one moment ritual sems to be the source, at another it is entertainment. They are gemini acrobats, tumbling over one another, neither one always on top, neither one always first.

Even at this more or less quiet moment* it's clear that orthodox dramaturgy – the theater of plays behind prosceniums, in fixed settings, for a settled audience, relating stories as if they were happening to others – is finished. At least this kind of theater doesn't meet the needs of many people, needs as old as theater itself, combining ritual and entertainment. These needs also include group interactions as one of the remedies for runaway mechanistic technologies. I am not against technology – I haven't yet traded in my Manhattan loft for a Vermont cabin. But I know a need exists for encounters that are neither just informal person-to-person gatherings like parties nor formal, mediated programmed routines like office or factory work – or watching. TV and movies for that matter.

Theater is a middle world where groups actually interact not only through audience participation but by subtler means of audience inclusion and environmental staging. Theater combines artistic-composed

---

* 1974; revised 1986 (still pretty silent).

behavior (what I call "restored behavior," see Schechner 1985) with everyday-spontaneous behavior. Theater people are moving into areas once occupied mostly by practitioners of religion and politics. Priests and politicians will doubtlessly continue to pick up techniques from the theater. But whether they will be able to restore public confidence in their professions is questionable. If not, will theater in the west become again a big avenue rather than the side road it's been for the past 300 years?

NOTES

1 Whether to use the present or past tense in discussing the kaikos of the Tsembaga is a problem. The data is from 1962–3. Swift and irrevocable changes have occurred in Papua New Guinea from that time to this, including independence, pacification of warring tribal groups, and various kinds of "modernization." I don't know if the kaikos continue roughly as they were, have been transformed, or have been extinguished. Basically, I use the past tense to describe events from 1962–3 and the present tense when theorizing from these events. However, inconsistencies remain and these reflect an uncertainty concerning the status of such ritual entertainments in Papua New Guinea, and elsewhere.

2 In describing the kaiko I follow the account of Rappaport (1968) whose study is a paradigm of how to examine ritual performances within an ecological context.

3 A fight package is a small bundle containing "the thorny leaves of the males of a rare, unidentified tree growing in the *kamnunga*, called the 'fight tree,' and personal material belonging to the enemy, such as hair, fragments of leaves worn over the buttocks, and dirt scraped from the skin" (Rappaport 1968: 120). It is said that pressing the package to the heart and head will give a man courage and improve his chances of killing an enemy. Materials used in fight packages are acquired from neutrals who have relatives among the enemy. Fight packages are items of trade. Their use in peaceful dancing shows the relationship between the dancing and combat. In many parts of Asia perform-ance forms have arisen from martial arts, still use martial arts as training, and display routines of the martial arts in the repertory. The reverse is also true: some of the style and feel of the martial arts are derived from, or at least closely linked to, dance.

4 Spencer and Gillen's *The Native Tribes of Central Australia* has the advantage over later works that the tribes described were relatively intact, having just been contacted by the invading Europeans. In Australia, even more than in North America, contact meant extermination, or nearly so, both culturally and demo-graphically. In recent years there has been an attempt at redress, both in material terms and in constructing historical and scholarly accounts that give

Aboriginals a strong say. In this regard the Australian Institute of Aboriginal Studies, Canberra, has led the way.

5 This rhythm of relatively long preparations followed by a brief performance with a series of performances given on a single day is common in Australia. See Elkin, Berndt, and Berndt 1950, and Berndt and Berndt 1964. Although this rhythm is acceptable in western music and dance, it is alien to western theater where Aristotelian injunctions demand that a work be of a "certain magnitude" with a clear "beginning, middle, and end." Otherwise, the piece is not thought "serious." The emergence of performance art in the 1970s and 1980s has successfully amended, if not wholly repealed, the Aristotelian law.

6 In Oceania it is not unusual – or was not until the eradication of traditional ways – for ritual performances to be the core of a person's life. Van Gennep's (1908, repr. 1960) classic analysis of rituals as crisis moments preceded and followed by longish periods of relative calm describes the situation in Papua New Guinea and Aboriginal Australia. The performances are peak experiences, while preparations for them continue over months and years infiltrating and frequently dominating the daily lives of the people. See my discussion in chapters 2 and 5 as well as Victor Turner 1969, 1974, 1982, and 1985.

7 See Eliade (1965) for a discussion of "reactualization" and its relation to the Dreamtime.

8 An excellent account of the intimate association among events, landmarks, and body decorations is given by Gould (1969: 120–8). See also Roheim (1969). Aborigines continue to feel very strongly about the land, as do many native Americans. The struggle for Uluru – Ayers Rock to European Australians – is emblematic of the issue. The story of Uluru, and how finally in November 1983 the Euro-Australians recognized Aboriginal title to it, is told in Layton (1986).

9 The Eastern Highlands consist of a central valley and many spur valleys surrounded by mountains rising to 15,000 feet. The whole area is about 300 miles long and 150 miles wide. As of around 1970, the Highlands were populated by less than 3 million persons with each village averaging 400 inhabitants. Because of the terrain, many local groups have little contact with each other – and there is much local warfare and feuding. There are about 500 languages spoken, most of them mutually unintelligible, and the largest of them spoken by only 130,000 people. English and pidgin are the basic *lingua franca*. For more detailed information, see Ward and Lea (1970).

10 For a critique of the best-known of these archeological-anthropological reconstructions – the theories of the "Cambridge anthropologists" – see chapter 1 of this book. For an alternative speculation concerning Greek theater, see Dodds (1951).

11 Joan MacIntosh, a member of The Performance Group, was my partner on the 1971–2 trip to Asia that forms the experiential ground of this essay. In addition to Papua New Guinea we visited India, Sri Lanka, Thailand, Malaysia, Indonesia, the Philippines, Hong Kong, and Japan.

12 Burns (1972: 132). This way of looking at ordinary experience as theater has roots, of course, in ancient traditions of *teatrum mundi*. But systematically examining what this means has only recently begun. Key observations have been made by Goffman (1959, 1967, 1971, and 1974). See also Geertz (1973, 1980a, and 1980b); Victor Turner (1974, 1982, and 1986); Schechner (1982 and 1985).

13 See Brustein (1974). According to him, news theater is "any histrionic proceeding that results from a collaboration between newsworthy personalities, a vast public, and the visual or print media (television, films, book publishing, magazines and newspapers). News theater, in other words, is any event that confuses news with theater and theater with news" (p. 7). I think Brustein's description is accurate, but that he is wrong when he says that "news" and "theater" should be kept distinct. How can this be when the two are inherently interdependent? Both are public, action-centered, and crisis-seeking. Furthermore, as the means of news transmission abandons print and relocates in the visual media, they approximate theater at the technical level. The problems stirred up are not solved by bemoaning the inevitable. Only in finding ways of understanding and then controlling what's happening will a satisfactory outcome be achieved. Take one limited but decisive area – the ethics of news reporting. I refer to the ways in which reporting shapes people's responses to events. We all know that so-called "objective" reporting is anything but objective; that context, not to mention editing, shapes content. But is reporting distorted simply through the evil designs of news managers, or is there at work a deep structure which dooms to failure every attempt at objectivity? Drama has long had an ethical purpose which is expressed not only overtly but in dramatic structure. News broadcasting uses the same structures but without consciously conceding their ethical purposes. Or maybe I should say their rhetorical purposes, their intentions to persuade. An ethic that remains unconscious, that is, unexamined, will automatically reinforce the status quo. Or, as Brecht put it, to remain neutral is to support the stronger side. The need then is to make the theatrical structures of news reporting more and more visible, to force reporters and editors alike to acknowledge and deal with the value-systems inherent in their line of work. Whether such consciousness will result in advancing the causes of the people or in further repressing/oppressing them remains in doubt. See also my "News, Sex, and Performance Theory" in Schechner (1985).

14 This is true even of war, where a perpetual imbalance of casualties must be maintained. In both pig-kill exchanges and combat the excess of repayment is often rhetorical – the emphatic claim that the payback exceeds the debt. The permissibility of rhetoric insures a discontinuation of perpetual escalation. Instead, everyone feels that things are imbalanced, always in need of redress. Would that the defense departments of various "great powers" would learn the same lesson.

15 Ketchak is a "monkey dance song" popular in Bali. It combines old-style Balinese elements with modern techniques designed to please tourists.

While listening to the Highlanders I wondered about the Melanesian layer of Balinese culture.

16 Konrad Lorenz (1967) discusses at some length the development of "appeasement ceremonies" in animals. More technical descriptions are given by Eibl-Eibesfeldt (1970). Lorenz describes a special kind of ceremony that is analogous to what I saw in Papua New Guinea.

> Of all the various appeasement ceremonies, with their many different roots, the most important for our theme are those appeasing or greeting rites which have arisen from redirected aggression movements. They differ from the already described appeasement ceremonies in that they do not put aggression under inhibition but divert it from certain members of the species and canalize it in the direction of others. This new orientation of aggressive behavior is one of the most ingenious inventions of evolution, but it is even more than that: wherever redirected rituals of appeasement are observed, ceremony is bound to the individuality of the participating partners. The aggression of a particular individual is diverted from a second, equally particular individual, while its discharge against all other anonymous members of the species is not inhibited. Thus discrimination between friend and stranger arises, and for the first time in the world personal bonds between individuals come into being.
>
> (Lorenz 1967: 131–2)

Or, as the Tsembaga say, "those who come to our *kaiko* will also come to our fights." It is also important to note that the ceremonies Lorenz focused on were greeting ceremonies. The dances in the Highlands may correctly be called greeting dances.

17 See E. T. Kirby (1975). Kirby sees shamanism as "the 'great unitarian artwork' that fragmented into a number of performances arts" (p. 6). Also see the chapter "Shaman," in my *Environmental Theater* (Schechner 1973).

18 Performance activities that go far beyond what is normally thought of as "community theater" exist in both Europe and America. The wide-ranging work of Anna Halprin, Eugenio Barba, and Augusto Boal are but three examples. See Lawrence Halprin (1969), Halprin and Burns (1974), Barba (1979 and 1986), and Boal (1979). Also see *TDR, The Drama Review* 27 (2) (1983), an issue devoted to "grass roots theater." Of course, what is a "movement" in Europe and America is the most widespread kind of theater and dance in many parts of Africa and Asia.

19 Jerzy Grotowski has been the leading pioneer, but by no means the only practitioner, of paratheater. See Kolankiewicz (1978), Burzynski and Osinski (1979), Kumiega (1985), and Osinski (1986).

20 See Kaprow (1966b and 1983) and Montano (1981). As Kaprow says:

> A supposed conflict between art and life has been a theme in Western art at least since ancient Rome. . . . Simplistically put, artlike art holds that art

is separate from life and everything else, while lifelike art holds that art is connected to life and everything else. . . . The root message of all artlike art is separateness and specialness; and the corresponding one of all lifelike art is connectedness and wide-angle awareness.

(Kaprow 1983: 36, 38)

Kaprow goes on to enunciate eight points that "summarize the characteristics of an emerging lifelike art." Key among these is the shift in locale of where art can take place – away from museums, theaters, concert halls to "anywhere else in the real world"; the intentional blurring of the "possible boundaries between lifelike art and the rest of life"; and the "therapeutic purpose" of lifelike art: "to reintegrate the piecemeal reality we take for granted. Not just intellectually, but directly, as experience – in this moment, in this house, at this kitchen sink" (Kaprow 1983: 39).

21 Of many documents available, see especially Emile Zola's "Naturalism in Theater" (1880) and August Strindberg's "Naturalism in Theater" (1888), both reprinted in Becker 1963.

22 FACT met in Princeton June 2–6, 1974. It brought together more than two hundred leaders of the American theater, very heavily tilted toward producers, managers of regional theaters, and professional administrators. Only a relatively few actors, directors, and designers were there. Also the conference was weighted toward New York, organized as it was by Alexander H. Cohen, the New York producer. Eleven panels discussed various problems confronting the theater, but the real action went on offstage where individuals and interest groups exchanged – or failed to exchange – ideas and opinions. The Theatre Communications Group (TCG) has taken up where FACT left off, organizing once every two years or so meetings of alleged theater leaders. The problem with these meetings is that they are self-perpetuating. People never included in any numbers are those who work with community groups, who are politically radical, who are experimental. A few such always attend, to season the sauce. But the preponderance are regional theater people. Underlying FACT and the TCG meetings is a growing awareness of a contradictory reality: theater is marginal economically speaking but it has enduring roots in society. Means are therefore necessary to bring the disparate wings of the theater together for a common rumination on basically economic issues relating to the survival of theater at the institutional level. Whether politics can, or should be, kept out of such meetings is another question. As for aesthetics, forget it.

23 As I later learned, things are not, nor can they ever be, so simple. Anthropologist Edmund Carpenter wrote me a letter in which he said that the performance of the mudmen does not originate in Makehuku practice at all. "These [mudmen] were invented by a TAA [Australian] travel agent. They have no antiquity, no foundation in New Guinea aesthetics, no parallels elsewhere." Wanting to resolve the matter, I wrote to the National Library in Boroko, Papua New Guinea. The response didn't help. The reference librarian checked holdings in Boroko and contacted both local anthropologists and theater people. No data

resolving the contradiction between the two "origin stories" of the mudmen turned up. Finally, the people in New Guinea referred me to the Museum of Natural History in New York – where Margaret Mead was curator and from whom I had got the "threatened-by-attack-evil-spirit" hypothesis in the first place (Mead 1970).

24 Brook's anecdote is a fine example of what I mean by "preparations" rather than rehearsals. Rehearsing is a way of setting an exact sequence of events. Preparing is a constant state of training so that when a situation arises one will be ready to "do something appropriate" to the moment. Preparations are what a good athletics team does. Too often those wanting to improvise feel that an improvisation can arise spontaneously out of the moment. Nothing is further from the truth. What arises spontaneously is the moment itself. The response to that moment is selected from a known repertory, rearranged, adapted to the immediate given circumstances; when done without anxiety this response joins with the moment to give the impression of total spontaneity. Many ritual performances are not rehearsed, they are prepared.

25 The headman's invitation was based on my reputation on the island for being a clown. Although I was in Bali for only two weeks, I used to play games with children in which I would imitate animals. I did one act that especially amused the kids: making my hands into horns, I would charge them as if I were an enraged bull. On several occasions while riding a bus to a remote village some children would spot me and make the horn gesture while laughing. Probably I was regarded as an outlandish foreigner, a bit crazy. At Tenganan the dance I did at the public performance was a variation on the animal game. MacIntosh's professional-level singing was appreciated everywhere. People would get angry if she refused to sing. In New Guinea especially, almost anything – an object, a relationship, an event, a performance – can be an item of trade; there are no neutral or valueless occurrences.

26 The late 1960s and early 1970s saw a number of performances based on this premise. A family in Greenwich Village sold admission to their apartment where spectators watched them in their daily lives. Of course the Loud Family epic on television carried this style of documentary drama to its logical end: the feedback from the weekly series actually affected the life the Louds lived, and so we watched the family change under the impact of their knowledge that they were being watched. In the 1980s performers like Linda Montano and Allan Kaprow are further breaking down the "art/life" barrier or, perhaps it is better to say, interdigitating the two kinds of experience (see Montano 1981 and Kaprow 1983).

27 This kind of overlapping non-exclusivity is increasingly in use in the sciences. "Classifications need not be hierarchic and the clusters may overlap (intersect). The whole idea of hierarchic, nonoverlapping (mutually exclusive) classification which is so attractive to the human mind is currently undergoing reexamination. From studies in a variety of fields the representation of taxonomic structure as overlapping clusters or as ordinations appears far preferable" (Sokal

1974: 1121). One "locates" a performance by using the coordinates of efficacy and entertainment.

28 In TPG's *Commune* there was one night an interruption of more than three hours. During that time the spectators and the performers came to know and interact with each other in ways much more actual than is usual in a theater. When *Commune* resumed there was a feeling surrounding the performance that added power to it – a ritual sense of having gone through something and now needing to complete the show. The supper in *Mother Courage* was an attempt at building in the kind of interaction/relationship between performers and spectators that occurred only occasionally – and usually as conflict – in *Commune* (see Schechner 1973: 49–56).

29 Grotowski's paratheatrical work is described in detail in Burzynski and Osinski 1979, Kumiega 1985, and Osinski 1986. Paratheater involved not only Grotowski but members of his company working on their own on such projects as *Acting Therapy, Vigil, Meditations Aloud*, and *Soundings*. The events took from a few hours to several weeks and used all kinds of spaces from rooms where workshops were held to pilgrimages through the countryside.

5

TOWARD A POETICS OF PERFORMANCE

HUNTING CIRCUITS, CEREMONIAL CENTERS, AND THEATERS

The earliest human societies were hunting and gathering bands. These bands were neither primitive nor poor; the best evidence suggests an abundance of food, small families (birth control was practiced), and an established range. Humans did not live in one spot, neither did they wander aimlessly. Each band had its own circuit: a more or less fixed route through time/space. I say "time/space" because the hunting schedule was not gratuitous; it took into account the movement of game according to its own feeding and mating patterns. The cultural level – at least in terms of painting and sculpting – was very high: the masterpieces of the caves of south-west Europe and the mobile art of Eurasia are testimony enough. Cave art from very far back exists in many parts of the world, though nothing comparable to Lascaux, Altamira, and the others has been uncovered elsewhere. In brief, humans occupied an ecological niche that kept bands on the move in regular, repetitious patterns, following game, adjusting to the seasons, creating art/ritual.

Repetitious beyond modern calculation: evidence shows that certain decorated caves were in constant use for more than 10,000 years. What kind of use? Human bands did not number more than 40 to 70 individuals, and more than one band used adjacent and overlapping ranges. For most of the year bands probably met only occasionally, by chance, or perhaps to exchange information and goods. Maybe relations between some bands were hostile. But indications are that at special times – when game was assembled in one area, when certain edible fruits and nuts were ripe for gathering – a concentration of bands took place. This still happens among the few hunting and gathering peoples left, in the Kalahari with the !Kung, at the corroborees of the Australian Aborigines. The farming and hunting tribes of Highlands New Guinea stage elaborate "payback" or exchange ceremonies on a regular basis (see chapter 4). Pilgrimages, family reunions marked by feasting and the exchange of gifts, potlatches, and "going to" the theater are other variations on this same action of concentration, exchange or give-away, and dispersal.

V. and F. Reynolds report a strikingly similar phenomenon among the chimpanzees of the Bundongo Forest in Uganda. The Reynolds' account makes me want to root "going out to the theater" or "ceremonial gathering" in behavior common to humans and certain other species.

> Garner (1896: 59–60) wrote that, according to native hearsay, "one of the most remarkable habits of the chimpanzee is the *kanjo* as it is called in the native tongue. The word . . . implies more of the idea of "carnival." It is believed that more than one family takes part in these festivities." He went on to describe how the chimpanzees fashion a drum from damp clay and wait for it to dry. Then "the chimpanzees assemble by night in great numbers and then the carnival begins. One or two will beat violently on this dry clay, while others jump up and down in a wild grotesque manner. Some of them utter long rolling sounds as if trying to sing . . . and the festivities continue in this fashion for hours." Apart from the question of the drum, the account given above describes quite well what occurred in the Bundongo Forest in its extreme form, as we heard it six times, once when we were very close to the chimpanzees. Only twice, however, did this happen at night; the four other times it lasted for a few hours during the daytime.

The "carnivals" consisted of prolonged noise for periods of hours, whereas ordinary outbursts of calling and drumming lasted a few minutes only. Although it was not possible to know the reason for this unusual behavior, twice it seemed to be associated with the meeting at a common food source of bands that may have been relatively unfamiliar to each other.

(Reynolds and Reynolds 1965: 408–9)

The Reynolds aren't sure what the carnivals were for – they think it may signal a move from one food source to another: it occurs when certain edible fruits are ripe. The nineteenth-century report indicating some kind of entertainment (singing, dancing, drumming) apparently romanticized and anthropomorphized the gathering of chimpanzees. But the Reynolds confirmed the nineteenth-century report of a mood of excitement and well-being permeating the meeting of animals from different bands who are on friendly terms with each other.

Calls were coming from all directions at once and all groups concerned seemed to be moving about rapidly. As we oriented the source of one outburst, another came from another direction. Stamping and fast-running feet were heard sometimes behind, sometimes in front and howling outbursts and prolonged rolls of drums (as many as 13 rapid beats) shaking the ground surprised us every few yards.

(Reynolds and Reynolds 1965: 409)

Aren't these "carnivals" prototypes of celebratory, theatrical events? Their qualities are worth nothing: 1) a gathering of bands – not individuals – who are neither living with nor total strangers to each other; 2) the sharing of food or, at least, a food source; 3) singing, dancing (rhythmic movement), drumming: entertainment; 4) use of a place that is not "home" for any group as the grounds for the gathering. (In regard to the last point I note that even in our own culture parties held in the home use rooms specially marked out or decorated "for the occasion," while other rooms are more or less off limits.)

The entertainment aspects of gatherings are of special importance. Western thinkers have too often split ritual from entertainment privileging ritual over entertainment. It has been accepted wisdom to assert that ritual comes first (historically, conceptually), with entertainment arising later as a derivation or even deterioration of ritual. Ritual is "serious" while entertainment is "frivolous." These are prejudiced culture-bound conclusions. As I tried to show in chapter 4, entertainment and ritual are braided together, neither one being the "original" of the other. At celebratory gatherings people are free to engage in behavior that would otherwise be forbidden. Even more, special non-ordinary, otherwise forbidden (frequently promiscuous) behavior is not only permitted, but encouraged, prepared for, and rehearsed. Behavior during carnival combines or alternates with prescribed spontaneity with large-scale public performances.

Where two or more groups meet on a seasonal schedule, where there is abundant food either available or stored, and where there is a geographical marker – cave, hill, waterhole, etc. – there is likelihood of a ceremonial center (see figure 5.1). Of the many differences between

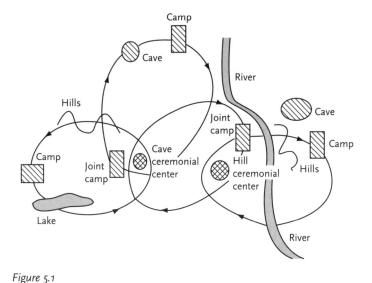

Figure 5.1

Note

At places where seasonal hunting places intersect at a landmark, ceremonial centers arise.

human and ape ceremonial centers none is more decisive than the fact that only humans permanently transform the space by "writing" on it or attaching a lore to it. The art in the caves of south-west Europe and the stories of the Aborigines about the landmarks in their range are means of transforming natural spaces into cultural places: ways of making theaters. But every architectural construction or modification is the making of a cultural place – what is special about a theater?

A theater is a place whose only or main use is to stage or enact performances. It is my belief that this kind of space, a theater place, did not arrive late in human cultures (say with the Greeks of the fifth century BCE) but was there from the beginning – is itself one of the characteristics of our species. The first theaters were ceremonial centers – part of a system of hunting, following food sources according to a seasonal schedule, meeting other human bands, celebrating, and marking the celebration by some kind of writing on a space: an integration of geography, calendar, social interaction, and the proclivity of people to transform nature into culture. The first theaters were not merely "natural spaces" – as is the Bundongo Forest where the chimpanzees stage their carnivals – but were also, and fundamentally, "cultural places." The transformation of space into place means to construct a theater; this transformation is accomplished by "writing on the space," as the cave art of the Paleolithic period demonstrates so well.[1] This writing need not be visual, it can be oral as with the Aborigines. The Aborigines are a people with few material possessions but possessing a culture rich in kinship systems, rites, myths, songs, and dances. With them the transformation of space into place cannot be seen so much as it can be heard. Or, similarly but in an environment as different as can be imagined from the desert home of the Aborigines, the central-African Mbuti move confidently through their sacred tropical forest singing and dancing their Molimo (see Turnbull 1962, 1985, 1988). What characterizes Mbuti Molimo ritual is the sound of the Molimo wooden trumpet and the pattern of the dances associated with it. The Molimo, hidden "vertically in a tree near the sacred center of the forest moves toward the camp, relocating the sacred center as it breathes air, drinks water, is rubbed with earth, and finally manifests itself over fire. At this point the sanctity of the forest center envelops the camp" (Turnbull 1985: 16). Remembering the Aborigines and the Mbuti we must be cautious when assuming an area that has left little visual evidence of high art is necessarily artistically impoverished.

The functions of the ceremonies – the performances – at the ceremonial centers, and the exact procedures, cannot be known precisely. Heel-marks left in the clay in at least one of the caves indicate dancing; authorities generally agree that performances of some kind took place.[2] But more often than not the reconstructions suit the tastes of the reconstructor: fertility rites, initiations, shamanist-curing, and so on. My own tastes run toward "ecological rituals" such as outlined by Roy A. Rappaport: performances which regulate economic, political, and religious interaction among neighboring groups whose relation with each other is ambivalently collaborative and hostile. In fact, Rappaport (1968) discusses war as part of a total ecological system. My own views are close to Rappaport's:

> ritual, particularly in the context of a ritual cycle, operates as a regulating mechanism in a system, or set of interlocking systems, in which such variables as the area of available land, necessary lengths of fallow periods, size and composition of both human and pig populations, trophic requirements of pigs and people, energy expended in various activities, and the frequency of misfortunes are included. . . . Underlying these hypotheses is the belief that much is to be gained by regarding culture, in some of its aspects, as part of the means by which animals of the human species maintain themselves in their environments.
>
> (Rappaport 1968: 4–5)

Rappaport is writing about a contemporary New Guinea people; I am trying to reconstruct performances of Paleolithic hunters – I think both bear on patterns within modern and postmodern societies. Extrapolating from Rappaport, from the pictorial and other evidence within the caves, and from patterns within contemporary theater I say that the performances at the ceremonial centers occurring where hunting bands met functioned in at least the following ways:

1. To maintain friendly relations.
2. To exchange goods, mates, trophies, techniques.

3.   To show and exchange dances, songs, stories.

Furthermore, I think these performances followed rhythms familiar to us in:

1.   Gathering.
2.   Playing out an action or actions.
3.   Dispersing.

In other words, people came to a special place, did something that can be called theater (and/or dance and music because all three genres are always performed together in such situations), and went on their way. Simple and obvious as this constellation of rhythmically organized events may seem to be, they are not inevitable when two or more groups approach each other. The groups could avoid each other, meet in combat, pass each other by as travelers do on a road, and so on. The pattern of gathering, performing, and dispersing is a specifically theatrical pattern.

This pattern occurs "naturally" in urban settings. An accident happens, or is caused to happen (as in guerrilla theater); a crowd gathers to see what's going on. The crowd makes a circle around the event or, as in the case of accidents, around the aftermath of the event. Talk in the crowd is about what happened, to whom, why; this talk is largely interrogative: like dramas and courtroom trials, which are formal versions of the street accident, the event itself is absorbed into the *action of reconstructing what took place*. In trials this is done verbally, in theater analogically: by doing again what happened (actually, fictionally, mythically, religiously). The questions asked in the crowd are those which Brecht wanted theater audiences to ask of theater.[3] The shape of this kind of street event – a heated center with involved spectators fading into a cool rim where people come, peer in, and move on – is like that of some medieval street theater.[4] Accidents conform to the basic performance pattern; even after the event is "cleaned up" some writing marks the site: for example, bloodstains, knots of witnesses and the curious. Only slowly does the event evaporate and the crowd disperse. I call such events "eruptions" (see figure 5.2).

An eruption is like a theatrical performance because it is *not* the

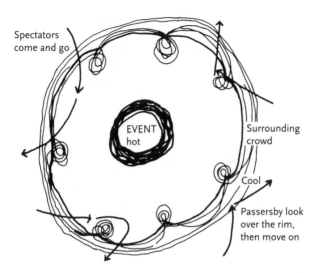

Figure 5.2 An eruption
Note
An "eruption" features a heated center and a cool rim, with spectators coming and going. The eruption occurs either *after* an accident or during an event whose development is predictable such as an argument, or the construction or demolition of a building.

accident itself that gathers and keeps an audience. They are held by the reconstruction or reenactment of the event. In the case of an argument or, at a much slower pace, the construction of a building watched by sidewalk superintendents, it is the unfolding of an event which can be measured against a predictable script (see chapter 3) that gathers and holds people. Totally unmanageable occurrences – a falling wall, sudden gunfire – scatters people; only after the wall has fallen or when the shooting stops does the crowd gather to make the theater.

Eruptions are one kind of "natural"[5] theater, processions are another. Understood as a coherent system they form a bipolar model of the performances that took place in the ceremonial centers which arose at points where Paleolithic hunting bands, moving across the terrain on their seasonal treks, met. In a procession (see figure 5.3) – which is a

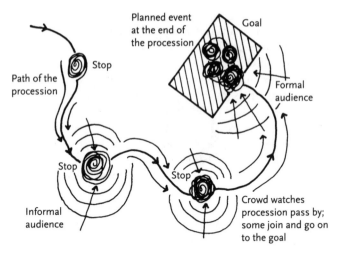

Figure 5.3 A procession
Note

A procession has a fixed route and a known goal. At several points along the way, the procession stops and performances are played. As spectators watch the procession pass by, some may join and go on to the goal.

kind of pilgrimage – the event moves along a prescribed path, spectators gather along the route, and at appointed places the procession halts and performances are played. Parades, funeral corteges, political marches, and the Bread and Puppet Theater are processions.[6]

Usually a procession moves to a goal: the funeral to the grave, the political march to the speakers' stand, the circus parade to the big top, the pilgrimage to the shrine. The event performed at the goal of the procession is the opposite of an eruption: it is well planned for, rehearsed, ritualized.

However, eruptions and processions can occur simultaneously, especially when large numbers of people are involved and the leadership of a group is flexible. The meeting of bands of chimpanzees in the Bundongo Forest is both eruptive and processional: at a known place in a known circuit, the abundance of food coupled with the encounter with strange bands triggers an eruption of the "carnival." It is my belief that a roughly similar thing happened countless times on the hunting circuits of Paleolithic humans. Out of these hunting circuits developed ritual circuits, meeting places, ceremonial centers, and theaters.

Everywhere theater occurs at special times in special places. Theater is but one of a complex of performance activities which also includes rituals, sport and trials (duels, ritual combats, courtroom trials), dance, music, play, and various performances in everyday life (see chapter 1). Theater places are maps of the cultures where they exist. That is, theater is analogical not only in the literary sense – the stories dramas tell, the convention of explicating action by staging it – but also in the architectonic sense. Thus, for example, the Athenian theater of the fifth century BCE had as its center the altar of Dionysus. When the chorus danced around the altar it was located between the audience and the men who played the dramatic roles. The Greek theater's semicircular tiers of seats – not individuated as in modern theaters but curving communal benches as in modern sports stadiums – literally enfolded the drama, containing its agons within the Athenian solidarity (see figure 5.4). Conceptually this pattern of solidarity-containing-agon was repeated in the contest among the poets and actors for the best play and best performance. The proscenium theater of the eighteenth to twentieth centuries in the west also shows a definite, but very different, sociometric design (figure 5.5).

The Greek amphitheater was open. Beyond and around it the city could be seen during performances which took place in daylight. It was the city, the polis, that was tightly boundaried geographically and ideologically. On the other hand, the proscenium theater is a tightly boundaried, closed individual building with access from the street strictly controlled. Within the part of the structure where the performance takes place and is viewed much effort is spent in directing attention only to the stage; everything not in the show is hidden or sunk in darkness. The building, like the events within it, is compartmentalized; the time for the audience to look at each other is regulated and is limited to before the show and to intermissions.

The proscenium theater is divided into five precincts (see figure 5.5). Theater workers enter through a backstage door unseen by the ticket-buying patrons. This is a version of the industrial practice of separating the factory where goods are produced from the store where

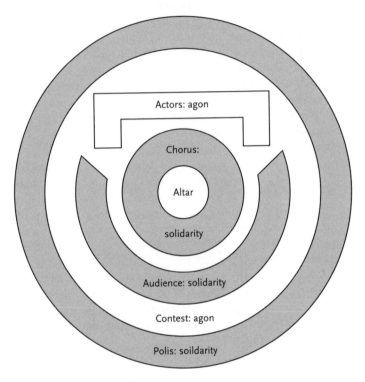

Actors: agon

Chorus:

Altar

solidarity

Audience: solidarity

Contest: agon

Polis: soildarity

Figure 5.4 The Athenian theater
Note
Nested at the center of the Athenian theater was the open eye of the Altar of Dionysus. Around it danced the Chorus, giving a core of solidarity for the agonistic actions of the actors. The audience nested both Chorus and actors. But the agon of the contest among poets and actors for the prizes surrounded the whole theatrical event. Yet the solidarity of Athens, the polis, provided the ultimate nest for the entire sequence of performances and contests. Each agon was literally held in a nest of solidarity. The outer nest – the polis – was not metaphorical: there were definite geographical, ideological, and social limits to Athens; and each person knew what it was to be a citizen. The shape of the theater was a version of the social system which alternated agon and solidarity; it was open to debate and interrogation, but closed about who was or was not a member, a citizen.

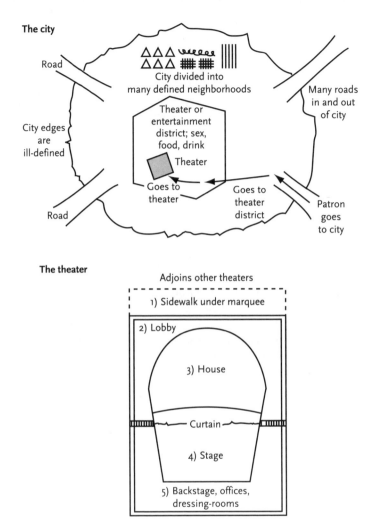

Figure 5.5 The proscenium theater

Note

The modern theater building is not in itself a central structure at the heart of a clearly boundaried polis. That structure – if it exists at all – is the stadium or Superdome. Theaters are built in "theater districts," one neighborhood in a rather ill-defined "urban area." The proscenium theater itself is divided into five areas: 1) sidewalk under marquee, 2) lobby, 3) house, 4) stage, and 5) backstage. Fixed seating points the audience toward the stage. The stage floor is open and often slightly raked, tilting the action toward the house. Stage machinery is hidden in the wings and flies, making quick scene changes possible. The lobby, which extends into the street under the theater marquee, is a gathering place for the audience before the performance and during intermissions.

they are sold. In a way the proscenium theater combines factory and store in one building but with clearly defined areas. The spaces occupied by the public – marquee area, lobby, and house – are gaudily decorated reflecting an ambition to appear "aristocratic" or "high-class." The spaces occupied by the workers – stage and backstage – resemble industrial workspaces, functional, sparsely decorated, raw, and full of necessary equipment.

The house is divided into different classes of seats, some better than others, but even the cheap seats are individual units. (In older proscenium theaters the cheap seats were literally benches, only the rich were entitled to individual places.) The box seats are placed so that patrons sitting there can be seen by other spectators.[7] Before the play begins a curtain conceals most of the stage facing the seats. However, even when this temporary barrier is lifted, patrons are no longer allowed on stage as they were during the Restoration, nor do they usually see the actual walls of the theater building. These are masked by flats or sets: false architectural elements depicting various scenes.

The stage is architecturally separated from the house by the proscenium arch, the proscenium theater's most unique and dominating feature. The arch is actually a framed wall with its center portion removed so that literally the audience is in one room and looking into another. The wall separating the two rooms is only *partially* removed. The arch itself emphasizes this incomplete removal. As the proscenium theater developed from the seventeenth through the twentieth centuries the forestage jutting into the house receded until it all but vanished, eliminating any sharing of space between the stage and house. The open-theater movement of the twentieth century has once again made the playing space part of the viewing space. This has been attempted in many variations – thrust stage, arena, environmental theater. In the proscenium theater the part of the stage visible to the audience is a surprisingly small portion of the area behind the proscenium. In the Greek theater almost every space was visible, as well as the city and countryside behind and around the theater. In the proscenium theater the wings, flies, dressing-rooms, offices, and storage bins are all concealed. The stage and backstage portions of the building usually occupy more than half the area of the theater, but from the house the stage looks much less spacious than the house. Flies and wings were developed to facilitate quick changes of scenery – visual surprises. Additional storage space was necessary as productions involving bulky scenery were kept for future productions; dressing-rooms became more ornate as costumes and makeup increased in complexity. The stage space of the proscenium theater is an efficient engine for quick scene changes and mounting sumptuous effects; this theater produces "numbers" and *coups de théâtre* like a many-course meal at an expensive restaurant. Usually every attempt is made to hide how effects are achieved. Dramas written for the proscenium usually include one or two intermissions because it's necessary for patrons to see each other, evaluate the product they've purchased, drink, smoke, and re-experience the thrill and surprise of the rising curtain.

Theaters are located in a theater district; performances are offered at the edge of workdays, "after work" or on weekends and general holidays: theater is a place to go when work is finished, it is not meant to be a rival of work. Because it is a model of the mercantile process, and a product itself of the working middle-class, the modern theater can't impede that process. Nor is it proper for the theater to entice patrons from their jobs (except on Wednesday afternoons, matinées traditionally reserved for blue-haired non-working ladies). Movies and baseball are different: they are offered as alternatives to work, though night ball is the accommodation of the big leagues to the workday. The theater district – often also a sex and restaurant district – stimulates consumer appetites by offering a series of shows just as each show offers a sequence of scenes. Competition is fierce among theaters – this competition is for customers not prizes; when prizes are given they are used to attract more customers. Regardless of their artistic quality, most shows fail (which means they don't attract buyers), but hits run as long as people will pay to see them. Thus, in all these ways, the proscenium theater is a model of capitalism. Today, as capitalism evolves into corporatism, new kinds of theater arise. Cultural centers and regional theaters – art fortresses run by impresarios overseen by boards of directors – are examples of corporatism. Environmental theaters – built in cheap hit-and-run spaces, often in out-of-the-way neighborhoods – exemplify a resistance and alternative to the conglomerates. But environmental theaters exist only in the creases of contemporary society, living off the leavings, like cockroaches.

Creases are not marginal, on the edge, but liminal, in between. They run through the actual and conceptual centers of society, like faults in the Earth's crust. Creases are places to hide, but more importantly they signal areas of instability, disturbance, and potentially radical changes in the social topography. These changes are always "changes in direction," that is, changes of something more than technique. In the urban environment, in places abandoned, or not yet reclaimed, individuals and small groups can still work. Even in large, apparently smooth operations like corporations and universities, creases exist; look for them, quite literally, in "out of the way places." Crease phenomena do not transform existing neighborhoods instantly, as when bulldozers herald the erection of a new cultural center whose monuments rest on murdered neighborhoods, but step by step through infiltration and renovation. At the time when a balance/tension exists between several classes, income levels, interests, and uses – as was the case in the 1960s and 1970s in New York's SoHo district – crease phenomena – experimental art, bars, cafés, and clubs, lively street performances, parties where artists congregate – peak. But when a threshold of visibility and "stability" is crossed, the neighborhood freezes in a new form, becomes an "attraction" (like the theater district which draws most of its life from outside its own precinct) and the crease is smoothed out. Then artists – and others who need a crease environment – follow along, or create, a new fault.

Theaters everywhere are scenographic models of sociometric process. Pointing out that "most of the traditional theater performances [of India] are open-air events, organized on the level ground, a platform stage, or as a mobile processional spectacle," Suresh Awasthi goes on to say:

> They are presented in fields after the harvest, streets, open spaces, outside town (often permanently designated for performances), fairs, markets and – especially for the Ramayana and the Krishna legend shows – temple gardens, riverbanks, market squares, and courtyards. . . . The performances are social events not separated from the community activity. The actor is an active member of his community. He is also a farmer, a mechanic, a carpenter, a fruit vendor, a vegetable hawker. . . . An important factor that determines the nature of the

scenography in this theater is the nonrealistic and metaphysical treatment of time and place.

(Awasthi 1974: 36–8)

Traditional Indian theater is very like western medieval theater – and modern avant-garde or experimental theater. The performer often has a second or third occupation, but this does not mean that his skills as a performer are amateurish; far from it, a connection to a community may deepen all aspects of his art. The flexible treatment of time and space – the ability of one space to be transformed into many places through the skills of the performer more than through the illusionistic devices of the scenographer – goes hand in hand with a transformational view of character (role doubling, role switching) and a close contact with the audience (the performer both as character and as story-teller, the use of such devices as the aside and direct address to the audience). This connectedness – a mobility among spheres of reality rather than social mobility in the modern sense – is an important quality of traditional performances, and even the avant-garde. This kind of total theater is nowhere better expressed than among the Aborigines:

> The daily life of the Aborigines is rewarding but routine. There is a kind of low-key pace to the everyday round of living. In their ritual lives, however, the Aborigines attain a heightened sense of drama. Sharp images appear and colors deepen. The Aborigines are masters of stagecraft and achieve remarkable visual and musical effects with the limited materials at hand. . . . Gradually I experienced the central truth of Aboriginal religion: that it is not a thing by itself but an inseparable part of a whole that encompasses every aspect of daily life, every individual and ever time – past, present and future. It is nothing less than the theme of existence, and as such constitutes one of the most sophisticated and unique religious and philosophical systems known to man.

(Gould 1969: 103–4)[8]

We are accustomed to a theater that locates "the real" in relationships among individual people; but most of world theater takes a broader, and deeper, view of what's real. Modern western theater is mimetic. Traditional theater, and again I include the avant-garde in this category, is *transformational*, creating or incarnating in a theater place what cannot take place anywhere else. Just as a farm is a field where edible foods are grown, so a theater is a place where transformations of time, place, and persons (human and non-human) are accomplished. Aborigine scenography creates theater out of a combination of natural and built elements. Each rock, waterhole, tree, and stream is embedded in a matrix of legend and dramatic action. Thus a particular place is where a ceremony takes place, where a mythic event has happened in the past, where beings manifest themselves through songs and dances, and where everyday and special actions converge – for example, a waterhole is both a place where people come to drink and where ceremonies are enacted. Simple modifications of space transform the drinking place (or some other multiple-use space) into a theater: clearing the area of small rocks, doing sand or rock paintings, for example; or a space may become a theater by being "learned" – a novice is taught the legends, songs, and dances associated with a particular place: geography itself is socialized; the uninitiated see nothing but an outcropping of rock or a waterhole; while the initiated experience a dense theatrical setting. This technique of creating a theater place by poetic means is used by Shakespeare and the makers of guerrilla theater alike.

TRANSFORMANCES

Victor Turner (1974) analyzes "social dramas" using theatrical terminology to describe how disharmonic or crisis situations are dealt with. These situations – arguments, combats, rites of passage – are inherently dramatic because participants not only do things, they *show themselves and others what they are doing or have done*; actions take on a reflexive and performed-for-an-audience aspect. Erving Goffman (1959) is as direct as Turner in using the theatrical paradigm. Goffman believes all social interactions are staged – people prepare their social roles (various personae or masks, different techniques of role playing) "backstage" and then enter the "main stage" areas in order to play out key social interactions and routines. For both Turner and Goffman the basic human plot is the same: someone or some group begins to move to a new place in the social order; this move is acceded to or blocked; in either case a crisis occurs because any change in status involves a readjustment of the entire scheme; this readjustment is effected performatively – that is, by means of theater and ritual. Turner writes:

> Social dramas are units of aharmonic or disharmonic process, arising in conflict situations. Typically, they have four main phases of public action. . . . These are: 1. *Breach* of regular, norm-governed social relations. . . . 2. *Crisis* during which . . . there is a tendency for the breach to widen. . . . Each public crisis has what I now call liminal characteristics, since it is a threshold between more or less stable phases of the social process, but it is not a sacred limen, hedged around by taboos and thrust away from the centers of public life. On the contrary, it takes up its menacing stance in the forum itself and, as it were, dares the representatives of order to grapple with it. . . . 3. *Redressive action* [ranging] from personal advice and informal meditation or arbitration to formal judicial and legal machinery and, to resolve certain kinds of crisis or legitimate other modes or resolution, to the performance of public ritual. . . . Redress, too, has its liminal features, its being "betwixt and between," and, as such, furnishes a distanced replication and critique of the events leading up to and composing the "crisis." This replication may be in the rational idiom of a judicial process, or in the metaphorical and symbolic idiom of a ritual process. . . . 4. The final phase. . . . consists either of the *reintegration* of the disturbed social group or of the social recognition and legitimization of irreparable schism between contesting parties.
>
> (Turner 1974: 37–41)

This way of growing by means of conflict and schism Bateson calls "schismogenesis" (1958: 171–97). It is a major agency of human cultural growth.

Turner's dramatic approach is interesting on many levels. The replication of the redressive action phase is, of course, a theatrical performance, a formal restaging of events. The four-phase process as a whole is a drama in the Euro-American tradition – this scheme can be discerned in Greek tragedies, Shakespearean plays, or the dramas of Ibsen or O'Neill. It is less easy to find in Chekhov, Ionesco, or Beckett – but it is there; the way it is distorted gives an insight into dramatic structure. For example, in *Waiting for Godot* there is breach (the separation from Godot) and crises (waiting, the arrival of the Boy at the end of each act to tell Gogo and Didi that Godot will not come). There is a negative but extended redressive action: the doing of various bits of "nothing" – talk that has no effect on the dramatic action, vaudeville routines that fill up time but achieve nothing: these routines emphasize all that the characters can (not) do. But in *Godot* there's no reintegration, nor is there a schism. The play simply stops and if any future is suggested it simply continues the present indefinitely. Significantly the play ends with stage direction "They do not move." Most other dramas, the plays of Shakespeare and Ibsen, for example, end either with a journey – to get crowned, to go to the grave to dispose of corpses, to go to the authorities to relate what's happened – or with some reintegrative gesture such as Tesman's determination, at the close of *Hedda Gabler*, to reconstruct Lövborg's manuscript. Life literally "goes on." This movement which ends so many dramas is akin to the *Ita, missa est* which concludes the Mass: it is a dismissal of the audience, a signal within the drama itself that the theatrical event is coming to a close, that the spectators must prepare to move on. The audience disperses, spreading the news (good or bad) of the show. Even a play as non-conventional and non-religious as *Mother Courage and Her Children* follows this nearly universal pattern. The play climaxes in scene 11 with the murder of Kattrin, Courage's last child. The next and final scene shows Courage, by means of the lullaby and funeral arrangements, taking leave of her daughter. The play's tag – comparable to the final couplets of Shakespearean drama – is Courage's shout as she hitches herself to her wagon, "I've got to get back into business. Hey, take me with you!" The last action of the play is Courage marching off, on the move again. The song is the same as that which started the play, but played at a slower tempo: is this stubborn determination or tragic stupidity? Whatever the meaning of the last sight and sound – and meanings will vary according to different *mises-en-scène* – the action is clear: Courage is on the road, walking and working.

Turner further asserts that the liminal phases of the rites of tribal, agrarian, hunting, and traditional societies are analogous to the artworks and leisure activities of industrial and post-industrial societies.

These Turner (1982, 1985) calls "liminoid," meaning they are like liminal rites but not identical to them. Basically liminal rites are obligatory while liminoid arts and entertainments are voluntary. However, the question remains: is Turner's four-phase pattern of breach, crisis, redressive action, and reintegration (or schism) actually a theatrical universal – or is it an imposition of a western concept? Turner shows how the social process of the Ndembu of Uganda conforms to this dramatistic paradigm. I could show how Aborigine, Papua New Guinea, and Indian theater also conform. But what is the cost of this conformity? As Clifford Geertz notes, "the drama analogy . . . can expose some of the profoundest features of social process, but at the expense of making vividly disparate matters look drably homogeneous" (1980a: 173).

I want to go beyond what may be, after all, just an elaborate tautology. The basic performance structure of gathering/performing/dispersing underlies and literally contains, the dramatic structure:

Breach–Crisis–Redressive action–Reintegration

GATHERING   PERFORMING   DISPERSING

The bottom line is solidarity, not conflict. Conflict is supportable (in the theater, and perhaps in society too) only inside a nest built from the agreement to gather at a specific time and place, to perform – to do something agreed on – and to disperse once the performance is over. The extreme forms of violence that characterize drama can be played out only inside this nest. When people "go to the theater"[9] they are acknowledging that theater takes place at special times in special places. Surrounding a show are special observances, practices, and rituals that lead into the performance and away from it. Not only getting to the theater district, but entering the building itself involves ceremony: ticket-taking, passing through gates, performing rituals, finding a place from which to watch: all this – and the procedures vary from culture to culture, event to event – frames and defines the performance. Ending the show and going away also involves ceremony: applause or some formal way to conclude the performance and wipe away the reality of the show re-establishing in its place the reality of everyday life. The performers even more than the audience prepare and then, when the show is over, undertake "cooling-off" procedures. In many cultures this cooling off involves rituals to retire props or costumes or to assist performers out of trance or other non-ordinary states of being. Too little study has been made of how people – both spectators and performers – approach and leave performances. How do specific audiences get to, and into, the performance space; how do they go from that space? In what ways are gathering/dispersing related to preparation/cooling off?

The "theatrical frame" allows spectators to enjoy deep feelings without feeling compelled either to intervene or to avoid witnessing the actions that arouse those feelings. A spectator better not prevent the murders occurring in Hamlet. Yet these stage murders are not "less real" but "differently real" than what happens in everyday life. Theater, to be effective, must maintain its double or incomplete presence, as a *here-and-now performance of there-and-then events*. The gap between "here and now" and "there and then" allows an audience to contemplate the action, and to entertain alternatives. Theater is the art of enacting only one of a range of virtual alternatives. It is a luxury unaffordable in ordinary life. *Oedipus* would be much different if there were a plague afflicting the town where the drama was being played and the audience believed the plague would end if the murderer of their former mayor – a murderer they knew to be concealed in their midst – was found and brought to judgement here and now.

Some people want performance to achieve this level of actuality. As theater approaches this limit it changes fundamentally: small real actions are substituted for big fictional semblances. A female has her body scarred or a male is circumcised. These "real actions" are themselves emblems or symbols. But when the theatrical frame is imposed strongly it permits the enactment of "aesthetic dramas," shows whose actions, like Oedipus poking out his own eyes, are extreme but recognized by everyone, including the performers, as a "playing with" rather than a "real doing of." This "playing with" is not weak or false, it causes changes to both performers and spectators.

People who want to make "everything real," including killing animals, the "art" of self-mutilation, or "snuff films" where people are actually murdered,[10] are deceiving themselves if they think they are approaching a deeper or more essential reality. All of these actions – like the Roman gladiatorial games or Aztec human sacrifices – are as symbolic and make-believe as anything else on stage. What happens is that living beings are reified into symbolic agents. Such reification is monstrous, I condemn it without exception. It is no justification to point out that modern warfare does the same, killing "things" at a distance. Nor will these blood performances act as a cathartic: violence replicated, or actualized, stimulates more violence. It also deadens people's abilities to intervene outside the theater when they see violence being done.

Turner locates the essential drama in conflict and conflict resolution. I locate it in *transformation* – in how people use theater as a way to experiment with, act out, and ratify change. Transformations in theater occur in three different places, and at three different levels: 1) in the drama, that is, in the story;[11] 2) in the performers whose special task it is to undergo a temporary *rearrangement* of their body/mind, what I call a "transportation" (Schechner 1985: 117–51); 3) in the audience where changes may either be temporary (entertainment) or permanent (ritual). All over the world performances are accompanied by eating and drinking. In New Guinea, Australia, and Africa feasting is at the very center of theater; in modern western theater a show without something to eat or drink at intermission or just before or after the theater is unusual. This action recalls not only the chimpanzee carnivals but the hunting circuit; it suggests that theater stimulates appetites, that it is an oral/visceral art (see Kaplan 1968). And, as Lévi-Strauss has shown, the basic transformation from raw to cooked is a paradigm of culture-making: the making of the natural into the human.[12] At its deepest level this is what theater is "about," the ability to frame and control, to transform the raw into the cooked, to deal with the most problematic (violent, dangerous, sexual, taboo) human interactions.

At all levels theater includes mechanisms for transformation. At the level of the staging there are costumes and masks, exercises and incantations, incense and music, all designed to "make believe" in the literal sense – to help the performer make her/himself into another person or being, existing at another time in another place, and to manifest this presence here and now, in this theater, so that time and place are at least doubled. If the transformation works, individual spectators will experience changes in mood and/or consciousness; these changes are usually temporary but sometimes they can be permanent. In some kinds of performance – rites of passage, for example – a permanent change in the status of the participants is accomplished. But all these changes are in the service of social homeostasis. Changes affecting individuals or groups help maintain the balance of the whole system. For example, it's necessary to change girls into women (in an initiation rite) because somewhere else within the system women are being changed into dead people (in funeral rites); a vacancy exists that must be filled. These vacancies don't occur on a simple one-to-one basis, but according to system-wide probabilities. It is less easy to see how this works in an aesthetic drama, say a performance of Eugene O'Neill's *Long Day's Journey into Night*.

The key difference between social and aesthetic dramas is the performance of the transformations effected. Some kinds of social drama such as feuds, trials, and wars effect permanent change. In other kinds of performance which share qualities both of social and aesthetic drama – rites of passage, political ceremonies – changes in status are permanent (or at least cannot be undone except through more ritual) while changes in the body are either temporary – the wearing of some costume – or not severe: piercing an ear or septum, circumcision. The ordeals which are features of initiation rites, though extreme relative to ordinary experience are temporary. But the idea of these body markings, alterations, and ordeals is to signal and/or mark and enforce a permanent change in the participants. In aesthetic drama no permanent body change is effected. A gap is intentionally opened between what happens to the figures in the story and what happens to the performers playing that story. To play a person in love, or someone who murders or is murdered (common enough in western theater), or to be transformed into a god, or to go into a trance (common enough in non-western theater) involves fundamental, if temporary, transformations of being, not mere appearance.

Aesthetic drama works its transformations on the audience. In aesthetic drama the audience is separated both actually and conceptually from the performers. This separateness of the audience is the hallmark of aesthetic drama. In social drama all present are participants, though some are more decisively involved than others. In aesthetic drama everyone in the theater is a participant in the *performance* while only those playing roles in the drama are participants in the *drama* nested within the performance (see chapter 3). The performance as distinct from the drama is social, and it is at the level of performance that aesthetic and social drama converge. The function of aesthetic drama is *to do for the consciousness of the audience what social drama does for its participants*: providing a place for, and means of, transformation. Rituals carry participants across limens, transforming them into different persons. For example a young man is a "bachelor" and through the ceremony of marriage he becomes a "husband." His status during that ceremony, but only then, is that of "groom." Groom is the liminal role he plays while transforming from bachelor into husband. Aesthetic drama compels a transformation of the spectators' view of the world by rubbing their senses against enactments of extreme events, much more extreme than they would usually witness. The nesting pattern makes it possible for the spectator to reflect on these events rather than flee from them or intervene in them. That reflection is the liminal time during which the transformation of consciousness takes place.

The situation for the actor in aesthetic drama is complicated because the drama is repeated many times and each time the actor is supposed to start from nearly the same place. In other words, in western theater at least, although spectators come and go, and they are encouraged to change, techniques have been developed to prepare actors for, and bring them down from, the experience of playing relatively unchanged – no more changed than any ordinary career changes a person. Metaphorically speaking, the actor is a circular printing press who, in rolling over makes an impression on her audience; but she is not ready to roll over again until she is back in her original position. For each performance there is a new audience on whom an impression is to be made. The actor makes a journey that ends where it began, while the audience is "moved" to a new place. In aesthetic drama techniques have been developed to transform the actor into the role and other techniques are used to bring her back to her ordinary self. In some ritual theater the officiators are very like actors in aesthetic drama: the shaman working a cure must effect change in the patient, and often does this by transforming into another being; but at the end of the performance the shaman must return to her/his ordinary existence. It is the ability to "get into" and "get back from" that makes the shaman a continually useful person, not a person to be used once only. Thus there are at least three categories of performance: 1) aesthetic, where the audience changes consciousness while the performer "rolls over"; 2) ritual, where the subject of the ceremony is transformed while the officiating performer "rolls over"; 3) social drama, where all involved change (see Schechner 1985: 117–50).

The ambiguity of theater since 1960 regarding whether or not an event is "really happening" is an outcome of the blurring of the boundaries between the categories of performance. Television has made it possible to theatricalize experience by editing even the most intimate or horrendous events into "news" so that people feel nothing strange about a complementary actualization of art (see Schechner 1985: 295–324). The boundaries between "art" and "life" are blurry and permeable. When people watch extreme events knowing these are 1) actually happening and 2) edited to make the events both more dramatic and more palatable, fitting them into a "showtime" format, but also knowing 3) that as observers they are stripped of all possibility of intervention – that is, they are turned into an audience in the formal sense – the reaction of anger quickly dissolves into paralysis and despair, or indifference. Maybe appetites are aroused, but these can't be satisfied except by going on the shopping sprees the commercials insist are necessary for happiness. Emotional feedback is not possible while watching TV. TV is not a two-way communications system as live theater is. Some people react by making and/or enjoying art that's more "real," introducing into aesthetics the interventions and feedback eliminated from ordinary life.

Thus it is no longer strange in theater or performance art to involve the audience directly in the story, to stage actual encounters among people, and to use theatrical events as the first step in a process of religious retreats and meetings (as Grotowski did). These are attempts to regain some balance between information – which today overwhelms people – and action, which seems more and more difficult to effect. Terrorism, as opposed to ordinary street violence, is a way of getting the attention of society, of making a show; it is a symptom of the basic dysfunction of the communication–feedback–consequent action process. The actualization of art – the existence of theater combining the social with the aesthetic – is traditional in many parts of the world. Thus avant-garde and political theater find already prepared paths.

I have tried in my work with The Performance Group and since, and in my teaching, to place the actuality of performances in the immediate theatrical event I am staging. I emphasize the gathering and dispersing aspects of performance. Upon entering the theater spectators are greeted, either by me or by the actors. Spectators see the performance being prepared – actors getting into costume, musicians tuning up, technical equipment checked, etc. Intermissions, and less formal breaks in the narration such as scene shifts, are underlined. In *Mother Courage* a full meal was served during intermission – during this break in the narration the performance was carried on by other means, by mingling performers and audience, by encouraging spectators to use parts of the space otherwise and at other times reserved for the performers (see chapter 4). I try to establish non-story-telling time as an integral part of the whole performance scheme, while clearly separating this time from the drama. When the drama is over I speak to spectators as they are leaving. I direct many of them to where the performers are so that the experience ends not with a dramatic moment, or even the curtain call, but with discussions, greetings, and leave-takings.

The history of intermissions in the western theater is an interesting example of the importance of the underlying social event as a nest for the theatrical event. When performances were staged outdoors (Greek, medieval, Elizabethan) the spectators could see each other in daylight. The court performances of masques and dramas in the Renaissance were so lit that spectators could see each other as well as the actors. This kind of general illumination, and a mixing of focus including spectators as well as actors, continued throughout the seventeenth and eighteenth centuries. But as scene changes began to necessitate complicated machinery which producers wanted to mask from the audience, the front curtain was introduced and step by step the forestage was eliminated. Also changes in lighting, especially the introduction first of gas and then electricity in the nineteenth century, widened the gap between stage and house until the stage was brightly lit and the house dark. In this situation naturalism arose, with its slice-of-life and peep-ing-Tom staging. Along with these conventions came the intermission: a formal period when the house was illuminated and the spectators, either remaining in the house or trouping to lounges and restaurants, had the opportunity to see and mingle with each other. The intermis-sion served a purpose, not necessary either in outdoor or fully lit theaters: that of giving the spectators a chance to see themselves. Intermission confirms the existence of the "gathering," a group assembled specifically to attend this particular theatrical event. Why don't movies have intermissions? Because movies lack a group of live entertainers on stage, they are barely social at all. Sporting events are social, and feature intermissions (halftime, seventh-inning stretch, a card of bouts or races). Performances which keep the audience in the dark with no intermission generate anxiety and contradict the social impulses of theater. I do not condemn such performances, but note that they run against the grain of the western tradition; in the deepest sense they are unconventional.

My directing is intended to show the audience that "a story is being played for you, all around you, needing your active support." These techniques emphasize the "performance nest" inside which the drama happens. Performers in The Performance Group were trained to display their double identities: as themselves and as the characters they were playing. By keeping these both out front spectators see performers not only acting but *choosing to act*. Even "being in character" is seen as a choice not an inevitability. Thus the spectator, too, is encouraged to choose how to receive each action. There is no fixed seating, several actions go on simultaneously – spectators can shift focus from one aspect of the performance to another. By no means are all these aspects concerned with the drama: a spectator can focus on a performer chan-ging costume (that is, becoming another character), the technical crew, other spectators, etc. Instead of working for a unanimity of reaction, as in orthodox theater, I strive for a diversity of opportunities. These encourage spectators to react intellectually and ideologically as well as emotionally. What is "really happening" is a gathering of spectators of different ages, sexes, classes, and ideologies watching a group of per-formers tell a story by theatrical means. Within this context The Per-formance Group explored the most radical theatrical means we could handle: audience participation, environmental staging, multi-focus, etc. These were combined with the traditional theatrical means of our culture: narration and characterization.

WHAT PERFORMERS DO: THE ECSTASY/TRANCE WHEEL

Looking at performing worldwide, two processes are identifiable. A performer is either "subtracted," achieving transparency, eliminating "from the creative process the resistance and obstacles caused by one's own organism" (Grotowski 1968a: 178); or s/he is "added to," becoming more or other than s/he is when not performing. S/he is "doubled," to use Artaud's word. The first technique, that of the shaman, is ecstasy; the second, that of the Balinese dancer, is trance. In the west we have terms for these two kinds of acting: the actor in ecstasy is Ryszard Cieslak in *The Constant Prince*, Grotowski's "holy actor"; the actor in trance possessed by another, is Konstantin Stanislavsky as Vershinin, the "character actor."

To be in trance is not to be out of control or unconscious. The Balinese say that if a trance dancer hurts himself the trance was not genuine. In some kinds of trance the possessed and the possessor are both visible. Jane Belo describes a Balinese horse dance where

> the player would start out riding the hobbyhorse, being, so to speak, the horseman. But in his trance activity he would soon become identified with the horse – he would prance, gallop about, stamp and kick as a horse – or perhaps it would be fairer to say that he would be the horse and rider in one. For though he would sit on the hobbyhorse, his legs had to serve from the beginning as the legs of the beast.
>
> (Belo 1960: 213)

This is the centaur; and it is an example of the performer's double identity. When, in western theater, we speak of an actor "portraying a role," using a metaphor from painting where the artist studies a subject and produces an image of that subject, we slide away from the main fact of theatrical performance: that the "portrayal" is a transformation of the performer's body/mind – the "canvas" or "material" is the performer. Interviewing Balinese performers of *sanghyangs*, village trance performances, Goesti Made Soemeng (GM), a Balinese member of Belo's research team, probed the way trance possession happens:

GM: What is your feeling when you are first smoked?[13]

Darja: Somehow or other suddenly I lose consciousness. The people singing I hear. If people call out, calling me "Tjittah!" [a pig call] like that, I hear it too. If people talk of other things, I don't hear it.

GM: When you are a sanghyang pig, and people insult you, do you hear it?

Darja: I hear it. If anyone insults me I am furious.

GM: When you finish playing, how do you feel, tired or not?

Darja: When it's just over, I don't feel tired yet. But the next day or the day after that, my body is sick . . .

GM: When you become a sanghyang snake, what is the feeling like, and where do you feel your body to be?

Darma: When I'm a sanghyang snake, suddenly my thoughts are delicious. Thus, my feelings being delicious suddenly I see something like forest, woods, with many many trees. When my body is like that, as a snake, my feeling is of going through the woods, and I am pleased . . .

GM: And if you're a sanghyang puppy, what does your body feel like? Where do you feel yourself to be?

Darja: I just feel like a puppy. I feel happy to run along the ground. I am very pleased, just like a puppy running on the ground. As long as I can run on the ground, I'm happy.

GM: And if you're a sanghyang potato, where do you feel yourself to be, and like what?

Darma: I feel I am in the garden, like a potato planted in the garden.

GM: And if you're a sanghyang broom, what's it like, and where do you feel?

Darma: Like sweeping filth in the middle of the ground. Like sweeping filth in the street, in the village. I feel I am being carried off by the broom, led on to sweep.

(Belo 1960: 222)

Belo notes that "a considerable crowd had to be present to insure that the trancer did not get out of hand." She tells of the time when a man playing a pig escaped from the courtyard. He was not caught until the next morning. "He had by that time ravaged the gardens, trampled and eaten the plants, which was not good for the village. He had also, being a pig, eaten large quantities of excreta he had found in the roadways, which was not good for him" (Belo 1960: 202).

Belo finds these accounts "surprisingly satisfactory," and I do too. They show that trance performing is a kind of character acting: being possessed by another = becoming another. Eliade says that shamans, too, are often possessed by animals.

> During seances among the Yakut, the Yukagir, the Chukchee, the Goldi, the Eskimo and others, wild animal cries and bird calls are heard. Castagne describes the Kirgiz-Tartar *baqca* running around the tent, springing, roaring, leaping; he "barks like a dog, sniffs at the audience, lows like an ox, bellows, cries, bleats like a lamb, grunts like a pig, whinnies, coos, imitating with remarkable accuracy the cries of animals, the songs of birds, the sound of their flight and so on, all of which greatly impresses his audience." The "descent of the spirits" often takes place in this fashion.
>
> (Eliade 1970: 97)[14]

And, as I noted in chapter 4, this kind of performing associated with trickster figures and hunters arose very early in human history (see La Barre 1972: 195–6).

Balinese trance, shamanic possession, and the trickster are not examples of acting from the Stanislavsky tradition. But nor are they essentially different. Stanislavsky developed exercises – sense memory, emotional recall, playing the through-line of action, etc. – so that actors could "get inside of" and act "as if" they were other people. Stanislavsky's approach is humanist and psychological, but still a version of the ancient technique of performing by becoming or being possessed by another.

Belo (1960: 223) says that the pleasure of the "trance experience is connected with the surrendering of the self-impulse. . . . Being a pig, a toad, a snake, or a creepy spirit are all enactments of the feeling of lowness in a very literal, childish and direct manner." She thinks that "urge to be low" is one of the foundations of trance.[15] To be low is to take the physical perspective of a child. To be filthy – playing with excrement and mud – is a regression to infantile behavior. It opens a channel to farce – and farce is probably more ancient than tragedy.[16] Finally, to be low is to escape from rigid mores – being low is a way to be free.

But these phenomena are only half of the dialectic of performing. The other half is ecstasy: a soaring away from the body, an emptying of the body. Eliade:

> The shamanic costume tends to give the shaman a new, magical body in animal form. The three chief types are that of the bird, the reindeer (stag) and the bear – but especially the bird. ... Feathers are mentioned more or less everywhere in the descriptions of shamanic costumes. More significantly, the very structure of the costumes seeks to imitate as faithfully as possible the shape of a bird. ... Siberian, Eskimo and North American shamans fly. All over the world the same magical power is credited to sorcerers and medicine men. ... An adequate analysis of the symbolism of magical flight would lead us too far. We will simply observe that two important mythical motifs have contributed to give it its present structure: the mythical image of the soul in the form of a bird and the idea of birds as psychopomps.
>
> (Eliade 1970: 156, 477–9)

Aborigine "Dreamtime" songs and dances are examples of this kind of performing. A person, often in sleep but sometimes wide-awake, is transported to the original "timeless mythical past during which totemic beings traveled from place to place across the desert performing creative acts" (Gould 1969: 105). Some of these beings are natural species such as kangaroo and emu, some are special beings like Wati Jutjars (the Two Men) and Wanampi (the Water Snake). "Although they lived in the past, the dreamtime beings are still thought of as being alive and exerting influence over present-day people" (Gould 1969: 106). Performances are passed on down the generations. When new material is added it is learned by "dreaming": a man participates with the mythical beings in their ceremonies, then he teaches his comrades what he has learned. Aborigine performances are staged with extreme care, especially regarding scenography, body decorations, and the execution of song and dance routines. This care is not a matter of beauty in our sense – smoothness, efficiency – but of making sure that all the prescribed steps are taken in proper order. Propriety is more important than artistry in the Euro-American sense. If the material is new every care is taken that it is learned exactly and passed on intact.

During his poor theater phase (1959–68) Grotowski followed a procedure close to that of the Aborigines. But instead of seeking material in the Dreamtime (archeology, history), Grotowski's performers sought it in their own experiences.

> In our opinion, the conditions essential to the art of acting are the following, and should be made the object of a methodical investigation:
>
> (a) To stimulate a process of self-revelation, going back as far as the subconscious, yet canalizing this stimulus in order to obtain the required reaction.
>
> (b) To be able to articulate this process, discipline it, and convert it into signs. In concrete terms, this means to construct a score whose notes are tiny elements of contact, reactions to the stimuli of the outside world: what we call "give and take."
>
> (c) To eliminate from the creative process the resistances and obstacles caused by one's own organism, both physical and psychical (the two forming a whole).
>
> (Grotowski 1968a: 128)

Using this method Grotowski composed "gesticulatory ideograms" comparable to the signs of medieval European theater, Peking Opera, ballet, and other highly codified forms. But Grotowski's ideograms were "immediate and spontaneous . . . a living from possessing its own logic" (1968a: 142). This was because his actors were transparent: they were able to let impulses pass through them so that their gestures were at one and the same time intimate and impersonal. Grotowski, his scenographers, and the performers of Dr Faustus, Akropolis, The Constant Prince, and Apocalypsis cum Figuris (first version) achieved a total iconography of body, voice, group composition, and scenic architecture. The totality was so complete that western audiences felt uncomfortable: even Oriental performances as tightly structured as noh or kathakali allow open spaces for audience inattention. The productions

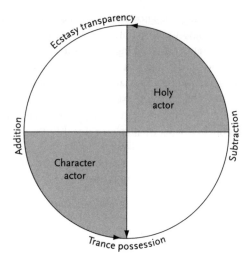

Figure 5.6
Note
The ecstatic flight of the shaman leaves the body empty and transparent: absolutely vulnerable. Cieslak travels by means of *subtraction* toward ecstasy when he plays the Prince in *The Constant Prince*. The trance dancers of Bali are possessed or "taken over" by whomever or whatever possesses them. Olivier travels by means of *addition* toward possession; he systematically converts the "as if" of his Hamlet into a "becoming of" Hamlet. Those techniques of performer training which begin with a movement toward ecstasy – psychophysical exercises, yoga, etc. – help the performer "follow impulses," that is, yield and become transparent. In this state a performer may suddenly "drop into" his role because the vulnerability of ecstasy can be suddenly transformed into the totality of trance possession.

of the Polish Laboratory Theater were totally without "noise." Such clarity of signal evoked anxiety as well as pleasure.

No performing is "pure" ecstasy or trance. Always there is a shifting, dialectical tension between the two (figure 5.6).

REHEARSAL PROCEDURES

Every aspect of gathering/performing/dispersing needs careful examination both from the point of view of the performers and that of the spectators. In expanding our knowledge beyond drama to performing and beyond performing to the whole performance process much will be learned not only about art-making (for theater, as Alexander Alland pointed out to me, is the only art where the creative process is by necessity visible) but also about social life because theater is both intentionally and non-consciously a paradigm of culture and culture-making. In this concluding section I will look briefly at a decisive aspect of the large problem: what rehearsal is. I think I will be able to show that *the essential ritual action of theater takes place during rehearsals.*

At the 1957 Macy Foundation Conference on Group Processes Ray Birdwhistell explained the following model:

> We have been running trajectories on dancing and other acts described as graceful behavior.

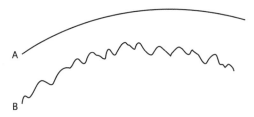

> Note B and A are trajectories of an arm or leg or body. A is a smooth curve; B is the zigzag line. The sizes of these zigzags are unimportant. It is the shape of the movement with which I am concerned. A and B express the same trajectory. However, ultimately trajectory A shows minimal variation or adjustment within the scope of the trajectory. In A there is a minimum of messages being reacted to in process. This is "grace." In B multiple messages are being introduced into the system and there is the zigazg. The things we call graceful are always multi-message acts in which the secondary messages are minimized, and there the role of the whole is maximized.
>
> (Birdwhistell, in Lorenz 1959: 101–2)

Lorenz pointed out that:

> with the elimination of the noise in the movement, when the movement becomes graceful, it becomes more unambiguous as a

> signal. . . . The more pregnant and simple the movement is, the easier
> it is for it to be taken up unambiguously by the receptor. Therefore,
> there is a strong selection pressure working in the direction of making
> all signal movements, these releasing movements [Innate Release
> Mechanisms or learned gestalts], more and more graceful, and that is
> also what reminds us [in animal behavior] of a dance.
>
> (Lorenz 1959: 202–3)

Grace = simplification = increasing the signal efficiency of a movement = a dance.

But some artworks, even performances, are notoriously complex, ambivalent, and "inefficient." Great masterpieces are not necessarily minimalist. The *Ramayana*, the Bible, the *Odyssey*, the plays of Shakespeare, the spectacles of Robert Wilson, the paintings of Brueghel, the sculptings at Konarak, etc. – are these less "graceful" (that is, less artistic) than the plays of Beckett, the paintings of Mondrian, or *haiku* poetry? Clearly a single, normative standard for "evaluating art" abolishes various cultural, historical, or evolutionary perspectives. The difficulty is solved by relocating the question of simplification (grace) from a comparison of finished works in their exhibition phase to works in the process of being made: the selection-of-what's-done-as-against-all-other-possibilities phase. It is not a matter of comparing one work to other works, or to the world. Important and revealing as such comparisons are they yield nothing concerning the issue Birdwhistell raises. One must fold each work back in on itself, comparing its completed state to the process of inventing it, to its own internal procedures during that time when it was not yet ready for showing. Although all arts have this phase, only performance requires it to be public, that is, acted out among the performers as rehearsal. Comparing a work to its own process of creation applies not only to single-authored works but to multi-authored works such as the Homeric epics, the Bible, medieval cathedrals, and all other projects that extend beyond a single person's attention or life-span. In these cases the process of making the work has an extra step, that of arriving at a "finished form" that cannot be known with certainty beforehand. This solidification may take many generations and be ratified historically in structures which, under different circumstances, may have turned out differently. For example, Notre Dame in Paris has only one "finished" tower; but how "wrong" it would be to finish the "incomplete" structure. As an ideal cathedral the building lacks a tower; as Notre Dame it is complete only as it now stands. In all cases the process of solidification, completion, and historical ratification is a process of rehearsal: how a work is reworked until it crosses a threshold of "acceptability" after which it can be "shown."

The theater is unique in that all its works, even the most traditional, are produced by means of the rehearsal process. That is, all theatrical works change over time as they are adjusted to immediate circumstances. Sometimes these changes are tectonically slow when a dogma is fixed as, say, the Roman Catholic Mass is. But even the Mass has been suddenly readjusted, most recently by Vatican Council II. And, on the local level, the Mass is always accommodating the given circumstances of its various celebrations. In the aesthetic genres such as modern Euro-American theater delight is taken in reinterpreting the classics; but there are also unspoken limits – if a theater group goes beyond these it is not praised for being inventive but attacked for "violating" the material. Such was the reaction of some critics and spectators to The Performance Group's productions of *Dionysus in 69* (Euripides' *The Bacchae*) and *Makbeth* (Shakespeare's *Macbeth*). But even when doing a brand new play tensions arise between the author's intentions and what finally happens on the stage. This happened in TPG's production of Sam Shepard's *The Tooth of Crime* (see chapter 3). Sometimes, as in the famous disputes between Anton Chekhov and Stanislavsky, Tennessee Williams and Elia Kazan, these tensions reach a breaking point.

But what exactly is the "rehearsal process"? At the Macy Conference W. Gray Walter commented on Birdwhistell's model:

> Grace may be the result of efficiency in a goal-directed movement. In the case of an artificial animal or guided weapon, the early guided weapons and some modern ones, when they are searching and are not goal-directed, have a trajectory with a messy curve like B [203]. They perform a hunting movement, which looks quite random and is certainly not very graceful. It is jerky and disjointed, incoherent, often a series of cycloid loops. But the moment the goal or target is perceived,

the trajectory becomes a graceful parabola or hyperbola. So, the appearance of a goal will transform a graceless, and exploratory mode of behavior (which may have a high information potential in it, in the sense that it is looking in many directions) into one which has only one bit of information, if the target is there, but looks smooth and pretty.

(Walter, in Lorenz 1959: 202)

Early rehearsals, or workshops, are jerky and disjointed, often incoherent. The work is indeed a hunt, full of actions with "high information potential," but very low goal-orientation. Even in working on texted material this kind of "looking around" marks early rehearsals: actors try a variety of interpretations, designers bring in many sketches and models most of which are rejected, the director doesn't really know what s/he wants. And especially if the project is to develop its own text and actions the basic question of the early work is an anxiety-laden, "What are we doing?" If, by a certain time, a target is not visible (not only a production date but a vision of what is to be produced), the project falters, then fails. A director may maintain confidence by imposing order in the guise of set exercises; s/he may do this too soon and cut down the chances of discovering new actions. A balance is needed. Comparable processes occur in traditional societies. John Emigh writes about a rehearsal of a ceremony in a village on the Sepik River, Papua New Guinea:

As the rehearsal proceeded an old man would stop the singing from time to time to make suggestions on style or phrasing or, just as often, just as much a part of the event being rehearsed, he would comment on the meaning of the song words, on the details of the story. The rehearsal was at once remarkably informal and absolutely effective. A middle-aged woman with an extraordinary, searing voice seemed to be in control of the singing. She would start and stop at whim, repeating phrases, checking points with the old man, pausing to hear his explanation. . . . As the rehearsal proceeded, men and women would occasionally drift by. The assembled singers and drum beaters and witnesses practiced the movements of the dance to accompany the mother's lament.[17]

We are used to rehearsals for weddings, funerals, and other religious and civic ceremonies. In every case the rehearsal is a way of selecting from the possible actions those to be performed, of simplifying these, making them as clear as possible in regard both to the matrix from which they have been taken and the audience with which they are meant to communicate. Along with this primary task the secondary work of rehearsal is to have each performer perform her/his part with maximum clarity. Farce is interesting in this regard because it turns one kind of clarity on its head. Charlie Chaplin staggering drunkenly across the street is acting "messy" but with consummate skill – just as a clown performs a graceless pratfall gracefully. The signal sent reads "graceless" but this signal is sent clearly – i.e. gracefully. Audiences admire the ease with which great farceurs play at being clumsy. The same may be said about dissimulation of all kinds so popular in theater: lies, disguises, double plots, ironies. In every case the performer's problem is to be clear about the lie, to be convincing in both aspects of the situation so that an audience can see around the action and perceive it and its opposite, text and metatext, simultaneously.

Comparable to rehearsal, but not exactly identical to it, is preparation. The Aborigines spend many hours preparing for a ten-minute dance. They carefully lay out all the implements of the dance, they paint their bodies, they prepare the dancing area. Before each performance members of The Performance Group took two hours or more warming up their voices, doing psychophysical exercises, dance steps and yoga, reviewing difficult bits from the show, etc. The Moscow Art Theater was famous for the preparation period each actor practiced immediately before going onto the stage. Every performer I know goes through a routine before performing. These preparations literally "compose" the person and the group: they are a kinesic recapitulation of the rehearsal process allowing for a settling into the special tasks at hand, a concentration that shrinks the world to the dimensions of the theater. These preparations are the ritual frame surrounding, setting off, and protecting the time/space of the theater.

Both rehearsal and preparation employ the same means: repetition, simplification, exaggeration, rhythmic action, the transformation of "natural sequences" of behavior into "composed sequences." These means comprise the ritual process as understood by ethologists. Thus it is in rehearsals/preparations that I detect the fundamental ritual of theater.

I find nothing disturbing about relating the finest achievements of human art – indeed, the very process of making art: the ritual actions of rehearsal and preparation – to animal behavior because I detect no break between animal and human behavior. And especially in the realm of artistic-ritual behavior I find homologies, continuities, and analogies. Activities thicken – get more complicated, dense, symbolic, contradictory, and multivocal – along a continuum of expanding consciousness. The human achievement – shared by a few primates and aquatic mammals but not elaborated by them – is the ability to make decisions based on virtual as well as actual alternatives. These virtual alternatives take on a life of their own. Theater is the art of actualizing them, and rehearsal is the means of developing their individual shapes and rhythms. By turning possibilities into action, into performances, whole worlds otherwise not lived are born. Theater doesn't arrive suddenly and stay fixed either in its cultural or individual manifestations. It is insinuated along a web of associations spun from play, games, hunting, slaughter and distribution of meat, ceremonial centers, trials, rites of passage, and story-telling. Rehearsals and recollections – preplay and afterplay – converge in the theatrical event.

NOTES

1   See Marshack (1972), Giedion (1962–4), and La Barre (1972).

2   Ucko and Rosenfeld (1967: 229) summarize thought on the subjet: "The relative frequencies of animals, the absence of representations of vegetation, and also the evidence . . . which shows that many representations were intended to be viewed, suggest that 'theater' may well be behind some of the parietal representations." Although there are many disputes in the field of cave art, all authorities believe that performances of some kind (rites, theater, dance, music) took place in the caves. The antiquity, one can almost say the primacy, of performance is clear. For an extended investigation of these ideas, see Pfeiffer (1982).

3   See Brecht's "The Street Scene" in Brecht (1964: 121–9).

4   In England, the medieval cycle plays were staged on wagons which moved from site to site. The wagons were used as stages, backdrops, and dressing-rooms. The audience gathered around as the play moved from the wagons to the street, employing both the raised space of the wagons and the flat space of the

street. Spectators stood in the street or looked from rooftops and windows of buildings surrounding the narrow roadways. Playing began at dawn and continued throughout the day. There must have been much coming and going among the spectators. This mixing of the social, the religious, and the aesthetic marks such contemporary performances as the ramlilas of north India (see Schechner 1985: 151–213).

5 I use the word "natural" to mean the kind of theater that happens in everyday life. There is no need to stage or (re)create it. When an accident happens or a dispute is played out in public, people will watch. The media, if alerted, will replay such "newsworthy" events. When something sumptuous passes by, people turn to watch, whether it be an ocean liner steaming down river or a head of state motorcading up an avenue.

6 For extended discussions of a number of processional performances in different cultures, see *TDR, The Drama Review* 29 (3) (1985), a special issue edited by Barbara Kirshenblatt-Gimblett and Brooks McNamara.

7 Box seats developed from earlier practices where VIPs sat onstage. When this was recognized as a disruption the theater could no longer tolerate, boxes came into fashion. It is interesting how in environmental theater the presence of everyone, or anyone, on stage – or in the same area where the players play – is a democratization of the presence on stage of the VIPs.

8 See also E. T. Kirby (1972: 5–21).

9 By "going to the theater" I mean something more than the Euro-American practice. I mean whatever arrangements are made so that a performance can occur: for example, adhering to a ritual calendar; preparing a special place or making an ordinary place such as a market square special; rehearsing; making sure that the necessary spectators are in attendance.

10 The ultimate theater of violence (along with documentary movies of war, torture, and mayhem) are pornographic "snuff films." In these, someone is hired to make a porn movie but at the moment of climax the person is killed. The camera records the shock and agony of the victim and the actions of the murderer(s). The film is then exhibited for high admissions at private parties. Sometimes, it's said, the victim agrees for a handsome price to be killed. The comparison of snuff porn to Roman gladiatorial games is obvious, as is the decadence of both kinds of entertainment. As for the cathartic effect of viewing violent actions, studies reported by Eibl-Eibesfeldt (1970: 329, 331–2) indicate that the cathartic effects, if any, are short-lived: "In the long run, the possibility of discharging aggressive impulses constitutes a kind of training for aggression. The animal becomes more aggressive."

11 Drama is about the changes that happen to the characters. Take any drama and compare who, where, and what each character is at the beginning to what s/he is like at the end: the resultant map of the changes is a summary of the drama's action.

12 Lévi-Strauss's (1969b) seminal and complicated work elaborates the "two contrasts – nature/culture, raw/cooked" (p. 338). In terms of theater, the "cooked

action" is not an imitation of problematic behavior. It is new behavior analogic-ally or metaphorically related to its "raw" precursor. Rites of passage "cook" kinds of behavior that need socialization as well as "work on" individuals who need to be transported from one status to another. See Schechner (1985: 35–116, 261–94).

13   Often Balinese trance dancers are "smoked" by inhaling fumes of burning incense. As far as I can determine, the smoke itself is not psychoactive. It does not "cause" the trance, but inhaling it is a decisive moment in the process of achieving trance. When only part of the body is to go into trance – for example, the hand which is to become the broom – only that part is smoked. This smoking is not confined to Bali. I saw it in Sri Lanka too.

14   Eliade says of the shaman's transformation: "It is the shaman who *turns himself* into an animal just as he achieves a similar result by putting on an animal mask" (1970: 93).

15   Belo (1960: 223):

> The feeling of lowness, which Darma described as delightful, fits in with the whole constellation of ideas about being mounted, being sat on, and so forth, wherein the pleasurable quality of the trance experience is con-nected with the surrendering of the self-impulses. This is one aspect of the trance state which seems to have reverberations in the trance vocabulary in whatever country these phenomena appear – and the aspect which is perhaps the hardest for non-trancers to grasp.

This "surrendering of the self-impulses" is a giving over to a specific Other: an animal, spirit, person, god, etc. In ecstasy, it is a pure giving up to noneness/oneness of being, as in Zen meditation.

16   Although I don't have space to expound on it here, the brevity characteristic of farce, as well as its swift, violent action and surprising reversals, offer internal evidence for the antiquity of farce. Farce's universality also indicates its antiquity. Every culture has farce, while only relatively few have tragedy in the sense of the Greeks or the Japanese.

17   From a letter John Emigh distributed to several of his colleagues. Emigh observed the rehearsals in 1974. For a further discussion of this particular rehearsal, see Schechner (1985: 52–4).

6

SELECTIVE INATTENTION

RELATIONSHIP BETWEEN SOCIAL AND AESTHETIC DRAMA

Victor Turner (1974) locates four actions as the nubs of social drama: 1) breach, 2) crisis, 3) redressive action, and 4) reintegration. A breach is a situation that schisms a social unit – family, work group, village, community, nation, etc. A crisis is a precipitating event that can't be overlooked, that must be dealt with. Redressive action is what's done to overcome the crisis – the crisis itself having arisen out of the breach. Reintegration is the elimination of the original breach that mothered the crisis. Reintegration comes in two ways, either by healing the breach or by schismogenesis (see Bateson 1958).

Apply Turner's model to an actual social situation, say the November, 1975 dismissal of cabinet members by President Gerald Ford. The breach is the fact that Ford as an appointed rather than elected president carried in his cabinet a number of Nixon people. Thus Ford was forced to defend policies he might dislike as well as bear the stigma of a disgraced administration. At the same time Ford wished to seek the presidency on his own. The crisis came from a severe embarrassment to the "security community" through revelations of planned assassinations of foreign heads of state and phone-tapping of Americans as part of a widespread secret-police apparatus whose operations pinnacled under Nixon. Other items added to the crisis: the disagreement between Ford and Vice President Nelson Rockefeller over aid to New York City, the growing feeling nationally that Ford was stupid and indecisive; and, perhaps (though there is no direct evidence), Ford's feeling that he was not the master of his own administration. The redressive action, as described in the *New York Times* of Monday, November 3, 1975 was typically dramatic:

> President Ford has dismissed Secretary of Defense James R. Schlesinger and William E. Colby, Director of Central Intelligence, in a major shuffling of his top national security posts. Administration officials said that the President had also asked Secretary of State Henry A. Kissinger to relinquish his post as national security adviser in the White House, but to stay on as head of the State Department. White House officials said that Mr. Schlesinger would probably be replaced by the White House chief of staff, Donald H. Rumsfeld, and that Mr. Colby's likely successor would be George Bush, the present head of the American liaison office in China.

This redressive action did not end the crisis, but led to further surprising developments – as is often the case ("one thing leads to another"). Rockefeller told Ford that he would not in any case be a candidate for the vice presidency in 1976. And, in the Washington scheme of things, this apparent resignation by the Vice President was probably a firing by the President – the reversal of roles being a common face-saving device in American politics. Or it might have meant that Rockefeller would actively campaign against Ford for the Republican nomination. Finally, the Secretary of Commerce resigned and was replaced by the one person in the Nixon administration whose reputation was not only untarnished but enhanced: Elliott Richardson, the man who – when his Watergate prosecutor, Archibald Cox, was fired – resigned as Attorney General. The reintegration phase of this social drama took some time, as Ford established "his own" government in preparation for the 1976 elections.

The characteristic structure of this Turnerian four-phase operation is that the breach exists for a long time, the critical corrective action is sudden, even unpredictable because a precipitating event is often not something big in itself but a "straw that breaks the camel's back." Once the action is over analysts can look back and "see what happened" detecting an orderly development of events that follow Turner's scheme. The scheme looks like figure 6.1. The visible drama is in the crisis and redressive action. With hindsight, from beyond reintegration, the whole sequence can be easily reconstructed. The elegance of the whole pattern as reconstructed is where social drama and aesthetic drama coincide.

Apply Turner's model to an aesthetic drama, say Shakespeare's *Romeo and Juliet*. The breach is the long-standing feud between Montagues and Capulets. Thus wherever and whenever members of the two families meet a fight is likely to erupt. The streets of Verona are dangerous. The precipitating event is Romeo's sighting of Juliet and their love at first sight. Had Romeo just crashed the Capulets' party and not fallen in love with Juliet, or had Juliet not responded to Romeo, there'd be no drama. Romeo recognizes the crisis at once – having kissed her, then finding out who she is, he exclaims: "Is she a Capulet?/O dear account! my life is my foe's debt" (I. v. 22–3). Juliet is equally aware of the crisis: "My only love sprung from my only hate!" (I. v. 142).

Most of the rest of the play is taken up by the burgeoning crisis met by increasingly dangerous redressive actions. The crisis is the hot love affair compounded by Romeo's killing of Tybalt. Shakespeare brilliantly counterpoints each gesture of affection with a corresponding increase in the danger of discovery and the catastrophe that threatens. The redressive action is the answer to the question: how are they to find each other safely in a city and from families where they must only hate each other? Friar Laurence's plan to get them out of Verona is a classic strategy of schismogenesis: the founding of a new social unit in a new place in order to avoid or end conflict. Laurence knows that when Juliet

Figure 6.1

is presumed dead her suit with Paris is ended; after she is buried with the other Capulets, Romeo can find her in the tomb and carry her to Mantua where there is nothing to keep a Montague from marrying a Capulet. But this happy ending is not to be. Throughout the redressive-action phase the tension heightens between the lovers' passion for each other and their parents' hatred. The action of the play is strung like wires on a suspension bridge between these two opposite but identical poles: love and hate. What connects these poles is the power of passion flowing with equal force into both love and hate. Everyone in the play must take sides: Laurence with the lovers, the Nurse with the parents. The redressive action ends in tragedy because of a break in communication. Theatrically three deaths occur, not two: Juliet's (she isn't really dead but Romeo thinks so); Romeo's (he kills himself – sign of passion – instead of waiting a few minutes until Juliet wakes up); Juliet's (she acts as Romeo did, but in her case there is genuine cause). At this point the tragedy teeters on the edge of farce – think what Charles Ludlam could do with the death scene in the tomb.

As in all tragedy (and in some farce, the genre closest to tragedy) redressive action doesn't make life comfortable for the heroes: they end up dead, maimed, and/or exiled, separated from the community, but also sacrificed on behalf of the community. This sacrifice constitutes the occasion of the reintegration, forcing those blocking it to let it happen or, as in *Hamlet* and *Oedipus*, removing through death or exile any who would stand in reintegration's way. Discovering their beloved children dead Montague and Capulet agree to end their feud, and Verona is made whole again: "A glooming peace this morning with it brings" (V. iii. 305). It is a depressing drama indeed that does nothing to knit up the unraveled social order; that kind of drama we know from Samuel Beckett and other writers of the absurd, including Euripides. Beckett's *Waiting for Godot* is all redressive action, the character have even forgotten the breach and crisis.

What comparisons can I make between Ford's cabinet shakeup and *Romeo and Juliet*? The hidden structure of one is the visible structure of the other (figure 6.2). The "infinity loop" depicts dynamic positive feedback. Social dramas affect aesthetic dramas, aesthetic dramas affect social dramas. The visible actions of a given social drama are informed – shaped, conditioned, guided – by underlying

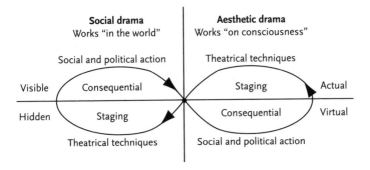

Figure 6.2

aesthetic principles and specific theatrical/rhetorical techniques. Reciprocally, a culture's visible aesthetic theater is informed − shaped, conditioned, guided − by underlying processes of social interaction. The politician, activist, militant, terrorist all use techniques of the theater (staging) to support social action − events that are consequential, that is, designed to change the social order or to maintain it. The theater artist uses the consequential actions of social life as the underlying themes, frames, and/or rhythms of her/his art. The theater is designed to entertain and sometimes to effect changes in perception, viewpoint, attitude: in other words, to make spectators react to the world of social drama in new ways. There is a flowing back and forth, up and down, characterizing the relationship between social and aesthetic dramas; specific enactments (shows) may "travel" from one hemisphere to the other, following the direction of the arrows.

The specific principles of both aesthetic and social drama will vary from culture to culture. Turner's four-part scheme of breach, crisis, redressive action, reintegration (or schism) is modeled on the Greco-European idea of theater − an idea that may also be found in other Indo-European theaters such as those forms derived from Sanskrit-Indian cultures. But, as Turner says, sometimes a phase of a social drama may seethe for years and years with nothing much happening on the surface. Sometimes there is no resolution even after a climactic series of events. Great excitement is followed by a sudden breaking off of turmoil, rather than resolution. In these cases, it might be better to apply the Japanese aesthetic notion of *jo-ha-kyu*, where a long festering breach may be seen as jo, the sudden eruption of crisis as ha, and the rapid rise to a climax that displays the conflict but does not resolve it as kyu. My point is that the infinity loop works, but what specifically constitutes the underlying aesthetic drama/social drama varies from culture to culture.

Victor Turner very much liked the infinity-loop model of the inter-action between social and aesthetic drama. He used the loop in two essays elaborating his theories of social drama (1982: 61–88, 1985: 291–301). In the second of these, Turner succinctly explicated the model:

> Notice that the *manifest* social drama feeds into the latent realm of stage drama; its characteristic form in a given culture, at a given time and place, unconsciously, or perhaps precociously, influences not only the form but also the content of the stage drama of which it is the active or "magic" mirror. The stage drama, when it is meant to do more than entertain – though entertainment is always one of its vital aims – is a metacommentary, explicit or implicit, witting or unwitting, on the major social dramas of its social context (wars, revolutions, scandals, institutional changes). Not only that, but its message and its rhetoric feed back into the *latent* processual structure of the social drama and partly accounts for its ready ritualization. Life itself now becomes a mirror held up to art, and the living now *perform* their lives, for the protagonists of a social drama, a "drama of living," have been equipped by aesthetic drama with some of their most salient opinions, imageries, tropes, and ideological perspectives. Neither mutual mirroring, life by art, art by life, is exact, for each is not a planar mirror but a matricidal mirror; at each exchange something new is added and something old is lost or discarded. Human beings learn through experience, though all too often they repress painful experience, and perhaps the deepest experience is through drama; not through social drama, or stage drama (or its equivalent) alone but in the circulatory or oscillatory process of their mutual and incessant modification.

(Turner 1985: 300–1)

To return now to President Ford and *Romeo and Juliet*. Ford's actions tell a story, contain an aesthetic component, follow a scenario. The President, both consciously and at a non-conscious level, arranged the release of information and timed the sequence of events to suit a sense of drama that in turn would portray him as a character of determination, self-will, strength, purpose, and independence: all qualities expected of a president by the American people. But bumbling Gerry Ford's social drama did not work out as he had planned it. This failure was clearly experienced in theatrical terms. From the *New York Times* of November 4, 1975:

> The strategy behind Vice President Rockefeller's withdrawal, the dismissal of Defense Secretary James R. Schlesinger and other possible moves yet to come is to put a distinct Ford imprimatur on his Administration's domestic and foreign policies, Administration sources said today. The first move was to be the announcement of Mr. Rockefeller's decision not to be Mr. Ford's running mate. . . . The second move – the removal of Mr. Schlesinger [and the others] had been scheduled to be announced this Wednesday. . . . But this carefully planned scenario went awry yesterday when the dismissals and switches were leaked prematurely to the press. In the absence of the Rockefeller announcement, the officials said, the leaks gave off highly undesirable and conflicting signals.

Thus the President and his stage managers had a script in mind, but newsmen compete with each other to ventilate as many leaks as possible. So a change designed to show a deft handling of affairs of state became a confused shakeup. If the President's "image" suffers, his theatrical ineptitude will have repercussions on his career. Unlike TV smoothy Ronald Reagan, Ford's public manner has always been slow, even dumb – not that there was much to choose from, theatrically speaking, in the 1976 match-up of Ford versus Jimmy Carter.

Reciprocally, underneath *Romeo and Juliet*'s sentimental love story is a political struggle that Shakespeare weaves into the play. Romeo is a Montague, Juliet a Capulet, thereby guaranteeing that their fates will have the profoundest effect on the fight between their families. In doing this Shakespeare plays to Renaissance sensibilities of class and order: if the lovers were commoners their plight would be as moving (as in *West Side Story*) but its repercussions more limited. The lovers' story is richer for being played out against and within the war of their parents. But *West Side Story* also embodies the politics of its social milieu, albeit one fascinating to audiences in love with America's democratizing myths. All tragedies, probably all dramas, have under their personal and idiosyncratic surfaces deep social sub-structures that guide the sequence of events.

At another level there is cross-feed. Ford took techniques from the theater: how to release news, how to manipulate the public's reactions, how to disarm his enemies; even how to make up his face, wear his costume, deliver his sentences. This is not a new preoccupation of political leaders. Nor is it restricted to the Louis XIVs of the world: Lenin, a New Guinea village headman, and George Meany practice stagecraft. Shakespeare, like the Greeks, is a master at deploying his dramas of persons in the field of state events. Like a spider's web, what touches one part sends vibrations through the whole. It is this wide field that Brecht understood and used but which the psychological naturalists and absurdists avoid or reject. This field is not an abstract legendary community – my objection to some of the Open Theater's and Bread and Puppet Theater's work is that it mythologizes and generalizes political power which is always and everywhere specific and concrete, dripping with local customs. The field is always the *polis*, full of castes, classes, cross-interests, rivalries, and struggle; this is true of drama in society not only in the west, but everywhere. Nor do certain eras have more social structure than others: systems change, they don't disappear. The "spontaneous communitas" Turner sees as anti-structure is temporary, liminal, a special performative circumstance carefully hedged. One of the beautiful ironies of theater is that it is a *communitas* infiltrated by structure, a liminal event refracting the tensions of social order and disorder. The conventions of performance are a latticework supporting the liberties of theatrical *communitas*.

THE INTEGRAL VS. THE ACCIDENTAL AUDIENCE

The best way to understand the relationship between ritual theater – such as initiation rites, marriage ceremonies, funerals, etc. – and aesthetic theater is to appreciate the variety of roles the audience plays. The audience is not an either/or stagnant lump. Changes in an audience occur during performances as well as from one performance to another. For example, in 1973 when The Performance Group played Sam Shepard's *The Tooth of Crime* at Amherst College in a barn used for horse shows, a male spectator began talking back to Hoss played by Spalding Gray. At first Gray responded to the man as Hoss, "in character." But it soon was evident that the spectator wanted to go on and on. Everytime Hoss/Gray began speaking the man began too; instead of a dialogue there was a blur of two voices. Finally, Gray dropped his characterization and spoke from the role of the performer not the character: "Look, I want to go on with the play, but I can't if you keep interrupting me. If you've got anything you want to say say it, and when you're finished I'll go on." The man demurred, "Go on, go on, I got nothing to say." But as soon as Hoss/Gray began the man started too. Then other spectators jumped in against the man. "Shut up! Let the actor act!" A person leaned over to me and said, "The guy's stoned," as if a chemical explanation would somehow make things alright. But as soon as some in the audience tried to quiet the man, others began shouting too: "Let him say what he wants! Don't shut him up!" The interchange in the audience went on until a clear sense developed that most of the people wanted to see the play. The heckler must have sensed this too, because when Hoss/Gray resumed he was not interrupted. An even longer interruption occurred during the run of *Commune*. (See Schechner 1973: 40–86 for a discussion of the varieties of audience participation.)

The Group's production of *Tooth* was open enough to accept the interruption and debate, but not enough to carry on the play and the interruption at the same time. On the other hand, the Living Theater's *Paradise Now* was designed to open up to (or break down into) audience–performer and audience–audience interactions. In the case of *The Tooth of Crime* Gray's only strategy was passive: he refused to go on until the man stopped. Gray enlisted the audience which finally mobilized itself on the side of the play as a play. In the case of *Paradise Now* the audience was mobilized on the side of the play as a lead-in to direct action. In both cases the performance was licensed by its audience which can, at any time, re-ratify or withdraw that license. This is true of all performances, though most of the time the audience doesn't know its own power – or is provoked only occasionally into exercising it.

This license is significantly different for "accidental" than for "integral" audiences. An accidental audience is a group of people who, individually or in small clusters, go to the theater – the performances are publically advertised and open to all. On opening nights of commercial shows the attendance of the critics and friends constitutes an integral rather than an accidental audience. An integral audience is one where people come because they have to or because the event is of special significance to them. Integral audiences include the relatives of the bride and groom at a wedding, the tribe assembled for initation rites, dignitaries on the podium for an inauguration. Avant-garde performers who send out mailings or who gather audiences mostly of people who have attended previous performances are in the process of creating an integral audience for their work, a supportive audience. Every "artistic community" develops an integral audience: people who know each other, are involved with each other, support each other. Kabuki actors hire spectators to exclaim admiring epithets at special moments during the show. Some integral audiences can be anti-audiences, people who come especially to heckle or attack the performance. Some audiences can be mixed – for example, public events like coronations or state funerals feature a closeup show witnessed by an integral audience of notables which is itself part of the spectacle for the general public. On TV the studio audience becomes part of the show for those watching at home. In short, an accidental audience comes "to see the show" while the integral audience is "necessary to accomplish the work of the show." Or, to put it another way, the accidental audience attends voluntarily, the integral audience from ritual need. In fact, the presence of an integral audience is the surest evidence that the performance is a ritual.

There aren't any hard boundaries between these different kinds of performances; but their relationship can be expressed schematically (figure 6.3). There's movement between the categories. A commercial production begins as an integral-audience event but lives the rest of its existence with accidental audiences – except when theater parties or benefits buy up the whole house. Rituals once thought to be inaccessible are now rented out on location or imported to urban centers

Integral-Aesthetic	Accidental-aesthetic
Invited audiences	Commercial productions publicly advertised
Opening nights	
Audience of those "in the know"	Audience of those who are interested
Integral-Ritual	Accidental-Ritual
Audiences at weddings, funerals, etc.	Tourists watching a ceremony
Inaugurations, signing of treaties, state matters	Imported rituals performed in theaters

Figure 6.3

where they are exhibited in public theaters (see chapter 4). Select mailing lists and word-of-mouth performances are popular in New York now: a kind of not-so-secret society of those in the know. An attempt is being made for theater to fill a niche abandoned by religion: solidarity, mutual supportive belief, gathering in the catacombs, etc. Even within the same performance an audience can change from accidental to integral. At the end of *Over Here!*, a light Broadway musical of the mid-1970s, the two Andrews Sisters came onto the stage and gave an encore of some favorite oldies. The audience immediately picked up on the apparent "special performance" and the theater was aglow. (Even I was taken in. I later inquired whether the Sisters did this every night, or only the night I was there. Every night.)

Interestingly, the behavior of people as spectators differs greatly depending on whether these individuals comprise an integral or accidental audience – and this difference is not what one would expect. By and large, *the accidental audience pays closer attention than does an integral audience.* This is for four reasons: 1) the accidental audience chooses to attend, has often paid to attend; 2) its members attend as individuals or in small clusters so that large crowd action is unlikely – each spectator or small group is a stranger among strangers. 3) An integral audience often knows what's going on – and not paying attention to it all is a way of showing off that knowledge. Sometimes, as during the reading of the Torah prior to the bar mitzvah boy's performance, the featured event is heightened by ignoring the preliminaries. The same thing happens for preliminary bouts preceding a championship boxing match. 4) Sometimes the duration of a performance is so long that it isn't possible to pay attention throughout; ritual performances have a program to fulfill and cannot be fit in between supper and the 11 o'clock news. Performances for accidental audiences are designed to fit convenient time-slots; ritual performances allow their audience to demonstrate their devotion by pilgrimages, duration, and/or ordeals.

SELECTIVE INATTENTION: RITUALIZING AESTHETIC DRAMA

For the December, 1973 performances of Robert Wilson's *The Life and Times of Joseph Stalin* at the Brooklyn Academy of Music opera house, the Le Perq space – a room about 150 feet by 80 feet – was set up with tables, chairs, refreshments: a place where people went not only during the six 15-minute intermissions but also during the acts of Wilson's seven-act opera which began at 7 p.m. and ran more than twelve hours. I remember coming back to Manhattan at about 8.30 a.m., stopping at Dave's Corner at Broadway and Canal to have an early-morning egg cream: a re-entry ritual into New York's ordinary life. Each of *Stalin's* seven acts had been performed before, either as part of Wilson's earlier works or as independent pieces. Thus the twelve-hour performance in the opera house was in a sense a retrospective. Most of the people in the audience had previously seen at least some of Wilson's work (an assertion I can't prove, but looking around the house convinced me): they assembled at BAM to re-experience the work, to try an all-night performance, to meet again with old friends – using the performance of *Stalin* not only as a thing in itself (accidental audience) but as a ritual experience (integral audience).

The behavior in the Le Perq space was not the same throughout the night. During the first three acts the space was generally empty except during intermissions. But as the night went on people came to the space and stayed there, speaking to friends, taking a break from the performance, looping out of the opera, later to re-enter. About two-thirds of the audience left BAM before the performance was over; but those who remained, like repeated siftings of flour, were finer and finer examples of Wilson fans. The audience sorted itself out until those of us there for the whole opera shared not only the experience of Wilson's work but the experience of experiencing it, and the experience of experiencing it with other resilient comrades. The opera was advertised and tickets sold publicly. But the accidental audience was winnowed into an integral audience by the long hours, the socializing in the Le Perq space, and the fact that the performance was a retrospective.

A loop developed between the Le Perq space and the opera house. The house was a place of silence, attention on the performance, and – as the night went on – a more and more spatially scattered audience, until at the end maybe one-fifth of the 2,200 seats were occupied. As evening deepened into late night the tables and chairs in the Le Perq space were rearranged according to the size and needs of the parties using them; the space was used continuously until, at around dawn, there were about half as many people in Le Perq as in the opera house. Special people claimed, or were accorded, special places – for example, a little crowd ringed Allen Ginsberg's table.

What happened during *Stalin* was unusual for orthodox American theater but common in many parts of the world. People selected for themselves what parts of Wilson's opera to pay attention to, and what parts to absent themselves from. When they went into the Le Perq space to rest, socialize, have a refreshment, prepare for a return to the opera house, or whatever, the spectators were not ignoring the performance, they were adding a dimension to it. The social end of the loop was as important to *Stalin* as the aesthetic end.

Similarly, in Madras, in 1971, I was impressed by the behavior of the audience at a concert of classical Carnatic music. People came and went, stood outside the hall, re-entering when a musician they wanted to hear played. The festival lasted more than a week, and during each phase – individual concerts, individual performances within concerts, individual passages within performances, individual moments within passages – attention and inattention alternated. There was no necessity to maintain, or appear to maintain, a single-focus high-tension attention. But at the same time the use of selective inattention led not to a feeling of laxness or "I don't care," but to a selective discipline on the part of the audience. Connoisseurs knew precisely what and who they wanted to hear. As I wrote in my notebook on December 2, 1971:

> Just now the flute and violin are trading and talking and mirroring musical phrases. I've heard this before with voice and violin. But this is the most *profound* I've ever heard it – there is here an *essential dialogue*. Also the audience's close attention and applause makes me think I am in Athens at the great drama festivals and contests. This audience is *sitting in judgement* – but that judgement is based on its knowledge and love of the music – and somehow the judgement supports the musicians – the way the sharp, but willingly adoring eye of the sports spectator supports the athlete. Only these musicians can do what they're doing – but only this audience can do what it can do: IMMEDIATELY REWARD THE PERFORMER. No amount of delayed praise or end of the show applause can approach the now-support of an audience that is really with it, and not jealous, not "let me do that too," not worshipful – but genuinely appreciative. The lights stay on here so the audience can see each other, and feel together, and so the musicians can see the audience.
>
> Also this kind of appreciation takes knowledge of what the performer is trying to do – a real sense of the task at hand: the audience can't do it, but they know what's to be done. We've yet to educate our theater audiences sufficiently – so they can really demand excellence, and not just "an experience." Again, this is a function of a tradition – for an educated audience, and I don't mean academically educated, arises in the midst of a living tradition which people experience from birth. A *living* tradition is one with roots and branches among the people. It can be studied at school but kept alive only in the streets.
>
> Here the music is everywhere: at weddings, in the shouts of the vegetable sellers in the streets, in side alleys where kids bang home-made drums, and at hundreds of concerts happening formally and informally all the time.
>
> It's different from a rock concert. The audience here is not swept away. They are not after ecstasy or oblivion or something *other than the music*. The music is not a means, it is the thing itself. They remain in contact with it, in touch with the musicians. Spectators keep their critical faculties intact. This doesn't mean they aren't moved – but

> they're *moved into the music not beyond it.* The audience isn't quiet. I
> mean they not only accompany the music, they talk to each other – not
> loudly, but there's always a buzz. Also "tsk-tsk," "oooos," the slapping
> of hands on the thighs keeping the rhythms, the bursts of applause
> (always selective, that is, always just a portion of the audience), the
> low talking. Somehow the collective effect of all this is not distracting
> – it is natural, business-like: like eating hot dogs at a ball game.

In chapter 3 I described the rhythms of an all-night performance of a
thovil healing ceremony in Sri Lanka. The audience comes and goes,
and there are several hours when the performance all but stops as only
a few spectators listen to the music or watch occasional dances. In
Australia, Papua New Guinea, Africa, and American Indian villages this
same pattern exists. It is not necessarily tied to long performances or
cycle plays that take a long time to unfold, although these kinds of
episodic or loosely tied bundles of events seem to need selective
inattention.

In the American theater not only Wilson but Peter Schumann, Douglas Dunn, other "new dancers," and, in a modest way, The Performance Group, have experimented with selective inattention. The parades
and outdoor spectacles of the Bread and Puppet Theater necessarily
encourage selective inattention. As a procession goes by a spectator
either follows it or not, and during large-scale performances such as
Domestic Resurrection (an annual show I saw in 1970) it isn't possible to
keep your eye on all that's going on. More than that, the outdoor
setting (a meadow in Vermont), the crowd shifting from place to place,
the people in the audience that I knew – going to Vermont to see the
piece was a pilgrimage – meant that greetings, short conversations, and
looking at rather than *being swept away by* was how I watched the performance. Even when a boat was made from a great sail and streamers of
cloth, and I, along with many other spectators, accepted the invitation
to climb on board by walking inside the hull of cloth, as if we were
passengers escaping the great flood, I felt involved and separate,
celebratory and critical simultaneously.

Douglas Dunn's 101 (1974) was a unique experience for me as a
spectator. In his 25 × 75 × 12 feet high loft Dunn built a maze/
honeycomb of loading sleds gleaned from the streets of SoHo. This

resulted in a wooden structure that completely filled the loft, wall to wall, ceiling to floor. The performance was sparsely attended – Dunn announced he would be "on" from 2 p.m. to 6 p.m., Wednesdays through Sundays, October 2 through 13. People dropped in one or two at a time. Upon entering the loft I signed a guest book (putting me on Dunn's mailing list) and donated a couple of dollars. Then I walked into the honeycomb. I was alone. I wandered through, thinking my own thoughts, and then (I don't know why) I looked up and saw a body lying on a sled near the ceiling. I was shocked, scared. I climbed up and saw Dunn. He wore a touch of eye makeup, was dressed all in white, and lay absolutely still. From the corner of his mouth was drawn, very realistically, a trickle of blood. I leaned close to his face and felt his breath: it was reassuring. Though I knew he was alive, it was good to have my knowledge confirmed. I wanted to touch him but thought this would violate some convention, so I did nothing but contemplate him. Then I went to a corner of the loft, at ceiling level (on a plane with Dunn) and dozed. A few other spectators arrived and left. I napped and sometimes lay half-awake for nearly two hours, as afternoon gave way to evening. Then the woman at the desk came to the entrance of the performing space and said that the performance was ending. I climbed down and left the honeycomb. I stayed in the kitchen and when Dunn came out about 20 minutes later we talked for a little while. Talking to him was important, comforting – as was quietly walking home alone. I felt contemplative, rested.

Dunn told me that sometimes spectators tugged at him, pinched him, tried to make him move or scream. I remembered what Judith Malina and Julian Beck told me about the body-pile scene from the Living Theater's *Mysteries*:

> *Malina*: In Europe, it was more common to be treated aggressively. I have been kicked, stomped, tickled, had my fingers bent back and my hair set on fire.
>
> *Schechner*: My God, why, do you think . . .
>
> *Beck*: To get her to move.
>
> *Malina*: To get me to move.
>
> *Beck*: To get the corpse not to be a real corpse.
>
> *Malina*: Only in America have we been comforted. Isn't it strange?

> *Schechner:* Well, in America you are, for better or worse, an American; in
> Europe you are, for better or worse, an American.
>
> (Malina and Beck 1969: 34)

In retrospect I think Beck's interpretation was correct: people are uncomfortable even in the presence of simulated death. With Dunn's 101 the relationship to him in his honeycomb (or ought I say catacomb?) was ambiguous: Dunn was still but not "actively dead," as the Living was in the plague scene of *Mysteries*. Spectators could choose their own relationship to Dunn, his performance, the space.

In The Performance Group's production of Brecht's *Mother Courage and Her Children* (1974–7), a reverse kind of selective inattention was tried. I encouraged the performers to drop their characterizations when they were not involved in a scene – to move from the realm of the story to that of the audience: simply sit and watch, or relax (read, talk quietly, prepare for their next scene) in a small area fully in view of the audience which we called the green room (though it really wasn't one). I took the idea, I think, from work the Open Theater and other groups did in the 1960s where performers not in a scene sat to the side, usually in a quiet, almost formal manner, and then rose to join the scene – something like athletes coming into the game from the bench. I wanted to use this idea but in a more traditionally theatrical way – thus the green room. Up to a point the experiment worked. The audience saw performers neither playing roles nor pretending to pay attention to the play. For example, when Mother Courage leaves the performing area in scene 3 to go shopping, Swiss Cheese takes the cash box, runs away with it, and is arrested. Joan MacIntosh (Courage) and Stephen Borst (Chaplain) are in the green room. Clearly they aren't continuing the story offstage – they are not seen, for example, pantomiming buying things at the market. They're just sitting down, as Joan and Steve, while a few feet away Spalding Gray (Swiss Cheese) and Leeny Sack (Kattrin) are performing the story of the cash box. It seems to me that just as a spectator can drop in and out of a drama so the performers can drop in and out of character. The challenge is to arrange, not so much the time for this to happen, the drama will fix that, but the place for it, and in what way it's to be observed. In *Mother Courage* what happened was that the audience's ability to see into the green room set up a pressure for still another, really private space: performers drifted out of the green room to a space behind the light board that spectators couldn't see into – there the performers talked, smoked, and prepared for their next entries. Only some performers, and only some of the time, used the public green room. I had exactly the same experience in my 1987 production of *Don Juan* at Florida State University in Tallahassee.

During the performance of *Mother Courage* performers could find themselves in five different situations: 1) In the midst of a scene which needs tension to carry the narrative – for example, that part of scene 3 where Courage is bargaining with Yvette for the life of Swiss Cheese. 2) As an observer of the scene, but doing work indirectly related to the narrative action of the scene – for example, while Courage is haggling in scene 3, the Chaplain and Kattrin are setting up tables, cups, trays, and flatware for the supper that will be served to the audience after the scene is over. This supper is both part of the story (Courage is preparing to sell lunch to the troops) and part of the performance event (The Performance Group is preparing to sell supper to the audience). While working, Borst and Sack concentrate on their tasks quietly and with as little stage business as possible except for those moments that explicitly call for participation in the drama of the scene such as when the Chaplain drops a cup and Courage yells at him. 3) As performers in the space but not in the scene. During the same scene, James Clayburgh hauls Swiss Cheese up into the air using the pulley system he, as one of the Group's environmentalists, designed. Once Clayburgh finishes his work he remains visually in the scene but he isn't "in character," he doesn't "do" anything except watch the action: a kind of intermediary between the spontaneous attentiveness of a spectator and the planned participation of a performer. 4) In the visible-to-the-public green room. 5) In the private space out of sight of the public.

This graded and sometimes relaxed inattention of the performers allows for a subtle infiltration of their everyday lives into the dramatic reality of the performance. Some critics consider this mixture a serious breach of convention. I insist on it for several reasons: it is like the readiness of athletes not only on the sidelines but on the field before a play or a down; it shows the double person of the performer, the "myself" and the "person-of-the-character"; it serves as a bridge between the audience and the performers. Some spectators are disturbed by the "lack of energy" of this kind of performing. But when an engaged action occurs, the energy resources, not having been squandered, can be spent more powerfully. Some spectators find themselves falling into parallel rhythms of focused attention and selective inattention. As their attention "wanders" people begin picking up on events and images that would otherwise escape notice, or be merely blurred side visions: movements of spectators, gestures of performers not at the center of the scene, overall arrangement and dynamics of space. The performance can be contemplated; the spectator can choose to be in or out, moving her attention up and down a sliding scale of involvement. Selective inattention allows patterns of the whole to be visible, patterns that otherwise would be burned out of consciousness by a too intense concentration. It is this sometimes very subtle manifestation of what Anton Ehrenzweig calls the "primary process" that interests me. Through selective inattention spectators co-create the work with the performers. It is this that struck me in Madras. In a real way the spectators become artists. As Ehrenzweig says:

> How often have we not observed how an artist suddenly stops in his tracks without apparent reason, steps back from his canvas and looks at it with a curiously vacant stare? What happens is that the conscious gestalt is prevented from crystallizing. Nothing seems to come into his mind. Perhaps one or another detail lights up for a moment only to sink back into the emptiness. During this absence of mind an unconscious scanning seems to go on. Suddenly as from nowhere some offending detail hitherto ignored will come into view. It had somehow upset the balance of the picture, but had gone undetected. With relief the painter will end his apparent inactivity. He returns to his canvas and carries out the necessary retouching. This "full" emptiness of unconscious scanning occurs in many other examples of creative work.

> (Ehrenzweig 1970: 38)

I agree with Ehrenzweig's stressing the importance of unconscious scanning. I disagree when his artist corrects the "offending detail." In theater, at least, these disruptions and disturbances, these variations – often brought on by unpredictable interactions with spectators – are what make this or that particular performance interesting. The process by means of which a performance grows over a period of time is analogous to evolution by natural selection working from accidental genetic variations. Ehrenzweig recognizes these changes:

> A performer may readily change the inarticulate micro-elements of his interpretation from performance to performance. But this instability does not make them arbitrary. Any change forces the performer to recast his interpretation of the whole work on the spur of the moment. This total integration can only be controlled by the empty stare of unconscious scanning which alone is capable of overcoming the fragmentation in art's surface structure.
>
> (Ehrenzweig 1970: 49)

Audiences as well as performers employ unconscious scanning. More than in "product arts" (painting, sculpting, writing, film) "process arts" (live performing) are co-created by performers and spectators. A reader may complete a written text in each reading, but only during live performances do artists and audiences *co-create together* in exactly the same time/space.

This relaxed unconscious scanning – selective inattention – is nowhere more clearly seen than in observing people at a performance of *noh*. Noh is the exquisitely articulated masked theater of Japan that "developed from a variety of sacred rituals and festival entertainment arts . . . brought to a state of refinement and maturity during the Muromachi period (1336–1568)" (Komparu 1983: xv). The Japanese say that the proper way to "watch" noh is in a hypnagogic state between waking and sleeping. Among the noh audience are many whose eyes are closed, or heavy-lidded. These experts are "paying attention" by relaxing their consciousness, allowing material to stream upward from their unconscious to meet the sounds/images streaming outward from the noh stage. In this state of porous receptive inattention each individual spectator is carried along in noh's dreamlike rhythms. Often images and sounds are shared by *shite* (leading actor), chorus, musicians, and spectators so that the principal character is constructed by, distributed to, and shared among a number of participants. As Komparu notes:

> the viewer participates in the creation of the play by individual free association and brings to life internally a drama based on individual experience filtered through the emotions of the protagonist. The shared dramatic experience, in other words, is not the viewer's adjustment of himself to the protagonist on stage but rather his creation of a separate personal drama by sharing the play with the performer. Indeed, he becomes that protagonist.
>
> (Komparu 1983: 18)

Among the Japanese this kind of experiencing, based on Buddhist principles, is called "detached vision."

Related to selective inattention is the question of "presence." What gives to some performers a special allure, and why do audiences confer this status and seek out those who have it? It isn't only a western phenomenon, this idea of being a star; and it isn't always related to the skills of the performer. While watching the thovil ceremony in Sri Lanka I was told that one of the dancers, a very old man, was the village's most powerful "devil dancer," a kind of exorcist. This aged person executed a few steps and chanted. His dancing and singing were poor by western standards of energy, precision, invention, duration. But he commanded the complete attention of the previously noisy, socializing crowd. His presence, not his theatrical skills, carried power: he was an agent, a funnel, a conduit for power, and it was that power, showing meagerly through him – a brilliant light almost obscured by obstacles in a long tunnel, that held the audience. Also, as someone told me, people recalled the old man's youth when he'd danced some furious dances, as another young man would do later the same night. So the crowd's attention was also due to respect for what this old man had once been, the memories of the community embodied in him. The same may be said concerning many of the world's political or religious stars. Some may project a powerful figure and great oratory. But others, for example Emperor Hirohito, command respect by virtue of their position. Or a feeble-voiced, trembling, and off-key pope presiding at a Mass brings to the performance the authority and history of his office not merely his skills as a performer. Or Mao in the 1970s appearing briefly in public, stooped with age, barely able to raise his hand: still he is an emblem of the Chinese revolution, a pinnacle of its power.

Being a star is to be a person whose very presence transcends whatever activity s/he may be absorbed in. In the case of the devil dancer, Hirohito, the pope, and Mao the role transcends the performer. In the case of movie stars the person transcends the role – so no matter what movie she is in Marilyn Monroe is Marilyn and Clark Gable is Gable. The fact that these stars are dead adds to their allure: their performances, their lives, are finished, as paintings by a dead painter are finished, and their whole careers can be studied as completed trajectories. But even while alive their performances converge on their lives, the two are one, and the mere presence of a star in a film makes that movie important.

There are two kinds of presence: the kind where an office, as an emblem or conduit of power, confers on whoever holds it star quality; and the kind where publicity, manipulation of the public, or some hard-to-define-but-visible quality in a person vibrates through the public so that a presence is felt, as in movie stars. These apparently opposite examples of presence are in fact very closely connected. There are two roads to power – through work, and through being called (elevated by accident of birth or some other circumstance). The work path is progressive, step by step, from priest to bishop, to cardinal, to pope; from party worker, to cell leader, to commissar, to chairman. The magic path is to be "discovered" in Schwab's drugstore. Of course we know the path to stardom is strewn with difficult and dirty tasks. But the myth is of apotheosis. In fact, being a movie star means to fulfill the wishes of the public even as the public is being manipulated into having the kind of wishes movie stars fulfill. Underneath apparent differences the two paths to power – pope's, movie star's – are linked by the continuous, conscious manipulation of the public.

This relates to selective inattention in an interesting way. Presence becomes a kind of absence, a lack of anything complicated to do. In a certain way the star must practice doing very little, actually falling out of character in so far as this character interferes with a direct communication of personality to the spectator. Thus the non-dependence of the star, the absolute absence from any specific role, is what creates star quality. I think this is true of official stars as well as movie stars. Mao is seen at a distance, waving; or a picture is released of a president signing a bill, or shaking hands; a pope kisses the earth or blesses the crowds: the actual work these people do, if any at all by the time they have ascended to their ultimate positions, is hidden from the public. The ironically comforting revelation of the Nixon tapes was that presidents curse, fumble, speak as humans do; that their policies are forged through prejudice and arguments.

This star quality is something Genet understood better than most other dramatists. His plays – especially *The Maids* and *The Balcony* – examine the gaps and links between the gestures/costumes of power and the personalities of those who put on these accoutrements. The appearance of stars – their empty but emblematic look and gestures – encourage the public to project onto them every kind of expectation and fantasy. The stars are in fact blank screens. Ehrenzweig's primary process is not the property only of artists and scientists, the general public participates in it too.

The blank screens, the underlying rhythms, the absence of focus which constitute the operative processes of stardom relate back to the infinity-loop model. What is blank, undifferentiated, hypnagogic, relaxed – in a word, inattentive – is actually the bottom or hidden half of the loop. When the noh spectator enters and co-creates the performance by absenting herself from too close or narrow a focus on what's coming from the stage, she is encouraging hidden or underlying unconscious material to blend with her conscious experience. In a way, she is relaxing in order to be creative. This kind of experiencing happens – or can happen – during a wide range of performances. Spectators can be trained to enjoy being selectively inattentive. A large enterprise of contemporary experimental performance is to make visible this creative process – to reposition it at the top half of the loop. In experimental performance, what then is underneath? Nothing other than the orthodox genres and tropes – narrativity, parody, lyrical description, etc. On the surface a Robert Wilson opera, a Merce Cunningham dance, a Pina Bausch dance-theater piece eschew orthodox genres. But if a spectator is selectively inattentive, narratives, social commentaries, "pure" or simply beautiful movements and spectacles emerge and merge with her own reveries. To a certain degree the works of these artists converge at the point where the loop's intersecting energies meet – "between the eyes" of the loop. This Shiva-like meditative yet burning third eye is where the hidden and the visible cross each other. Paradoxically, the intensity of this third eye cannot be experienced unless one's focus is open – relaxed, inattentive – to the whole dynamic process.

In today's (mid-1970s) performances I see two divergent tendencies. One is the short, intense, you-must-pay-attention kind of work characteristic of Richard Foreman's *Sophia-Wisdom* series; also the kind of work Grotowski did from 1959 through 1968 (his poor theater phase). These intense pieces need a silent, attentive, hard-working audience. But another kind of theater has emerged – longer, episodic, loosely constructed. These pieces might appear to be like Piscator's and Brecht's epic theater but actually they are more like the ceremonies and celebrations of non-western theater, or like performances in the west that attract integral audiences. Spectators come and go, pay attention or don't, select what parts of the performance to follow. These habits may be further trained by television – because the ubiquitous sets are always turned on but often not looked at; or by the radio and phonograph which also encourage selective inattention. In work such as Dunn's 101 the action is minimal, the piece being essentially meditative rather than dramatic. The use of selective inattention encourages a kind of alpha-rhythm performance that evokes deep relaxation rather than tension (see chapter 8). Or, as in the episodic pearls-on-a-string pageants of Wilson, a long-wave rhythm stimulates dropping in, dropping out: a different kind of meditation. The experiment I made with performer inattention in *Mother Courage* only partially succeeded. We in the west still have neither an educated audience nor performers and directors confident enough of their work – that is, well-enough trained in both doing and not doing – to drop in and out of a performance with ease and skill. Perhaps someday we will learn that the full scope of performing, like living, involves not only the push of doing but the release of undoing, the meditation of non-doing.

7

ETHOLOGY AND THEATER

ANIMAL–HUMAN PERFORMANCE CONTINUITIES

Darwin first proposed a continuity of behavior from animals to people in *The Expression of the Emotions in Man and Animals* (1872). For a long time his speculations lay fallow, but they are now being followed up. We want to know how much of "body language" is genetically fixed and how much learned. The underlying assumption is that an inclusive web includes both human and animal behavior. Is there also a cultural web? How are human religions, customs, and arts extensions, elaborations, and transformations of animal cultures? I want to explore this question as it pertains to theater. But I propose that the theatrical paradigm is a key to understanding larger plans of human social interaction.

Theatrical performances consist of ritualized gestures and sounds. These may be displays of non-daily behavior as in kabuki, kathakali, ballet, or the dances of Australian Aborigines. Or they may be replications of ordinary behavior as in naturalistic theater. Theater trades on recognizable moments and on sequences of behavior that succinctly "tell stories." I think all kinds of theater – that on show in theaters or churches, that of rites of passage, that of sports, that accompanying official displays of power, and that happening on a microsocial level in play and daily routines – comprise a single system of script, scenarios, disguises, displays, dances, impersonations, and scenes.

Studies of this system have been made by people whose knowledge of theater is from the outside. My experience, and therefore my perspective, is from the inside, as a theater director.

Both "fun" and "rehearsal" seem to be part of the performance sequences of the great apes. In his studies of the mountain gorilla of central Africa, Schaller says the functions of the chest-beating sequence include the discharge of excitement and showing off. Young males "occasionally displayed with great abandon, then sat quietly, and looked all around as if to judge the effectiveness of the behavior" (1963: 227). The chest-beating display also repels intruders and maintains group hierarchy. It thereby combines efficacy and entertainment (see chapter 4); but so does "professional theater" with its combination of money-making, ambition, fame, and art. The function of discharging excitement among gorillas is parallel to the cathartic function of theater proposed by Aristotle and Artaud, an ancient, persistent, and robust therapeutic tradition of performance. Schaller notes that "the primary causation of the chest-beating sequence appears to be the build-up of tension (excitement) above a certain threshold. After the display, the level of excitement temporarily drops below the threshold, and the animals behave calmly until a new accumulation of tension erupts in display" (Schaller 1963: 233). The build-up of tension does not lead to fighting but to display; potential disruption is transformed into entertainment. This outcome is very much like human theatrical performances. There too violence is present in both themes and gestures; but the process of theatricalization renders this violence less harmful than it would be if actualized "in life." The resulting performance is entertaining.[1]

The chest-beating sequence, and other displays among primates, use drumming and dancing: making and then moving to self-made rhythms. These displays occur among individuals and among groups; they are often accompanied by hooting and other vocalizations; they create and modify moods. Among the many functions of these displays, fun appears to be the connecting link. I can't define fun, except to say that it's related to entertainment, to showing off, playing around, exploring, and pretending (becoming bigger, smaller, other, different). Fun happens when the energy released by an action is more than the anxiety, fear, or effort spent either on making the action or on overcoming the obstacles inhibiting it. I shall return to this theme later.

To perform acts that are otherwise forbidden – punished, taboo, unthought of – is a way of "making fun." In human cultures these acts are often violent and sexual. This is as true of the obscene real-life dramas of the Kogu in Papua New Guinea as it is of Aristophanes; of the insulting song-duels of the Tiv in Nigeria as it is of the Eskimos of Alaska or Greenland. And if similar actions occur where there is no chance of cultural diffusion, these are evidence of the deep structures of human social, aesthetic, and biological organization. Rehearsals – whether these be the exploratory seeking for and repeating of actions characteristic of the modern theater, or the formal preparations that precede many rituals – are times of intense fun. During rehearsals performers play with the interface between the private and the public, pushing and pulling the porous boundaries. A big part of the fun of rehearsal is in trying out what may never be shown, a way of enacting the forbidden.

The apes may not rehearse, but they do practice and improve their performances through repetition. Goodall describes the display of Mike, a male chimpanzee of the Gombe Stream Reserve in Tanzania. (These chimps are not tamed or trained animals; the significance of studies like Schaller's and Goodall's is that they were made among wild animals.)

> All at once Mike calmly walked over to our tent and took hold of an empty kerosene can by the handle. Then he picked up a second can and, walking upright, returned to the place where he had been sitting. Armed with his two cans Mike continued to stare toward the other males. After a few minutes he began to rock from side to side. At first the movement was almost imperceptible, but Hugo and I were watching him closely. Gradually he rocked more vigorously, his hair slowly began to stand erect, and then softly at first, he started a series of pant-hoots. As he called, Mike got to his feet and suddenly he was off, charging toward the group of males, hitting the two cans ahead of him. The cans, together with Mike's crescendo of hooting, made the most appalling racket: no wonder the erstwhile peaceful males rushed out of the way. Mike and his cans vanished down a track, and after a

few moments there was silence. . . . After a short interval that low-pitched hooting began again, followed almost immediately by the appearance of the two rackety cans with Mike closely behind them. Straight for the other males he charged, and once more they fled. This time, even before the group could reassemble, Mike set off again; but he made straight for Goliath [the alpha male] – and even he hastened out of his way like all the others. Then Mike stopped and sat, all his hair on end, breathing hard.

(Goodall 1972: 122–3)

Obviously Mike was challenging Goliath's alpha rank; and not long after this display Mike replaced Goliath. But the challenge – like so many encounters between animals about dominance, territory, food, and mates – came not as a direct attack or life-and-death fight but wrapped in ritual, played out as a theatrical event. Just as "making fun" can be an indirect attack on the authorities, so Mike's charge, driving the kerosene cans ahead of him, was a rehearsed, yet still indirect attack on Goliath's dominant rank.

Mike's performance can be analyzed in two ways. Either the sequence was a performance during which Mike worked himself up step by step in front of the whole band until finally he confronted Goliath in a chimp version of the game of chicken; or the showing off and charge at the low-ranking males were rehearsals, try-outs, preparations for the main event, the challenge to Goliath. In theater I have often seen similar "unconscious" discoveries – where improvisations, or simply "fooling around," during or between work periods in rehearsals uncover images/actions later used in performance. The activity of doing things, repeating where necessary, changing, improvising, and including even mistakes in the performance, is common in theater. Robert Wilson tape-records workshops and rehearsals, videotaping when possible, in order to retain business that is repeated and built on. Spalding Gray constructs his "real-life" monologs by performing, tape-recording his performances, listening to what he's done, editing, and performing again and again. The choreography of much postmodern dance is invented through improvisations and perfected through repetition: the emotional core of a work is not known in advance and then "expressed," it is uncovered through action.

This is the way Grotowski worked during his poor theater phase (1959–68), the way Peter Brook and Joseph Chaikin developed their works. I used this method in all of my productions with The Performance Group (1967–80). Rehearsals are no longer what they were in Max Reinhardt's day when the director marched in with all the actions inscribed in a *Regiebuch*. Rehearsals have become centers of psychophysical, sociological, and personal research. The only thing known in advance is that maybe a performance will happen sometime during, not after, the process, and that an audience will enter the space to watch or interact with the performers. Working this way puts a new burden on the performers. They are intermediaries, masters of ceremony, inventors; they must show themselves even as they interpret their roles. And interpretation is more complicated when performance texts are radically deconstructed–reconstructed.

All this has been implicit in western theater since the end of the nineteenth century. Stanislavsky was the first to put the training of the performer at the top of the theatrical agenda, a training that finally led to the deconstruction of performance texts. During the more than ninety-year course of this development western theater became increasingly ritualized, moving into areas of human interaction once reserved for religion. As society cyberneticizes, programming the contacts people make with each other, theater gains importance as a live activity, oscillating between relatively unstructured interactions, say at a party, and totally formalized or mediated exchanges, say a job interview. Theater can be semi-formal, narrative, personal, direct, and fun. Its methods encourage audience participation on many levels, some not so obvious. This aspect of theater has heavily influenced politics, sports, and religious ceremony, all of which have become more theatricalized in recent years. On the other hand, movies, despite their apparent immediacy, are a flat, framed medium, projected into a darkened room, ineluctable and non-participatory. Environmental theater – implicit in the "fourth wall" of Antoine and Stanislavsky, explicit since Meyerhold's productions of the early 1920s – needs performers trained in semiotics, that is, in consciously managing the representational signs of their trade. This kind of training is intrinsic to the traditional performance genres I studied in India, Java, Bali, and Papua New Guinea. It is also there in Africa and native America. But in modern and postmodern performance, new "ideograms" have to be invented or discovered for each production. As Grotowski says:

> It is not, however, a question of seeking fixed ideograms as, for example, in the Peking Opera in which, in order to portray a particular flower, the actor makes a specific unchangeable gesture inherited from centuries of tradition. New ideograms must constantly be sought and their composition appear immediate and spontaneous. . . . The final result is a living form possessing its own logic.
>
> (Grotowski 1968a: 142)

The first fruits of this method were the stiff biomechanics of Meyerhold; next came the carefully arranged, though ordinary-appearing, compositions of Brecht (available for study in his model books). Then Grotowski developed exercises that helped actors "confront" texts, discovering meeting places between their own psychophysical impulses and the logic of the texts. The framed, pictorial exactness of Richard Foreman's theater is different, there is nothing spontaneous about it. Foreman consciously emphasizes the thought-out-before quality of his productions. But in Wilson's super-slow imagery spectators can predict moves and follow their trajectories through time–space. Also some actions are repeated so many times that the spectator is forced to look at different aspects of the action. Similarly, in the postmodern dances of Dunn, Forti, Jonas, Paxton, and others,[2] as well as in the performance art of Allan Kaprow and many others, ordinary human actions are isolated, displaced, stopped, slowed or accelerated, repeated: all ritualizations ethologically speaking.

The movie camera has given artists the ability to stop action, examine gesture frame by frame, go forward and backward, repeat, and study compositions as they condense and evaporate; these techniques have reshaped theatrical imagination. A theoretical basis for these examinations exists in the work of "human ethologists" such as Eibl-Eibesfeldt, Birdwhistell, and Ekman.[3] The kind of ritualization they study does not focus on social organization so much as on micro-gestures: glances, eyebrow flashes, smiles, hand gestures, shoulder lurches, pelvic thrusts, etc. To be alive is to dance.

Chimpanzee Mike probably didn't have a strategy or a goal in mind when he began his challenge of Goliath. What Mike meant to do emerged as he was doing it. The same thing often happens to human performers. At the January 11, 1976 performance of Brecht's *Mother Courage and Her Children* – at least the eightieth performance of that play by The Performance Group – Spalding Gray as Swiss Cheese let out four terrified screams as he was captured and hauled into the air during scene 3. Gray's screams were those of a 2-year-old boy. At that performance I realized for the first time that Gray's Swiss Cheese was just a big baby, that this baby believed his mother was omnipotent, and that he would never be separated from her. When the Sergeant arrests him, Swiss Cheese knew his mother would fix things up. But as he is hauled into the air Swiss Cheese had a revelation: his mother's power is limited. His screams combined rage, terror, and disappointment. At age 33 Swiss Cheese suffered his first attack of separation anxiety. It took all those performances before Gray discovered, through his body, what Swiss Cheese felt, and how this big baby might react to his revelation. The screams "completed" Swiss Cheese's character even as they indicted his mother who never prepared him to live, or die, in the adult world. Probably Mike began his performance as unknowing of its end, or its significance, as Gray did his. Mike never could achieve Gray's level of reflexive self-understanding. Maybe Mike only felt a tension vis-à-vis Goliath, a tension there in his body whether or not Mike could conceive of its presence. Each step of the performance both relieved the tension and built new tension, until the final direct charge at Goliath. This kind of performance is one where the actions are discovered during rehearsals, where rehearsals are not designed to express what's known but to discover what's to be done. Such doings are not "improvisations" but variations.

In chapter 3 I cited Goodall's description of the chimpanzee "rain dance." This performance is both a prototype and a parallel to human theater. The spectacle Goodall saw, and other observations made in the field, confirm how fundamental the performer–spectator dyad is. In fact, we may be speaking of a triad: protagonist–antagonist–spectator. The dyad is the basic performance relationship, the triad the basic dramatic-theatrical relationship. What a sclerotic western aesthetics has done is freeze who should play what role in the triad. Among animals and many human societies, the roles shift during performance: this moment's observer may be the next moment's protagonist, while this moment's antagonist may be the next moment's spectator. But can I say with any assurance that the young male and female chimps sitting in the trees oserving the mature males rushing with branches down the hillside in the midst of the terrific thunderstorm – the event Goodall saw – are spectators? And in what sense are the mature males performers? The display is most parsimoniously explained as a performance, a kind of playing.

Lorenz connects animal and human performances in this way:

> The formation of traditional rites must have begun with the first dawning of human culture, just as at a much lower level phylogenetic rite formation was a prerequisite for the origin of social organization in higher animals. ... In both cases, a behavior pattern by means of which a species in the one case, a cultured society in the other, deals with certain environmental conditions, acquires an entirely new function, that of communication. The primary function may still be performed, but it often recedes more and more into the background and may disappear completely so that a typical change of functions is achieved. Out of communication two new equally important functions may arise, both of which still contain some measure of communicative effects. The first of these is the channeling of aggression into innocuous outlets, the second is the formation of a bond between two or more individuals. In both cases, the selection pressure of the new function has wrought analogous changes on the form of the primal, nonritualized behavior. It quite obviously lessens the chances of ambiguity in the communication that a long series of independently variable patterns should be welded into one obligatory sequence. ... The display of animals during threat and courtship furnishes an abundance of examples, and so does the culturally developed ceremonial of man. ... Rhythmical repetition of the same movement is so characteristic of very many rituals, both instinctive and cultural, that it is hardly necessary to describe examples. ... This "mimic exaggeration" results in a ceremony which is, indeed, closely akin to a symbol and which produces that theatrical effect that first struck Sir Julian Huxley as he watched his Great Crested Grebes. ... There is hardly a doubt that

all human art primarily developed in the service of rituals and that the autonomy of "art for art's sake" was achieved only by another, secondary step of cultural progress.

(Lorenz 1967: 72–4)

I doubt whether there ever was any "art for art's sake." Implicit in Lorenz's "history" is the idea that theater is a model of, or an experimentally controlled example of, human interactions. It is something else too: a reflection of, or mediation among, these interactions, freed as they are by theatrical convention from being "really real." Instead, actions are segregated "in the theater" where through exaggeration, repetition, and metaphorization they can be displayed and handled. The interactions played out in the theater are those which are problematical in society, interactions of a sexual, violent, or taboo kind concerning hierarchy, territory, or mating.[4] This is not a characteristic of western theater only, but of theater everywhere. In my view drama is not a model of all human action, but of the most problematical, difficult, taboo, liminal, and dangerous activities. The theatrical actions vivifying drama are rhythmic, repetitive, exaggerated; the body adornments and physical deeds of theater are spectacular: everything in theater is ritualized, if we understand ritual the way ethologists do. Drama arises where clarity of signal is needed most: where the risk is greatest and the stakes highest, where redundancy of signal is an advantage. Drama, the narrative core of theater, links two basic human actions: 1) misunderstanding, a break in communication, a confusion of messages, a layering of ironies; 2) the violence that results when sexual and political desires collide; such violence (in farce as well as tragedy) often takes the shape of a rebellion against authority and decency.

The second point in Lorenz's statement is the link between aggression and aggregation. He suggests the underlying effect of releasing aggressive behavior ritually is not to separate individuals but to bond them. I've seen this confirmed in Papua New Guinea (see chapter 4) as well as in my own workshops and rehearsals where the release of "bad feelings" during exercises (local rituals) leads to the strengthening of strong bonds among participating group members. Thus on two levels simultaneously – the level of drama and the level of theater –

aggression and groupness often support each other, if the aggression is expressed in/as ritual.

Furthermore, the dramatic event at the core of the performance is itself a ritualized way of presenting to the assembled community, the audience, "difficult" material. In this sense, every drama is a story enacted for those who are, directly or indirectly, the subject of the story they are seeing, who are doubly represented – as characters and as spectators. Or, as Geertz said of the Balinese cockfight, it is "a story they tell themselves about themselves" (1973: 448). It is no accident that Shakespeare's plays are not only full of metatheatrical plays-within-plays and references to the stage but also thematically return again and again to questions of personal-vs.-state interests. Or that nineteenth–twentieth century naturalist dramas focused on the disparity between individual needs (often sexual and creative) and the grinding routine of the socioeconomic order of things. It's been my experience that the more risky the actions dealt with in performance – the more physical the actions, the more taboos revealed or violated – the stronger the bonds formed among the group making the performance. The limits here are ethical: what the group itself, or its leaders, determine are the boundaries of what will be acted out. Gangs, even political parties, have in "real life" carried such bonding to grisly extremes. If one of theater's functions is to model interactions resulting from the release of repressed material, another is to form groups that can control, through ritualization and play, this explosive material. In this way, theater can be a laboratory of group process.

Lorenz concentrates on the finished artwork. He doesn't differentiate between theater and the other arts. In the overall span of human history, written literature is a late development; painting goes back at least to Paleolithic times. But human culture extends back how far? Several hundred thousand years, a million or more years? Theater, dance, and music – these must precede the material arts whose remnants we possess. Ethological analogy suggests that people, like other primates, vocalized and danced before they spoke or told stories. The surviving Paleolithic sculptings and paintings were more of an "action art" than a "gallery art." Much of the cave art is located deep in unlit chambers difficult of access; other work is superimposed one image over another, forming rich palimpsests. This indicates that the cave art was designed to accompany performances or was executed as performances. Making the images was more important than looking at them when complete. If Lorenz were more familiar with theater, he would see that rehearsal is the link between animal ritual and human art. I discuss this connection in chapters 3 and 5.

PHATIC THEATER

All animals, including Homo sapiens, exist within the same ecological web. But animals are not all alike. Analogies must be put forward cautiously. I don't call the "dance" of a male cichlid defending his territory against other males while at the same time enticing a female to his nest a dance in the human sense; nor would I call the patterned waggle and footwork of bees communicating to other bees where the honey is, a dance in the human sense. Where everything is genetically determined, where no genuine learning takes place, where no improvisation or variation is possible, where error and/or conscious lying cannot easily occur, art is not. Of course, people may imitate these patterns and make dances (or other things) based on them. Also, almost all animal performances lack crafted performance places and tools – specially prepared places, props, costumes, etc. But by the time we get to chimpanzee Mike's performance with the kerosene cans we are at the threshold of human theater. It only remained for Mike to do his act with another chimp playing Goliath while Goliath looked on, for us to have a chimp version of Hamlet's mousetrap. Mike combined fixed elements characteristic of his species – swaying, pant-hooting, drumming, charging – with improvised elements and props: the kerosene cans, charging out of sight to allow for a temporary respite and rising suspense, a steadily increasing intensity of action climaxing in the confrontation with Goliath. The cichlid does something else, "releasing" identical behavior everytime he's properly stimulated. Mike interacts in ways that are only generally predictable: he will display, someday he will probably challenge Goliath. Mike composes his own scenario as he goes along, combining the fixed with the found. Aside from its non-repeatability and the lack of an audience, Mike's display is very much like human dance-theater. This dance-theater does not assume a "psychology" for Mike – his performance is not an "expression of" feeling but an action which is the feeling.

Schaller points out that people in a stadium watching sporting events display in much the same way as great apes do:

> Various aspects of the chest-beating display sequence are present in the gibbon, orang-utan, chimpanzee, and man, although the specificity is sometimes lacking. . . . Man behaves remarkably like a chimpanzee or a gorilla in conflicting situations. Sporting events are ideal locations for watching the behavior of man when he is generally excited and emotionally off-guard. A spectator at a sporting event perceives actions which excite him. Yet he cannot participate in them directly, nor does he want to cease observing them. The tension thus produced finds release in chanting, clapping of hands, stamping of feet, jumping up and down, throwing of objects. This behavior is sometimes guided into a pattern by the efforts of cheerleaders who, by repeating similar sounds over and over again, channel the displays into a violent, synchronized climax. The intermittent nature of such behavior, the transfer of excitement from one individual to the next, and other similarities with the displays of gorillas are readily apparent.
> (Schaller 1963: 235)

Our century is not alone in giving testimony that such displays can be manipulated by politicians, preachers, entertainers. People dramatically display their moods by throwing things when angry, kicking the wall, jumping up and down with enthusiasm, clapping or stamping the feet to show strong feelings, etc. These "mood displays" change character when they are ritualized into mass actions such as spectator sports, political rallies, or militarized parades; then individual expression rigidifies, is channeled into exaggerated, rhythmically coordinated, repetitive actions, while emphasis shifts from the free expression of feeling to an evocation and channeling of aggression for the benefit of the sponsor: the team, corporation, politician, religion, party, or state.

In the 1960s and 1970s "phatic theater" – performances based on evoking mood displays – re-emerged in the west. This kind of theater is present in mass spectacles and their opposite: quasi-theatrical therapies where individuals learn again, or for the first time, how to let their feelings "out." Groups theatrical and therapeutic are extended pseudo-families where intra-family feelings, especially violent or other taboo feelings, are let out. This often occurs in a make-believe situation. The actual person(s) to whom the heretofore repressed feelings are addressed are present only by proxy. An actor or fellow member of the therapeutic group "takes the place of" mother, father, sister, brother, lover – whoever.

Displays I've seen, and sometimes invoked, in workshops and group therapy are versions of what's no longer (or never was) permitted in general Euro-American society. These displays were framed and controlled – artfully presented – as part of theater training or therapy healing. The displays were managed with the greatest art in theater where they were rehearsed and scored. But what happens in therapy is also artful because the therapist monitors and coaches the patients, while the patients frequently present "numbers," actions and feelings they have played before. In many cases, abreaction is encouraged by therapists.

A very radical integration of therapy into theater was Robert Wilson's work in the 1960s–1970s. Wilson drew also on non-western performances, especially trance dancing, selective inattention, and extended performance time/space. Wilson's approach to therapy was like what Australian Aborigines do. Wilson didn't try to convince the patient – a protagonist not necessarily in the narrative but in the kinesthetic sense – to "adjust" to the ordinary world, the world which the protagonist has in some way rejected or been rejected by. Instead, Wilson brought other performers into the protagonist's world, creating a secure nest inside which the protagonist's own construction of reality could be played out.

> In his therapy workshops, Wilson provides movement exercises for participants and at the same time he learns from them – from their particular ways of expression, communication, and sensibility. His observations are applied to his theater workshops and performances. From the early stages, his performances have been influenced to a great extent by his work with exceptional children. During workshops for *The King of Spain* (1969), Wilson began to work with an almost totally deaf boy, Raymond Andrews. . . . [Quoting from Wilson's *The*

King of Spain Production notes:] "Raymond with his special sensibility and unusual ways of communication, provided a rich alternative and inspiration for the work. In spite of his near total deafness and virtually no vocabulary, he immediately became a jovial, out-going, convivial and even communicative member of the group. For instance, the movement sections – he is more lively in them and often more imaginative in demonstrating an ability to be exceedingly and exceptionally sensitive to the feelings of others. Only he 'perceives' (and transmits) this through kinetic, or kinesthetic awareness rather than through discursive, or verbal dialogue. In these children, I sensed not only a deep, special talent but channels usually unknown for establishing lines of communication. Because of a bodily maladjustment in a certain sense, there was an extended range of feeling or, even, sensibility that, once uncovered, meant an expression of awareness and communication."

(Deák 1974: 69)[5]

It was Andrews' world that Wilson and his co-workers actualized so fully in *Deafman Glance* (1971). Wilson nested Andrews in a world of Andrews' own making. Instead of adjusting Andrews to the world – instead of insisting that Andrews' experience of the world was wrong, askew, abnormal and in need of adjustment – Wilson provided a theatrical world that harmonized with the perceptions of the protagonist–patient. This is close to how the Aborigines dance their Dreamtime into being. Or to the way some native Americans on a vision quest receive and transmit what they find. The dream visions are enacted and then re-enacted by the band or tribe. In Wilson's theater, as in therapies following the same principle (and Wilson once was a therapist working with autistic children), the protagonist–patient reciprocates by granting a degree of validity to the world of her/his partners, thereby opening a channel of communication. Wilson, at this stage of his career, often chose to work with, and privilege, people with problems of communication, Andrews and later Christopher Knowles. By letting the deaf or brain-damaged person know that they can "do their own world" and that the others will follow, Wilson made possible an exchange where the protagonist–patient finally says, "OK, now it's your turn to do your world and I'll follow." A favorite exercise of

Wilson's in workshop was the game of follow-the-leader. Or he asked people to pick up on rhythms and movements of others. He did many variations on mirror exercises – but not in a mechanical way: people improvised on the basis of mirroring.

I'm uncomfortable using the word "patient" for Andrews or for Knowles who worked with Wilson on The Life and Times of Joseph Stalin (1973), The $ Value of Man (1975), and DIA LOG/Curious George (1980). Patient signals stigma, abbreviated or twisted personhood, while it was by granting whole personhood – or even the enhanced status of protagonist, of hero, that Wilson created the environment out of which his extraordinary art grew. When working with Knowles on Stalin, other performers followed him, imitated him, played with him on his own terms: in this nest of experiences, people began to come out, showing idiosyncratic aspects of their own personalities. The gap between them and Knowles, and between each other, both grew and diminished. Paradoxically, these deeply private worlds proved "universal," a widely shared repertory of actions, many based on recognizable versions/distortions of ordinary experience slowed down or exaggerated. Individuals showed each other fantasies they would usually hide or trash as "unacceptable." In the actions Wilson received from the performers he worked with, the private, the social, and the species-wide converged. Breaking away from the idea of a normative, single world-view, Wilson opened the possibilities of multiple worlds coexisting and interacting in the same performance time/space. Maybe this is only a late-twentieth-century version of traditional American Utopian projections. It certainly has a pluralistic ring to it. But may be too it creates on stage the interplay between genetically fixed (universal) patterns and culturally invented (learned) ones both as recast by individual fantasy.

Wilson's method has four steps: 1) creating a secure nest for the protagonist, making her/him feel that her/his world-view/experience is authentic and worth sharing; 2) playing with the world-views of some, many, or all the other performer-participants; 3) integrating these multiple world-views into the vision of the protagonist; 4) subsuming all these to the over-view of the auteur, Wilson himself.

Spectators say that Wilson's work is comforting, even healing. I think this is because Wilson unfolds his images very slowly, evoking alpha rhythms, "slowing" the brain down, engaging the trophotropic right hemisphere (see chapter 8). Also because his performances are vast, truly epic world visions, they are all-encompassing, reassuring. While traditional western art since the Renaissance has been obsessively single-minded, monoscopic, intensive, and dialectical, Wilson's work is many-minded, multiscopic, extensive, and varilectical.

Wilson's methods, and their results, are like some shamans' performances which also use the sick in a drama of adventure while opening multiple channels of communication. I pointed out how Aborigines construct ceremonies from what a shaman "sees" either while asleep or alone in the desert. He returns to his people and shares with them what he experienced – a dance, a narrative, a song. The others participate with him in enacting a ceremony that is both new and old. To "see" while sleeping is different but not less real than seeing while awake. Performances made from vision-quests, drug-induced visions, or dreams are treated by many of the world's peoples with special respect precisely because they hinge two spheres of reality. A shaman is a professional link connecting disparate but interacting reality spheres. One of the ways a person knows s/he is going to become a shaman is when s/he experiences visions that can be translated into performances. Isaac Tens, a shaman of the north-west Pacific, tells how he was called:

> Thirty years after my birth was the time. . . . My heart started to beat fast, & I began to tremble, just as had happened before, when the shamans were trying to fix me up. My flesh seemed to be boiling, & I could hear su—. My body was quivering. While I remained in this state, I began to sing. A chant was coming out of me without my being able to do anything to stop it. Many things appeared to me presently: huge black birds & other animals. . . . These were visible only to me, not to the others in my house. Such visions happen when a man is about to become a shaman; they occur of their own accord. The songs force themselves out complete without any attempt to compose them. But I learned & memorized those songs by repeating them.
>
> (Rothenberg 1968: 51–2)

See Eliade (1970) and Lévi-Strauss (1963) for other versions of how the call comes, and what shamans do with the skills they acquire. The one unifying factor is that the shaman after receiving the call in a flash, a crisis, a sudden sickness, later learns through difficult detailed training a specific technique which is a performance.

Earlier I mentioned "phatic theater," a kind of performance where the evocation and expression of a group mood is the most important thing. La Barre defines "phatic communication in man as in apes" as "the establishment of similar subjective states in a group of animals – which is why the shaman's message need not be notably rational cognitively, and very often is not" (1972: 343). La Barre sees verbal language developing from phatic cries, especially as humans improved their hunting skills:

> The greater complexity of hunting as compared with fruit eating, and the swiftly changing contingencies of the hunt, also evidently favored a change from closed, species-wide "phatic" ape cries – closed in the sense that each monolithic one of these cries can serve to display in the individual ape, and diffuse to the group, only one endocrine phatic state each: fear, anger, amorousness, and the like – into the more elaborated communications of merely group-wide articulate speech. Hominid hunters need language. But not only in the hunt. The adaptive necessity of intense group life among aggressive hunters also demands better communication and management of both aggressive and erotic drives in early man.
>
> (La Barre 1972: 77)[6]

La Barre underestimates the complexity of social life among the great apes. The same cries and gestures, in different circumstances, can mean different things. The multivocality of ape communication is close to human phatic expressions. Shouting, laughing, sobbing, plaintive whining, jumping up and down, foot-stamping, raising the fist, etc., are all communications emitted from that confused area between culturally specific expressions and universal human signaling. The cry of a frightened child, the moaning of grief, the scream of pain, the gasp of terror, and other phatic expressions – as well as the body configurations, gestures, and facial displays accompanying these – probably constitute universal signals; yet each culture, each family, each person plays this pan-species repertory with singular skill, manipulating meaning and effect.

Rappaport tells us that in the Highlands of Papua New Guinea:

> When pigs are sacrificed to them, spirits are usually addressed in a peculiar screaming style. The message is delivered in staccato phrases, interrupted with increasing frequency by meaningless, loud, sharp yells until, just before the pig is struck on the head with the club, the staccato "Ah! Ah! Ah! Ah!" has replaced words altogether.
>
> (Rappaport 1968: 128)

Here cognitive discourse – usually about how fat the pig is, how suitable for repaying an obligation – is transformed into pure phatic expression. Ordinary speech everywhere is immersed in a sea of exclamatory sounds, stutterings, repetitions, ohs, ahs, and uhs; as well as variations in rhythm, pitch, and volume – a whole language of metaverbal communication giving to each utterance its unique and unrepeatable shape and significance. In any situation of strong feeling this infrastructure erupts into dominance: the cognitive value of words is submerged in a rising tide of phatic expression. The center of speaking actually shifts downward to where diaphragmatic breathing controls how sound is released automatically as sheer breath. Not enough is known about this transformational process, about how cognitive speech becomes metaverbal sounding.

In opera, Indian raga, and jazz "meaningless" vocables temporarily replace words at moments of intense expressivity. The extension of sounds built on modulations of pitch, volume, and duration characterizing the aria, the raga, and the jazz riff is a formal way of giving over to the phatic quality of "pure music." In left-brain/right-brain terms, the utterance that begins as left-hemisphere-dominant arouses the right hemisphere so strongly that the original cognitive function is overwhelmed – the singer, and the audience too, is "swept away," "moved," "overcome," "touched" – all dynamic and sensuous metaphors appropriate to the right hemisphere. A time of free play ensues during which the left hemisphere abdicates authority until a formal resolution restores its dominance. This structure, so clear in music, is implicit in many human encounters. Greek tragedy, with its fierce agons of pure staccato speech bracketed by the longer rhythms of the choric odes, is another example of this pattern.

Andrei Serban and Elizabeth Swados in their *Fragments of a Trilogy* (1975) – based on *Medea, Electra,* and *The Trojan Women* – carried experiments in phatic language and sounds very far. Serban worked with Peter Brook and Ted Hughes in the creation of *Orghast* (1971, see Smith 1972). *Orghast* was a performance for which Hughes invented-constructed a "new language" emphasizing its phatic qualities. In *Orghast* words "felt" rather than "meant." For the *Trilogy* Serban preferred not to invent a new language but to work with ancient Greek – a language neither the performers nor the audience understood. As Serban said:

> The reason we used ancient Greek was to really examine what is hidden in those sounds – in those particular sounds. What is there is the potential for a special energy to be acted, to be rediscovered again after being buried for 2000 years.
>
> (Serban, in Blumenthal 1976: 107–8)

I saw/heard *The Trilogy.* Language was pulled and screamed, chanted and pushed up against a wide array of percussive sounds composed and performed by Swados. Also the vocal range of the performers – especially Priscilla Smith's deep gutturals and shrieks – displaced the ancient Greek, transforming it into a medium of direct phatic communication between performers and spectators. Whatever the language, it's Greek to us so the effect of the performance is of receiving it "concretely," as ways of finding sounds that embody the terror of the tragic actions. The text is used as a tool to dig sound out of the performers. They do not "interpret" or "read" the text. They do not "express" it, it extrudes phatic sounds from them.

Eibl-Eibesfeldt points out the relationship between inborn releasing mechanisms and artistic expression, especially music. Breathing and heartbeat can be brought into harmony with metronomes or melodies; drumming raises body temperature.

> By the artistic manipulation of the releasing stimuli the composer can create and dissolve tensions in the listener. The highs and lows of

emotional experience are touched in an ever-changing pattern that cannot be experienced in everyday life.

(Eibl-Eibesfeldt 1970: 440)

Of course anyone who has ever wept at a performance of *Romeo and Juliet*, or a soap opera, or while reading, knows how susceptible humans are to an artistic induction of feelings. Brecht struggled against these reactions, wishing to highlight thinking or sitting in judgement. If even the tame shows of western theater are capable of inducing such strong reactions think how much more thorough are total theater performances – dreamed of by Artaud but realized mainly outside the Euro-American context. Outside if we consider only what we call theater. Certainly charismatic churches, rock concerts, and some sports events achieve every bit as much phatically speaking as the ritual performances of non-western cultures. Of many non-western examples available, I will cite two to show how thoroughly spectators are involved in the construction of total theater performances. S. M. Shirokogoroff, the Russian anthropologist who studied Siberian shamanism in great detail and depth, reported that:

The rhythmic music and singing, and later the dancing of the shaman, gradually involve every participant more and more in a collective action. When the audience begins to repeat the refrains together with the assistants, only those who are defective fail to join the chorus. The tempo of the action increases, the shaman with a spirit is no more an ordinary man or relative, but is a "placing" (i.e. incarnation of the spirit; the spirit acts together with the audience, and this is felt by everyone. The state of many participants is now near to that of the shaman himself, and only a strong belief that when the shaman is there the spirit may only enter him, restrains the participants from being possessed in mass by the spirit. . . . When the shaman feels that the audience is with him and follows him he becomes still more active and this effect is transmitted to his audience. After shamanizing, the audience recollects various moments of the performance, their great psychophysiological emotion and the hallucinations of sight and hearing which they have experienced. They then have a deep satisfaction – much greater than that from emotions produced by theatrical and musical performances, literature, and general artistic phenomena of the European complex, because in shamanizing the audience at the same time acts and participates.

(Shirokogoroff, in Lewis 1971: 53)

And as Kenneth E. Read, an anthropologist who lived with the Gahuku of Papua New Guinea, said of a prenuptial ceremony:

The extraordinary effect of the next half hour is difficult to describe. The house was packed to its capacity, but in the blackness I was unable to discover so much as a single feature of the man who sat beside me. Almost immediately, enveloped in disembodied voices, I felt the first stirrings of a curious panic, a fear that if I relaxed my objectivity for as much as a moment I would lose my identity. At the same time the possibility that this could happen seemed immensely attractive. The air was thick with pungent odors, with the smell of unwashed bodies and stranger aromatic overtones that pricked my nostrils and my eyes. But it was the singing, reverberating in the confined space and pounding incessantly against my ears that rose to cloud my mind with the fumes of a collective emotion almost too powerful for my independent will. . . . The songs followed one another without a perceptible break, a single shrill and keening voice lifting now and then to point the way to a new set. As the others joined in strongly, I felt close to the very things that eluded me in my day-to-day investigations, brought into psychical confrontation with the intangible realm of hopes and shared ideas for which words and actions, though they are all we have, are quite inadequate expressions. In analytic language, the situation could be accommodated under the rubric of a rite of separation — an event by which a young girl in her father's house, surrounded by her kinsmen, was brought to the morning of the day on which she must assume a new status and be transferred to her husband's people, but its quality could not be conveyed in any professional terms. While the voices swelled inside the house, mounting to a climax, the barriers of my alien life dissolved. The sound engulfed me, bearing me with it beyond the house and into the empty spaces of the revolving universe. Thus sustained, I was one of the innumerable companies of men who, back to the shrouded entrance of the human race, have sat at night by fires and filled forest clearings and the wilderness with recitals of their own uniqueness.

(Read 1965: 251–2)

From a late-1980s perspective these accounts could be deconstructed, revealing romantic yearnings, assumptions about the ahistoricity of non-western peoples, and so on. But the accounts can also yield information if taken at face value. For all the differences, Shirokogoroff and Read report the same pattern: a collective performance, rising to an epiphanic climax, then subsiding into a calm that leads to a "recollection in tranquility" of what it all means. This same pattern characterizes charismatic church services, rock concerts, and maybe even the waltz or tarantella in their heyday. These events each require not "spectators" but "participants," even "congregations," assemblies of believers who co-create the world of the performance. Such a social unit is something more than a random assembly of ticket buyers, though they may start out as that. Listen to Abbie Hoffman describe the 1969 Woodstock festival:

They were all piled up on People Hill and saw the spotlight burn down on Creedence Clearwater, hypnotizing them, driving them into an orgiastic fury that shook the whole mutherfucking stage. It felt like the last scene from *Frankenstein* performed by the Living Theater. . . . Every once in a while a straight dude from the Construction Company or the Safety Department or something like that would rush up to someone who looked like he was in charge and yell "We must stop this! The stage will collapse! Everybody must get off!" And always some shaggy-haired freak would hug him and say "Swingin baby, we're gonna fly up here forever!" and the swingers and the faith healers and the astrology freaks were all right that Saturday night up there. That was one of the eerie things about WOODSTOCK NATION, every nut in it was right, even the Meher Baba buffs. . . . There is a way of integrating your own ego trip with a sense of community, with a concept of the "we." I feel a sense of this most strongly in these massive events, in what Artaud refers to as the "festival of the streets."

(Hoffman 1969: 86, 5–6)

Hindsight discredits Hoffman as a predictor of political trends in the USA. But he is an accurate reporter of the phatic sense of things circa Woodstock 1969. And the "concept of the 'we' " he describes may not be limited to humans. In chapter 5 I discussed the chimpanzee "carnivals" V. and F. Reynolds observed in the Bundongo Forest of Uganda. These

> "carnivals" consisted of prolonged noise for periods of hours ... stamping and fast-running feet ... howling outbursts and prolonged rolls of drums (as many as 13 rapid beats) shaking the ground. ... Although it was not possible to know the reason for this unusual behavior, twice it seemed to be associated with the meeting at a common food source of bands that may have been relatively unfamiliar to each other.
>
> (Reynolds and Reynolds 1965: 409)

The meeting of bands at a time when there is an abundance of fruit fits nicely with Woodstock and other human celebrations: theater so often occurs when divergent groups assemble to share food.

LYING AND PRETENDING

A great difference between human and non-human performers is the ability of humans to lie and pretend. There is plenty of deception in the animal world: mimicry, camouflage, and the like. But most, if not all, of these body modifications and behaviors are hard-wired, genetically determined. A chameleon can't choose not to change colors anymore than a parrot can decide not to mimic certain sounds. What marks human behavior is its lability, its unfinishedness. People can choose to do, or not do; to adorn or transform their bodies, or not to; to wear masks, or to go bare-faced. Hamlet's very basic "to be or not to be" is a question only humans can ask – and answer in the negative if a person so decides. But lability does not equal liberty. Often enough people get drawn deeply into schemes of their own construction. There probably isn't any over-riding human destiny; each person, mostly unconsciously, constructs a destiny for her/himself. Take Quesalid, a Kwakiutl whose story Claude Lévi-Strauss

(1963) tells. Quesalid wanted to debunk the shamans, revealing their fakery.

> Driven by curiosity about their tricks and by the desire to expose them, he began to associate with the shamans until one of them offered to make him a member of their group. Quesalid did not wait to be asked twice, and his narrative recounts the details of his first lessons, a curious mixture of pantomime, prestigiation and empirical knowledge, including the art of simulating fainting and nervous fits, the learning of sacred songs, the technique for inducing vomiting, rather precise notions of auscultation and obstetrics and the use of "dreamers," that is, spies who listen to private conversations and secretly convey to the shaman bits of information concerning the origins and symptoms of the ills suffered by different people. Above all, he learned the *ars magna* of one of the shamanistic schools of the Northwest Coast: the shaman hides a little tuft of down in a corner of his mouth, and he throws it up, covered with blood, at the proper moment – after having bitten his tongue or made his gums bleed – and solemnly presents it to his patient and the onlookers as the pathological foreign body extracted as a result of his sucking and manipulations.
>
> (Lévi-Strauss 1963: 175)

Quesalid wanted to expose his teachers but before he could he was called by the family of a sick person who had dreamt that Quesalid cured him. Using the techniques he learned Quesalid was successful. This was the first of many cures, and as time went by Quesalid became known as a great shaman – but he credited his success to psychological factors. No matter, over the years, he came more and more to believe in his own methods, to discriminate against practices that were more false (in his view) than his own.

> While visiting the neighboring Koskimo Indians, Quesalid attends a curing ceremony of his illustrious colleagues of the other tribe. To his great astonishment he observes a difference in their technique. Instead of spitting out the illness in the form of a "bloody worm" (the concealed down), the Koskimo shamans merely spit a little saliva into their hands, and they dare to claim that this is "the sickness." What is

the value of this method? What is the theory behind it? In order to find out the "strength of the shamans, whether it was real or whether they only pretended to be shamans" like his fellow tribesmen, Quesalid requests and obtains permission to try his method in an instance where the Koskimo method has failed. The sick woman then declares herself cured.

(Lévi-Strauss 1963: 176)

Thereafter Quesalid is invited to test his method against all others, and he invariably triumphs. Other shamans come to him and confess their tricks. Quesalid no longer refers to the technique of the bloody down as a trick: he says nothing about it, while continuing to proclaim its superiority over all other methods. "He seems to have completely lost sight of the fallaciousness of the technique which he had so disparaged at the beginning" (Lévi-Strauss 1963: 178).

How different is Quesalid's opinion concerning his act than Pete Townshend's of The Who?

We did a thing at Detroit and we got to the end and I thought, Jesus, we've taken it completely the wrong route and we've already finished with what we normally finish with, we'd done that, we'd done the big ending, we've done the guitar spinning, we've leaped in the air, we're exhausted, we've gone thru every musical brain-wave we could possibly go thru and yet they, out there, don't think we're finished. So what do we do now? . . . So we play, like B sides of remote singles, and bit by bit we take the audience down and down and down and down and down until they're so desperate, right, we've got 'em, they're down where we are, they're desperate, where we are, then all we've got to do is jump three times in the air, spin a guitar and bang it on the ground, then kick a drum over and we're finished!

(Somma 1969: 134–5)[7]

Both Quesalid and Townshend wholly own their techniques. They are able to open a gap between performer and performance. They are not swept away by the performance as the audience is; they are not taken in by what they are doing. Or if they are, as Quesalid was, it comes by observing the effect the performance has on others, measuring this against the less effective means of rivals. Or, as in Indian *rasa* theory, both performer and spectator experience the performance together. The performer, responsible for making the performance happen, also reacts to it and displays that reaction. The *rasa* – the juice or flavor of the performance – is co-created, it exists *between* performer and spectator and is shared by them. In the performances of Quesalid, Townshend, and those working according to rasa theory, a double gap is opened: 1) between the performer and the performance; 2) between the performance and the audience. Quesalid cures his patients which affects the audience of supporters and rival shamans. Townshend manipulates his performance on the spot, changing plans in order to bring the audience down to where the set can end. This double gap is inconceivable in any species other than the human. Once this gap opens, in spills the drama.

RITUALIZATION, BLOCKED DISPLAY, AND PERFORMANCE

Before considering drama, farce especially, which is a unique creation of our species, I want to look at more parallels between animal and human theatrical behavior. Up to now I've said that phatic behavior in humans is both homologous and analogous to the phatic behavior of the great apes. This behavior is performative, including mood displays, drumming, dancing, shouting. Sometimes the displays include rehearsals, or at least trial runs and preparations. The mood displays are interactive, often contagious, and, when celebratory, associated with the meeting of bands and the sharing of food. Correlations between animal and human performances occur at deeper levels too, in events ethologists call displacement activities, redirected activities, and ritualization. In humans, these behaviors are linked to internal experiences: fantasies, day and night dreaming, and (for lack of a better term) the imagination up to and including sports, simulations, and stage dramas. Who knows if non-human animals fantasize? My argument does not depend on the existence of such fantasies. I say only that human fantasies are evolutionary developments of animal pre-human ritualizations and displays.

To ethologists a ritual is a behavior sequence which over the course of evolutionary time and through the process of natural selection is transformed in the following ways (adapted from Eibl-Eibesfedt 1970: 100–1):

1. Behavior changes function.
2. Movements become independent of their original causes and develop their own releasing mechanisms.
3. These movements are exaggerated and at the same time simplified; they frequently freeze into postures; they become rhythmic and repetitive.
4. Conspicuous body parts develop such as the peacock's tail and the moose's horns. These parts become important elements in behavioral displays.

In chapter 5 of this volume I argue that ritualization in the theater is not a function of content or even of "origins" (if ever these could be determined, which I doubt) but of the rehearsal-to-performance sequence, the periodicity of performances, and on the microsocial level, the prevalence of conventions designed to remove ambiguity from the communication. In chapter 3 I connect the action of drama to play and to hunting behavior. Here I want to discuss ritualization from the point of view of the performer's process and the spectator's response.

The debate concerning whether there is a "universal" body language is now running in favor of such a conclusion. A look of surprise, a belly laugh, a howl of pain, a child's cry, the outstretched arms of a mother, and so on, are all understood everywhere. Paul Ekman (1972, 1980, 1983, Ekman, Friesen, and Ellsworth 1972) has shown how facial displays associated with six emotions – surprise, disgust, sadness, anger, fear, and happiness – are universally recognized. (See chapter 8 for a discussion of how these facial displays affect the autonomic nervous system and relate to stage acting.) There appears to be a developmental continuity of behavior among primates. Surely certain human behavior sequences are enacted everywhere in the same way; these may constitute a basic repertory of mini-dramas: the child running for protection into the arms of its mother; the open-palm greeting; freezing in place when a suspicious noise or an unknown threat is perceived; taking cover by means of hiding, crouching, or flattening when an overwhelming force is encountered. There is a large repertory of universally recognized situations eliciting equally recognizable responses. Theater plays with these situations and responses, often twisting ironies out of misunderstandings and misinterpretations. For with the ritualization of signals comes the possibility, among humans particularly, of irony, tricks, lies, and the dissemination of misinformation. Iago preceded Ronald Reagan in this regard. Double and triple misunderstandings spark drama: such is the trap Oedipus falls into when he runs from Corinth in an effort to escape the fate the oracle has predicted for him; or Romeo's misreading Juliet's drugged sleep as death, even though she doesn't look dead: "Death, that hath sucked the honey of the breath/Hath had no power yet upon thy beauty" (V. iii. 92–3). Theatrical costuming and gesturing are exaggerated, sometimes even outlandishly so as in kabuki, kathakali, and melodrama. But even in so-called naturalist theater the gestures are not natural – that is, as in ordinary life. And the Euro-American avant-garde from the nineteenth century to the present never tires of appropriating the styles, masks, and "hieroglyphs" (as Artaud called the gestures of Balinese dance) of non-western genres.

There are two kinds of body language. The first is the "natural language" of animals in the wild studied by ethologists and the microsocial exchanges among humans studied by scholars such as Ekman, Goffman, and Birdwhistell.[8] The second is the artificial languages of ritual and art. Separating these two kinds of body language is not easy; perhaps with humans it's impossible. Human social life affects human biology at a very deep level.

But let us look again at the Paleolithic cave art of south-west Europe (which I've discussed in chapters 3 and 5). Already in this art the human body is exaggerated, distorted, transformed, masked, and abstracted. Most of the art is of animals – but these animals are depicted in groupings that don't fit what goes on "in nature." Predators and prey are shown together in non-agonistic arrangements; some species are painted together that do not run together in nature; and a few paintings are of imaginary animals such as the unicorn-like figure at Lascaux. At least one figure depicts a person dressed in an animal skin and mask. This is the "sorcerer" or "shaman" of the Les Trois Frères cave. As I noted previously, the cave art, and the mobile art of the period too, suggests theater, dance, and music: an art of physical action. Certainly the cave paintings weren't there solely or even mainly to be looked at, as in an art gallery. The paintings were executed in torch-light, some of the chambers are extremely difficult to get to. Footprints frozen in clay floors suggest circular dancing in at least the caves of Niaux, the Grotte d'Aldène, and Tuc d'Audoubert where adolescent initiation may explain the "smaller-than-adult heel prints, as though in a ritual walk or dance, surround[ing] a clay effigy of copulating bisons" (La Barre 1972: 162). The presence of imaginary animals, masked human dancers, and, outside the caves, "Venus" figures with intentionally exaggerated hips, thighs, and breasts all show a big capa-city for an art that used meaningful distortion/transformation: a kind of conceptual-ritual complex. To be in the world, as all animals are, is one thing; to present this being is something else; to transform it is something else again. And to transform it as a way of constructing its potential, its "as if," is the heart of the theatrical process.

Thus from the earliest art we can know about with certainty, and continuing to the present, ironies, contradictions, transformations, and imaginary beings and situations are part of art — while art itself is fundamental to religion and other belief systems. People make what isn't there, combine elements from fantasy, actualize situations that occur only as art or performance. These actualizations in the service of social organization, thought, ritual, or rebellious anti-structure con-tain, transmit, and (dare I say it?) *create* the very circumstances they purport to depict.

The way this process works is different, or at least inordinately more complex, for humans than for animals. The "innate releasing mechan-isms" of animals — hard-wired in their nervous systems — cause the display of a sequence of behavior that is predictable and in many cases invariable. A stimulus — an interaction with another animal, or some-thing else — releases an animal's display (figure 7.1). These displays can be fancy — threats, stamping, dances, etc. — or plain ongoing social interactions. The fancy displays — those that ethologists call ritualiza-tions — usually concern mating, hierarchy, territory: arenas of conflict and misunderstanding where clear signaling is to the advantage of both the individual and the species. In people interaction also stimulates

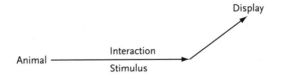

Figure 7.1

displays, but often these displays are blocked from full expression. Human interactions are so dense, multivocal, ambivalent, and ambiguous that individuals learn early to hold back, to redirect their impulses either redirecting them inward or displacing them. This is not just a "problem" of modern industrial societies but a characteristic of all human groupings.

Art, custom, religion, and social convention flow from and cluster around these arenas of blocked display. In animals "the dammed-up excitation sparks over, so to speak, into another channel and there finds its discharge" (Eibl-Eibesfeldt 1970: 17). In people, dammed-up excitation is frequently redirected inward where it happens as a fantasy (figure 7.2). The fantasy is not necessarily – in fact, rarely – a literal translation of the blocked display. The fantasy picks up and elaborates on materials associated with the blocked display. The fantasy is like a dream, consisting of clusters of apparently unrelated stuff. But actually the material is all connected. Ultimately, in some cases where an acceptable channel exists, or can be made, the fantasy plus its associated material from "other channels" re-emerges as a display. This display, a

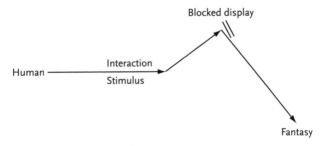

Figure 7.2

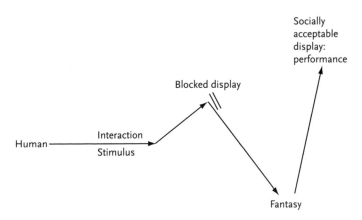

Figure 7.3

performance, is a public way to show private stuff (figure 7.3). In this way many performances have a restorative function for the performer analogous to the cathartic function for the spectator.

Performances can get at, and out, two sets of material simultaneously: 1) what was blocked and transformed into fantasy; 2) stuff from other channels that otherwise might have a hard time getting expressed at all. Seen this way, performing is a public dreaming. Conversely, dreaming is an interior drama. It is not only psychoanalysis that assumes as much. In many cultures dreams open to highly valued worlds where skilled humans – shamans, visionaries, dream-seekers – acquire definite knowledge that they bring back and share with the community. Just as dream work combines the day's event with the dreamer's interior life, creating a symbolic drama with an audience/ participator of one, so rehearsals combine verbal texts, music, and choreography with individual fantasies. Displays that are blocked, that "can't happen," happen, but in disguised form. No matter how weird the public performance, if it is public it's found its niche. Some performances of the avant-garde, of religious ceremonies, of shamanism, of initiation rites, and so on feature actions that are taboo. A balance is struck among the public, the private, and the secret. It's no accident that many cultures link performance to dreams: vision quests, hallucinations, trances, Dreamtime, surrealistic automatic creation, and so on. Fantasy is interiorized display and performance is exterior-ized fantasy.

The interior and exterior are open to each other, the borders between them are porous and fluid. Human art and religion deal in imaginary realities which have had the greatest possible influence on social organization. The ritual process of animals is the basis for but by no means the limit of these human symbolic expressions. The languages of culture – verbal, mathematical, musical, pictorial, architectural, theatrical – are continually interacting with and transforming ritual body language. Who can say what is "primary" and what "secondary" of these? They are continually constructing–deconstructing–reconstructing each other.

DRAMA, DISPLACEMENT, AND REDIRECTION

Drama is a narrative dialogic text written to be performed. The high points of drama include Greek tragedy, Indian Sanskrit plays, the Eliza-bethan theater, Japanese noh. Periods of drama come and go in this culture and that; in chapters 3 and 4 I discuss some of the vagaries of drama as an historical phenomenon. Here I want to deal not with drama itself but with what E. T. Kirby (1975) calls "ur-drama," the process of transforming social conflict into aesthetics. Some of the most interesting kinds of ur-drama are trials – which are often enter-tainments as well as judicial procedures. Included as "trials" are not only courtroom proceedings where lawyers clash by day but also ritual combats, obscene farces, world duels, "soundings," and praise-singing. In all these encounters, combatants test their skills before juries whose reactions – formal or otherwise – clearly determine winners and losers.

These events are analogous to what ethologists call "displacement" or "redirected" activity. As Lorenz describes it, "a redirected activity is just this: if I am furious with my boss, my fear may inhibit my aggres-sion against him, so I release my aggression toward the underdog or toward anything else" (1959: 187). The high incidence of sex and violence in theater can be partially explained as redirected activities. Some performers enter the profession (or become shamans) because of their excitability. It is even possible to find whole theatrical traditions that arose as redirected activities. Among peoples of the Highlands of

Papua New Guinea, tribal warfare was banned first by Australian colonial authorities and later by the Papua New Guinea government. What has arisen in its place are performances. As Rappaport tells us:

> It is said that dancing is like fighting. The visitors' procession is led by men carrying fight-packages,[9] and their entrance upon the dance group of their hosts is martial. To join a group in dancing is the symbolic expression of willingness to join them in fighting.
>
> (Rappaport 1968: 196)

Of course many military displays all around the world are dances. The aggressive potential of a "great power" is advertised in its parades which display armies and armaments. Among the Kogu of Papua New Guinea, observed by Ronald M. Berndt in the 1950s, warfare and cannibalism were replaced by local courts. By the mid-1980s there was debate regarding whether cannibalism ever was practiced in Papua New Guinea or anywhere else.[10] But the Berndts accepted it as fact.

"Dead human flesh, to these people, is food. . . . 'Cut my body,' a dying man or woman may say, 'so that the crops may increase. Eat my flesh so that the gardens may grow' " (Berndt 1962: 271–2). Enemies were eaten for their protein and their power. Cannibalism is the ultimate occupation of another's territory: it obliterates the other by transforming him into the eater. It is also a eucharistic feast. According to Berndt, the Kogu practiced two kinds of cannibalism: aggressive/celebratory cannibalism, where an enemy was ingested with much shouting, dancing, and feasting; and "ordinary" cannibalism, where a fellow villager was slaughtered because she or he was old, sick, or defenseless.

The cruelty with which the Kogu dispatched their enemies is reminiscent of Greek myths. A wounded enemy, Kricme, was taken prisoner:

> As they entered their district, they were greeted by all the women and children dancing and singing around them. They put Kricme in the center of the village clearing, where the people danced around him. It is said that he must have been in great pain, for the arrow with which he had been shot was still protruding. Nasecompa then came forward with a steel ax and began cutting at his knee; Kricme cried out, but

Nasecompa severed the limb and threw it to one side. A woman danced forward singing, picked up the leg and danced away. Still Kricme cried as Nasecompa cut off the other leg and threw it to a man who danced forward, singing, and carried it away. The same was done with one arm, then the other; still Kricme cried, until Nasecompa with a stroke of his ax severed the head, which was caught by a dancing man and carried away. Then the trunk was cut up and various parts distributed. When the feast was finished the bones were tied up in croton leaves and fastened to the Moiife stockade.

(Berndt 1962: 280–1)

Kricme's fate is uncannily like that of Pentheus of Euripides' *The Bacchae*. In a case of adultery – also reminiscent of Greek myth – a Haita man, Auglimu, found his wife with a lover. He shot the man, sliced his flesh while he was still living, severed both his arms, and left him to bleed to death. Then he took his wife, and her lover's arms, back to her house where they roasted the arms, ate a meal of them, and slept together. Berndt comments:

Whether the cutting up of a victim while he is still alive is deliberate cruelty, as in the case of the husband who killed his wife's lover, is difficult to say. There is little doubt, however, that the people who participated . . . appear to have enjoyed watching the man's suffering and hearing him cry as his limbs were hacked off. A number of men who took part in this particular feast [the killing of Kricme], including Nasecompa himself, thought it great fun and laughed uproariously discussing it, with no sign of embarrassment.

(Berndt 1962: 281)

Berndt reports that when warriors came home with a corpse often "many men and women indulge[d] in uncontrolled behavior, assaulting the corpse and fighting over the best portions of meat" (Berndt 1962: 283). If the victim was a young woman, men would copulate with the corpse before cutting it up. The men acted openly and their women

far from resenting it, apparently enjoyed watching them. It is said that they themselves often squat over dead men, pretending to have coitus with them or playing with the penes of corpses. Both men and women smear themselves with blood and hang from their head and shoulders various parts of the body in much the same way as is done with the meat of pigs during the pig festival.

(Berndt 1962: 283–4)

Such incidents seem more suited to pornographic horror films than ethnography. One event Berndt describes, were it acted on a stage in proper Grand-Guignol style by Charles Ludlam, would surely be farce. Groups of Aguara, Moiife, and Kogu men and women gathered around corpses taken in battle to cut them up. Unapicna began on a woman named Pazucna – but instead of cutting her up he fucked her. A Kogu woman, Aria, accused him of taking too long and because Unapicna ignored her she began to cut up Pazucna. "She cut further in and across, hacking away at the flesh; and since Unapicna's penis was in the woman's vagina, she cut most of it off." Aria blamed Unapicna: "You sit there copulating, not bothering to cut her up properly. . . . Thus I cut off your penis!" Unapicna screamed at Aria, but then she removed the penis from the corpse, "popped it into her mouth, and ate it, and then continued with the cutting. Unapicna was helped back to his house where he rested. Ovens were made and the meat cooked, amid dancing and singing. Unapicna was given Pazucna's vulva and surrounding flesh to eat" (Berndt 1962: 283).

In 1976 when I originally wrote this chapter I accepted as factual these accounts of the cruel, bizarre actions of the Kogu. But in 1987 the debate concerning the existence of cannibalism made me think the "data" over again.

In the preface to his book, Berndt says, "My wife and I, together or singly, were able to observe the majority of features discussed in this volume, some of them not once or twice but many times, in Kogu and various adjacent districts, as well as in the Busarasa-Moke area" (1962: xii). He then gives a long list of what they saw. Finally he says:

There was, however, as there must always be, much that we could not see: for example, violence during cannibal feasts, sharp fighting and confusion when a village was raided, certain extra-marital ventures, and so on. Although by all accounts these were still taking place south of Wanevinti, it would have been unwise and dangerous to attempt research there at that time.

(1962: xiii)

So the detailed descriptions of cannibalism and necrophilia previously presented turned out to be "by all accounts"; they were not witnessed by the ethnographers. The uproarious laughter in "discussing" Kricme's death and dismemberment might have been directed at the gullible ethnographers.

I find this even more interesting than if these events could be proven to have happened exactly as Berndt reports them.

The Rabelaisian extremes of the actions, the delight with which some of the incredible cruelties are described, the parallels to farces performed in the area − all indicate that what the Kogu informants chose to display to the Berndts were bloody, cruel stories: elaborate displays of fact-mixed-with-fantasy: a Hieronymus Bosch of Highland Papua New Guinea life, as the Kogu chose to present it to themselves and to the Berndts. Why would the Kogu display themselves in this light?

The accounts the Berndts accept as raw data I now interpret as displays analogous to how some of our artists depict American life in films, writings, and visual arts. Any prime-time night on TV, or the *Rambo* or Schwarzenegger films, or the dozens of horror movies full of bloody murder, ghouls, dismemberment, cannibalism, and corpse-fucking, will yield very similar information to what the Berndts gathered from the Kogu, if what is presented in the American media is accepted as raw data.

It is data, of course: not of events done, but rather of events dreamed, fantasized, and desired. These representations − of the Kogu, of American popular entertainment − must be analyzed critically. They are evidence of the violence of desire, its twisted and dangerous possibilities. After all, we live in the epoch of Auschwitz and Cambodia. Or these entertainments can be regarded as cathartic displays, healthy blowouts of fantasies everyone has. In either case, such accounts − true or false at the level of events − point to the violence of human possibility and imagination. Such violence is not, I think, a local event assignable to the Papua New Guinea Highlands.

Among the Kogu, co-existent with cannibal facts and/or stories, were "informal courts" where dramas were acted out. As Berndt sees it, once the Kogu were prevented from warring with and eating their enemies, "the official court was seen by these people as an alternative mode of settling differences, of righting wrongs and of obtaining compensation for injury" (Berndt 1962: 314). The court also was theater:

> The informal court is held in the village clearing, or in front of the men's house. . . . The presiding authority takes the central position, flanked by other dignitaries. . . . In front of them on one side sits the complainant, on the other the accused (or defendant); each may be supported by patrikin . . . or others. The audience disposes itself as it pleases. It is all very informal; the complainant may be nursing a child, and children may play among the audience. Various witnesses are heard and sometimes cross-questioned. The complainant may give an impassioned speech or may leave the matter entirely in the hands of others (witnesses or kin). He may be interrupted at will by the court leaders, who will go over and over the matter. Repetition in discussion is the delight of such meetings, especially when the affair concerns sexual matters or when amounts of settlement are to be determined. Proceedings may continue for a couple of days or longer, usually depending on the entertainment value of the evidence.
>
> (Berndt 1962: 323)

If Berndt is right, then the court is a redirected activity. Supporting this thesis is the appetite for verdicts that provide spectators with violent entertainment something they previously got from warfare and maybe from cannibalism.

> Many means of achieving excitement have been done away with through the banning of warfare and cannibalism; but some of the emotions expressed in these are diverted into the informal court, and in this respect there is great similarity between them. Prior to alien contact, violence was recognized as a necessary part of ordinary social life. Now, under the aegis of the informal court, it has been concentrated, as it were, and highlighted.
>
> (1962: 325)

Sexual cases are especially relished. In such cases the court proceedings closely resemble traditional farces. For example, Jowajaca's husband caught her in the act of adultery. The court established that the adultery took place at least five times, but that Jowajaca had some cause: her husband didn't have sex with her often enough. Part of the judgement was that he copulate with her at once while the crowd watched. Throughout one night they were made to fuck many times, always in front of witnesses. The next day Jowajaca was punished this way:

> Her skirt was cut off and she was told to sit down naked before the people. A large tin was obtained and filled with stones and a special ceremonial emblem was made. She was made to stand up and a man's fringed skirt was fastened around her, but not concealing her pubes. The wooden end of the emblem was then inserted into her vagina so that it protruded out and upward. Attached to the skirt behind her was a similar emblem. She was then told to place the tin of stones on her head and dance up and down. She began to dance to and fro cross the village clearing, the emblems shaking as she did so. People crowded around to look at her, even coming from other villages and districts. They joked and laughed. Children rushed up and down with her, crying out and shouting obscenities. When she stopped dancing or showed signs of exhaustion she was threatened with a bow and arrow and urged on. Throughout the day she continued to dance, holding the tin of stones on her head; sweat poured from her body, and her head was swollen from the weight she carried. During late afternoon she could hardly move and showed extreme exhaustion. Her mother and father began to wail, and the latter called out, "Oh, my daughter what is this that you are doing? Give her back to us. Stop this punishment." But they did not intervene because they were afraid of Ozazecna [headman of the court].

> (Berndt 1962: 332–3)

At sunset Ozazecna stopped Jowajaca's dancing and summoned her husband, Anaga. Ozazecna asked Jowajaca if she wanted to go back to her husband or with her lover, Aguvi. She chose Aguvi and was beaten. The next morning Ozazecna ordered Aguvi to pay Anaga five items of wealth; then Jowajaca was declared free to marry Aguvi. The court was adjourned.

But Jowajaca didn't marry Aguvi. She went back to her house in Anaga's village. She cooked for him, but he always left her food untouched. After a few weeks they resumed sexual relations. When this had gone on for some time Jowajaca called all the men of the village together and said: "Other men continually copulate with their wives at night. Anaga always comes to me and copulates!" The men laughed. They said: "He puts his finger in his nose, yet he still copulates with her. You two continue copulating." Anaga was then considered to have remarried Jowajaca (Berndt 1962: 334).

Taken as a whole, this incident is both a social and an aesthetic drama. The characters are real people, the events took place. At the same time the trial is an entertainment – the story, the sexual enactment, the cruel dance, and even the outcome are suitably theatrical. Is this just an outsider's opinion? No, because the Kogu themselves think of the events as entertaining.

An even clearer convergence of court drama and traditional farce is when prominent performers help act out the punishment. The case involved Urolni, who said she disliked her husband, Ameja. She refused to have sex with him. Ameja brought Urolni to court and the headman decided that her punishment would be plural copulation with Urolni. But this is what happened:

> Nomaja, a prominent performer in erotic farces and generally considered a great wit, squatted before Urolni and taking up her hands pretended to eat them. "Ah! This tastes good!" Then he pulled her labia majora and made as if to eat, remarking how good they were. The onlookers applauded. But at this juncture Urolni grabbed one of Nomaja's testes and pulled. Nomaja let out a cry. She tugged at it again and Nomaja pretended to eat her face, making sucking sounds. "How good this tastes. Oh my vulva. Loose me now – it pains!" But Urolni pulled it again, and Nomaja fell over, pretending to die. "You have killed me now!" Urolni, becoming afraid, released his testicle. Nomaja jumped up and began to play with her vulva, passing remarks as the occasion demanded. Finally he picked her up in his arms and carried her to a nearby stream. Here he threw her into the shallow

> water and began to copulate. . . . Afterwards she said to him, "I have
> left my child behind. I will go and get it and come to you. I will leave my
> husband."
>
> (Berndt 1962: 362–3)

Urolni went to Nomaja the next day, but she was beaten and returned
to her husband with whom she remained. The action of this trial is like
that of a well-known traditional farce (see Berndt 1962: 148–9).

It's not only in Papua New Guinea that trials and dramas converge,
offering entertainment to the people. Public trials in Europe or America are ostensibly about crime and punishment, but often they are as
entertaining as the "informal court" of Kogu. People delight in juicy
stories such as Jean Harris's jealous murder of Herman Tarnower or in
events of great pathos like determining who will have custody of Baby
M. Until this century public executions were more occasions for cruel
joking and picnicking than they were solemn warnings against crime.
Earlier still in medieval Europe disputes among the upper classes were
frequently settled by duels or jousts waged by "champions," combatants who substituted themselves for those they represented. This practice developed in two directions: into sports contests where individuals
and teams are "champions" representing clubs, universities, or cities
(at least on the surface because in fact, of course, modern athletics are
big business); and into modern legal practice where the champion
of the state is the prosecutor while the champion of the accused is
the defense attorney. The modern trial presents two dramas
simultaneously, as Richard Harbinger points out:

> When one observes an adversary trial, he [sic] sees a play; when he
> observes a while longer, he perceives a play within the play. . . . And
> from this form all else naturally proceeds: double plots, double casts,
> double settings, double audiences and double effects. . . . The "play
> without" stages the legal combat between the prosecuting attorney
> and the defense attorney. . . . The "play within" tells the story of the
> alleged killing [or whatever the accused is accused of].
>
> (Harbinger 1971: 122–3)

What Harbinger calls the "play without" is a ritual combat; the "play within" is a drama. I do not say that drama "comes from" trials, or vice versa. Such a simple evolution is absurd. Both drama and trials are theatrical events of great entertainment value. And the two can be easily confounded. Currently on American TV there are several daily programs based on the courtroom, including *People's Court* and *Divorce Court*. In *People's Court* real disputes are adjudicated (by a retired judge) and cash settlements paid out. Participants sign agreements making these settlements binding: entertainment swallows the legal process whole.

Ritual combats often employ theatrical means. Farb tells us that among the Eskimos of both Alaska and Greenland it was traditional for

> all disputes except murder . . . [to be] settled by a song duel. In these areas an Eskimo male is often as acclaimed for his ability to sing insults as for his hunting prowess. The song duel consists of lampoons, insults and obscenities and the disputants sing to each other and of course, to their delighted audience. (Incidentally, the West Indies calypso, now sung as an entertainment for tourists, similarly originated as a song of ridicule.) The verses are earthy and very much to the point; they are intended to humiliate, and no physical deformity, personal shame or family trouble is sacred. As verse after verse is sung in turn by the opponents, the audience begins to take sides; it applauds one singer a bit longer and laughs a bit louder at his lampoons. Finally, he is the only one to get applause, and he thereby becomes the winner of a bloodless contest. The loser suffers a great punishment, for disapproval of the community is very difficult to bear in a group as small as that of the Eskimo.
>
> (Farb 1969: 68–9)

Far from improvising, the Greenland singer prepares for the contest by singing his songs to his family until they know them all perfectly. "When the actual contest is in full swing, his householders reinforce his words in chorus" (Hoebel 1967: 259). Song duels are sometimes accompanied by head-butting and punching.

The Tiv of northern Nigeria use a similar kind of theatricalized combat. Bohannan tells how early in the spring of 1950 Torgindi and Mtswen started feuding over the repayment of a debt.

> Torgindi went back to his compound [after the men exchanged angry words] and made up a song in which he said what a skunk Mtswen was. That night, when all was quiet, he drummed and sang the song as loud as he could, for the whole countryside to hear – including Mtswen, who lived a little over a quarter of a mile away.
>
> (Bohannan 1967: 263)

Torgindi repeated the song the next night – and everyone in his compound and some from other compounds in his lineage joined in the chorus.

> The only thing for Mtswen to do was to make up a song of his own against Torgindi. But knowing he wasn't much of a songmaker, he hired the best songmaker in Shangev Ya to stay at his place and compose scurrilous songs about Torgindi and all his kinsmen and wives.
>
> (Bohannan 1967: 263)

Torgindi responded by hiring his own songmaker. Soon the men were sponsoring songs and dances each night – "they each brewed beer and made food in order to attract dancers to come and dance and sing the songs directed at the other" (Bohannan 1967: 264). There were no fixed rules for composing the songs, except that incidents referred to must be true. If an accusation is false the slandered person calls a jir, foul, and the accusation is withdrawn. But if the accusation could not possibly be true then it can't be the basis of a jir. For example, "one of the catchiest tunes . . . told how Torgindi changed himself into a pig at night and made it unsafe for every sow in the countryside" (Bohannan 1967: 264). Everyone agreed that Torgindi couldn't transform himself, therefore he wasn't entitled to call a jir. This rule encouraged combining painful truths with wild fantasies.

The song duel between Torgindi and Mtswen went on nightly for more than three weeks before the village elders decided that to continue would lead to violence. The elders summoned both men and their supporters to a central place where they were told to sing and drum: the elders would decide who was the victor. The elders went from one performing group to the other, listened to all the songs, and then retired to consider the case. After two hours they ruled that

Torgindi had won the case, but that Mtswen had the better songs. A decision worthy of Solomon.

"Sounding" is a less elaborate but possibly historically related word duel common in American black neighborhoods. Soundings are formal tradings of ritual insults – also called "the dozens" or "signifying." According to Labov "the ways in which sounds are delivered, and the evaluation of them by the group, follow a well-established ritual pattern" (1972: 127). Sounds are "evaluated overtly and immediately by the audience" (Labov 1972: 144). The mark of winning is laughter. And when a traditional sound is rendered incorrectly the spectators yell "Mistake!" Among adolescent gangs the members know who the best sounders are and will rarely engage them in a duel. To be a good sounder is to be a leader in the group. The sounds, often rhymed couplets, are almost always sexual, and they usually involve insults concerning mothers or fathers – if these insults were made outside the context of sounding, that is, "for real," a fist-fight or worse could break out. Some examples of sounds collected by Labov:

> Iron is iron, and steel don't rust,
> But your momma got a pussy like a Greyhound bus.

> I hate to talk about your mother, she's a good old soul
> She got a ten-ton pussy and a rubber asshole.

These are two traditional sounds selected from a large collection many of which would be recited in a given contest. The winner would be the boy with the best memory. Other sounds may be improvised. These are usually less elegant:

> Your mother so old she can stretch her head and lick her ass.

> I went in David house, I saw the roaches walkin' round in combat boots.

> Money got a head like a tornado mixed with a horse.

Traditional sounds are obscene, but improvised ones often aren't. They range across myriad subjects suitable for insulting: housing, work, looks, eating habits, poverty, school. The performance structure of sounding is like that of the song duels of the Eskimo or Tiv. A boy sounds and the audience evaluates: his adversary sounds and the audience evaluates. Soon enough a winner is evident. As Labov notes,

> The audience . . . is an essential ingredient here. It is true that one person *can* sound against another without a third person being present, but the presupposition that this is public behavior can easily be heard in the verbal style. Sounds are not uttered in a direct, face-to-face conversational mode. The voice is raised and projected, as if to reach an audience.
>
> (Labov 1972: 157)

The amount of sounding crammed into a short time is amazing. Labov reports that when thirteen members of the Jets were crowded into a minibus, 138 sounds were deciphered from a tape of the 35-minute ride (Labov 1972: 130).

The structure of sounding resembles a boxing match where two opponents trade punches before a partisan audience. "There are three participants in this speech event: antagonist A, antagonist B, and the audience. A sounds against B; the audience evaluates; B sounds against A and his sound is evaluated" (Labov 1972: 146). The participation of the audience as judge insures the formal progression of the ritual combat which takes the shape of a duel. It is important that the speakers do not overlap or cancel each other out. The audience has to hear every word in order to judge who the winner is.

Sounding feeds on the aggressive tendencies of laughter – which in its breathing pattern shares much with the derisive-triumphant pant-hoots of our fellow primates. What begins structurally as a contest between equals becomes an unequal battle. The audience soon creates a disparity among the opponents: laughter supports the stronger sounder, silence is a clear sign of rejection. But the laughter greeting the stronger sounder is only apparently "with" him, it is really an aggression *against* his opponent. The stronger sounder enlists the audience in his attack on the loser. This is the root structure of a certain kind of theatrical dialogue, from stichomythia, the short, give-and-take dialogic assaults of classical Greek theater, to the punning wit and quick-flying obscenities enjoyed by such Shakespearean characters as Beatrice and Benedick, through to the laconic exchanges of Pinter. The audience's participation may not be heard (except in comedy and farce), but their judgemental presence is decisive. They are always being solicited to take sides.

Labov thinks the ritual nature of sounding – like ritual in general – offers a "sanctuary" where "we are freed from personal responsibility for the acts we are engaged in" (Labov 1972: 168). What a neat definition of what performers are allowed to do, how they "get away with" the actions they enact, the words they speak.

The Kogu informal court, the Eskimo and Tiv song duels, and sounding are all examples of "redirected activity." They may also be examples of "displacement activity," a deep-level behavioral process that Lorenz explains this way:

> Displacement activity happens if two mutually inhibiting motivations result in such a perfect equilibrium as to block each other completely. What happens then is that another movement, which is usually inhibited by both of them, becomes disinhibited because the other two neutralize each other. So, if a bird wants to attack and is afraid in more or less perfect equilibrium of these two motivations, he may start to preen or to scratch, or to perform other activities which are inhibited both by attack and escape, attack and escape being at the moment mutually inhibited.
>
> (Lorenz 1959: 188)

In the examples I've cited, the sexuality, violence, conflict, and obscenity are transformations, redirections, of behavior prevented their full expression. But other behaviors – laughter, feeling "entertained" – are "displacements" in the ethological sense. What are the "mutually inhibiting motivations" behind the Kogu, Eskimo, medieval, Tiv, ghetto, and by extension all other "real life" "drama-like" performances? In every case, forbidden or extremely dangerous relationships – adulterous, incestuous, warlike, cannibalistic – are blocked by law or custom even as they are desired. Drama condenses around the "I-want-but-can't/shouldn't-do"; or around the "I-do-but-will-pay-for." If the forbidden relationships are consummated in fact (as they sometimes are) the social order may be threatened. When the social order is threatened, even by fantasies and desires, a special kind of public performance is called for, one that uses "real people" acting out "real events" (the Kogu trial); or sometimes the principals can find "champions" to act in their behalf (the Tiv song duel, or Euro-American trials); or often enough the desires manifest themselves in wholly fictionalized transformations of the forbidden events (dramas). But in all cases what must be performed are the forbidden acts which are thereby both released and contained. The formal nature of these ur-dramas – the Kogu court or farce, the joust, the song duel, the trial, the rhymed couplet, the sounding – guarantees some measure of control over the impulses being enacted.

Also the ur-dramas suggest their own elaboration into full-fledged theater. The fundamental opposition is between individual desire and social order: these inhibit each other. The resulting displaced activity – entertainment eliciting laughter and/or tears from the audience – is as different from its causes as a bird's preening is from is mutually blocked impulses to fight and flee. Instead of causing further anxiety the performance of forbidden relationships relaxes tensions. Even among the Kogu, the court and the farces it resembles so closely are less fearful than war. As for cannibalism, I don't know where to place it: as an historical fact now redirected and displaced, or as a fantasized desire of extreme violence, itself a redirection and displacement – perhaps of rage against the intrusions of first colonial and then Papua New Guinea's national authority.

LAUGHTER AND FREUD

So much violence is expressed in laughter. Cruel farces probably preceded tragedy. Laughter preserves the ambivalence of the conflicts that give rise to displacement activities. As such laughter is both aggressive and aggregating. Eibl-Eibesfeldt notes that: "The rhythmic vocalizations [of laughter] remind one of similar sounds made by primate groups when they threaten in unison against an enemy. . . . In its original form laughing seems to unite *against* a third party" (1970: 132). Thus laughter presupposes, even creates, a "we" that opposes a "them."

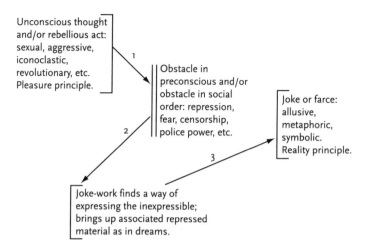

Figure 7.4

In 1905 Freud explained "joke-work" by offering a model analogous to his ideas concerning "dream-work." Freud thought dreams and jokes worked in much the same way, expressing/concealing unrecognized desires. Freud's model (interpreted by me in figure 7.4) explains how farce especially, and maybe all theater, accomplishes the complicated task of uniting an in-group, threatening an out-group, and bringing repressed materials to the surface. Joke-work condenses, inverts, and displaces images, actions, and associations. A successful joke – and a farce is a string of successful jokes comprising a coherent structure that is itself a joke – is an extremely dense, specially coded communication. In releasing laughter the joke liberates laughter's double purpose of threat and bond. It also stunningly erases the gap between audience and performer: the audience hears the performers, laughs as a response; the performers hear the audience laughing, perform as a response; and so the farce progresses. As Freud wrote:

> And here at last we can understand what it is that jokes achieve in the service of their purpose. They make possible the satisfaction of an obstacle that stands in its way. They circumvent this obstacle and in that way draw pleasure from a source which the obstacle had made

inaccessible. . . . The repressive activity of civilization brings it about that primary possibilities of enjoyment, which had now, however, been repudiated by the censorship in us, are lost to us. But to the human psyche all renunciation is exceedingly difficult, and so we find that tendentious jokes provide a means of undoing the renunciation and retrieving what was lost.

(Freud 1963: 100–1)

Interestingly, Freud sees the pleasure in joking much the way Schaller sees the chest-beating sequence in gorillas: as a discharge of energy. In overcoming the obstacle a joke makes a short-circuit – a connection that is both surprising and delightful as it suddenly brings to consciousness the repressed unconscious desire. The energy spent on inhibition, on keeping the obstacle in place, is released all at once. "This yield of pleasure corresponds to the psychical expenditure that is saved" (Freud 1963: 118).

But what purposes do jokes serve? First, there is "criticism against persons in exalted positions who claim to exercise authority. The joke, then, represents a rebellion against that authority, a liberation from its pressures" (Freud 1963: 105). And then there is delight in celebrating the obscene. It is clear how this works both in the Kogu court and in Euro-American trials. The court, like Kogu farce, is authorized rebellion: the adultery reproduced in public is behavior temporarily sanctioned "as evidence" but enjoyed "as entertainment." It is the same with trials in America where the "play within" (to use Harbinger's suggestive nomenclature) is always the description of a forbidden (illegal) act. In aesthetic farce there is no need even to pretend to deplore the crimes, outrages, and reversals of social order. Satire, parody, ridicule, and caricature are all species of hostile joking. These are the heart of farce, different from "comedy of manners" which maintains a façade of politeness. In farce, the young ridicule the old, prodigality laughs away prudence, promiscuity overturns marriage, the poor rule the rich, the underdog lords it over the overdog. From Kogu to the Marx Brothers, Aristophanes to the Tiv, Harlem to Chaplin: a bedlam anti-structure as well as *Sacer Ludus* marks farce. But only temporarily: "for the time being."

Farcical actions can by mocking authority become strong political weapons. On March 20, 1968, Colonel Paul Akst, director of New York City's selective service system, was talking to Columbia University students about the tough new draft law put in force at the height of the Vietnam war.

> As Akst began fielding questions from the floor, a group of students created a diversion at the rear of the auditorium, and as everyone in the audience turned around, an unidentified assailant walked up to the colonel and pushed a lemon meringue pie squarely in his face.
>
> (Avorn 1968: 32)

A pie in the face is not just any action, but one drawn from the stock repertory of burlesque and early movies. The student uprisings of 1968 in Europe and America combined farce and eroticism with radical thought and action. The first phase of a victorious revolution – look at France in 1792, the USSR in 1917 – is often a carnival; the next phase is a vituperative bloodbath.

Ludwig Jekels, a follower of Freud, interprets comedy in a unique way. If the Oedipus complex is the basis of tragedy, he argues, then its opposite underlies farce: "the feeling of guilt which, in tragedy, rests upon the son, appears in comedy displaced on the father; it is the father who is guilty" (Jekels 1965: 264). Once the father – the authority of the old (state) – is done away with "we find the ego, which has liberated itself from the tyrant, uninhibitedly venting its humor, wit, and every sort of comic manifestation in a very ecstasy of freedom" (Jekels 1965: 264). In revolution the liberation is actual, if temporary; in aesthetic theater, in even the Kogu court and other "near-dramas," the liberation is monitored, controlled, overseen by authorities who give permission for the temporary suspension of the usual order of things. In this way rebellion is co-opted, serving the powers that be.

IN-GROUP, OUT-GROUP

From an ethological perspective rituals evolve as a way of improving communications, removing ambiguities, making signals clear. These signals are preponderantly directed at conspecifics. Behavior in relation to animals of another species is likely to be more "direct": fight, flight, hide, kill. Rituals are biologically necessary because conspecifics need to mate, organize in stable social hierarchies, share territory. Interactions determining how these are to be achieved are likely to cause trouble. Rituals mediate these difficult interactions by creating a second reality more compelling than direct action. This second reality is performance.

These performances are just as aggressive as direct action but less deadly. Among animals, in fact, two separate kinds of aggression operate: that directed against prey is unemotional and deadly, while that directed against conspecifics is emotional but ritualized. Eibl-Eibesfeldt reports:

> An oryz antelope will never use its horns to gore another oryz but fights according to strictly observed rules. It does, however, stab lions [with its horns]. A giraffe uses its short horns to fight rivals [other giraffes], but uses its hoofs in defense against predators. A predator fights differently with a species member than with a prey and by electrical brain stimulation it could be shown in cats that these two types of behavior have different neural substrates in the brain.
>
> (Eibl-Eibesfeldt 1970: 314)

In humans, substitute in-group and out-group for "my species" and "other species." Many languages reflect this division by naming the home culture "human," relegating all others as non-human or barbarian.

A stunning example of this is provided by Ruesch and Bateson. Just before Europeans arrived in numbers in Java a large white monkey was washed up on the coast. It was taken to the court of the raja whose experts told him that the monkey was from the court of the god of the sea who had expelled him in anger by causing a great storm. The raja ordered that the white monkey be chained to a stone.

> Doctor Stutterheim [Dutch government archeologist in Java] told me that he had seen the stone and that, roughly scratched on it in Latin, Dutch, and English were the name of a man and a statement of his shipwreck. Apparently this trilingual sailor never established verbal communication with his captors. He was surely unaware of the

premises in their minds which labeled him a white monkey and therefore not a potential recipient of verbal messages; it probably never
occurred to him that they could doubt his humanity. He may have
doubted theirs.

(Ruesch and Bateson 1951: 204–5)

Of course, humans can also treat other species as prey: Homo sapiens
appears to specialize in the extermination of species.

In humans as in other animals, separating in-groupers from out-
groupers gives rise to two complementary conflict systems: 1) aggressive
conflict against outsiders ("not my people"); 2) aggressive solidarity
for insiders ("my people"). These two systems express themselves
everywhere, but especially in war, business, and sports. Murder seems
to contradict this division because insiders often murder each other.
But war is more "impersonal" than murder and, statistically speaking,
more deadly, decimating whole populations, bloodily soaking up the
wealth of nations, winners and losers alike.

Conflict-resolution systems – mediation, courts, and diplomacy –
try to convert the first kind of aggression into the second: widening the
circle of insiders. Often the conflict-resolution process is a mirror or
reduction-transformation of the conflict to be resolved: a theatrical
playing out of the conflict.

In human theater the subject matter and actions include the most
horrible deeds; bloody conflicts between people, gods, beasts, and
demons; war and murder; atrocities; torture: every violent action
imaginable. But all this is acted out as ritual and/or play. This is because
redirected behavior and displacement activities in people create complicated sequences of transformations, different in each culture, maybe
in each individual, but interculturally recognizable as make-believe.
Audiences can enjoy watching/participating and performers can enjoy
playing out what otherwise would be dangerous, forbidden, or
inhibited. Acting out the troubles of Oedipus, the murders of Macbeth,
the adventures of Rama, the crucifixion of Jesus, the struggle of a
shaman against the disease-causing demons, the farces or informal
courts of the Kogu all yield great pleasure. In serious drama or tragedy as well as farce, the pleasures derive from the excess of energy
released when obstacles to seeing/participating in taboo actions are

suddenly removed. The sound of laughter is triumphantly, celebratorily, aggressive.

All human theater is created by processes analogous to dream-work/joke-work. Dream-work/joke-work, in turn, are versions of redirected activities and displacement. Thus human theater arises precisely where animal rituals do and serve analogous needs. These performances are liminal events existing to *mediate or explore for pleasure interactions that are potentially risky and disruptive*. Where transitions/transformations are dangerous what Van Gennep calls "rites of passage" are invented; where trouble is liable to break out, theatrical fun eases the way.

CONCLUSIONS

Scientists have long been prejudiced in favor of mathematical and verbal languages. But semiotics reveals many different kinds of language – kinesic, visual, spatial, sonic, etc. Symbol-making often involves transformation of the body, and the spaces around it, into full fields of communication. And transformation, not conflict, is the root of theater. When Mike displayed with the kerosene cans he was transforming them. When Robert de Niro plays Jake La Motta in *Raging Bull* he is transforming himself.

Many animals, including humans, employ disguises; prepare special places for habitation, mating, and ritual combat; drum, dance, and sing; display spectacular manes, plumages, antlers, etc. Some, like fiddler crabs, even appropriate other animals' bodies. Humans imitate whatever they see: a shaman puts on a bear's skin, a woman wears a hat with feathers, a singer whistles like a bird. Non-human animals can't imitate so freely. Although a few species specialize in "deceit," most animal performances are automatically released, fixed, and stereotyped. There is no irony, no pliable back-and-forth play between the role and the performer, no trilogical interaction linking performer to performer to spectator. Even among non-human primates and dolphins – the most intelligent and playful of animals – performances lack the kind of intricate mimetic fantasy-loving free-play we expect from our own species. And in all animal performances to lose is to lose, while among humans to lose is often to win: theatrical careers are built by the skill with which roles are played, not by the events of the story. No one shuns the actors who play Oedipus or Richard III. Among the Kogu the guilty often gained status when they were forced to perform their punishments publicly. Real-life criminals become celebrities – especially when given the chance to tell their stories publicly; that is, to theatricalize their lives.

Ethological thinking is the application of evolutionary theory to behavior and culture. On several levels human and animal performances converge and/or exist along a continuum: 1) on the structural level where performances are redirected activities, displacement activities, and/or improvements of signal functions; 2) on a processual level of dream-work/joke-work; 3) on the level of technique where drumming, rhythmic vocalization, dancing, and visual displays are used to create, spread, and share moods; 4) on a cultural level where performances are means of social control providing avenues for the discharge of aggression or providing ways of mobilizing people either to maintain or change a given social order; 5) on a mimetic level where animals imitate animals and people imitate animals – even appropriating skins, feathers, faces, gaits, gestures, and sounds; 6) on a theoretical level where animals and humans are included in reciprocal social structures as in totemism. (Ironically, a criticism of ethologists is that they anthropomorphize.) These similarities and convergences offer a basis for re-examining human theater from the perspective of animal performances. A re-examination not of two opposing systems but of a single bio-aesthetic web.

NOTES

1   There is a question of whether performances excite or discharge violent feelings. My experience as a theater director and spectator tells me that performances do both. They uncover hidden feelings, arousing them in the extreme. But this arousal does not lead to action, rather to a cathartic discharge and ultimate calm. Even when extremely worked up – as by the Living Theater in the 1960s and 1970s – spectators did not seriously agitate in the streets. Rather they went outside to play.

2   See Rainer (1974), Forti (1974), and *TDR, The Drama Review* 16 (3) (1972) and 19 (1) (1975).

3   See the References for specific titles. The unifying idea is the belief that visible behaviors, and what we can learn of deep behaviors through analysis of brain structure and activity, skin temperature, glandular secretion, and so on,

correlate with what is happening socially, that is, between individuals and among groups. This kind of study is a holistic behaviorism. See chapter 8.

4   See Girard (1977), Ehrenzweig (1970), and Schechner (1986a).

5   For a very interesting take on Wilson's work from *The Life and Times of Sigmund Freud* (1969) through *I was Sitting on My Patio* (1977), see Stefan Brecht (1978).

6   Marshack (1972) shows how early mathematical systems developed as seasonal markers and accurate calendars. He finds these widely scattered over Eurasia and dates them as early as the earliest cave paintings. If correct, Marshack establishes for humans a complicated notation system – writing – coexistent with the first surviving artworks.

7   Scott Powell of Sha-Na-Na observed The Who on tour. Powell wrote the following description of their finale in Philadelphia's Spectrum in 1975, showing how consistent The Who's performance is and how it affects audiences:

> The stage grows black. The synthesizer is playing through the dark hall. It continues for five minutes, and it seems as if the concert is over, with the expectation that the houselights will come up and the synthesizer will continue playing as exit music. But suddenly white spotlights simultaneously pick up Townshend in mid-air leaping from on top of his amplifiers, and Daltrey at the front of the stage, belting out a scream that fills the hall. The landing lights explode through the darkness; the lasers pierce to the ceiling once again. With the entire audience on its feet clapping, singing, and dancing to the music, the band leads the audience through several choruses of the song, and hits a final chord. Townshend has his guitar by the neck and is beating it into the stage. Feedback and distortion ring through the hall. Daltrey flies feet first into a stack of amplifiers, toppling them back off the stage. Moon kicks though his drum-head and hurls his tom-tom at the rest of the kit. Townshend attacks his stack of amplifiers with a flying kick and they fall off the back of the stage. Entwhistle stands by the side of the stage and watches the destruction. Then, with a final kick at the guitar, clapping each other on the back, The Who disappear from the stage, and the houselights come up.

> (Unpublished paper, 1976)

8   See Ekman (1972, 1980, and 1983); Ekman, Friesen, and Ellsworth (1972); Birdwhistell (1952, 1964a, 1964b, and 1970); and Goffman (1959, 1961, 1963a, 1963b, 1967, 1969, and 1974).

9   A fight-package is a bundle of sacred/magic materials carried into battle. The package is said to protect the fighter and to bring him victory.

10 Since writing this essay in the mid-1970s, the debate concerning cannibalism has sharpened. Some anthropologists doubt that there is, or ever was, cannibalism – except out of the need for sheer survival (shipwrecks, for example). The debate is reported in *Science*.

> What [William] Arens concluded after investigating countless accounts of cannibalism is that there are no reliable first hand witnesses to this

practice. Even in New Guinea where cannibalism is presumed to have spread the slow virus disease kuru, there is no good evidence for cannibalism, Arens and others say. . . . "If I'm right, [Arens says,] anthropologists are engaged not in a lie, not in a hoax, but in a myth. They are retelling what is always assumed to be true."

(Kolata 1986: 1497)

But others strongly disagree with Arens. "D. Carleton Gajdusek . . . who won a Nobel prize for his studies of kuru in New Guinea, says that the evidence of cannibalism in New Guinea is so clear that 'it's beneath my dignity to answer the argument' " (Kolata 1986: 1497).

Factual or not, cannibalism exercises a powerful hold on the human imagination and, like incest, is a primary taboo. Cannibalism – either "barbaric" or, for example, Christian (the Eucharist) – is a strong component of many cultures' belief systems; there is an undeniable link between what is eaten and what "becomes part of." To share food is to contract friendship; to share that food which is the loved/hated other is to acquire power. And is it too much to suggest that mother's milk – the first food – is mother herself? What exactly is the nipple the infant takes into its mouth? A myself who is another. See Winnicott (1971) on transitional objects and phenomena.

8

MAGNITUDES OF PERFORMANCE

A FIGURE FOR ALL GENRES

At the descriptive level there is no detail of performance occurring everywhere under all circumstances. Nor is it easy to specify limitations on what is, or could be treated as, performance. Figure 8.1 is an exemplary but somewhat serendipitous panorama of just how diverse and extensive the performance world is. Criteria for inclusion in the chart were: 1) events called performances in this or that culture; 2) events treated "as performance" by scholars. I limited myself as much as possible to events that I have either seen or studied. I wanted to fight the tendency to seek "origins" or "sources" in performances below the horizons of field work or reliable historical research. I took my cue from anthropological field work: the evidence I sought was *in vivo*, ready at hand. I know that another person could make another time/space/event chart populated by different items. But I believe the outcome would be a similar riot of apparently disparate particulars. What hope is there of unifying such a figure?

If "universals" are wanted, they might be found in processual models explaining how one set of genres, ritual performances for example, becomes other sets. Does ritual "evolve" into dance, theater, and sports, and if so how? This search for universals occupied Victor Turner during much of his life. Turner felt his social drama/liminal-to-liminoid model[1] worked universally. In one of his last essays – "Are There Universals of Performance in Myth, Ritual, and Drama?" (1985) – he said as much:

> Theater is but one of the many inheritors of that multifaced system of preindustrial ritual which embraces ideas and images of cosmos and chaos, interdigitates clowns and their foolery with gods and their solemnity, and uses all the sensory codes to produce symphonies in more than music: the intertwining of dance, body languages of many kinds, song, chant, architectural forms (temples, amphitheaters), incense, burnt offerings, ritualized feasting and drinking, painting, body markings of many kinds, including circumcision and scarification, the application of lotions and drinking potions, the enacting of mythic and heroic plots drawn from oral traditions. And so much more. Rapid advances in the scale and complexity of society, particularly after industrialization, have passed this unified liminal configuration through the analytical prism of the division of labor, with its specialization and professionalization, reducing each of these sensory domains to a set of entertainment genres flourishing in the leisure time of society, no longer in a central, driving place. The pronounced numinous supernatural character of archaic ritual has been greatly attenuated.
>
> (Turner 1985: 295–7)

Turner regrets what he calls the "*sparagmos*" of ritual, but he detects "signs that the amputated specialized genres are seeking to rejoin and to recover something of the numinosity lost in their . . . dismemberment" (1985: 297). I pursued a similar theme in chapter 4, where I suggested that the development of theater from ritual was only one way in a two-way process, that rituals emerge from theater (or other performative genres).

Turner's idea fits nicely the approach of the "Cambridge anthropologists" who, during the first decades of the twentieth century, thought they had found a "primal ritual," what Murray called a *Sacer Ludus* as the source of classical Greek theater. (See chapter 1 for a fuller discussion of

Figure 8.1 Performance Time/Space/Event Chart

	Aesthetic theater	Sacred ritual	Secular ritual	Sports	Social drama	Minutes or less	Hours
Private & restricted	Theater on Chekhov Street[1]	Initiation rites	Executions in USA	Sports played at home	Election of pope	Execution	Theater on Chekhov Street
Private but open	Happenings & performance art	Bar mitzvah	Ph.D. orals	Sandlot baseball	Murder trial	Puja at Hindu temple	Happenings; ball games, etc.
Local	Ordinary theater & dance	Teyyam	Macy's Thanksgiving's parade	Big league baseball	Turnerian social drama	Stuart Sherman[4] street spectacle	Ordinary theater & dance
General	National network TV drama	Pilgrimage	Inauguration of US president	Olympics	Hostage crisis; wars	TV commericals	Feature films
Sacred space	Bread & Puppet Theater in St. John the Divine	Religious events; Aborigine landscape	Town meeting in church	Aztec ball game	Church where pope is elected	Puja; Eucharist	Ordinary church service
Secular space	Ordinary theater & dance	Jewish circumcision; home wedding	Macy's Parade; Olympics	Playing fields	Town square; legislative hall	Stuart Sherman; Jewish circumcision	Ordinary theater & dance
Found space	Rooftops, beaches, streets, galleries	Sacred trees, rocks, rivers	Parade routes	Sandlot ball	Wars; US embassy during hostage crisis	Some happenings	Parades; some happenings
Transformed space	Stage set; environmental theater	Churches; Ramlila environments	Courtroom; execution chamber	Stadiums	Courtroom; throne-room	Execution	Ordinary theater & dance
Indoor space	Theaters	Churches, temples	Courtroom; execution chamber	Field-houses[2]	Courtroom, legislative hall	Some happenings; execution	Ordinary theater & dance
Outdoor space	Greek or Elizabethan theater	Aborigine initation grounds	Parade route; US inauguration	Stadiums	Tiwi "duel"[3]	Stuart Sherman	Greek or Elizabethan theater
Single space	Ordinary theater & dance	Church service	Courtroom	Stadiums, fieldhouses	Courtroom; legislative hall	Execution	Ordinary theater & dance
Multispace	Many happenings; environmental theater	Pilgrimage	Parades	Marathon running; Olympics	Hostage crisis	Some happenings; some guerrilla theater	Some happenings

Days	Months or more	Single time: once only	Repeated	Multitime: segmented	Calendrical cycle	Event-generated time	Symbolic time
Election of pope	Some initiations	Execution	Theater on Chekhov Street	Election of pope	Some Aborigine performances	Election of pope	Theater on Chekhov Street
Some happenings	Tehching Hsieh's "Year-long" performances[5]	Bar mitzvah		Some happenings	Puja at Hindu temple	Some happenings; sandlot baseball	Some happenings
Ramlila; Yaqui Easter cycle[6]	Orokolo	Some happenings	Ordinary theater & dance	Yaqui Easter; Ramlila	Macy's Parade; Ramlila	Big league ball	Ordinary theater & dance
Olympics	TV soaps	Boxing title match	Feature films	Olympics	World Series; Olympics	World Series	Feature films
Election of pope; Aborigine ceremonies	Pilgrimage	Bar mitzvah		Yaqui Easter; Ramlila	Yaqui Easter; Ramlila		Yaqui Easter; Ramlila
Wilson's Ka Mtn[7]	Hostage crisis	Wilson's Ka Mtn; hostage crisis	Ordinary theater & dance	World Series; Olympics	World Series; Olympics	Baseball	Ordinary theater & dance
Wilson's Ka Mtn	Brook's theater in Africa[8]	Many happenings & perform-ance art		Aborigine ceremonies	Macy's Parade; Aborigine ceremonies	Sandlot baseball	Schechner's Philoctetes on beach[10]
Murder trial	Orokolo cycle; pilgrimage	Some happenings	Ordinary theater & dance	Yaqui Easter; Ramlila	Yaqui Easter; Ramlila	World Series	Ordinary theater & Dance
Murder trial	Tehching Hsieh's "Year-long" performances	Some happenings	Ordinary theater & dance	Murder trial	Church services; folk Bugaku[9]	Indoor sports	Ordinary theater & dance
Wilson's Ka Mtn	Orokolo cycle; pilgrimage; Tehching Hsieh's "Year-long" performances	Some happenings	Elizabethan theater	Yaqui Easter; Ramlila	Yaqui Easter; Ramlila	Baseball	Elizabethan theater
Murder trial		Boxing title match	Ordinary theater & dance	Murder trial	Folk Bugaku	Indoor sports	Ordinary theater & dance
Olympics; Yaqui Easter; Ramlila	Orokolo cycle; hostage crisis	Hostage crisis	Yaqui Easter; Ramlila	Yaqui Easter; Ramlila	Yaqui Easter; Ramlila	World Series	Yaqui Easter; Ramlila

Notes

The chart lists examples anecdotally. That is, many more examples could be given for almost every category. What the chart shows is the great diversity of performative events in terms of genre and use of time and space; and it shows the interrelatedness of events–time–space.

The chart can be read as a grid. For example, a Ph.D. oral examination is an example of private but open secular ritual; a town meeting held in a church is an example of a secular ritual taking place in a sacred space; the Macy's Thanksgiving Day Parade is a calendrical/cyclical event taking place in found space. And so on. All items can be located according to three axes: event, time, space.

Not all items are so explained, but they can be. And some items, obviously, occur in more than one category. So, Ramlila is multitime: segmented plus calendrical/cycle plus symbolic time plus days in duration. But Ramlila is not so easy to locate in terms of whether or not it is aesthetic theater or sacred ritual or social drama: it is all of these, and at some moments more one than the others. Thus the chart's weakness: it categorizes whereas many performances transform from one category to another, or slip across categorical boundaries. Still I have found making the chart helpful in organizing my thinking about performance; and I hope that it will be of use to others.

1 The Theater on Chekhov Street is one of several in Moscow operating privately outside the control of censorship. A description of it, and other private performances, is found in Law (1979). Private restricted performances are common in places where public free expression is limited; it is also the mark of certain kinds of ritual that can be attended by certain people only.

2 Fieldhouses, as the name suggests, are indoor spaces that attempt to bring the outdoors inside. Even more out front in this intention are domed stadiums whose astroturf looks like grass.

3 The Tiwi settle certain disputes by using a ritual duel staged in the main village square. The duel is described by Hart and Pilling (1966). Using their account, I discuss the Tiwi duel in chapter 2. The Tiwi duel is a near perfect example of Victor Turner's "social drama."

4 Stuart Sherman stages "spectacles" on street corners, in theater lobbies, in various other places not usually thought of as performance spaces. His spectacles are theatrically modest: a small table, an assembly of props all of which can fit in an attaché case, no dialog; a total elapsed time of under thirty minutes. As he became more successful, Sherman began to work inside theaters, on stage, in more orthodox ways.

5 Tehching (formerly Sam) Hsieh is a performance artist who specializes in "one-year performances." According to Barry Kahn: "On 30 September 1978, Sam Hsieh began a year of solitary confinement inside an 11'–6'' × 9' × 8' cell which he built within his studio. 'I shall not converse, read, write, listen to the radio or watch television until I unseal myself.' A friend, Cheng Wei Kwang, took charge of his food, clothing, and waste. At 5.00 p.m. on 11 April 1980, Sam Hsieh punched in on a standard industrial time clock he had installed in his studio, an act which he repeated every hour on the hour until 6.00 p.m. on 11 April 1981. And on Saturday 26 September 1981, Sam Hsieh began his third one year performance: 'I shall stay outdoors for one year, never go inside. I shall not go in to [sic] a building, subway, train, car, airplane, ship, cave, tent. I shall have a sleeping bag,' his statement said" (1982: 41). From July 4, 1983 until July 4, 1984 Hsieh was attached to performance artist Linda Montano by an eight-foot rope. Their joint statement read in part: "We will stay together for one year and never be alone. . . . We will be tied together at the waist with an eight-foot rope. We will never touch each other during the year." During his year-long performances Hsieh schedules certain times when the public can view him.

6 The Orokolo of Papua New Guinea used to perform a cycle play that took years to complete. It is described by Williams (1940); and also discussed by me in chapter 2. Extended performances – or connected cycles of performances – are not uncommon. A sports season can be thought of as a cycle of performances. Major League baseball is certainly this way – with several high points: opening games, All Star Games, "important series" near the end of the season, "traditional rivalries," playoffs, and World Series.

7 Robert Wilson staged this seven-day performance as part of the Shiraz Festival in 1972. It involved 50 persons and took 168 hours. It was staged on a mountain and took the form of a kind of ascent or pilgrimage. *Ka Mountain* is described by Trilling (1973: 33–47) and Langton (1973: 48–57).

8 From December, 1972 through February, 1973, Peter Brook and thirty actors, technicians, and support persons traveled by Landrover through Africa from Algiers, across the Sahara, into Niger, Nigeria, Dahomey, Mali, and back to Algiers. During their trip they staged improvisations, exchanged theatrical items (songs, dances, skits, techniques, etc.) with Africans, and showed their own work. They played in many different situations. A uniting, and signaling, item was their "performance carpet." "We got out [of our vehicles]," said Brook, "unrolled our carpet, sat down, and an audience assembled in no time. And there was something incredibly moving – because it was the total unknown, we didn't know what could be communicated, what couldn't. All we discovered after was that nothing had ever happened resembling this before on the market [at In-Salah, in Algeria]. Never had there been a strolling player or some little improvisation. There was no precedent for it. There was a feeling of simple and total attentiveness, total response and lightning appreciation, something that, perhaps in a second, changed every actor's sense of what a relation with an audience could be" (Gibson 1973: 37–51).

9 In December, 1979 I observed Dianichi-do Bugaku in northern Japan (Kazano City) at a Shinto shrine. Peasants, wearing traditional masks, including a famous golden one said to possess great power, dance for about three hours on a makeshift square, elevated stage – like a boxing ring without ropes – set up in the center of the interior of the shrine. It was said that this same performance is done each year, and dates back many hundreds of years.

10 In 1960 I staged Sophocles' *Philoctetes* on the beach of Truro, Massachusetts (near Provincetown, where I was running a summer theater). The audience had to walk over a mile of sand dunes to reach the place where the performance took place. Philoctetes himself roamed the dunes; Neoptolemus and Odysseus arrived by boat (we had launched them about a half-mile further down the beach). The Truro dunes really conveyed the sense of desert island that the Sophocles play asks for.

the Cambridge thesis.) But the "origin" of the theater, dance, and music could as well be healing, or fun-making, or story-telling, or initiations, or nothing at all. Performance may be coexistent with the human species.[2]

Ritual has a broader scope than the Cambridge group supposed. Ethological and neurological approaches to ritual are extremely important for performance studies. From the ethological perspective, rituals are behavioral displacements, exaggerations, repetitions, and transformations that communicate and/or symbolize meanings not ordinarily associated with the behavior displayed. As Irenaus Eibl-Eibesfeldt writes, "ritualization is the process by which non-communicative behavior patterns evolve into signals. . . . In a ritual expressive movements are integrated in a more complex event which is structured in a rule-governed way" (1979: 14, 10).

But let me back up.

Figure 8.1 lays out the time, space, and event parameters of performances without regard to culture or genres. I wanted to take an intergeneric, intercultural perspective and see what the "limits" of performance were. I tried to think of performances of different magnitudes, from the very longest, lasting months or even years, to split-second events; from the largest, spanning millions of miles, to the smallest "brain events" of conceptual art – performances making no spatial claims at all; from clear examples of theater, dance, and music to what Clifford Geertz might lift his eyebrows at as the blurriest of genres: the Iranian hostage crisis of 1979–80, a bar mitzvah, famous murder trials (like those of Klaus von Bulow or Jean Harris), Hindu temple services, title boxing matches, TV soap operas, the Yaqui Easter Passion play, orthodox Euro-American theater and dance, noh drama, ramlila, etc. Some of these performances are one of a kind while others are generic; some are rituals, some entertainments; some take months, others are over in a matter of minutes or take no time at all. What figure 8.1 expresses is my triune thesis: 1) there is a unifiable realm of performance that includes ritual, theater, dance, music, sports, play, social drama, and various popular entertainments; 2) certain patterns can be detected among these examples; 3) from these patterns theorists can develop consistent broad-based models that respect the immediacy, ephemerality, peculiarity, and ever-changingness of individual performances, runs, and genres.

In the essay that follows I will develop only a few aspects and consequences of the time/space/event chart. My aim is to indicate what the magnitudes of performances are, where each magnitude of performance takes place.

INSIDERS, OUTSIDERS[3]

Erving Goffman built his work on the basis that everyday life is framed and performed. Early in his investigations he wrote, "All the world is not, of course, a stage, but the crucial ways in which it isn't are not easy to specify" (1959: 72). Not easy because everyday life is suffused with interactions that are rule-bound, conventions that are networks of reciprocal expectations and obligations.

> The legitimate performances of everyday life are not "acted" or "put on" in the sense that the performer knows in advance just what he is going to do, and does this solely because of the effect it is likely to have. The expressions it is felt he is giving off will be especially "inaccessible" to him. But as in the case of less legitimate performers, the incapacity of the ordinary individual to formulate in advance the movements of his eyes and body does not mean that he will not express himself through these devices in a way that is dramatized and pre-formed in his repertoire of actions. In short, we all act better than we know how.
>
> (Goffman 1959: 73–4)

Goffman goes on in this early, but decisive, enunciation of his core idea to say that in cultures where trance is practiced – such as Haiti (he could have added Korea and Bali, as well as certain African, Afro-American, and Euro-American religious sects) – the entranced person will

> be able to provide a correct portrayal of the god that has entered him [because of all the contextual knowledge and memories available; that] the person possessed will be in just the right social relation to those who are watching; that possession occurs at just the right moment in the ceremonial undertaking, the possessed one carrying out his ritual obligations to the point of participating in a kind of skit with persons possessed at the time with other spirits.
>
> (Goffman 1959: 74)

Goffman emphasized that his observations are usually not shared by the possessed people. "Participants in the cult believe that possession is a real thing and that persons are possessed at random by gods who they cannot select" (1959: 74).

This break between the experience of the observer and that of the participant is one of the most interesting things about trance possession from the point of view of performance theory. This break is on a continuum with the less radical but still distinctly observable breaks between the experiences of performers and audiences in all kinds of performances. In terms of trance a very few examples must suffice as indicators of a general tendency.

> *Insiders*: Shakers of St Vincent: "Power is a breeze descended that comes as a rushing wind into the heart. When It leaves, you feel something leaving you."
>
> (Henney 1974: 59)

> *Outsiders*: Shakers of St Vincent: Three "levels" of trance are perceived. "The first external sign of dissociation may be a convulsive jerk of one or both arms, of one or both shoulders, or of the head. It may be a shudder, shiver, or trembling; a sudden shout, sob, hiss, or series of unintelligible sounds. . . . As more and more individuals throughout the church become involved in the random symptoms of the first level . . ., a subtle change of behavior characteristic of the second level takes place. . . . Idiosyncratic movements and sounds, and breathing

peculiarities become less conspicuous because of the concerted attention persons in possession trance give to the same rhythm pattern. ... Sooner or later the second level of possession trance changes. The smoothly patterned phenomenon in which each individual submits to the group-impressed rhythmic beat is disrupted as the dissociated persons emit loud sighs and yells, and breathe with complete disregard for the previous regular timing. ... All movements and sounds again become individualistic. ... That the Shakers themselves are aware of differences in possession-trance levels came to my attention when I played for them some of the tapes I had made."

(Henney 1974: 61–3)

Insiders: Balinese *sanghyang* trance: "GM [Jane Belo's Balinese assistant]: what is the feeling like when you are beginning to be smoked [put into a trance]? Soekani: When I am just being smoked my ears are stopped up, hearing the song. After that I immediately lose consciousness, I feel as if I were all alone. When I am about to come to myself suddenly I know where I am ... Darja: When I've gone in trance, my thoughts are delicious, but I do not remember them. What's more, my whole body is very hot. And then, if I am touched with holy water, my thoughts are like a crazy person's. ... Darma: When I'm a *sanghyang* snake, suddenly my thoughts are delicious. ... When my body is like that, as a snake, my feeling is of going through the woods, and I am pleased. GM: And if you're a *sanghyang* broom, what's it like, and where do you feel? Darma: like sweeping filth in the middle of the ground, like sweeping filth in the street, in the village, I feel I am being carried off by the broom, led on to sweep."

(Belo 1960: 221–2)

Outsiders: "The hypnotic threshold, the selective awareness of certain stimuli and imperviousness to others irrelevant to the situation, wellknown in hypnosis experiments, is illustrated in the players' remarks about hearing the song, but not hearing people talking of other things, not seeing the singers, but trampling upon them when angered. The feeling of lowness, which Darma described as delightful, fits in with the whole constellation of ideas about being mounted, being sat on, and so forth, wherein the pleasurable quality of the trance experience is connected with the surrendering of the self-impulses. This is one aspect of the trance state which seems to have reverberations in the trance vocabulary in whatever country these phenomena appear – and the aspect which is perhaps the hardest for non-trancers to grasp."

(Belo 1976: 158–9)

Even further outside are analyses like Chapple's (1970) and Lex's (1979):

Voodoo drums, the regular and driving rhythms of revivalistic cere-monies, the incessant beat of jazz or its teenage variants in rock and roll, must synchronize the rhythms of muscular activity centered in the brain and the nervous system. Combined with the dance or with other rhythmic forms of synchronized mass movement – stamping the feet or clapping the hands over and over again – the sound and action of responding as the tempo speeds up clearly "possess" and control the participant. The external rhythm becomes the synchronizer to set the internal clocks of these fast rhythms.

(Chapple 1970: 38, in Lex 1979: 122)

The *raison d'être* for rituals is the readjustment of dysphasic biological and social rhythms by manipulation of neurophysiological structures under controlled conditions. Rituals properly executed promote a feel-ing of well-being and relief, not only because prolonged or intense stresses are alleviated, but also because the driving techniques employed in rituals are designed to sensitize or "tune" the nervous system and thereby lessen inhibition of the right [cerebral] hemisphere and permit temporary right-hemisphere domination, as well as mixed trophotropic-ergotropic excitation, to achieve synchronization of cor-tical rhythms in both hemispheres and evoke trophotropic rebound.[4] Furthermore, it is difficult to separate the impact of repetitive behaviors on the brain from their influence on the rest of the nervous system because the various driving techniques simultaneously excite numerous neural centers. In a given ritual one specific practice alone may be sufficient to establish a state of trance; that several techniques are engaged concomitantly or sequentially indicates redundancy, to guarantee reliability, potentially affecting the entire group of participants. In other words, manifold driving techniques accommodate individual differences in experience and genetic makeup. However, any complete interpretation of ritual trance also recognizes the symbolic qualities of human behavior.

(Lex 1979: 144–5)

These differences are not just exercises in the "emic-etic"* pitfalls of field work. The great big gap between what a performance is to people inside and what it is to people outside conditions all the thinking about performance. These differences can be as great within a single culture as they are across cultural boundaries. In fact, in my own experience, performers from different cultures are more likely to understand each other – and be able to exchange techniques, anecdotes, information – than they can understand, and be understood, by people within their own culture who have not themselves either been performers or gone out of their way to understand what performers experience. Performance experience – unlike eating, housing, speaking/listening, etc. – is something the outsider has to specifically go out of her/his way to get from the inside. This curiosity concerning experience prompted Turner to experiment with "performing ethnography."[5]

The situation of the "professional performer" – a person who reflexively masters the techniques of performance (whether or not s/he gets paid for it) – is very different from the "Goffman performer" who is likely to be unaware of her/his own performance.[6] The theorist in Goffman's world is always an outsider because the theorist exposes precisely what the Goffman performer conceals or is unaware of: the very fact that s/he is performing. There are actually two kinds of Goffman performer: the ones who conceal, as conmen do; and the ones who don't know they are performing. Of this second type there are two subdivisions: ordinary people playing their "life roles" as waitresses, doctors, teachers, street people, etc. And those whose particular actions have been framed as a performance in documentary film, shows like *Candid Camera*, or on the 6 o'clock TV news. The woman whose children have perished in a fire in Brooklyn pours out her grief and

* Emic and *etic* are anthropological terms often used together, meaning, respectively, "to experience a culture from the inside"; "to experience a culture from the outside."

bewilderment in front of and for whom? For the cameras, and behind them, invisible but present, the "public." Perhaps, even, for herself as later she watched replays of her own grieving. A person in a similar plight who does not "make the news" has not become a performer. There are real-life consequences: the woman on TV is likely to have offered to her the assistance of viewers moved by her circumstances, while an unbroadcast person in a similar fix will have to depend on her own resources and official aid only.[7]

Clearly, there are several bands of participation and reception, and these define what kind of performance is going on. The comparisons among framed-as performers, Goffman performers, and professional performers are depicted in figure 8.2. Using figures 8.1 and 8.2 together, one can situate performances of different cultures and genres. The main question one asks is whether a performance generates its own frame – is reflexive (self-conscious, conscious of its audience, the audience conscious of the performer being conscious of being a performer, etc.); or whether the frame is imposed from the outside, as when TV crews arrive at the scene of a "tragedy." In between these extremes are many gradations of purposeful concealment or information sharing – even what the US Government calls "disinformation" (what the Nazis called propaganda, what Madison Avenue calls a "campaign"). Concomitantly, there are degrees of publicly articulated performance conventions, staging, and training.

BIRDWHISTELL AND EKMAN

Ray Birdwhistell locates the sources of some of what Goffman discussed in very minute behavior observable only by studying human interactions as they are recorded and therefore susceptible to being slowed down, stopped, and repeated on film and tape.[8] Can we call the facial gestures that Birdwhistell says happen in milliseconds – such as eyebrow flashes, the turn of the lips that characterize certain smiles, tongue flicks, etc. – "performances"? Birdwhistell says these "kinemes" are culture-specific. There is an American way of flashing the eyebrows – or, perhaps it is more accurate to say, there is an American cultural context within which brow flashes communicate culture-specific meanings. But kinemes are not under anyone's conscious control –

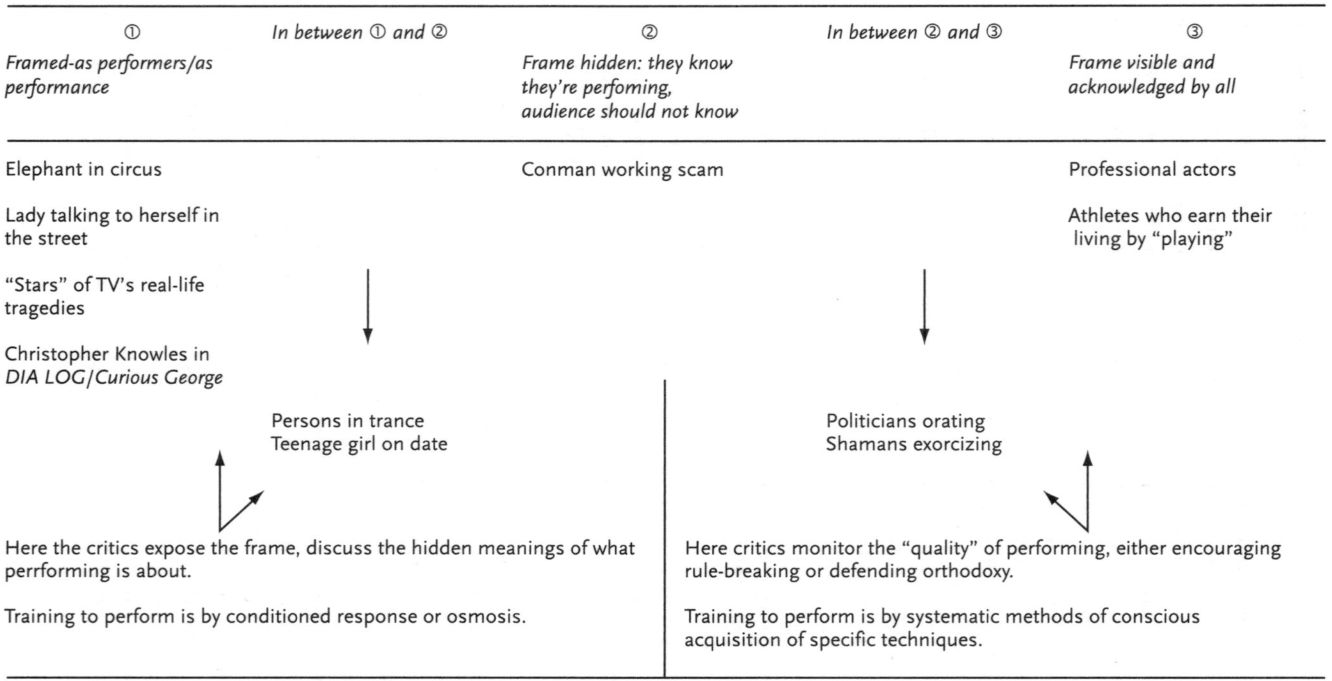

①	In between ① and ②	②	In between ② and ③	③
Framed-as performers/as performance		Frame hidden: they know they're performing, audience should not know		Frame visible and acknowledged by all
Elephant in circus		Conman working scam		Professional actors
Lady talking to herself in the street				Athletes who earn their living by "playing"
"Stars" of TV's real-life tragedies				
Christopher Knowles in DIA LOG/Curious George				
	Persons in trance		Politicians orating	
	Teenage girl on date		Shamans exorcizing	

Here the critics expose the frame, discuss the hidden meanings of what performing is about.

Here critics monitor the "quality" of performing, either encouraging rule-breaking or defending orthodoxy.

Training to perform is by conditioned response or osmosis.

Training to perform is by systematic methods of conscious acquisition of specific techniques.

Figure 8.2

unless, that is, you study them in slow motion, learn what muscles are involved, and train yourself to execute the gestures, as Birdwhistell himself has done (and as, I would suppose, many actors have done from the days of Delsarte onward[9]). Birdwhistell is an animated lecturer precisely because he can demonstrate in terms of facial displays a midwestern American teenage female's mode of greeting as distinct from that of a teenager from the deep south. As Birdwhistell points out there is a difference between understanding kinemes as expressing meaning and situating those kinemes in the various cultural settings that give them distinct social meanings. The number of kinemes is limited: "the [American] kinemic catalogue will probably contain between fifty and sixty items" (Birdwhistell 1970: 27). But these items can be combined with each other in various social contexts to yield the full range of "American" body languages. Birdwhistell's work has been used in conjunction with Goffman's as the basis of many workshops in body language and management of expressive behavior – what Arlie Hochschild (1983) calls "deep acting."[10]

Maybe the "deepest" acting goes on at the neurological level. Paul Ekman's work in this area, though apparently inimical to Birdwhistell's (the two have debated each other), actually meshes productively with it. Ekman believes that there are universally recognized facial displays of "target emotions." Ekman and his colleagues are currently detailing relationships between the autonomic nervous system (ANS) and acting. Here I mean acting as done by professional stage actors, though I do not doubt that similar results would be obtained using Goffman performers. In fact, the evidence is accumulating that the difference between "ordinary behavior" and "acting" is one of reflexivity: professional actors are aware that they are acting.[11]

Ekman's experiments show that the six "target emotions" of surprise, disgust, sadness, anger, fear, and happiness elicit "emotion-specific activity in the ANS" (figure 8.3). He got these data in two ways, using actors from San Francisco's American Conservatory Theater. In one, subjects "were told precisely which muscles to contract . . . constructing facial prototypes of emotion muscle by muscle"; in the other, "subjects were asked to experience each of the six emotions . . . by reliving a past emotional experience for 30 seconds" (Ekman 1983: 1208–9). This reliving of a past emotional experience is the

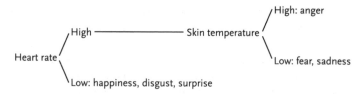

Figure 8.3 Emotions that Ekman (1983: 1209) distinguishes on the basis of heart-rate and skin-temperature differences

classic acting exercise from the turn of the century, called "emotion memory" or "affective memory" by the Russian theater director Konstantin Stanislavsky (see note 10). Stanislavsky developed this exercise to help actors actually live on stage the emotional lives of the characters they were portraying. The same exercise, with modifications, is practiced today by many actors following the Method of Lee Strasberg and his Actors' Studio in New York.[12] In fact, Ekman wrote, "The idea of studying actors was suggested to me by Lee Strasberg some years ago. Although I never met Strasberg, we corresponded at some length about how our research might be used to explore the nature of the physiological changes that can occur when the 'method' is used" (Ekman 1983: personal communication).

The actors who made Ekman's faces were not aware of what emotions they were constructing; rather they were coached muscle by muscle as they looked at themselves in mirrors.[13] Their work was a flagrant demonstration of "mechanical acting" – the kind despised by most American performers, but exactly what is learned by Indian young boys beginning their studies as performers in kathakali dance-theater. There a most rigorous system of body and facial training is followed, one that more or less adheres to the ancient Sanskrit text on theater, the *Natyasastra*, which I will discuss below in connection with Ekman's work. What should be noted now is that the facial and body displays practiced by students of kathakali are not "natural" but exaggerated, wholly composed "deconstructions/reconstructions" of human behavior (see Schechner 1985: 213–60 and Zarrilli 1984). If the kathakali displays also elicit changes in the ANS, might this not indicate that the human neurological system accepts a very deep emotional learning? That is, human "fixed action patterns" or "ethological rituals" might be specifically transformable – a Batesonian play frame built into the brain.

As noted, reliving emotions from past experience is an exercise familiar to anyone who has studied acting in America. It is so common, in fact, that many people working in experimental theater eschew it, detesting its clichés, lack of spontaneity, and underlying mechanistic approach to human feelings: the performer is drawn away from the actual present circumstances onstage, concentrating instead on a "there and then" experience bootlegged into the present. On the other hand, such powerfully relived feelings generate performances in many ways similar to trance.

What is truly surprising about Ekman's experiment is not that emotional recall works, but that "producing the emotion-prototypic patterns of facial muscle action resulted in autonomic changes of large magnitude that were more clear-cut than those produced by reliving emotions" (Ekman 1983: 1210). That is, mechanical acting worked better that getting the actor to feel. This is absolutelly contrary to the Stanislavsky–Strasberg canon. It also suggests that Hochschild's "deep acting" exists at the ANS level. And it asks for Birdwhistell's kinemes to be tested: do culture-specific facial displays also affect the ANS? Just how labile are humans, and to what level of the nervous system? Acting – professional and/or Goffman types – may be more than a neocortical event; acting may engage the old-mammalian and reptilian brains.

Ekman's experiment adds a new dimension to a growing body of evidence that suggests:

1. There are universal signals that not only repeat signifiers but signifieds: a "universal language," if you will, of "basic emotions" (see especially Eibl-Eibesfeldt 1979).
2. This "language of emotions" is nonverbal and consists mostly of facial displays, vocal cries, body postures (freezes), and movements (stamping, rushing, reaching).
3. There is a corresponding universal system in nerve and brain process – and this system probably underlies what anthropologists have called ritual (see Turner 1985 and d'Aquili, Laughlin, and McManus 1979).
4. The culture-specific kinemes that Birdwhistell finds are built on top

of and out of the "universal language of emotions." That is, the universal language is neither static nor fixed but transformable – the more so, the more conscious individuals are of it. Professional performers – from shamans to actors in soap operas – skillfully manipulate the relationships between the two corresponding systems, the universal and the culture-specific.

Thus performances "take place" all along the continuum from brain events to public events of great spatial and temporal magnitude.

Ekman's findings do not invalidate what Birdwhistell and like-minded researchers have been saying: that each culture has its own way of encoding, using, contexting, and making into art the multi-channeled systems of non-verbal and paraverbal expressions. I want to go further. Each human group – family, circle of friends, work group, ensemble – develops its own dialect of movement. Artists are particularly adept at constructing variations of basic codes. This is what "style" is all about. What a theater work is – not all it is, but the core of its "originality" – is how far a work can speak its own language without becoming unintelligible. Works called avant-garde or experimental sometimes go beyond this boundary, are rejected, only to be later incorporated into the canon as mainstream codes catch up with the avant-garde and critics and public learn what the previously rejected works were "about." That is, they learn to context the works, to relocate the boundaries of accepted conventions to include works that were previously out of bounds. If this doesn't happen, the works are forgotten.

THE NATYASASTRA

The Natyasastra, compiled in India between the second century BCE and the second century CE, describes in great detail various facial and

---

Plates 8.1–8.9

Plates on left The nine rasas performed in kathakali. (Photographs by Phillip Zarrilli)

Plates on right The six key emotions as expressed in the face according to Paul Ekman. (Photographs courtesy of Paul Ekman and Wallace V. Friesen)

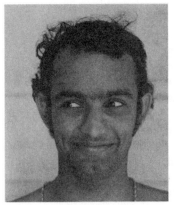

1 Śrngāra: love, happiness

Ekman: happiness

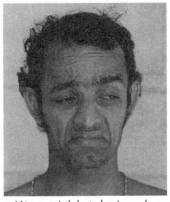

2 Hāsya: mirth but also impudence

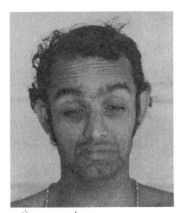

3 Ḱaruna: sadness

Ekman: sadness

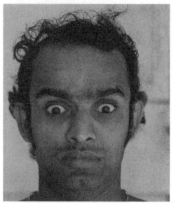

4 Raudra: anger, violence

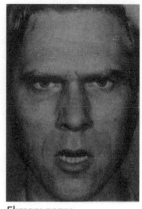

Ekman: anger

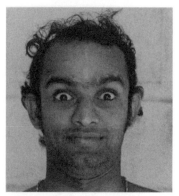

5 Vīra: vigor, heroism

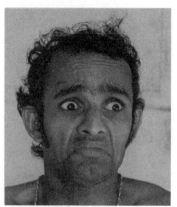

6 Bhayanaka: fear, guilt

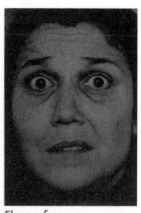

Ekman: fear

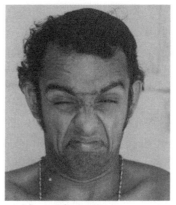

7 Bibhasta: disgust

Ekman: disgust

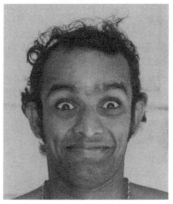

8 Adhuta: surprise, excitement

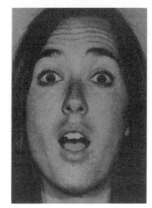

Ekman: surprise

9 Śānta: peace, meditation

bodily poses and expressions needed to perform the "eight basic emotions" of classical Indian dance-theater: love, happiness, sadness (or grief), anger, energy, fear, disgust, and surprise. A ninth emotion, peace or sublime tranquility (śānta) was added later (see plates 8.1–8.9). Humankind has countless gods, but I would be very surprised if there were not some agreement concerning the "basic emotions." Love, energy, and peace are not on Ekman's list, possibly because he considers them to be "mixed" or composite emotions.

Compare one of Ekman's muscle-by-muscle descriptions with what the Natyasastra instructs the actor to do. Ekman (1983: 1208) says the fear face is made by raising the eyebrows and pulling them together, raising the upper eyelids, and then stretching the lips horizontally back toward the ears. The Natyasastra deals with several kinds of fear and different classes of characters each of which reacts differently to fear. But there are some possible generalizations. In Ghosh's translation (Bharata-muni 1967: 144): "Fear is to be represented on stage by . . . shaking of the narrow limbs, body tremors, paralysis, goose pimples, speaking with a choked voice." Regarding the eyes and surrounding musculature, of which Ekman makes so much, the Natyasastra states: "the eyelids are drawn up and fixed, and the eyeballs are gleaming and turned up" (p. 155); and "the eyes are widely opened, the eyeballs are mobile in fear and are away from the center [of each eye] (p. 157). Also, "the glance in which the eyelids are drawn up in fear, the eyeballs are trembling, and the middle of the eye is full blown due to panic is called Trasta [frightened]" (p. 159). But the Natyasastra is not entirely consistent. Its authors are always quoting slokas (sacred couplets). Sometimes these say that fear is to be represented by half-closed eyes. The Natyasastra is not a scientific study but a compilation of the stage experience by many actors over a span of centuries. A wide variety of emotions is conveyed by specific facial and bodily gestures for the eyes, eyelids, eyebrows, nose, cheeks, lower lip, chin, mouth, and neck; there are also sixty-seven gestures for the hands and many gestures for other parts of the body.

No one knows exactly how, in its day, the Natyasastra was put into action. Most probably it was a text like Stanislavsky's books or Jerzy Grotowski's Towards a Poor Theatre (1968a), a collection of examples of what proved successful on stage. As such the Natyasastra serves as a node

Plate 8.10 Two kathakali trainees at the Kerala Kalamandalam are massaged in order to give their bodies flexibility, shaping their bodies into proper kathakali instruments. (Photograph by Sangeet Natak Akademi, New Delhi)

or transfer point linking previous practice with future practice. A hiatus of several centuries divides the Sanskrit theater of the *Natyasastra* with even the oldest of the still-performed Indian dance-theater, the *kutiattam* of Kerala. But in kutiattam, as in its sister genre, kathakali, a rigorous training continues the tradition of the *Natyasastra*. In kathakali there are numerous exercises for the eyes and facial mask (see plates 8.10–8.12).

> In these exercises the forehead, eyebrows, eyelids, cheeks, and lips are all manipulated independently to gain individual control of the muscles like that demanded of the eyes. The eyebrows are exercised up and down while the eyes remain fixed on one point. While keeping the eyebrows raised and the eyes open and fixed on a point, the eyelids are independently articulated and fluttered. The lips and cheeks are exercised by practicing a closed-lip smile. . . . Similarly the muscles

must be exercised to gain the pliability to give a broad frown. . . . While the facial mask is exercised, the young student must also learn the nine basic facial expressions which correspond to the nine permanent *bhavas* [feelings] and the corresponding *rasas* [emotions aroused in performer and spectator]. At first each facial expression is taught in purely technical terms.

(Zarrilli 1984: 133)

In the hands of a kathakali master these disciplines are not constraints, but the means to precise and spontaneous performances.

The *Natyasastra* – and the arts based on it – insist on what Ekman's experiments show: there are links between "mechanical acting" and feelings; the causal chain can go in both directions: feelings can lead to stage action while the practice of specific stage exercises can arouse feelings in the actor. In a definable way the performer can be moved by

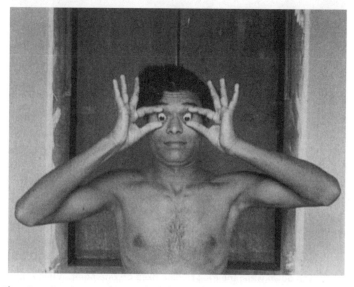

Plate 8.11 A trainee at the Kerala Kalamandalam practicing his eye exercises. Facial expression, including precise control of the eyes, is essential in kathakali. (Photograph by Richard Schechner)

Plate 8.12 A fully made up kathakali face, ready for performing. Even with the extreme stylization of the makeup, gesturing with the face is a very important part of expressing the role. (Photograph by Clifford R. Jones)

her/his own performance. Thus the performance – the psychophysical score of a scene, dance, piece of music, etc. – occupies a space *between* the performer who is doing the action and the spectator who is receiving it. The performer performing can be the "objective correlative" T. S. Eliot finds in the enunciable literary text.[14] Reading the *Natyasastra* and studying the dance-theater forms using it reveals that *abhinaya* – acting – is not only the means by which the audience gets the performance but also the way in which the actors get it – the "it" being not only gestures but the feelings as well, feelings which are aroused by the practice of the proper gestures.

Take kathakali, for example.[15] The basis for becoming a kathakali performer is mastering a certain body configuration with its attendant steps, gestures of the hands, feet, torso, and face – especially the mouth, forehead, eyebrows, and eyes – in what to an American appears to be a very mechanical way. Boys begin training between the ages of 8 and 16, the younger the better. They train for six or more years as their bodies are literally massaged and danced into shapes suited to kathakali. Even as they are learning the stories – taken mostly from the *Ramayana*, the *Mahabharata*, and the *Puranas* – their faces, feet, hands, and backs are learning by rote the sequences that add up to the finished performances. These sequences do not "make sense" by themselves; they equivocate concerning Ekman's assertions of universals. But these sequences can be thought of as aesthetic ritualizations of already ethologically ritualized "natural" displays. To a person educated in kathakali's face and hand language, the dancing makes sense, gestures convey specific meanings – as concrete and definite as American Sign Language. As they begin their training the boys have little idea, except as spectators, about these finished performances. But somewhere along the way the training "goes into the body" (as the Balinese, who use similar methods of training, say). An illumination of sorts occurs: what is being written in the bodies of the dancers is read *from the inside* by each of them.

What was rote movement, even painful body realignment, becomes second nature – a full language capable of conveying detailed and subtle meanings and feelings. The maturing performer now begins to internally experience his role with a force every bit as powerful as what an American Stanislavsky-trained actor might experience. I believe that if such a kathakali performer were tested for ANS variation the results from the composed, performed facial displays would not be less pronounced or in any way markedly different from those of the muscle-by-muscle enactment of the "natural" emotions tested by Ekman. Aesthetic acting, learned from the outside, "composed" and culturally determined, penetrates deep into the brain. What was at the start of training an external effect becomes during the course of training an internal cause. As Padmanathan Nair, one of the best kathakali actors, told me in 1976: "A good actor is the one who understands the character very well, thus becoming the character itself. . . . [But] we should not forget ourselves while acting. While acting, half of the actor is the role he does and half will be himself." Bertolt Brecht, so affected by Chinese acting, would have been very pleased with Nair's answer. The "half actor" who is the role is the one who has internalized the fixed gesture patterns of kathakali; the "half actor" who is himself is the one observing, manipulating, and enjoying the actions of the other half. To achieve this kind of acting it is necessary to assimilate into the body the precise second-by-second details of performing. In kathakali, at least, this kind of mastery begins mechanically, à la Ekman; "feeling" at the experiential and/or ANS level comes later.

LYING AND THE PERFORMER'S THREE HALVES

A depiction not merely of emotions, but of emotions that can easily be recognized, that can be composed and communicated – the raw material of theater wherever it is found – is also the stuff lies are made of. As Ekman points out the face is not only a truth-teller but a liar without peer. And lying, as much as truth-telling, is the stock in trade of theater.

> The face appears to be the most skilled nonverbal communicator and perhaps for that reason the best "nonverbal liar," capable not only of withholding information but of simulating the facial behavior associated with a feeling which the person is in no way experiencing.
> (Ekman 1972: 23)

Here the Ekman of 1972 does not yet know what the Ekman of 1983 found out: that the "mechanical" construction of a face in the configuration of a "target emotion" elicits an ANS response, i.e. an "experience." Thus lying is a very complicated business in which the skilled liar – a person who can make a convincing face – knows he is lying but feels he is telling the truth (see Ekman 1985). Exactly Nair's (and Brecht's) response. The half actor who "does not forget" himself is the knower, the half who "becomes the character itself" is the feeler. Exactly how this works neurologically remains to be investigated. Possibly there is a right-brain/left-brain operation going on.

This would suggest, even, that a skilled performer has "three halves." Both the ergotropic and trophotropic systems are aroused, while the "center" of the performer, the "I," stands outside observing and to some degree controlling both the knower and the feeler. Clearly a complex operation engages both the cognitive and the affective systems simultaneously, without either one washing out the other. A similar "triple state" accompanies some kinds of trance, while in other kinds of trance the feelings may be so powerful that they blot out entirely both the "knowing half" and the "observing/controlling" half of the performer.

Actor training in many cultures is largely about manipulating, controlling, manifesting, and communicating exact gestures, sounds, and other behaviors that elicit in the spectators particular rasas or feelings. It is not always expected that the actor experience the rasa s/he is producing. Of course, in some systems, both in the west and elsewhere, "authentic" feelings are asked of the performer.

The degree of authenticity required by varying genres of behavior (you see, I am going beyond "theater" and into "life") gets back to figure 8.2. Sometimes there is a mix of contexts and manipulations where ambivalence and ambiguity are delighted in. For example, animals at the circus are not aware of the varying human social and cognitive contexts of their behaviors. But it is these contexts that make the show enjoyable to the human spectators. The elephant bowing at the end of "his" act is not saying "thank you" although the spectators receive the elephant's behavior as such and applaud even louder accordingly. But how is what the elephant does different from what Laurence Olivier did when, in blackface, as Othello, raging, "Down, strumpet!" he takes up the pillow to murder Desdemona? The difference is that Olivier's knowing half knows he is just acting and as such controls his gestures so that he does not injure the actress playing Desdemona. Even more, Olivier feels and does not feel rage against that actress. Olivier is absorbed in the task of "performing the actions that communicate to himself and to his audience the emotions required." The whole bundle is necessary in order to understand this kind of acting. The Balinese dancer in trance is in a middle position. She might not know at the time that she has been dancing, that the *dedari* (gods) have possessed her. But before and after dancing she knows what trance is (in her culture), what the proper gestures are, what behavior is acceptable *while in trance* (even how far "out of control" to get). The trancer's situation is very different from that of the crazy lady shouting to the wind on a street in Manhattan. The crazy lady is talking so convincingly to an absent Other that around her has gathered an absorbed, amused crowd. She may be performing the gestures of a great monologist, but prompted by some interior cue she is no better off than the circus elephant. Worse, even, because no trainer can get her to stop "acting," no shout of "Fire!" will make her quit the stage for a safe exit.

Or take Christopher Knowles, the "brain-damaged" or "non-ordinary" or "specially creative" boy (depending on one's point of view regarding the ancient and widespread tradition of using such people as entertainers) who worked with Robert Wilson in the 1970s. They did a two-person show, *DIA LOG/Curious George*, where Knowles was – like the circus elephant or the lady in the street – just "being himself." Wilson contexted his interactions with Knowles as a performance for the public who paid fancy prices to witness and admire it. Sometimes Knowles' responses – his way of retelling the children's story, and Wilson's questions to Knowles, were very funny, wise, ironic, appropriate: one of those Simpleton Saints. Saint or not, Knowles was an elephant bowing at the circus – whatever his remarks meant to members of the audience they meant, or were, something else to Knowles. Because Knowles couldn't lie, he couldn't be an actor – he could only be *situated and displayed as if he were an actor* inside of Wilson's show.

BRAIN LATERALIZATION AND PERFORMANCE

But how can one specify the differences between performances that are so only contextually and those that the performer is conscious of manufacturing? Could the difference be in how the brain is used? D'Aquili and his colleagues (1979) note that the left side of the brain is ergotropic and the right side trophotropic. They say that

> there is something about the repetitive or rhythmic emanation of signals from a conspecific that generates a high degree of limbic arousal. ... There is something about repetitive rhythmic stimuli that may, under proper conditions, bring about the unusual neural state of simultaneous high discharge of both [the sympathetic and parasympathetic] autonomic subsystems. ... [The excited ANS] supersaturates the ergotropic or energy-expending system ... to the point that the trophotropic system not only is simultaneously excited by a kind of spillover but also on rare occasions may be maximally stimulated, so that, briefly at least, both systems are intensely stimulated.
>
> (d'Aquili, Laughlin, and McManus 1979: 157, 175)

Such maximal stimulation gives that feeling of the inexpressible which sometimes accompanies not only religious ritual and solitary meditation but large and small gatherings of many different kinds – from football games to Samuel Beckett's plays, from Nazi rallies to the soft rhythmic panting-chanting I teach as part of a theater workshop.

In 1971 Roland Fischer devised what he called "a cartography of the ecstatic and meditative states" (figure 8.4), wherein the spectrum of arousal is outlined from trophotropic (hypoaroused) states such as Yogic *samadhi* and Zen meditation through the normal "I" states of daily routine, on to ergotropic (hyperaroused) states such as schizophrenia and mystical ecstasy. Fischer, like d'Aquili, speaks of a "rebound" from one extreme to another.

> In spite of the mutually exclusive relation between the ergotropic and trophotropic systems, however, there is a phenomenon called "rebound to superactivity" or trophotropic rebound, which occurs in response to intense sympathetic excitation, that is, at ecstasy, the peak

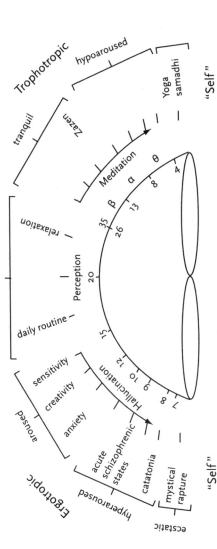

Figure 8.4 Fischer's (1971) cartography of the ecstatic and meditative states

Note

Fischer explains: "Varieties of conscious states [are] mapped on a perception–hallucination continuum of increasing ergotropic arousal (*left*) and a perception–meditation continuum of increasing trophotropic arousal (*right*). These levels of hyper and hypoarousal are interpreted by man as normal, creative, psychotic, and ecstatic states (*left*) and Zazen and samadhi (*right*). The loop connecting ecstasy and samadhi represents the rebound from ecstasy to samadhi, which is observed in response to intense ergotropic excitation. The numbers 35 to 7 on the perception–hallucination continuum are Goldstein's coefficient of variation . . ., specifying the decrease in variability of the EEG amplitude with increasing ergotropic arousal. The numbers 26 to 4 on the perception–meditation continuum, on the other hand, refer to those beta, alpha, and theta EEG waves (measured in hertz) that predominate during, but are not specific to, these states" (1971): 898). The figure is reproduced here by permission of the American Association for the Advancement of Science. Copyright 1971 by the AAAS.

of ergotropic arousal. A rebound into samadhi at this point can be conceived of as a physiological protective mechanism. . . . Meaning is "meaningful" only at that level of arousal at which it is experienced, and every experience has its state-bound meaning. During the "Self"-state of highest levels of hyper or hypoarousal, this meaning can no longer be expressed in dualistic terms, since the experience of unity is born from the integration of interpretive (cortical) and interpreted (subcortical) structures. Since this intense meaning is devoid of specificities, the only way to communicate its intensity is the metaphor; hence, only through the transformation of objective sign into subjective symbol in art, literature, and religion can the increasing integration of cortical and subcortical activity be communicated.

(Fischer 1971: 902)

Theatrical performance – from trance to Olivier to kathakali – seems to be a peculiar human activity in which there is high arousal of both ergotropic and trophotropic systems while some of the center – the "normal I" – is held back as an observing-controlling self. Performance training is the development of a number of communicative skills plus learning how to arouse the two extremes of brain activity without canceling out the center "I" self; the theatrical performer never wholly loses self-control. Precisely how this is done in terms of neurobiology remains to be discovered, though I believe Ekman's work on the relation between the ANS and facial muscular control is a big step in the right direction. Strong theatrical performances are thus dangerous – on the edges – and yet playful; they are examples of psychophysical "deep play."[16]

Trance performances are on or even over the edge: self-control is reduced to a minimum or absent, thus the necessity for helpers – people who stay out of trance specifically to aid those who are in trance, preventing injuries, assisting the trancers as they come out of trance. The crazy lady in the street is not in trance because she has no way out. She has surrendered to, or been taken over by, schizophrenia. The normal "I" self has been permanently abolished. Christopher Knowles and the circus elephant have a "damaged" or non-existent "I."

Performing artists are forever playing around – not only with the codes, frames, and metaframes of communication – but with their own internal brain states. Although artistic and scientific creativity have long been thought to be similar, there is this decisive difference: scientists focus their work on external phenomena; even a neurobiologist works on somebody else's brain. Performing artists – and, I would say, meditators, shamans, and trancers too – work on themselves, trying to induce deep psychophysical transformations either of a temporary or of a permanent kind. The external artwork – the performance the spectators see – is the visible result of a trialog among: 1) the conventions or givens of a genre, 2) the stretching, distorting, or invention of new conventions, and 3) brain-centered psychophysical transformations of self.

PERFORMATIVITY, THEATRICALITY, AND NARRATIVITY

In other writings (Schechner 1985) I have described in detail the deconstruction/reconstruction process that performers use to effect transformations of self. This process, present in different cultures and genres under various names, is the "ritual process" Van Gennep first specified and Turner explicated. D'Aquili, Lex, and Fischer investigate the same process from a neurological perspective. From a theatrical perspective what happens is that a person enters training or workshop as a "fixed" or "finished" or "already-made" being. The training consists of specific methods of "beaking down" the neophyte, of rendering her/him psychophysically malleable. Quite literally the performer in training (or workshop) is taken apart, deconstructed into bits. The "bit" is not only computer jargon but a venerable theater term meaning the smallest repeatable strip of action. Bits are as important to *commedia dell'arte* as they are to naturalistic or even formalistic acting; a bit is a molecule of action. The boys learning kathakali repeat the same bits over and over. Directors are always telling actors to "take that bit again" because it is at the bit level that acting can be "worked on" from the outside. Stanislavsky, co-founder of the Moscow Art Theater and progenitor of the first and still the most influential school of modern acting and directing, broke down the scores of his *mises-en-scène* into bits (sometimes translated into English as "beats"[17]).

Once bits are freed from their attachment to larger schemes of action, they can be rearranged – almost as the frames of a film being edited are rearranged – to make new actions. This rearranging is not mechanical, for it is accompanied by varying degrees of self-conscious, reflexive reconstruction. How these rearrangements are accomplished in different cultures and genres varies. Sometimes the methods are kept secret as in noh theater or in some initiation rites. Sometimes there is the opposite tendency – even a passion to spread the techniques as with many who make a career out of training actors and dancers. The devices of performer training go beyond the physical into realms of simulation, feigning, pretending, playing around with – all kinds of "as if-ing." Every performer knows that this kind of playing around is a dangerous game verging on self-deception accepted as truth.[18]

Human communications systems are not reducible to the static model of "sender–channel–receiver," or any variation thereof, that assumes the existence of discrete parts. The human system is an extremely subtle multiplex-feedback one in which the originator of feelings is also affected by the emotions s/he is expressing – *even if these emotions are a lie*. That is what Ekman's experiment, and good acting, are saying: the doing of the action of a feeling is enough to arouse the feeling both in the doer and in the receiver. Olivier need not work himself into a jealous rage against the actress playing Desdemona; but neither is he devoid of feelings; performing the actions of Othello will arouse Olivier. The so-called surface of emotion – the look on the face, the tone of the skin, the tilt of the body, the placement and moves of muscles – is also the emotion's "depth." Muscular, cortical, and subcortical routines are linked and can be mutually trained.

Ekman's work and the instructions of the *Natyasastra* should caution scholars against depending on linguistic models when it comes to figuring out what's going on during performances. There are no universals of spoken or written language – no phonemes or graphemes that mean the same thing everywhere. Nor are there performance details at the level of artistic expression that are the same everywhere. But there are certain looks, sounds, and movements – certain facial displays, screams, laughs, sobs, crouches, stamps, and arm movements – which, if not universally understood, come close to conveying the same *feelings* everywhere. Nor are these feelings trivial: they constitute the very heart of human performing art and ritual. What I'm saying is that performances of theater, dance, music, ritual by the very nature of their existence as behavior – as things are done – give us our best examples for the intercultural study of human communication.

In a clumsy but ironically accurate way governments recognize this: from the most simple to the most sophisticated, when one group wants to communicate to another across various boundaries (linguistic, political, cultural, geographical) the main initial signal is an exchange of performances, a mutual display of rituals. There is something about dance, music, theater, and ritual that needs no translating – even as there is very much that is so culturally specific that it takes a lifetime of study to understand the performances of a culture not one's own. What jumps borders are the rasas, the "universal target emotions" and what is so very culturally specific are the definite "texts" – the particular minute weaves of interaction made from these universal target emotions.

In figure 8.1 I offered examples of performances of the varying magnitudes from the point of view of mise-en-scène, the various ways of organizing time, space, and events. But existing within these mises-en-scène are Ekman universals. If Ekman is correct and there are certain facial expressions recognized universally, and if his work could be extended to include "target" gestures, moves, and sounds all studied from an ethological perspective, then we might be able to find out how performances use these universals. Do they build up from Ekman universals to Birdwhistell kinemes to specific genres to individual variations (the artist's "originality")? Or is context the determining factor – so that performances actually "build down" from larger meaningful units to smaller and smaller meaningless "performables"? Brain events, microbits, and bits (see below for an explanation of this terminology) are not themselves units of meaning – they are like phonemes and words that acquire meaning only as used in sentences or bigger semantic units. Thus performances of small magnitudes gather meaning from their contexts. Or perhaps it is more complicated. Meanings may be generated and transformed up and down the various magnitudes.

Studies by Victor Turner (1985), Frederick Turner (1985), Melvin Konner (1982), and d'Aquili, Laughlin, and McManus (1979) signal a convergence of anthropological, biological, and aesthetic theory. The focus of this convergence is ritual. Ritual studies are turning from

looking at the "finished product" toward examining the "whole performance sequence": training, workshop, rehearsal, warm-up, performance, cool-down, and aftermath. When this whole sequence is
considered, it becomes clear that the ritual process is identical to what I
call "restored behavior," "twice-behaved behavior," behavior that can
be repeated, that is, rehearsed (see Schechner 1985: 3–150). Ritual
process is performance.

From this perspective, performance magnitudes are not only about
time and space but also about extensions across various cultural and
personal boundaries. Thinking this way raises provocative questions:
When is a performance a performance? How long does a strip of
behavior have to be before it can be said to be performable in the ritual
or aesthetic sense? When strips of behavior are taken from one context
and played in another does it make any difference if, in the replaying,
the strip means something entirely different from what it meant "originally"? These transformations of meaning are inevitable if context
determines meaning. But it's not so simple, because every strip, no
matter how small, brings some of its former meanings into its new
context. That kind of "memory" is what makes ritual and artistic
recombinations so powerful.

To jump still farther ahead, it seems to me that the human community taken as a whole is entering a postmodern phase where the
construction of intercultural aesthetics and ritual is essential. This ethnopoetics[19] occurs on three levels simultaneously: at the panhuman
Ekman level where research might lead to the confirmation of the
existence of some kind of behavioral version of Jungian archetypes; at
the sociocultural level of diverse, particular performances: what
anthropologists and performance theorists have until now focused
on; at an emerging posthumanist, postmodern level of the exchange
of information through multiplex channels – a kind of intercultural reflexivity.[20]

Stay with me a bit longer. Are we to call the facial gestures Ekman
described "performances"? Why not? Can't they be brought under
conscious control? So, too, we can call the vast social dramas that
Turner describes as "performances" – even though they may involve
whole societies for years. Surely the events in Lebanon over however
many decades make a well-knit Turnerian social drama, one that can

never get beyond crisis and failed redressive action. Media encourages these large-scale dramas to be viewed with varying degrees of anxiety and amusement by hundreds of millions of people. A "Rashomon effect"[21] occurs where the same data are woven into many different narratives according to cultural bias, editing, and individual interpretation – and these become parts of a Geertzian interpretation of cultures by different cultures.

The work for performance theorists now is to correlate a number of performance magnitudes identifying the transformational systems operating among them. Let me suggest seven "performance magnitudes" whose interconnectedness ought to be explored:

1   Brain event: the neurological processes linking cortical to subcortical actions; ANS; the ergotropic–trophotropic system. Ekman's recent work, the speculations of d'Aquili and Lex. Turner's last investigations concerned these processes (1983). "Deep acting" works on this level as well as on levels 2 and 3.

2   Microbit: seen only with the help of the slow-motion or stop-action camera. What Birdwhistell says delimits the kinemic vocabularies of discrete cultures.

3   Bit: the smallest unit of consciously controllable repeatable behavior. Ekman composes his subjects' faces bit by bit in order to affect their ANS at the brain event level. Directors and choreographers often work bit by bit, especially if they wish to compose images without interference by the performers' intentions.

4   Sign: composed of one or more bits and readable as an emotion, a piece of discrete information. Ekman claims that certain facial displays are universal signs. Ordinarily theater and dance deal with events at the sign, scene, or drama levels. It is at these levels that spectators consciously receive performances.

5   Scene: a sequence of one or more signs that make up a whole unit of interaction. Goffman studied these. Narrative structures are visible at this level.

6   Drama: a complex, multiplex system of scenes ranging from aesthetic dramas to Balinese cockfights to initiations to long cycle plays such as the Ramlila or the Yaqui Easter Passion play. Geertz and Turner have analyzed these from a narrative point of view.

7   Macrodrama: large-scale social actions viewed performatively –
     what Turner calls "social drama" where whole communities act
     through their collective crises.

As we understand the relationships among these seven magnitudes –
how, especially, the smaller are elicited, manipulated, and then composed into the larger and how the larger deport meanings down to
the smaller – I think theorists will be able to better distinguish
"performativity" from its close relations, "theatricality" and "narrativity." Performativity is present in all seven magnitudes but most
decisively at levels 1, 2, and 3: the brain event, microbit, and bit.
Theatricality begins with level 3, the bit, and is dominant at levels
4 and 5, the sign and the scene. Theatricality is absorbed *as scene*
into levels 6 and 7, dramas and macrodramas. Narrativity begins at
level 5, the scene, and is dominant at levels 6 and 7, the drama
and macrodrama.

Ekman's work centers on performativity. Birdwhistell focuses on the
area between performativity and theatricality. Goffman deals with theatricality. Turner, during most of his life, was concerned with narrativity – his theory of social drama can best be understood as a theory of
performed narrative. Toward the end of his life, Turner became more
and more interested in performativity, thus his speculations in "Body,
Brain, and Culture" (1983).

Performativity – or, commonly, "performance" – *is everywhere* in life,
from ordinary gestures to macrodramas. But theatricality and narrativity are more limited, if only slightly so. Differences in degree of magnitude do lead to differences in kind. Aesthetic genres – theater, dance,
music – are framed theatrically, signaling the intentions of their com-
posers to their publics. Other genres are frequently not so clearly
marked – but this does not make them any less performative. And
although performativity permeates all seven magnitudes, it doesn't
work the other way round. There is neither narrativity nor theatricality
in a brain event. Performer training begins below the level of theatricality or narrativity; workshops and rehearsals often deal at these sub-
theatrical, sub-narrative levels. Scholars who want to understand these
formative processes must not focus on shows put on for the public –
even Goffmanian performances of everyday life – but must attend to

the brain events, microbits, and bits that pre-exist performances of larger magnitudes.

There is a continuity of performance magnitudes, from interior brain events to bits of training and the making of signs and scenes – the deconstruction/reconstruction process of workshops and rehearsals – on to public performances of varying scales – the end point being performances of worldwide or even cosmic dimensions, such as the Olympics, the shooting down of KAL 007, or Lowry Burgess's *Quiet Axis*.[22] Some of these are media events, some social dramas, some artworks. We have entered the epoch where a performance can be both a social drama and a media event, for example, the Iranian hostage crisis of 1980. However limited their magnitude at their points and moments of origin – a lone 747 trailed by a single fighter, an artist conceiving an artwork – they soon catch a larger audience. Some net hundreds of millions of people in narrative and symbolic macrodramas unique to our own times and technologies. Others, like Allan Kaprow's recent private happenings,[23] remain intimate, almost dimensionless both spatially and temporally.

To what degree does our very survival as a species depend on how peoples and their leaders "act," not only in the sense of comportment but also in the theatrical sense? Exactly how a crisis is "handled" – played out, performed – becomes a matter of extreme importance. This brings me back to a basic paradox: humans are able to absorb and learn behavior so thoroughly that the new "performed" behavior knits seamlessly into ongoing "spontaneous" action. Performance magnitude means not only size and duration but also extension across cultural boundaries and penetration to the deepest strata of historical, personal, and neurological experience.

NOTES

1 See Victor Turner (1969, 1974, and 1982). For a discussion of why it might be better to apply not one but several performance theory templates in intercultural studies, see Schechner (1985: 3–34).

2 Evolutionary progressions applied to performance make me very uncomfortable. Why ought theater, dance, and professional and/or recreational sports "come from" ritual – as if ritual were the great unitarian artwork of prehistory shattered into the multiple genres of classical, modern, and postmodern

societies? Rather, ritual *as a genre* exists side by side with the other performative genres. As far as the *ritual process* is concerned, I've discussed elsewhere how ritual process = performance-making process; therefore the ritual process was always part of performance, as much at the beginning as now (see Schechner 1985: 35–116, 261–94).

3   For a recent discussion of the complex relationship between anthropologists and the cultures they study, see Marcus and Fischer (1986). For a particular example of what happened in Kerala, India, when a team of scholars and film-makers studied *agnicayana*, a "vedic ritual," see my discussion of the filming of the 1975 agnicayana, my review of Frits Staal's *Agni*, Staal's response to my review, and my response to Staal's response (Schechner 1985: 55–65, Schechner 1986b, Staal 1987, Schechner 1987a).

4   According to Lex, "*Ergotropic* response consists of augmented sympathetic discharges, increased muscle tonus, and excitation in the cerebral cortex mani-fested as 'desynchronized' resting rhythms; the *trophotropic* pattern includes heightened parasympathetic discharges, relaxed skeletal muscles, and syn-chronized cortical rhythms" (1979: 135). The ergotropic/trophotropic responses are related to the distinct functions of the two hemispheres of the frontal cortex. Brain studies show that the two hemispheres are each special-ized, though not as absolutely as the popular literature suggests. The right hemisphere is visual-spatial while the left is verbal and mathematical; tropho-tropic responses are associated with the right hemisphere, ergotropic with the left.

5   For Turner's discussion of "performing ethnography," see Turner (1986: 139–55).

6   See Goffman's extensive writing on this subject: (1959, 1961, 1963a, 1963b, 1967, 1969, 1971, and 1974). As people become aware of performance techniques, they learn how to manipulate them. Workshops teach people how to perform in everyday life. It goes without saying that media skills – and the professional staff to exploit them – are necessary to every politician's career. Those inter-ested in the classics of performance relevant to today's world ought to study not Aristotle's *Poetics*, but his *Rhetoric*.

7   See my "News, Sex, and Performance Theory" (in Schechner 1985: 295–324).

8   See Birdwhistell (1964b and 1970) and Scheflen (1973).

9   According to theater historian Marvin Carlson (1984), François Delsarte (1811–71)

> began his *Cours d'esthétique appliqué* in 1839. The unfinished work, handed down in sometimes contradictory forms by his disciples, gained a reputa-tion quite the opposite of what its originator intended. Delsarte, reacting against the mechanical and formalized actor training of his time, attempted to return to nature by carefully observing and recording those expressions and gestures produced not by art but by instinct and emotion. But when these were codified for his students, the result was yet another mechanical system, the formal details of which were so rigorously taught by Delsarte's disciples for the remainder of the century that even today his

system is almost a synonym for mechanical, arbitrary expressions and gestures, the very thing it was created to prevent.

(Carlson 1984: 218)

There is a lesson here. Human activity – both physical and mental – is so labile that whenever a system appears that is "based on nature" it invariably finally discloses itself as being a cultural construct. The so-called "natural system" develops sclerosis as its adherents defend it against inevitable cultural change. They think they are opposing nature to culture when no such opposition exists. At most, there is a continuous oscillation between genetic tendencies and cultural systems that rewrite these tendencies over and over again, each time somewhat differently. For an American interpretation of Delsarte's system – including many exercises – see Stebbins (1902).

10   As defined by Hochschild (1983), "deep acting" is acting done by a person with a "trained imagination." Using the work of Stanislavsky as her guide, Hochschild discusses Stanislavsky's particularly powerful "emotion memory" exercise, whereby a person imagines all the "given circumstances" of an event – for example, the room, the temperature, the people present, the time of day, the smells, and so on – and soon the emotions of the event are "spontaneously" relived in all of their original force. The parallels with Freud's "abreaction" are obvious. Hochschild shows how deep acting is used in everyday situations. "In our daily lives, offstage as it were, we also develop feeling for the parts we play; and along with the workaday props of the kitchen table or office restroom mirror we also use deep acting, emotion memory, and the sense of 'as if this were true' in the course of trying to feel what we sense we ought to feel or want to feel" (Hochschild 1983: 43). She then goes on to show how techniques of deep acting are used by corporations and other "emotion managers" who wish their employees – mostly people in service jobs – to actually feel what those managing the institution think the job requires them to feel if they are to be effective in their work. In such a setting, airline stewardesses and stewards are taught to enjoy being helpful, ambulance paramedics to remain cool and efficient in the face of life-and-death crisis, etc. Deep acting persists, even when the learned affect and behavior might be inappropriate. For example, when airline stewardesses using United Airlines, which fired them because either they had married or turned 32, appeared on the stand they "behave[d] more like hostesses than litigants. When the lawyer who is challenging their testimony stands up and says, 'I am Mark Bigelow, representing United Airlines,' the witness is as likely as not to lean forward with a big smile and say, 'Hi!' " (Lewin 1984: D1). Hochschild contrasts deep acting with "surface acting" where "the expression on my face or the posture of my body feels 'put on' " (1983: 36). Paul Ekman's experiment with "put-on" faces, discussed below, shows that a put-on expression may affect the autonomic nervous system every bit as much as a feeling deeply acted.

11   In Indian and Japanese dance-theater – kathakali and kabuki, for example – non-ordinary body techniques are employed. Every gesture, look on the face,

and move is codified. There is an extreme difference between the way each of these genres looks, but is there a corresponding interior difference? That is, were kathakali and kabuki actors portraying their stylized, codified displays of emotion tested, would their ANS show any, or as much, reaction as the actors Ekman tested? Or would the kathakali performers' responses differ from the kabuki performers'? That is, is it only "natural emotional displays" that yield ANS reactions, or will culturally composed displays do the same? My guess is that the culturally composed displays will affect the ANS.

12   For a discussion of the Method and other American variations of Stanislavsky's system of actor training, see two special issues of TDR, The Drama Review devoted to "Stanislavsky in America," 9 (1) and (2) (1964), and Christine Edwards' The Stanislavsky Heritage (1965).

13   Ekman told me that he had repeated the experiment without mirrors and obtained the same results. This, he says, shows that the subjects were not responding to seeing their own faces, but only to the muscle-by-muscle "making" of the faces.

14   Eliot in his essay on Hamlet states: "The only way of expressing emotion in the form of art is by finding an 'objective correlative'; in other words, a set of objects, a situation, a chain of events which shall be the formula of that particular emotion; such that when the external facts, which must terminate in sensory experience, are given, the emotion is immediately evoked" (1951: 145). This is precisely Stanislavsky's "emotion memory" exercise.

15   For detailed descriptions and analyses of the training techniques in kathakali as practiced at the Kathakali Kalamandalam, India's première kathakali school, see Schechner (1985: 213–60) and Zarrilli (1984).

16   See Geertz (1973: 412–53).

17   The Russian emigrés – Richard Boleslavsky, Maria Ouspenskaya, Michael Chekhov – who first taught Stanislavsky's system in America spoke with a heavy accent. When they said "bit" their students heard "beat." "Beat" seemed an appropriate musical metaphor, and so the new pronunciation stuck. But Stanislavsky meant "bit," a term familiar to vaudeville entertainers as well as to actors on the legitimate stage.

18   A classic example of this in the anthropological literature is Lévi-Strauss's (1963: 167–85) account of Quesalid, the Kwakiutl who set out to expose the fakery of shamanism but ended up as a renowned shaman in his own right, believing in the very techniques he had intended to debunk. See chapter 7.

19   Jerome Rothenberg used the term "ethnopoetics" at least as early as 1975 when he and his co-editor Dennis Tedlock put out the first issue of Alcheringa Ethnopoetics. In 1983, starting his "Pre-Face" to Symposium of the Whole: A Range of Discourse Toward an Ethnopoetics, Rothenberg said:

> The word "ethnopoetics" suggested itself, almost too easily, on the basis of such earlier terms as ethnohistory, ethnomusicology, ethnolinguistics, ethnopharmacology, and so on. As such it refers to a redefinition of poetry in terms of culture specifics, with an emphasis on those alternative

traditions to which the West gave names like "pagan," "gentile," "tribal," "oral," and "ethnic." In its developed form, it moves toward an exploration of creativity over the fullest human range, pursued with a regard for particularized practice as much as unified theory.

(Rothenberg and Rothenberg 1983: xi)

20   Efforts in this direction are visible both artistically and in terms of scholarship. The series of three conferences in 1981 and 1982, culminating in the World Conference on Theater and Ritual held in New York in August, 1982, is perhaps the clearest example of this effort. Chaired by Victor Turner and me, the conference brought together scholars and performing artists from Asia, Africa, Native America, and Euro-America who, over a nine-day period, discussed and saw performed examples of a number of genres. Attention was paid not only to the finished performances but to techniques of training, workshops, rehearsals, cool-down, and aftermath. The two other conferences in the series, involving fewer participants, considered Yaqui performing arts and contemporary Japanese theater. In the artistic sphere, a powerful "fusion movement" is combining Asian with western performance. This has resulted in a number of interesting productions and even a few new genres, such as Japanese *butoh* dance. And one must not forget the extremely active tourist promotion of performances. Most tourist performances are sub-genres sharing qualities of condensation and simplification and playing to audiences who want to be entertained. Some tours, however, blur into a kind of fieldwork, with qualified anthropologists and other experts setting up the programs. In all cases, there is a double pressure: to be "authentic" (a rotten term impossible to define), to modify what happens to suit the needs of the visiting group. Finally, many performing groups leave their home territories to bring their arts to strangers. This is not only a matter of western impresarios and organizations importing "native arts." Aboriginal Australian groups hold festivals where they can see each others' dances and exchange techniques. Once every four years an all-Pacific festival is held. Similar exchanges are increasing all around the world.

21   The "Rashomon effect" is named after Akira Kurosawa's 1950 film. In *Rashomon* a number of narrators present their version of an event whose "objective" truth can at best be vectored, not settled. As narrators change, so does "truth." But the "Rashomon effect," like the movie, is neither a celebration of relativism nor a skeptic's complaint. It is an unfolding of epistemological passion.

22   According to Burgess:

> *The Quiet Axis* is an aesthetic structure that opens a benevolent revelation into the cosmos from the far side of the moon to the Large Cloud of Magellan. There are seven zones or aspects of its manifestation beginning with the Inclined Galactic Light Pond in Bamiyan, Afghanistan (1968–1974) passing through the earth to the second work called The Utopic Vessel (1974–1979) in the South Pacific Ocean beside Easter Island and

from there extending into outer space and the southern heavens to the third realization called The Gate into Aether (1979–1988) and then returning through the earth and backward in time to the fourth twinned work called the Boundless Cubic Aperture (1980–1995). The fifth work, Memory and Forms of the Unmanifest, touches The Boundless Cubic Aperture on the far lunar surface. The sixth and seventh aspects address the center of the earth and violet stellar source that is centered in the Large Cloud of Magellan, a source 50,000 times more bright and energetic than the sun.

(Burgess, undated poster)

23 Kaprow distinguishes between what he calls "artlike art" and "lifelike art." Artlike art is familiar to people – galleries, theaters, opera houses, etc.: art that *is* art. Lifelike art is often indistinguishable from ordinary living. For example:

For each day of a week, around 3 p.m. when the wind rose on the dunes, a woman took a walk and watched her tracks blow away behind her. Every evening she wrote an account of her walk in her journal. To begin each successive day, she read her journal story and then tried to repeat exactly what had happened. She described this experience, in turn, as faithfully as possible, until the week elapsed. Half in jest, she wrote in one passage, "I wanted to see if I could stop change".

(Kaprow 1983: 100)

And then there are "conceptual performances" where events never happen at all: the thought process is enough.

9

RASAESTHETICS

Where in the body is theatricality located? What is its place? Traditionally in western theater, the eyes and to some degree the ears are where
theatricality is experienced. By etymology and by practice a theater is a
"place of/for seeing." Seeing requires distance; engenders focus or
differentiation; encourages analysis or breaking apart into logical
strings; privileges meaning, theme, narration. Modern science depends
on instruments of observation, of ocularity: telescopes and microscopes. Theories derived from observations made by means of ocular
instruments define the time–space continuum. From super-galactic
strings on the one hand to molecular and subatomic wave particles on
the other, we "know" the universe by "seeing" it. See = know; know =
see; speed = space; distance = time; diachronicity = story.

But in other cultural traditions there are other locations for theatricality. One of these, the mouth, or better said, the snout-to-belly-to-
bowel – the route through the body managed by the enteric nervous
system – is the topic of this essay. The snout-to-belly-to-bowel is the
"where" of taste, digestion, and excretion. The performance of the
snout-to-belly-to-bowel is an ongoing interlinked muscular, cellular,
and neurological process of testing-tasting, separating nourishment
from waste, distributing nourishment throughout the body, and eliminating waste. The snout-to-belly-to-bowel is the where of intimacy,

sharing of bodily substances, mixing the inside and the outside, emotional experiences, and gut feelings. A good meal with good company is a pleasure; so is foreplay and lovemaking; so is a good shit.

THE *POETICS* AND THE *NATYASASTRA*

Aristotle's *Poetics* and Bharata-muni's *Natyasastra*, a Sanskrit manual of performance and performance theory, occupy parallel positions in European and Indian performance theory (and by extension, throughout the many areas and cultures where European-derived or Indian-derived performing arts are practiced). Both ancient texts continue to be actively interpreted and debated, theoretically and in practice. Both are at or near the "origins" of their respective performance traditions, both have evoked "after-texts" or "counter-texts" aimed at enhancing, revising, or refuting their basic principles.

But similar as they are in some ways, the two texts differ profoundly. Aristotle was an historical figure (384–322 BCE), the author of many key philosophical texts affecting, even determining, western thought in various fields as far-ranging as the physical sciences, politics, social thought, aesthetics, and theology. The Macedonian-Greek philosopher's writings have been actively debated for nearly two-and-a-half millennia. He specialized in dividing knowledge into knowable portions; he formulated the syllogism. Bharata-muni is a mythic-historical figure, the name of the author or compiler of a very detailed compendium concerning the religious-mythic origins and practices of *natya*, a Sanskrit word not easily translatable, but reducible to dance-theater-music. The precise date of the NS remains in question – scholars have placed it anywhere from the sixth century BCE to the second century CE Exactly how much of the NS was the work of one person and how much the lore of many will probably never be known. Bharata-muni, whoever he was, if he was at all, wrote only the NS.

Furthermore, the NS is a *sastra*, a sacred text authorized by religion, full of narration, myth, and detailed instructions for performers. The *Poetics* is secular, focused on the structure of drama, and dependent on the logical thinking its author helped invent. The *Poetics* is so laconic, running in English translation about 30 pages, that some believe it to be lecture notes compiled by Aristotle's students after his death rather than the philosopher's own finished work. The NS takes the form of an extended disquisition (345 pages in the Rangacharya translation) by Bharata in answer to sages who asked him to explain natya. Bharata begins with the story of how natya came about, what its proper subjects are, and for whom it was made.[1] Then he goes on to detail everything from theater architecture to how to perform the various emotions to the structure of dramas, and more.

Some centuries after it was completed, the NS was "lost" – fragmented, submerged, misplaced, and unread. The NS comes to modern Indians not directly and not as a single text. The NS comes down in performance practice and as a series of interpretations. The most important interpreter is the tenth-century Kashmiri Saivite (worshiper of Shiva), Abhinavagupta. Through Abhinavagupta, scholars discern earlier interpreters such as Bhatta Lollata, Srisankuka, Bhatta Nayaka, and Bhatta Tauta. As for the NS "itself," according to Kapila Vatsyayan, "not many texts have been systematically collated and edited and published. Hundreds [. . .] lie as manuscripts in public or private collections, in India and abroad, and an equal or larger number are in fragments" (1996: 115).

But this fragmentation ought not to be read as "neglect." The NS tradition is active, oral, and corporeal. It is present in performers, their teachers, and their performances. We must distinguish the absence of the NS as a text (a book brought to light in modern times mostly by western orientalists)[2] from its presence in actual performances where it has been absorbed into, and forms the core of, a multiplicity of genres such as kathak, kathakali, odissi, and bharatanatyam which, taken together, comprise Indian classic theater-dance. The NS is much more powerful as an embodied set of ideas and practices than as a written text. Unlike the Poetics, the NS is more danced than read.

Thus the NS and the Poetics are different in style, intent, and historical circumstance. The Poetics, written nearly a century after Greek tragedy's heyday, constitutes only a small portion of Aristotle's enormous output. The Poetics lacks descriptions of actual performances; it is mostly about drama, not theater, focusing on one play, Oedipus, which Aristotle offers as a model for the right way to write plays. Framed as "rational" and "historical," the Poetics is not regarded as sacred, although it has been, and remains, remarkably influential. On the other hand, the NS is a hybrid of myth and down-to-earth performance knowledge, far-ranging and detailed. Its author and protagonist, the semi-divine Bharata-muni, is almost certainly a pseudonym for a collective oral tradition.

But the greatest difference between the *Poetics* and the NS is that the Indian book deals in detail with performance: emotional expression as conveyed by specific gestures and movements, role and character types, theater architecture, music. The NS considers drama (chapters 20–21), but that analysis is not the core of the sastra. Many Indian artists subscribe to the ideal of a theater that integrates drama, dance, and music. Traditional genres accomplish this integration in ways that do not privilege plot (as Aristotle advised) over dance, gesture, and music. And then there is *rasa*.

RASA, FIRST TAKE

Of rasa, the NS says:

> There is no natya without rasa. Rasa is the cumulative result of *vibhava* [stimulus], *anubhava* [involuntary reaction], and *vyabhicari bhava* [voluntary reaction]. For example, just as when various condiments and sauces and herbs and other materials are mixed, a taste is experienced, or when the mixing of materials like molasses with other materials produces six kinds of taste, so also along with the different *bhavas* [emotions] the *sthayi bhava* [permanent emotions experienced "inside"] becomes a rasa.
>
> But what is this thing called rasa? Here is the reply. Because it is enjoyably tasted, it is called rasa. How does the enjoyment come? Persons who eat prepared food mixed with different condiments and sauces, if they are sensitive, enjoy the different tastes and then feel pleasure; likewise, sensitive spectators, after enjoying the various emotions expressed by the actors through words, gestures, and feelings feel pleasure. This feeling by the spectators is here explained as the rasas of natya.

> (Bharata-muni 1996: 54–5)

There is a lot going on here, and I do not intend at this time to go into a detailed explication of rasa theory. I want here to outline an overall theory of flavor as it pertains to performance, what I call "rasaesthetics."

Rasa is flavor, taste, the sensation one gets when food is perceived, brought within reach, touched, taken into the mouth, chewed, mixed, savored, and swallowed. The eyes and ears perceive the food on its way – the presentation of the dishes, the sizzling. At the same time, or very shortly after, the nose gets involved. The mouth waters in anticipation. Smell and taste dissolve into each other. The hands convey the food to the mouth – either directly as in the traditional Indian way of eating with the fingers or somewhat indirectly by means of utensils (a latecomer everywhere). The whole snout is engaged. In the snout all the senses are well-represented. The lower part of the face contains the mouth, in the center is the nose, above are the eyes. The ears are side-center, but focused forward.

Rasa also means "juice," the stuff that conveys the flavor, the medium of tasting. The juices of eating originate both in the food and from the body. Saliva not only moistens food, it distributes flavors. Rasa is sensuous, proximate, experiential. Rasa is aromatic. Rasa fills space, joining the outside to the inside. Food is actively taken into the body, becomes part of the body, works from the inside. What was outside is transformed into what is inside. An aesthetic founded on rasa is fundamentally different than one founded on the "theatron," the rationally ordered, analytically distanced panoptic.

ETYMOLOGIES AND DISTANCED KNOWING

Before more on rasaesthetics, something on western notions of theater. The word "theater" is cognate with "theorem," "theory," "theorist," and such, all from the Greek *theatron*, itself from *thea*, "a sight"; and from *theasthai*, "to view"; related to *thauma*, "a thing compelling the gaze, a wonder"; and *theorein*, "to look at" (Partridge 1966: 710). Theorein is related to *theorema*, "spectacle" and/or "speculation" (Shipley 1984: 69). These words are thought to be related to the Indo-European root *dheu* or *dhau*, "to look at" (Partridge 1966: 710). The Indo-European root of "Thespis" – the legendary founder of Greek theater – is *seku*, a "remark" or "saying," but with the implication of a divine vision; and from seku derive such English words as "see," "sight," and "say" (Shipley 1984: 353). Greek theater, then, and all European types of theater derived from it, are places of/for seeing and saying. What marks this kind of theater (and after it, film, TV, and possibly the Internet) is its specularity, its strategies of "gazing."

These etymologies reveal the tight bond linking Greek theater, European epistemology, and seeing. This binding of "knowing" to "seeing" is the root metaphor/master narrative of western thought. If the humans in Plato's cave were ignorant, it was because all they saw of "truth" were shadows cast on the wall. True reality was so much brighter even than the sun that no human viewer could look at it directly. What Plato said could be known through dialectics, scientists since the Renaissance have tried to do by devising finer and finer instruments of observation. A single net holds Plato's allegory, Galileo's observations, the Hubble Space Telescope, electron microscopes, and the super-colliding super-conductor particle accelerator.

Where does seeing take place? Only at a distance from what is being seen. There is both a logical and a practical difference keeping what is observed separate from the observing instrument (and/or observer). "Objectivity" can be understood as the desire to keep things at enough distance from the eyes to allow whatever it is to "take shape" perceptually: to see things "in perspective," to "focus on" them. The "indeterminacy principle" linking the instrument of observation to what is observed does not dissolve the distance between observer and observed so much as it asserts that what is observed is indissolubly linked to the means of observing. What "moves" the particle is the light needed to observe it.

At a more everyday level, as an object is brought close to the face, one loses focus and finally the object blurs, loses its visual shape. And, of course, one mustn't put things into one's eyes. Poking out the eyes is a terrible thing both legendarily (Oedipus, Gloucester, et al.) and actually. But a child learns early on to see something, focus on it, reach for it, grasp it, and bring it to the mouth. The mouth replaces the eyes as the end point of exploring the "outer" world and relating it to the "inner" world. The "transitional object" (see Winnicott 1971) is how the infant first experiences the sameness/difference between the world outside herself and the world inside herself: from the breast, to the fingers, to the grasped-tasted-chewed whatever, to the security blanket, to the favorite object. Even before birth, as in-utero photographs show, the preborn suck their fingers and toes. Can we doubt that the pre-born enjoy this activity? Nor is the mouth a singular conduit connected solely to the brain (as the eye is via the optic nerve). The mouth opens to the nasal cavity and the whole digestive system; the mouth – including lips and tongue – intimately engages the senses of touch, taste, and smell. The ocular system is extraordinarily focused, while the snout system is wide open, combining rather than separating.

The Greek theater that Aristotle based his theories on was fundamentally a seeing place. Architecturally – as is evident from what is left of the Theater of Dionysus on the hillside of the Acropolis, the almost wholly intact theater at Epidaurus, and from other sites and restorations – the Greek theater was immense. Most scholars place the number in the audience at the ancient festivals between 14,000 and 17,000. And although Aristotle favored the drama over the theater, the actual experience of being in a classical Greek theater is full of spectacle – dancing, singing, and reciting. The Greek theater was also, and perhaps mostly, a focus of competition. The Athenians were an intensely competitive people. The *agon* was for them the motor, source, and energy of creation, a model of becoming.[3] Whatever Aristotle may have wanted, the living heart of Greek tragedy was not plot as such, but a particular kind of storytelling, the agon. To sort winners from losers, the judges (and those judging the judges – the spectators) had to see clearly and base their opinions on "objective" values. Of course, there may have been all kinds of politicking and pressures. Maybe even bribes and cheating. But, as in today's spectator sports (with or without instant replays), clarity in presentation and reception was absolutely essential. The goal of the shows was to determine winners and losers – both in the dramas and in the competitions among actors and poets.

THE PLEASURES OF RASIC PERFORMANCE

Rasic performance has as its goal not separating winners from losers, but extending pleasure – as in an endless banquet or an always-deferred "almost" sexual orgasm. It accomplishes this in a way comparable to cooking: the combination/transformation of distinct elements into a something that offers new and/or intense and/or favorite flavors or tastes. Rasic performance values immediacy over distance, savoring over judgment. Its paradigmatic activity is a sharing between performers and partakers (a more accurate term than "audiences" or "spectators," words that privilege ear or eye). The rasic performance event is more a banquet than a day in court. The NS puts it this way:

> Those who are connoisseurs of tastes enjoy the taste of food prepared from (or containing) different stuff; likewise, intelligent, healthy persons enjoy various sthayi bhavas related to the acting of emotions.
>
> (Bharata-muni 1996: 55)

The Sanskrit word translated as "connoisseur" is *bhakta*, which can also mean a person ecstatically devoted to a god, particularly Krishna who is celebrated by means of singing, dancing, and feasting. The sthayi bhavas are the "permanent" or "abiding" or indwelling emotions that are accessed and evoked by good acting, called *abhinaya*. Rasa is experiencing the sthayi bhavas. To put it another way, the sweetness "in" a ripe plum is its sthayi bhava, the experience of "tasting the sweet" is rasa. The means of getting the taste across – preparing it, presenting it – is abhinaya. Every emotion is a sthayi bhava. Acting is the art of presenting the sthayi bhavas so that *both* the performer and the partaker can "taste" the emotion, the rasa.

In chapters six and seven, the NS gives the eight rasas and their corresponding sthayi bhavas:

Rasa	Sthayi Bhava	English
sringara	rati	desire, love
hasya	hasa	humor, laughter
karuna	soka	pity, grief
raudra	krodha	anger
vira	utsaha	energy, vigor
bhayanaka	bhaya	fear, shame
bibhasta	jugupsra	disgust
adbhuta	vismaya	surprise, wonder

Abhinavagupta added a ninth rasa, *śānta*, "bliss." From Abhinava-gupta's time onward, many Indians speak of the "nine rasas." But shanta does not correspond to any particular sthayi bhava. Rather, like white light, shanta is the perfect balance/mix of them all; or *śānta* may be regarded as the transcendent rasa which, when accomplished, absorbs and eliminates all the others. A perfect performance, should one occur, would not transmit or express *śānta* (as it could transmit or express any of the other rasas), but allow *śānta* to be experienced simultaneously and absolutely by performers and partakers.

It is not my aim in this essay to investigate the many connections between the sthayi bhavas and the rasas. It is enough to note that "emotions" in the Indian aesthetic performance system, far from being personal – based on individual experience, or locked up and only accessible by means of an "emotional memory" exercise or a "private moment" (Stanislavsky and his disciples) – are to some degree objective, residing in the public or social sphere.

In the rasic system, there are "artistically performed emotions" which comprise a distinct kind of behavior (different, perhaps, for each performance genre). These performed emotions are separate from the "feelings" – the interior, subjective experience of any given performer during a particular performance. There is no necessary and ineluctable chain linking these "performed emotions" with the "emotions of everyday life." In the rasic system, the emotions *in the arts, not in ordinary life* are knowable, manageable, and transmittable in roughly the same way that the flavors and presentation of a meal are manageable by following recipes and the conventions of presenting the meal.

When I spoke to kathakali actors, for example, some told me they felt the emotions they performed, others did not feel the emotions. There is no yes or no answer to Diderot's question, "Do actors feel the emotions they communicate?" Feeling the emotions is not necessary though it is not a bad thing either. Whether it happens or not to any particular performer does not necessarily make the performance better or worse. What is relevant is making certain that each "partaker" receives the emotions, and that these emotions are specific and controlled. The emotions, the sthayi bhava, are objective; the feelings (what an individual performer or partaker experiences) are subjective. What is shared are the rasas of a single emotion or combination of emotions.

It is not easy to clearly differentiate "emotions" from "feelings." Basically, emotions are communicated by means of abhinaya; feelings are experienced. So the rasas themselves (as flavors of moods) are feelings, but what is communicated or transmitted by means of rasas are emotions. One "has" emotions even if one is not feeling them; one "experiences" feelings even if sometimes disconnected to emotions ("I don't know why I am feeling the way I feel"). The links between emotions and feelings are usually manifest, but not always. When an actor's abhinaya is strong, the emotions are communicated and audience members feel feelings – whether or not the actor is feeling something. In expressing the emotions by means of abhinaya one may or may not create feelings in oneself, but a good actor always creates feelings in the partakers (audience). In order for rasas to be shared, performers must enact the abhinaya of a particular emotion or concatenation of emotions according to the traditions of a specific genre of performance. The feelings aroused may be personal, intimate, and indescribable; but the emotions enacted are consciously constructed and objectively managed.

According to Stanislavsky-based Euro-American acting, one does not "play an emotion." One plays the "given circumstances," the "objectives," the "through-line of action," the "magic if." If this is done right, "real" feelings will be experienced and "natural" emotions will be displayed. But according to my interpretation of the NS rasic system, one can work directly on the emotions, mixing them according to "recipes" known to the great acting gurus (which means, simply, "teachers") – or even by devising new recipes. From a Stanislavskyan vantage, such direct work on the emotions will result in false or mechanical acting. But anyone who has seen performers thoroughly trained in the NS rasic system knows these performers are every bit as effective as performers trained in the Stanislavsky system.

If performing rasically is to offer emotions to partakers in the same way that a chef offers a meal to diners, then the effectiveness of the performance depends very much on an active response from the partakers. The NS is very emphatic in its insistence that natya appeal to people of all stations in life, affecting different people differently.[4] The more knowledgeable the partakers, the better the experience. To respond to the fullest, partakers need to be connoisseurs of whatever performance genre they are taking in – as wine tasters need to know vintages, bottling procedures, and ways of sampling in order to fully appreciate a wine. There is a sliding scale of how much one needs to know. In the rasic system, each person enjoys according to her abilities; the higher the level of knowledge, the greater the enjoyment (or disappointment, if the performance is not up to standards). Japanese *noh* actors study the audience immediately before entering the stage and then adjust their performances to the particular partakers on hand. All performers know this. The best performers save their best performances for the most discerning partakers and those who know the most expect the best. In India, at least, the active response of the partakers is expected. At dance or music concerts people quietly beat out the *tal*, or rhythm, sing under their breath, and sometimes move their hands in harmony with the *mudras*, or hand-gesture system. At the *Ramlila* of Ramnagar, many persons carry texts of Tulsidas's *Ramcaritmanas*, following along, even singing, as the Ramayanis chant. The same is true of sports or pop music connoisseurs. The "home team advantage" is a direct measurement of how the active participation of the crowd can impact the level of performance.

ORAL PLEASURES, RASICALLY

Fundamentally, the attainment of pleasure and satisfaction in a rasic performance is oral – through the snout, by combining various flavors and tastes; and the satisfaction is visceral, in the belly. How can this be since the Indian theater, like the western theater, is presented visually and sonically? First, the Indian theater, both in earlier times and today, is not based on the agon, on formally determining winners and losers, either within the dramas (in classic Indian plays often everyone wins) or in terms of competitions among dramatists and actors. There were no judges formally ensconced on front marble benches as in the Theatre of Dionysus. Thus there is no attempt to quantify the performing experience, to bring it under the theatron's aegis of visuality. Second, many performances were part of the feasts of the rich or royal, and continue to be offered at weddings or other happy celebrations. Religion itself has a feasting quality that interweaves performing, worshiping, and eating. Separating work from play, and the sacred from the profane, has always been more a western than an Indian phenomenon. Third, until the Mughal conquest and then the English, there was no anti-theatrical prejudice or Puritanism in India. Far from it – the arts, infused with intense sexual pleasure, were often part of the religious experience.

India today is less open to the rasic mix of art, sensuousity, and feasting than before the advent of the Mughals and the British. But imagining performances from the period of Sanskrit drama (4th–11th centuries CE) as indicated by sculptings and paintings at such sites as Khajuraho, the shore temple of Mamallapuram, or the "theater caves" of Ajanta can get us closer to the kind of experience I am talking about.

> The Ajanta style approaches as near as it is likely for an artist to get to a felicitous rendering of tactile sensations normally experienced sub-consciously. These are felt rather than seen when the eye is subordin-ate to a total receptivity of all the senses. [. . .] The seated queen with the floating hand is drawn so that we obtain information which cannot be had by looking at her from a single, fixed viewpoint. [. . .T]he logic of this style demands that movements and gestures can only be described in terms of the area or space in which they occur, we cannot identify a figure except by comparing its position with others around it. [. . .] It could be said that the Ajanta artist is concerned with the order of sensuousness, as distinct from the order of reason.
>
> (Lannoy 1971: 48–9)

Richard Lannoy argues that Sanskrit drama – some form of which is described and theorized in the NS – is like the Ajanta paintings:

> The structure and ornamentation of the caves were deliberately designed to induce total participation during ritual circumambulation. The acoustics of one Ajanta *vihara*, or assembly hall (Cave VI), are such that any sound long continues to echo round the walls. This whole structure seems to have been tuned like a drum.
>
> (Lannoy 1971: 43)

This tuning was not fortuitous. The Ajanta caves are human-made, excavated and carved out of solid rock. Lannoy continues:

> In both cases [the caves, the theater] total participation of the viewer was ensured by a skillful combination of sensory experience. The "wrap-around" effect [of] the caves was conveyed on the stage by adapting the technically brilliant virtuosity of Vedic incantation and

phonetic science to the needs of the world's most richly textured style
of poetic drama.

(Lannoy 1971: 54)

What the NS supplies are the concrete details of that style, which at
its core is not literary but theatrical, not plot-dominated or driven.
Indian classical theater and dance does not emphasize clear beginnings,
middles, and ends but favors a more "open narration," a menu of many
delectables – offshoots, side-tracks, pleasurable digressions – not all of
which can be savored at a sitting. The performances the NS refers to
took place over periods of days or weeks. They were festivals, part of
multifaceted celebrations that also featured feasting and audience participation integral to the whole performance complex. Some of this
continues today, as experienced in such popular religious festive forms
as Ramlila, Raslila, and bhajan-singing/dancing, with their circum-
ambulations, hymn-singing, trance-dancing, food-sharing, and wrap-
around or environmental theater staging.

It's not all one way or the other. There is a lot of movement – actual
and conceptual – from one kind of action to another. There are phases
of these festive performances where partakers stand back and watch or
listen and other phases where they participate. This blending of theater,
dance, music, food, and religious devotion is to many participants a
full, satisfying, and pleasurable experience that cannot be reduced to
any single category – religious, aesthetic, personal, or gustatory. This
kind of an event yields experiences that dissolve differences, if only for
a little while. This kind of experience is hard to measure from the
inside or observe from the outside. western aesthetics are derived from
the Greek theater as reinterpreted in the Renaissance. The outcomes are
variations of the drama-based proscenium or frontal-stage theater still
prevalent today. Rasaesthetics is very different. It is not something that
happens in front of the spectator, a vision for the eyes, but "in the gut,"
an experience that takes place inside the body specifically engaging the
enteric nervous system.

THE ENTERIC NERVOUS SYSTEM

Take a step into neurobiology. According to recent studies, there is a
brain in the belly, literally. The basic research in this area has been

conducted by Michael D. Gershon (see his *The Second Brain* 1998) whose work was summarized in the *New York Times* by Sandra Blakeslee:

> The gut's brain, known as the enteric nervous system [ENS], is located in sheaths of tissue lining the esophagus, stomach, small intestine, and colon. Considered a single entity, it is a network of neurons, neurotransmitters, and proteins that zap messages between neurons, support cells like those found in the brain proper and a complex circuitry that enables it to act independently, learn, remember, and, as the saying goes, produce gut feelings.
>
> (Blakeslee 1996: CI)

The ENS derives from the "neural crest," a bunch of related cells that forms in mammals and birds early in embryo genesis: "One section turns into the central nervous system. Another piece migrates to become the enteric nervous system. Only later are the two nervous systems connected via a cable called the vagus nerve" (Blakeslee 1996: C3). According to Gershon:

> The ENS resembles the brain and differs both physiologically and structurally from any other region of the PNS [peripheral nervous system].[5] ... Both the avian and mammalian bowel are colonized by émigrés from the sacral as well as the vigil level of the neural crest. ... The PNS contains more neurons than the spinal cord and, in contrast to other regions of the PNS, the ENS is capable of mediating reflex activity in the absence of central neural input. In fact, most of the neurons of the ENS are not directly innervated by a preganglionic input from the brain or spinal cord. The functional independence of the ENS is mirrored in its chemistry and structure.
>
> (Gershon et al 1993: 199)

And again, as summarized by Blakeslee:

> Until relatively recently, people thought that the gut's muscles and sensory nerves were wired directly to the brain and that the brain controlled the gut through two pathways that increased or decreased rates of activity [. . .]. The gut was simply a tube with simple reflexes. Trouble is, no one bothered to count the nerve fibers in the gut. When

they did [. . .] they were surprised to find that the gut contains two million neurons – more than the spinal cord has. Yet the vagus nerve only sends a couple of thousand nerve fibers to the gut.

(Blakeslee 1993: C3)

What this means is that the gut – esophagus, stomach, intestines, and bowels – has its own nervous system. This system does not replace

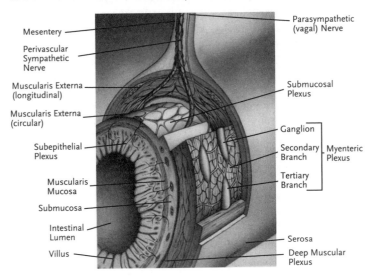

Figure 9.1 The enteric nervous system is composed of two ganglionated plexuses, or networks of gray masses of nerve tissue, that surround the intestines. The larger myenteric plexus is located between the circular and the longitudinal layers of the "muscularis externa," or outer muscles of the intestines. This plexus contains neurons responsible for movement and for mediating the enzyme output of adjacent organs. The smaller "submucosal" plexus contains sensory cells that "talk" to the motor neurons of the myenteric plexus as well as to the motor fibers that stimulate intestinal secretions. Note the vagus nerve in the upper center of the diagram. (Drawing by Michael D. Gershon and caption adapted from Gershon and Erde; courtesy of Michael Gershon)

or preempt the brain. Rather it operates alongside the brain, or – evolutionarily speaking – "before" or "underneath" the brain:

> The enteric nervous system is [. . .] a remnant of our evolutionary past that has been retained. [It] has been present in each of our predecessors through the millions of years of evolutionary history that separate us from the first animal with a backbone. [. . .T]he enteric nervous system is a vibrant, modern data-processing center that enables us to accomplish some very important and unpleasant tasks with no mental effort. When the gut rises to the level of conscious perception, in the form of, for example, heartburn, cramps, diarrhea, or constipation, no one is enthused. Few things are more distressing than an inefficient gut with feelings.
>
> (Gershon 1999: xiv)

But what about emotional feelings? In December 2000, I emailed Gershon about "rasaesthetics" and the ENS. He replied:

> Thank you for your letter. You touch a bit of raw nerve. You are certainly correct in that we in the West who consider ourselves "hard" scientists have not taken Eastern thought very seriously. The problem with a great deal of Eastern thought is that it is not based on documentable observation. You cannot quantify ideas about strong feelings or deep power. We therefore, either ignore Eastern ideas about the navel, or take them as metaphors, which are not very different from our own metaphors about "gut feelings." On the other hand, I have recently become aware of quantifiable research that establishes, without question, that vagus nerve stimulation can be used to treat epilepsy and depression. Vagus nerve stimulation also improves learning and memory. Vagus nerve stimulation is something physicians do and is not natural, but 90% of the vagus carries ascending information from the gut to the brain. It is thus possible that vagus nerve stimulation mimics natural stimulation of the vagus nerve by the "second brain." This relationship is particularly important in relation to the human condition of autism. Autism affects the gut as well as the brain. It is thus conceivable that autism could be the result in whole or in part of a disturbed communication between the two brains.

In short, I now take the possibility that the gut affects emotions very seriously. This seems much more likely to me now than it did when I wrote my book. A dialogue between us might be of mutual interest.

The dialogue has not yet progressed beyond the email quoted, but it is destined.

Let us suppose, in light of ENS research, that when someone says, "I have a gut feeling," she actually is experiencing a feeling, a neural response, but not one that is head–brain centered. Let us suppose that her feeling is located in, or emanating from, the "second brain," the brain in the belly. When expressed, this feeling is an emotion. Can such feelings be trained? That is, what are the systems converting "gut feelings" into expressible emotions? Gershon is interested primarily in the therapeutic value of vagus nerve stimulation, of causing or evoking feelings in autistics who suffer from lack of affect or lack of range of affect.

The presence and location of the ENS confirms a basic principle of Asian medicine, meditation, and martial arts: that the region in the gut between the navel and the public bone is the center/source of readiness, balance, and reception, the place where action and meditation originate and are centered. A related place is the base of the spine, the resting spot of kundalini, an energy system that can be aroused and transmitted up the spinal column. Gaining an awareness of and control over the gut and lower spine is crucial to anyone learning various Asian performances, martial arts, or meditations.

Phillip Zarrilli has for many years researched both in a scholarly and in a practical way the relationship between what in the Keralan martial art kalarippayattu is called the nabhi mula (root of the navel) and performance art training, psychophysical centering, and ayurvedic medicine. According to Zarrilli:

> When impulses originate from the nabhi mula [. . .they] are "grounded," "centered," "integrated," "filled out," "dynamic." The nabhi mula of kalarippayattu is identical to the svadhisthanam of classical yoga. Its location is two finger widths above the anus and two finger widths below the root of the navel. It is at this center that both

breath and impetus for movement into and out of forms originate.

(Zarrilli 1990: 136)

Zarrilli emphasizes that the nabhi mula is important "psychophysically," as the source of feeling-and-movement, a kind of "gripping" (*piduttam*) or firmness of body, spirit, and feelings that affect the whole human being. The Chinese notion of ch'i and the Japanese "activating force" ki are closely related to the nabhi mula and the sense of piduttam. In noh theater, the *tanden*, located "in the belly two inches below the navel" (Nearman 1982: 346) is the energy center. The point is that this "center" is a radiating spot:

> The actor is engaged in his total being in a psychophysical process where his internal energy, aroused in his vital center below the navel, then directed into and through the embodied forms of external gesture (body and voice) is of course fundamentally the same [in noh] as the interior process of the kathakali actor. This despite the fact that the exterior manifestation of the interior process is different.
>
> (Zarrilli 1990: 143)

I could cite many more examples. But it all comes down to what Zarrilli so nicely summarizes:

> In all such precise psychophysical moments, the "character" is being created – not in the personality of the actor but as an embodied and projected/energized/living form between actor and audience. These Asian forms assume no "suspension of disbelief," rather the actor and spectator co-create the figure embodied in the actor as "other." The "power of presence" manifest in this stage other, while embodied in this particular actor in this particular moment, is not limited to that ego. That dynamic figure exists between audience and actor, transcending both, pointing beyond itself.
>
> (Zarrilli 1990: 144)

The rasic system of response does not preclude the eye and ear during actual performance, but during training especially, it works *directly and strongly* on the ENS which, under different names, has been very important and well-theorized in various Asian systems of performance, medicine, and the martial arts – all of which are tightly related in Asian cultures. Thus, when I say the rasic aesthetic experience is fundamentally different than the eye-dominant system prevalent in the west, I am not talking metaphorically.

THE RASABOX EXERCISE

But if not metaphorically, how? Let me answer first in terms of training, then in terms of public performances. Over the past five years I and several of my colleagues at East Coast Artists,[6] especially Michele Minnick and Paula Murray Cole, have been developing the Rasabox exercise. For Minnick's and Cole's responses to the Rasabox exercise, see pp. 361 ff. This exercise is an application of some of the ideas in this essay, a kind of ENS training for artistic use.[7] It is based on the assumption that emotions are socially constructed while feelings are individually experienced.

The Rasabox exercise takes many hours to complete; in fact it is open-ended. It can't be done in one session. It continues from one day to the next. The exercise proceeds as an orderly progression of steps:

1. Draw or tape a grid of nine rectangular boxes on the floor. All rectangles are the same and each ought to be about 6' × 3'.
2. Very roughly "define" each rasa. For example, *raudra* means anger, rage, roaring; *bibhasta* means disgust, spitting up/out, vomiting.
3. In variously colored chalk, write the name of one rasa inside each rectangle. Use chance methods to determine which rasa goes where. Write the names in Roman alphabetized Sanskrit. Leave the center or ninth box empty or clear.
4. Have participants draw and/or describe each rasa inside its box. That is, ask each person to interpret the Sanskrit word, to associate feelings and ideas to it. Emphasize that these "definitions" and associations are not for all time, but just "for now." Emphasize also that drawings, abstract configurations, or words can be used. In moving from one box to another, participants must either "walk the line" at the edge of the boxes or step outside the Rasabox area entirely and walk around to the new box. There is no order of

progression from box to box. A person may return to a box as often as she likes, being careful not to overwrite someone else's contribution. Take as much time as necessary until everyone has drawn her fill. When a participant is finished, she steps to the outside of the Rasabox area. This phase of the exercise is over when everyone is outside the Rasabox area. Sometimes this takes several hours.

5. When everyone is standing at the edge of the Rasabox area, time is allowed for all to "take in" what has been drawn/written. Participants walk around the edge of the Rasaboxes. They read to themselves and out loud what is written. They describe what is drawn. But they can't ask questions; nor can anything be explained.

6 Pause. Silence.

7. Self-selecting, someone enters a box. The person takes/makes a pose of that rasa: for example, the pose of *sringara* or *karuna* . . . or whatever. The person can do as few as a single rasa or as many as all eight named rasas. (Remember the ninth or center box is "clear.") A person can move from box to box either along the edge or on the lines – in which case the movement is "neutral." But if a person steps into a box, he must take/make a rasic pose. This phase continues until everyone has had at least one chance to enter and pose within the Rasaboxes.

8. Same as 7, but now the pose is supplemented by a sound.

In steps 7 and 8, there is no "thinking." Just take/make a pose and/or a sound. Whatever is "there" in association to the rasa. Move rather quickly from one Rasabox to the next. Don't worry how "pretty," "true," or "original" the pose/sound is. Just do it. But once outside the boxes, reflect on how you composed your rasa and what it felt like to

RAUDRA	BIBHASTA	BHAYANAKA
KARUNA	ŚĀNTA (empty)	SRINGARA
HASYA	VIRA	ADBHUTU

Figure 9.2. The Rasabox grid with one rasa written in each box.

be in a composed rasa. In other words, begin the exploration of the distinction between feelings (experience) and emotion (public expression of feelings). Don't worry which came first. It is a chicken-and-egg question with no correct answer.

In fact, the first poses/sounds often have the quality of social clichés – of the "already known" that fit the rasas as casually understood. Big laughs for *hasya*, clenched fists for raudra, weeping for karuna, and so on. The distance between stereotype and archetype is not great. Sooner or later, the social stereotype/archetype will be augmented by gestures and sounds that are more intimate, personal, quirky, unexpected. Practice leads one toward these. The road from outer to inner = the road from inner to outer.

9. Move more rapidly from one box to the next. Quick changes, no time for thinking it out in advance.

Here we are beginning to grapple with Antonin Artaud's call for actors who are "athletes of the emotions." Actual athletic competitions

Figure 9.3 Paula Murray Cole (left) and Michele Minnick exchange an extreme facial gesture during the Rasabox exercise. (Photograph by Richard Schechner)

come to mind. A basketball player sits on the sidelines, quiet, a towel draped over his shoulder. But when called on to enter the game, he explodes with energy, performs at a high level of skill, and is entirely focused on his task. A whistle blows, and the athlete relaxes. The time-out is over, he jumps back into the game. One of the goals of the Rasabox exercise is to prepare actors to move with the same mastery from one emotion to another, in a random or almost random sequence, with no preparation between emotional displays, and with full commitment to each emotion. What happens at the feelings level is left indeterminate – as with the performers in India: some doers of the Rasabox exercise will "feel" it, others will not. See pp. 361–7 for what Cole and Minnick write concerning their experiences with the Rasabox exercise.

10. Two persons enter, each one in his or her own box. At first, they simply make the rasas without paying attention to each other. But then they begin to "dialogue" with each other using the rasas – and shift rapidly from one box to another. So, for example, sringara confronts vira and then vira moves to adbhuta; after a moment sringara rushes along the line to bibhasta and adbhuta jumps to bhayanaka.

At step 10, many new combinations appear. Participants begin to find things that are far from the social clichés. Those on the outside are often amused, sometimes frightened, or moved. "Something" is happening, though it can't be reduced to words. A few people are hesitant about going into the boxes at all. The exercise is both expressive and a scalpel that cuts very deeply into people. Paradoxically, in performing different emotional masks, the participants discover aspects of their beings that had remained hidden – sometimes even from themselves.

11. Participants bring in texts – that is, speeches from known plays or stuff written just for the exercise. Scenes from dramas are enacted by two or even three people. The text remains fixed, but the rasas shift – with no preplanning. So, for example, Romeo is all sringara but Juliet is karuna; then suddenly Juliet springs to bibhasta and Romeo to adbhuta. And so on – the possible combinations are nearly endless. Occasionally, Romeo and Juliet are in the same box.

At this stage, actors test out the many different possibilities of any given text. Or rather, the texts are revealed as not being fundamental, but permeable, open, wildly interpretable.

12. Scenes are enacted with one underlying rasa, on top of which are bits played in different rasas.

Here one begins to see how a whole production could be mapped as a progression of rasas. The progression could be scored or improvised each performance.

There are even more possibilities. The Rasabox exercise is designed to be unfinishable. It is not intended to be a "true example" of an NS-based performance. Indeed, what comes from the Rasabox exercise is not at all like what one sees at any traditional Indian performance. The exercise actually points to the creative possibilities suggested by the underlying theory of the NS. It "comes from" rather than "is an example of" that theory.

THE EMPTY BOX

What about the empty box at the center? Historically, there was no "shanta rasa" until Abhinavagupta added it some centuries after the NS was compiled. In the exercise, as in the historical development of rasa theory, the "ninth Rasabox" is special. What happens there? In the exercise, a person can enter that box – the *śānta* space – only when the person is "clear." What that means is not for the one directing the exercise to say. Each person will have her own criteria for total, whole clarity. In the years that I've directed the Rasabox exercise, "*śānta*" has been occupied very rarely, one or two times. There can be no challenge to such a position. So what if it is "not really so" that the person is "clear"? How can another person tell? And maybe it is so, maybe the participant has surpassed all *samsara*, all the clutter of feelings, the confusion of mixed emotions, the noise of change.

RASAESTHETICS IN PERFORMANCE

Now let me turn from training to performance. Indian theater, dance, and music are not banquets. In odissi, bharatanatyam, kathakali, kathak, and so on, performers dance, gesture, impersonate, and sometimes speak and sing. Occasionally, burning incense thickens the air with odor. But for the most part, the data of the performance is transmitted from performer to partaker in the same way as in the west (and elsewhere): through the eyes and ears. How is this rasic?

Watching traditional Indian genres, one sees the performer looking at her own hands as they form different *hastas* or mudras – precise gestures with very specific meanings. This self-regarding is not narcissism in the western sense. Abhinaya literally means to lead the performance to the spectators – and the first spectator is the performer herself. If the self-who-is-observing is moved by the self-who-is-performing the performance will be a success. This splitting is not exactly a Brechtian *Verfremdungseffekt*, but neither is it altogether different. Brecht wanted to open a space between performer and performance in order to insert a social commentary. The rasic performer opens a liminal space to allow further play – improvisation, variation, and enjoyment.

The performer becomes a partaker herself. When she is moved by her own performance, she is affected not as the character, but as a partaker. Like the other partakers, she can appreciate the dramatic situation, the crisis, the feelings of the character she is performing. She will both express the emotions of that character and be moved by her own feelings about those emotions. Where does she experience these feelings? In the ENS, in the gut – inside the body that is dancing, that is hearing music, that is enacting a dramatic situation. The other partakers – the audience – are doubly affected: by the performance and by the performer's reaction to her own performance. An empathetic feedback takes place. The experience can be remarkable.

In orthodox western theater, the spectators respond sympathetically to the "as if" of characters living out a narrative. In rasic theater, the partakers empathize with the experience of the performers playing. This empathy with the performer rather than with the plot is what permits Indian theater to "wander," to explore detours and hidden pathways, unexpected turns in the performance. Here rasa and *raga* (the classical Indian musical form) are analogous. The partakers' interest is not tied to the story, but to the enacting of the story; the partakers do not want to "see what happens next" but to "experience how the performer performs whatever is happening." There is no narrational imperative insisting on development, climax, recognition, and resolution. Instead, as in kundalini sexual meditation, there is as much deferral as one can bear – a delicious delay of resolution.

I am here expounding a theory of reception – even to the extent that the performer's self-regarding is a reception of her own performance. This needs further elaboration. One treatise on abhinaya instructs the dancer to sing with her throat, express the meaning of that song with her hand gestures, show how she feels with her eyes, and keep time with her feet. And every Indian performer knows the traditional adage: Where the hands go; the eyes follow; where the eyes go, the mind follows; where the mind goes, the emotions follow; and when the emotions are expressed, there will be rasa. Such a logically linked performance of emotions points to the "self." Not the self as personal ego, but the *atman* or profound absolute self, the self that is identical to the universal absolute, the *Brahman*.

Eating in a traditional manner in India means conveying the food directly to the mouth with the right hand. There is no intermediary instrument such as fork or spoon. Sometimes a flat bread is used to mop up or hold the food; sometimes rice is used to sop up a curry. But in all cases, the food on the index and third finger is swept into the mouth by an inward motion of the thumb. Along with the food, the eater tastes his own fingers. The performer regarding her mudras is engaging in a kind of "theater feeding." As with self-feeding, the emotions of a performance are first conveyed to the performer and the partakers by means of the hands.

Orthodox western performing arts remain invested in keeping performers separated from receivers. Stages are elevated; curtains mark a boundary; spectators are fixed in their seats. Mainstream artists, scholars, and critics do not look on synchronicity and synaesthesia with favor. Eating, digestion, and excretion are not thought of as proper sites of aesthetic pleasure. These sites – aside from rock concerts, raves, and sports matches – are more in the domain of performance art. In early performance art there were Carolee Schneemann, Allan Kaprow, Shiraga Kazuo, Hermann Nitsch, Chris Burden, Stelarc, Paul McCarthy, and others. Later came Mike Kelley, Karen Finley, Annie Sprinkle, Ron Athey, and Franko B. – all of whom insisted on making "the body" explicit (see Schneider 1997 and Jones 1998). Their work began to elide differences between the interior and the exterior; to emphasize permeability and porosity; to explore the sexual, the diseased, the excretory, the wet, and the smelly. Performances used blood, semen, spit, shit, urine – as well as food, paint, plastics, and other stuff drawn from the "literal" rather than the "make believe." On the surface, this work is not very Asian, but at an underlying theoretical level, it is extremely rasic.

These kinds of performances need to be studied in terms of rasaesthetics. That means paying attention to the increasing appetite for arts that engage visceral arousal and experience; performances that insist on sharing experiences with partakers and participants; works that try to evoke both terror and celebration. Such performances are often very personal even as they are no longer private.

What I'm asking for goes beyond performance art. Rasaesthetics opens questions regarding how the whole sensorium is, or can be, used in making performances. Smell, taste, and touch are demanding their place at the table.[8] Thus I am making a much larger claim – and sending out a more general invitation. I am inviting an investigation into theatricality as orality, digestion, and excretion rather than, or in addition to, theatricality as something only or mostly for the eyes and ears. I am saying that performance practice has already moved strongly into this place and now is the time for theory to follow.

NOTES

1   At the very start of the text, Bharata claims for the *NS* the status of a *veda* – the most sacred of ancient Indian texts. This is not all that unusual. Such claims to being the "fifth veda" were used to validate and strengthen a text. Of course tradition finally assigned the rank of *sastra* to the *NS*, a position well down the hierarchical ladder of sacred writings. As for the framing origin myth itself, which is told in chapter one – the story of Brahma's composition of the "fifth veda," its transmission to Bharata and his sons, and their performance of the "first natya" on the occasion of the Mahendra's flag festival (the victory

celebration of Indra's triumph over *asuras* and *danavas* [demons]) – much can be made of it. The demons are enraged by the performance of their defeat; they rush the stage and magically freeze "the speeches, movements, and even the memory of the performers" (Bharata-muni 1996: 3). Indra intervenes, thrashing the demons with a flagpole that is then installed as a protective totem. Brahma instructs the gods' architect Visvakarman to construct an impregnable theater, well-guarded by the most powerful gods. This having been done, the gods say it is better to negotiate with the demons than to forcibly exclude them. Brahma agrees, approaches the demons, and inquires why they want to destroy natya. They reply, "You are as much the creator of us as of the gods, So you should not have done it [omitted them from *natya*]" (4). "If that is all there is to it," Brahma says, "then there is no reason for you to feel angry or aggrieved. I have created the *Natyaveda* to show good and bad actions and feelings of both gods and yourselves. It is the representation of the entire three worlds and not only of the gods or of yourselves" (4). Thus natya is of divine origin, all-encompassing, and consisting of actions both good and bad. For an extended and highly sophisticated interpretation of the *NS* framing myth, see Byrski (1974).

2 According to Kapila Vatsyayan (1996: 32–6) and Adya Rangacharya, whose recent English translation of the *NS* is the most readable, the American Fitz Edward Hall unearthed and published several chapters in 1865. In 1874, the German Wilhelm Heymaun (or Haymann, as Vatsyayan spells it) wrote an influential essay that stimulated further translations of several chapters by the French scholar, Paul Reynaud (or Regnaud as Vatsyayan spells it). But it was only in 1926 that the Baroda critical edition was commenced. The whole text – in Sanskrit – was not in print until 1954.

> In spite of all these results, the final text is contradictory, repetitive and incongruent; there are lacunae too, hut, what is worse, there are words and passages that are almost impossible to understand. ... It is not only modern scholars who suffer this inability to understand; even almost a thousand years ago . . . Abhinavagupta . . . displayed this tendency.
>
> (Vatsyayan 1996: xviii)

Vatsyayan (1996: 180 ff.) provides a 'Database of the *Naryasastra*" locating and listing all 112 known extant texts and fragments. All the texts are in Sanskrit but are transcribed in a variety of scripts: Newari, Devanagari, Grantha, Telugu, Malayalam, Tamil, Kanarese. Thus we know that from an early time the *NS* was widely distributed across the subcontinent.

3 "In Presocratic thought the prerational notion of agon is used to describe the natural world as a ceaseless play of forces or Becoming" (Spariosu 1989: 13).

4 According to the first chapter of the *NS* Brahma created the natyaveda:

> to show good and bad actions and feelings of both gods and yourselves [humans]. It is the representation of the entire three worlds [divine, human, demonic] and not only of the gods or of yourselves. Now dharma [correct living], now artha [warring], now kama [loving], humor or fights,

greed or killing. Natya teaches the right way to those who go against dharma, erotic enjoyment to those who seek pleasure, restraint to those who are unruly, moderation to those who are self-disciplined, courage to cowards, energy to the brave, knowledge to the uneducated, wisdom to the learned, enjoyment to the rich, solace to those in grief, money to business-people, a calm mind to the disturbed. Natya is the representation of the ways of the worlds using various emotions and diverse circumstances. It gives you peace, entertainment, and happiness, as well as beneficial advice based on the actions of high, low, and middle people.

(Bharata-muni 1996: chapt. 1; English adapted from
Ghosh and Rangacharya translations)

5   The peripheral nervous system (PNS) consists of the many nerve cells throughout the body connected to the brain via the spinal cord. The PNS receives sensory input which is then transmitted to the brain where it is "interpreted" as various kinds of touch – heat/cold, pain, tickling, etc. Signals sent back from the brain result in bodily movements and so on. The ENS is part of the PNS, but is both structurally and operationally very different than the rest of the PNS. The ENS, for the most part, operates independently of the brain though it is connected to the brain via the vagus nerve.

6   East Coast Artists is a company I formed in New York in the early 1990s. Productions I've directed with ECA are *Faust/gastronome* (1992), *Three Sisters* (1997), *Hamlet* (1999), and *Yokastas* (2003). The Rasabox exercise was developed both during ECA rehearsal workshops and at workshops I ran at NYU in the 1990s. In the late 1990s, I worked very closely with Michele Minnick and Paula Murray Cole in relation to Rasaboxes. Minnick and Cole have led several Rasabox workshops in New York and elsewhere. The exercise is dynamic. It continues to change.

7   The exercise is not based on the theory, exactly; nor does the theory result from the exercise, exactly. Rather, there is a convergence and an interplay between what I am thinking and what I am doing. This interplay is open – that is why both the exercise and the theory are "in development" and not "finished."

8   The work of Constance Classen and David Howes and the group of scholars associated with them is well worth noting. They are developing an anthropology of and an aesthetics of the senses. See *The Varieties of Sensory Experience* (1991) edited by Howes, and Classen's *The Color of Angels* (1998). In April 2000, Classen, Howes, Jim Drobnick, and Jennifer Fisher convened "Uncommon Senses: An International Conference On the Senses in Art and Culture" at Concordia University in Montreal with 180 presenters. For papers adapted from this conference see Auslander (2001), Banes (2001), and Borsato (2001).

Rasaboxes Performer Training

Michele Minnick

Whether one accepts the idea of "rasa" as a literally gustatory experience, or simply understands food-rasa as a metaphor for the process of theater-rasa, the practical question still remains as to how one can achieve this shared experience between actor and spectator in the time-space of performance. What of *abhinaya* (the actual behaviors of a performance), the very concrete art of the actor? What are the "ingredients" at her disposal? How does she know when to add one thing, how much to add, how fast to stir it, how long to let it cook? And how does this idea of rasa as the space *between* serve the western performer? These questions can be partially answered by the Rasaboxes.

Fascinated with the idea of rasa, and challenged by Antonin Artaud's demand that the actor be an "athlete of the emotions," my teacher, colleague, and co-artistic director of East Coast Artists, Richard Schechner, designed the Rasaboxes exercise, in which the performer's emotional/physical/vocal expressivity and agility are trained. As we perform, direct, and teach workshops with East Coast Artists, Paula Murray Cole and I continue to develop this work, using it as a tool not only for training, but for performance composition.[a]

How do the Rasaboxes work? The key to their design is the spatialization of emotions. What makes our use of rasa "western" is that rather than codifying the expression of emotion through particular gestures and facial expressions that are always performed in the same way (as in classical Indian dance), we use space to delineate each rasa, and allow the individual performer to find her own expression of the emotion/s contained within it.

The first step toward movement improvisation involves getting into one box at a time and creating a "statue" or fixed pose for each rasa. We then establish the rule that a participant cannot be in a Rasabox without expressing it dynamically. Participants then move among the rasas, embodying each rasa by means of the pose they have chosen. The idea

(continued)

is to move from one box to another with no "daylight" – no period of transition – between them. This develops an emotional/physical agility the actor can use to transform instantly from expressing rage to love to sadness to disgust, etc. Once participants are comfortable with being statues, we introduce breath and then sound and finally movement and sound together. What starts as a fairly controlled exercise develops into a very free improvisation, involving a wide range of interactions or "scenes" between different people in different boxes.

Since being introduced to the Rasaboxes in 1996, I have been fascinated by their power to free performers (myself included) to experience ranges of physical and emotional expression that might have otherwise seemed unavailable to them. Through this training it is possible to develop an incredible range of expressiveness – from the filmic to the operatic or grotesque – without sacrificing the element of greatest concern to western performers: "sincerity" or "truth." I have found, in fact, that because of its focus on physical embodiment/expression, Rasaboxes training can serve to deepen a performer's ability to find authentic emotional connections.

The Rasaboxes externalize what is often considered an "internal" process, proving that "real" emotion does not have to be kept inside, but is actually a physical as well as a psychological process. In this way, rasa training serves as a bridge for the actor between his psycho-physiology and his expressiveness. Because it acts as a link between the actor's individual, physical body and emotions, and his emotional/physical relationship to the environment and other performers, rasa technique can serve as a multidirectional training ground where old habits and patterns can be brought to light and new ones can emerge. Unlike many other forms of actor training – in which the actor is encouraged to lose himself, to act on impulse, to give way to inspiration – the Rasaboxes encourage the actor to approach his craft as a conscious, body-oriented process to which he holds the keys and the tools for his own development. In drama therapy terms, she is the "observing ego," experiencing the process and observing the process at the same time. In Somatic Fitness terms, she develops "a body that knows itself."[b]

(continued)

When they first experience the Rasaboxes, people often comment on the "therapeutic" aspect of the exercises. Indeed, they are therapeutic; in my experience, many forms of actor training are therapeutic insofar as they promote health and balance, developing the body's energy-giving functions as well as its expressiveness. The Rasaboxes have, in fact, been adapted by some practitioners of drama therapy to provide their clients with a safe space in which to explore emotions. But in the context of performer training, the ultimate point of the exercises is to go beyond, rather than to indulge in, the personal side of emotion. When I am engaged in the work, I do feel the sense of being connected to a deep well – a kind of universal emotional source – which allows emotion to move me, and move through me and beyond me to an audience who can mutually share the experience. It is no longer "my" emotion. A paradox emerges: By going deeply into the intimate details of a particular body, we can go beyond that particular body, past the mundane personal/psychological realm to a transpersonal realm, even a mythic realm.

Ultimately, a performer experienced in Rasabox training can internalize the grid strucutre, and is able to transform from one rasic state to another without the physical map. It is possible for such a performer to change the emotional quality of a moment, a speech, or a scene at any point without necessarily changing her place in space. "Emotion," like space, time, and other elements of staging, becomes simply another tool to be used in the process of exploring and developing performance work. The Rasaboxes can free performers from questions about "motivation," allowing them to think of and use emotion in a more playful adventurous way. Finally, emotion – which is so often blocked, or internalized in western acting – moves into the body, where it can energize the space *between* one performer and another, and between performer and spectator.

The Rasaboxes are not meant to supplant other forms of actor training. Objectives, through-lines, creative improvisations, and other widely used western approaches can still be used to answer the "what" questions of acting, while the Rasaboxes can be used, in combination

(continued)

with them, to answer the "how" questions. Qualitative changes can be made by applying the idea of rasa to a character, a scene, even an entire play. At times it is useful to think of rasa as a kind of tonality, or rhythm of performance, which can be modulated as the pitch/key or the tempo/rhythm of a piece of music can be modulated.

One of the things I have discovered in working with the Rasaboxes is that, contrary to the training we have inherited from Stanislavsky, emotion, when fully played out through the body, can become action. Also, I have learned from this process that onstage, as in life, emotion is not necessarily psycho-"logical" in the simplistic sense that we often associate with realistic acting. In working on a scene or a monologue in the Rasaboxes, one discovers that often the least "logical" emotion is the one that makes the scene the most interesting. Sometimes, one discovers new layers of emotion; a scene played with laughter on the surface may have rage lurking beneath. The rasas can also serve as a kind of emotional baseline for character. A Blanche Dubois played with *karuna* (grief and compassion) as her baseline would be very different than a Blanche played with *raudra* (rage) or *bhayanaka* (fear) as the baseline. She would have a different breath, a different voice, a different body, and these details of her characterization would affect the tone of the entire character interpretation.

Now we are beginning to explore new material in the Rasaboxes. Composer/choreographer and East Coast Artists associate Liz Claire is working with music for a piece we are making about Russian poet Maria Tsvetaeva. The rich sounds and rhythms of Claire's violin sounding bhayanaka or karuna expand my work as a performer in those emotional spaces – pushing my body and voice into new territory, and multiplying the textural layers of the piece. Here, rasa becomes a terrain for dialogue between actor and musician, blurring the boundaries of our roles and the techniques available to us.

In my work as a movement analyst, I have also begun to explore the application of Laban ideas about movement to performers' work in the Rasaboxes. This detailed physical work can refine the body's work of emotional expression, challenging the performer to find Light, Quick

(continued)

rage, for example, or Bound, Strong fear. With its categories of Body, Space, Shape, Effort, and Relationship, Laban Movement Analysis provides the tools to take the performer beyond her "patterns," expanding the field of expressive possibility. The possibilities are endless. As Bharata says in the *Natyasastra*: "It is impossible [. . .] to know all about natya since there is no limit to bhava-s (emotions) and no end to the arts involved [in natya]. It is not possible to have a thorough knowledge of even one of them, leave alone so many of them" (Bharata-muni 1996: 53). It is with this spirit that I enter, and ask others to enter and re-enter the Rasaboxes, always knowing there are new worlds to be discovered there.

NOTES

a Rebecca Ortese worked with me for six months on developing the Rasaboxes as a rehearsal tool during the 1999 Mabou Mines Resident Artist Program.
b This idea was introduced to me by Martha Eddy, a Body–Mind Centering practitioner and teacher. *Somatic* refers to *soma*, or cell, which, according to this way of thinking, contains its own wisdom. This approach to the body's wisdom or knowledge is a wonderful way to approach the Rasaboxes, where the different parts of our bodies are in constant dialogue with one another as we search for ways to physically contain and express emotion.

Experience Rasaboxes

Paula Murray Cole

I'd like to describe what it feels like to experience the rasas as we explore them in the Rasaboxes exercise and apply them in our rehearsals and performances. First, however, let me help you to understand what a rasa experience feels like by relating something that recently happened to me.

Not long ago, I spent a week and a half studying the therapeutic uses of essential oils. As part of an introductory exercise, our class was asked to experience and respond to the smell and effects of various oils; to notice what parts of our bodies were most affected by each oil; what memories, images, or associations were evoked; and to guess each oil's therapeutic uses. During the exercise, I observed the expressions on the faces and bodies of my classmates as they related to each oil. I noticed that their responses were immediate and extremely physical. Robert took a whiff of German chamomile, a heavy dark blue oil, and was instantly, violently repulsed. His body jolted and jumped backward, his face contorted with disgust. "Auggghhhkk," he exhaled as he spat. He quickly replaced the cap on the bottle and put it far from his body. Steve uncapped the rosemary and his body and face widened, his spine lengthened, his breathing became large and even. "Wow," he said, and he reported that he felt stimulated, powerful, energized. We took turns smelling the substances. After about five minutes, the oils' essences were not only contained inside each bottle, but had diffused throughout the room, transfusing into our bodies and affecting our psychophysiology.

So it is with rasa. Rasa means "essence," and that essence has the power to move us, to transform and shape our responses. It comes from outside our bodies, is smelled, tasted, ingested. Its particular properties change us, transform our chemistry and shape our psychophysical expressive behavior.

In 1999, I played Ofelia in the East Coast Artists' production of

(continued)

Hamlet, directed by Richard Schechner at the Performing Garage in New York. I often used the rasa *karuna* (grief/anguish/compassion). Here's a description from my rehearsal notes about what it felt like to experience karuna:

I breathe in karuna, taste it, smell it. [. . .] My body folds on the first long exhale as my knees sink to the ground, my belly tightens and rounds my spine/my throat tightens/my breath heaves/my head bows [. . .]. One hand reaches up to cover my eyes while the other supports the rest of my weight as it drops further into the floor. I breathe in the karuna that is all around me. I sink into the feeling, my eyes well up with tears. I want to surrender my breath to the openness and expand- ing relief that sounding this pain would bring. [. . .] I tighten and fight against that feeling of vulnerability and exposure. The sound squeezes out anyway, a high keening noise. I breathe again and my mind rifles through the baggage of remembered and created associations I have with this feeling: A muscle memory? An emotional imprint? I can see the image of myself here on the floor. Then I see myself set out on the ice floe. [. . .] Then mourning the death of my father.

Now I am playing a bit of Ofelia's "mad scene":

The tears stream, I seek relief by crouching closer to the floor, squeezing my guts trying to support an insupportable sorrow. [. . .] The experience is as if it were happening to me, karuna is moving me according to its demands. I am not taking myself on an intellectual journey through my own personal psychology, to remember a time when I felt a similar feeling, though those memories may surface while I am working. I am simply and completely connecting with the rasa, working in relation- ship to the rasa, from the outside until it is the inside and back again.

REFERENCES

Aldena, Guillerno E. (1971) "Mesa del Nayar's Strange Holy Week," *National Geographic* 139 (6): 780–94.

American Anthropologist (1966) Issue on *The Ethnography of Communication*, 66 (6), part 2.

American Federation of Arts (1962) *The Ideal Theatre: Eight Concepts*, New York: American Federation of Arts.

And, Metin (1976) *A Pictorial History of Turkish Dancing*, Ankara: Dost Yayinlari.

—— (1979) *Karagoz: Turkish Shadow Theatre*, Ankara: Dost Yayinlari.

—— (1987) *Near Eastern Rituals and Performances*, New York: Performing Arts Journal Press.

Arieti, Silvano (1948) "Special Logic of Schizophrenic and Other Types of Autistic Thought," *Psychiatry* 11 (November): 325–38.

Aristotle (1961) *Aristotle's Poetics*, trans. S. H. Butcher, ed. Francis Fergusson, New York: Hill & Wang.

Arnott, Peter (1959) *The Theaters of Japan*, New York: St Martin's Press.

Aronson, Arnold (1981) *The History and Theory of Environmental Scenography*, Ann Arbor: UMI Research Press.

Arrowsmith, William (1959) "The Criticism of Greek Tragedy," *TDR, The Drama Review* 3 (3): 1–57.

Artaud, Antonin (1958) *The Theatre and Its Double*, trans. Mary Caroline Richards, New York: Grove Press.

Auslander, Philip (2001) "Looking at Records." *TDR* 45 (1) (T169): 77–83.

Avorn, Jerry L. (1968) *Up Against the Ivy Wall*, New York: Atheneum.

Awasthi, Suresh (1974) "The Scenography of the Traditional Theater of India," *TDR, The Drama Review* 18 (4): 36–46.

Bablet, Denis (1970) *Svoboda*, Paris: La Cité.

Bandem, I. Made and de Boer, Frederik Eugene (1981) *Kaja and Kelod: Balinese Dance in Transition*, Kuala Lumpur: Oxford University Press.

Banes, Sally (2001) "Olfactory Performances." *TDR* 45 (1) (T169): 68–76.

Barba, Eugenio (1965) "Theatre Laboratory 13 Rzedow," *TDR, The Drama Review* 9 (3): 153–71.

(1979) *The Floating Islands*, Holstebro, Denmark: Thomsens Bogtyrkkeri.

(1986) *Beyond the Floating Islands*, New York: Performing Arts Journal Press.

Barbeau, Marius (1958) *Medicine-Men of the North Pacific Coast*, Ottawa: National Museum of Canada, Bulletin 152.

Bateson, Gregory (1958) *Naven*, Palo Alto: Stanford University Press.

(1972) *Steps to an Ecology of Mind*, New York: Ballantine Books.

Bateson, Gregory and Mead, Margaret (1942) *Balinese Character: A Photographic Analysis*, New York: Special Publication of the New York Academy of Sciences, vol. 2.

Becker, George J. (ed.) (1963) *Documents of Modern Literary Realism*, Princeton: Princeton University Press.

Beckett, Samuel (1954) *Waiting for Godot*, New York: Grove Press.

Belo, Jane (1960) *Trance in Bali*, New York: Columbia University Press.

Berndt, Ronald M. (1962) *Excess and Restraint*, Chicago: University of Chicago Press.

Berndt, Ronald M. and Berndt, Catherine (1964) *The World of the First Australians*, Chicago: University of Chicago Press.

Berne, Eric (1962) *Transactional Analysis in Psychotherapy*, New York: Grove Press.

(1964) *Games People Play*, New York: Grove Press.

Bettelheim, Bruno (1962) *Symbolic Wounds: Puberty Rites and the Envious Male*, New York: Collier Books.

(1967) *The Empty Fortress*, New York: The Free Press.

Bharata-muni (1961) *The Natyasastra*, ed. and trans. Manomohan Ghosh, Calcutta: Asiatic Society, vol. 2, chs 28–36.

(1967) *The Natyasastra*, rev., ed., and trans. Manomohan Ghosh, Calcutta: Manisha-Granthalaya, vol. 1, chs 1–27.

(1996) *The Natyasastra*. ed. and trans. Adya Rangacharya, New Delhi: Munshiram Manoharlal Publishers Pvt. Ltd.

Birdwhistell, Ray L. (1952) *Introduction to Kinesics*, Louisville: University of Louisville Press.

(1964a) "Body Behavior and Communicaiton," *International Encyclopedia of the Social Sciences*, New York: The Free Press.

(1964b) "Communication Without Words," MS supplied by the Eastern Pennsylvania Psychiatric Institute, Philadelphia.

(1970) *Kinesics and Context*, Philadelphia: University of Pennsylvania Press.

Blakeslee, Sandra (1996) "Complex and Hidden Brain in the Gut Makes Cramps, Butterflies, and Valium," *New York Times*, January 23: C1–3.

Blumenthal, Eileen (1976) "Andrei Serban Makes Dead Languages Live Again," *Village Voice*, 26 Jan.: 107–8.

Boal, Augusto (1979) *Theatre of the Oppressed*, New York: Urizen Books.

Boas, Franz (1966) *The Mind of Primitive Man*, New York: The Free Press.

Bohannan, Paul (1963) *Social Anthropology*, New York: Holt, Rinehart, & Winston.

(1967) "Drumming the Scandal among the Tiv," in Paul Bohannan (ed.) *Law and Warfare*, Garden City: Natural History Press.

Bongartz, Roy (1970) "It's Called Earth Art – and Boulderdash," *New York Times Magazine*, February 1.

Borsato, Diane (2001) "Sleeping with Cake: And Other Affairs of the Heart," *TDR* 45 (1) (T169): 59–67.

Brecht, Bertolt (1964) *Brecht on Theatre*, New York: Hill & Wang.

Brecht, Stefan (1978) *The Theatre of Visions: Robert Wilson*, Frankfurt am Main: Suhrkamp Verlag.

Brook, Peter (1973) "On Africa," *TDR, The Drama Review* 17 (3): 37–51.

Brustein, Robert (1974) "News Theater," *New York Times Magazine*, June 16: 7 ff.

Burgess, Lowry (1986) "Program Note for *The Quiet Axis*," Chester Springs: Yellow Springs Institute.

(Undated) Poster for *Quiet Axis*.

Burke, Kenneth (1961) *The Philosophy of Literary Form*, New York: Vintage Books.

(1962) *A Grammar of Motives* and *A Rhetoric of Motives*, Cleveland: World Publishing Co.

Burns, Elizabeth (1972) *Theatricality*, New York: Harper & Row.

Burzynski, Tadeusz and Osinski, Zbigniew (1979) *Grotowski's Laboratory*, Warsaw: Interpress.

Byrski, Christopher (1973) *Concept of Ancient Indian Theatre*, New Delhi: Munshiram Manoharlal Publishers Pvt. Ltd.

Cage, John (1965) "An Interview with John Cage," *TDR, The Drama Review* 10 (2): 50–72.

Caillois, Roger (1961) *Man, Play, and Games*, New York: The free Press.

Campbell, Joseph (1956) *The Hero with a Thousand Faces*, New York: Meridian Books.

(1959–68) *The Masks of God*, New York: Viking Press, 4 vols.

Carlson, Marvin (1984) *Theories of the Theatre*, Ithaca: Cornell University Press.

Carpenter, C. R. (1964) *Naturalistic Behavior of Nonhuman Primates*, University Park: Pennsylvania State University Press.

Cassirer, Ernst (1946) *Language and Myth*, New York: Dover.

Castaneda, Carlos (1968) *The Teachings of Don Juan: A Yaqui Way of Knowledge*, New York: Ballantine Books.

(1971) *A Separate Reality*, New York: Simon & Schuster.

(1972) *Journey to Ixtlan*, New York: Simon & Schuster.

Chapple, E. D. (1970) *Culture and Biological Man*, New York: Holt, Rinehart & Winston.

Clark, La Verne Harrell (1966) *They Sang for Horses*, Tucson: University of Arizona Press.

Classen, Constance (1998) *The Color of Angels*, London: Routledge.

Cooper, David (1970) *The Death of the Family*, New York: Pantheon Books.

Cornford, Francis (1914) *The Origin of Attic Comedy*, London: Edward Arnold.

d'Aquili, Eugene G., Laughlin, Charles D., and McManus, John (1979) *The Spectrum of Ritual*, New York: Columbia University Press.

Darwin, Charles (1872) *The Expression of the Emotions in Man and Animals*, repr. 1965, Chicago: University of Chicago Press.

Deàk, Frantisek (1974) "Robert Wilson," *TDR, The Drama Review* 18 (2): 67–73.

Devore, I. (ed.) (1965) *Primate Behavior*, New York: Holt, Rinehart & Winston.

Diamond, Stanley (ed.) (1964) *Primitive Views of the World*, New York: Columbia University Press.

Dioszegi, Vilmos (1968) *Tracing Shamans in Siberia*, New York: Humanities Press.

Dodds, E. R. (1951) *The Greeks and the Irrational*, Berkeley: University of California Press.

Edwards, Christine (1965) *The Stanislavsky Heritage*, New York: New York University Press.

Ehrenzweig, Anton (1970) *The Hidden Order of Art*, St Albans: Paladin.

Eibl-Eibesfeldt, Irenaus (1970) *Ethology: The Biology of Behavior*, New York: Holt, Rinehart & Winston.

(1979) "Ritual and Ritualization from a Biological Perspective," in M. von Cranach, K. Foppa, W. Lepenies and D. Ploog (eds) *Human Ethology*, Cambridge: Cambridge University Press.

Ekman, Paul (1972) "Universal and Cultural Differences in Facial Expressions of Emotion," in *Nebraska Symposium on Motivation, 1971*, Omaha: University of Nebraska Press.

(1980) *The Face of Man*, New York: Garland STPM Press.

(1983) "Autonomic Nervous System Activity Distinguishes among Emotions," *Science* 221 (September 16): 1208–10.

(1985) *Telling Lies*, New York: W. W. Norton.

Ekman, Paul, Friesen, Wallace V., and Ellsworth, Phoebe (1972) *Emotion in the Human Face*, New York: Pergamon Press.

Elam, Keir (1980) *The Semiotics of Theatre and Drama*, London: Methuen.

Eliade, Mircea (1965) *Rites and Symbols of Initiation*, New York: Harper & Row.

(1970) *Shamanism: Archaic Techniques of Ecstasy*, Princeton: Princeton University Press.

Eliot, T. S. (1951) *Selected Essays*, London: Faber & Faber.

Elkin, A. P., Berndt, Catherine, and Berndt, Ronald (1950) *Art in Arnhem Land*, Chicago: University of Chicago Press.

Erikson, Eric H. (1959) *Identity and the Life Cycle*, Psychological Issues Monograph 1, New York: International Universities Press.

Euripides (1958) *Orestes*, trans. William Arrowsmith, in *Euripides IV*, Chicago: University of Chicago Press.

Evans-Pritchard, E. E. (1937) *Witchcraft, Oracles and Magic among the Azande*, London: Oxford University Press.

Fagan, J. and Shepherd, I. L. (1970) *Gestalt Therapy Now*, New York: Harper & Row.

Farb, Peter (1969) *Man's Rise to Civilization*, New York: Avon Books.

Feldenkrais, M. (1972) *Awareness Through Movement*, New York: Harper & Row.

Fergusson, Francis (1949) *The Idea of a Theater*, Princeton: Princeton University Press.

Firth, Raymond (1967) *Tikopia Ritual and Belief*, London: George Allen & Unwin.

Fischer, Roland (1971) "A Cartography of the Ecstatic and Meditative States," *Science* 174 (November 26): 897–904.

Fison, L. (1885) "The Nanga, or Sacred Stone Enclosure of Wainimala, Fiji," *Journal of the Royal Anthropological Institute* xiv.

Forti, Simone (1974) *Handbook in Motion*, New York: New York University Press.

Frankfort, Henri (1948) *Kingship and the Gods*, Chicago: University of Chicago Press.

Freud, Sigmund (1958) *On Creativity and the Unconscious*, New York: Harper & Row.

(1961) *The Interpretation of Dreams*, New York: John Wiley.

(1962a) *Totem and Taboo*, New York: W. W. Norton.

(1962b) *Civilization and Its Discontents*, New York: W. W. Norton.

(1963) *Jokes and Their Relation to the Unconscious*, New York: W. W. Norton.

Gardner, R. and Heider, K. G. (1968) *Gardens of War*, New York: Random House.

Garner, R. L. (1896) *Gorillas and Chimpanzees*. London: Osgood, McIlvaine & Co.

Gaster, Theodore H. (1961) *Thespis*, Garden City: Doubleday Anchor.

Geertz, Clifford (1973) *The Interpretation of Cultures*, New York: Basic Books.

(1980a) "Blurred Genres," *American Scholar* 49 (2): 165–82.

(1980b) *Negara: The Theatre State in Nineteenth Century Bali*, Princeton: Princeton University Press.

(1983) *Local Knowledge*, New York: Basic Books.

Gershon, Michael D. (1999) *The Second Brain*, New York: Harper Perennial.

(2000) Personal email correspondence. December.

Gershon, Michael and Erde, S. M. (1981) "The Nervous System of the Gut," *Gastroenterology* 80: 1571.

Gershon, Michael D., Chalazonitis, Alcmene, and Rothman, Taube P. (1993) "The Neural Crest to Bowel: Development of the Enteric Nervous System," *Journal of Neurobiology* 24 (2): 199–214.

Gibson, Michael (1973) "Brook's Africa: An Interview by Michael Gibson," *TDR, The Drama Review* 17 (3): 37–51.

Giddings, Ruth W. (1959) *Yaqui Myths and Legends*, Tucson: University of Arizona Press.

Giedion, S. (1962–4) *The Eternal Present*, New York: The Bollingen Foundation, 2 vols.

Girard, Rene (1977) *Violence and the Sacred*, Baltimore: The Johns Hopkins University Press.

Goffman, Erving (1959) *The Presesentation of Self in Everyday Life*, Garden City: Doubleday Anchor.

(1961) *Encounters*, Indianapolis: Bobbs-Merrill.

(1963a) *Stigma*, Englewood Cliffs: Prentice-Hall.

(1963b) *Behavior in Public Places*, Glencoe: The Free Press.

(1967) *Interaction Ritual*, Garden City: Doubleday Anchor.

(1969) *Strategic Interaction*, Philadelphia: University of Pennsylvania Press.

(1971) *Relations in Public*, New York: Basic Books.

(1974) *Frame Analysis*, New York: Harper & Row.

Goodall, Jane van Lawick (1972) *In the Shadow of Man*, New York: Dell.

Gordon, T. (1970) *Parent Effectiveness: Training Active Listening*, New York: Wyden.

Gould, Richard A. (1969) *Yiwara: Foragers of the Australian Desert*, New York: Scribner's.

Grotowski, Jerzy (1967) "Towards the Poor Theatre," *TDR, The Drama Review* 11 (3): 60–5.

(1968a) *Towards a Poor Theatre*, Holstebro, Denmark: Odin Teatrets Forlag.

(1968b) "An Interview with Grotowski," *TDR, The Drama Review* 13 (1): 29–45.

Haley, J. and Hoffman, L. (1967) *The Techniques of Family Therapy*, New York: Basic Books.

Hall, Edward T. (1969) *The Hidden Dimension*, Garden City: Doubleday Anchor.

(1970) *The Silent Language*, Greenwich: Fawcett.

Halprin, Anna (1965) "Yvonne Rainer Interviews Ann Halprin," *TDR, The Drama Review* 10 (2): 142–67.

(1968) "Mutual Creation," *TDR, The Drama Review* 13(1): 163–75.

Halprin, Lawrence (1969) *The RSVP Cycles: Creative Process in the Human Environment*, New York: George Braziller.

Halprin, Lawrence and Burns, Jim (1974) *Taking Part*, Cambridge, Mass.: MIT Press.

Hammel, E. and Simmons, S. (eds) (1957) *Man Makes Sense*, Boston: Little, Brown.

Hanna, Judith Lynne (1983) *The Performer–Audience Connection*, Austin: University of Texas Press.

Harbinger, Richard (1971) "Trial by Drama," *Judicature* 55 (3): 122–8.

Hardison, O. B. (Jr) (1965) *Christian Rite and Christian Drama in the Middle Ages*, Baltimore: The Johns Hopkins University Press.

Harrison, Jane Ellen (1912) *Themis: A Study of the Social Origins of Greek Religion*, Cambridge: Cambridge University Press.

(1913) *Ancient Art and Ritual*, New York: Henry Holt.

Hart, C. W. M. and Pilling, Arnold R. (1966) *The Tiwi of North Australia*, New York: Holt, Rinehart & Winston.

Hass, Hans (1972) *The Human Animal*, New York: Delta.

Hebdige, Dick (1979) *Subculture: The Meaning of Style*, London: Methuen.

Hed [Robert Head] (1966) "Kill Viet Cong," *TDR, The Drama Review* 10 (4): 153.

Henney, Jeannette H. (1974) "Spirit-Possession Belief and Trance Behavior in Two Fundamental Groups in St. Vincent," in Felicitas D. Goodman, Jeannette H. Henney, and Esther Pressel (eds) *Trance, Healing, and Hallucination*, New York: John Wiley, 1–111.

Herskovits, Melville J. (1950) *Man and His Works*, New York: Alfred A. Knopf.

Hochschild, Arlie Russel (1983) *The Managed Heart*, Berkeley: University of California Press.

Hoebel, E. Adamson (1967) "Song Duels Among the Eskimo," in Paul Bohannan (ed.) *Law and Warfare*, Garden City: Natural History Press.

Hoffman, Abbie (1969) *Woodstock Nation*, New York: Vintage Books.

Howes, David, ed. (1991) *The Varieties of Sensory Experience*, Toronto: University of Toronto Press.

Huizinga, J. (1955) *Homo Ludens*, New York: Beacon Press.

Hunningher, Benjamin (1961) *The Origin of the Theater*, New York: Hill & Wang.

Ionesco, Eugene (1958) *Four Plays*, New York: Grove Press.

(1966) *The Bald Soprano*, New York: Grove Press.

Jekels, Ludwig (1965) "On the Psychology of Comedy," in Robert W. Corrigan (ed.) *Comedy: Meaning and Form*, San Francisco: Chandler.

Jones, Amelia (1998) *Body Art: Performing the Subject*, Minneapolis: University of Minnesota Press.

Kafka, Franz (1954) *Wedding Preparations in the Country*, London: Secker & Warburg.

Kahn, Barry (1982) "One Year at a Time: Sam Hsieh's Annual Acts," *Live* 6/7 (1982): 40–2.

Kapferer, Bruce (1983) *A Celebration of Demons*, Bloomington: Indiana University Press.

Kaplan, Donald M. (1968) "Theatre Architecture: A Derivation of the Primal Cavity," *TDR, The Drama Review* 12 (3): 105–16.

(1969) "On Stage Fright," *TDR, The Drama Review* 14 (1): 60–83.

(1971) "Gestures, Sensibilities, Scripts," *Performance* 1 (1): 31–46.

Kaprow, Allan (1965) "Calling," *TDR, The Drama Review* 10 (2): 202–11.

(1966a) *Great Bear Pamphlet 7*, New York: Something Else Press.

(1966b) *Assemblages, Environments, and Happenings*, New York: Abrams.

(1968a) "Self-Service," *TDR, The Drama Review* 12 (3): 160–4.

(1968b) "Extensions in Time and Space," interview with Richard Schechner, *TDR, The Drama Review* 12 (3): 153–9.

(1983) "The Real Experiment," *Artforum* 22 (4) (December): 36–43.

Keisler, Frederick (1932) "——[?[," *Shelter Magazine*, May.

Kirby, E. T. (1972) "The Mask: Abstract Theatre Primitive and Modern," *TDR, The Drama Review* 16 (3): 5–21.

(1975) *Ur-Drama*, New York: New York University Press.

Kirby, Michael (1965a) "The New Theatre," *TDR, The Drama Review* 10 (2): 23–43.

(1965b) *Happenings*, New York: E. P. Dutton.

(1969) *The Art of Time*, New York: E. P. Dutton.

(1972) "On Acting and Not-Acting," *TDR, The Drama Review* 16 (1): 3–15.

(1973) "Richard Foreman's Ontological-Hysteric Theatre," *TDR, The Drama Review* 17 (2): 5–32.

Kirshenblatt-Gimblett, Barbara and McNamara, Brooks (eds) (1985) Special issue of *TDR, The Drama Review* on "Processional Performance," 29 (3).

Koestler, Arthur (1961) "Some Aspects of the Creative Process," in Seymour M. Farber and Roger H. L. Wilson (eds) *Control of the Mind*, New York: McGraw-Hill, 188–208.

Kolankiewicz, Leszek (ed.) (1978) *On the Road to Active Culture*, Wroclaw: Theater Laboratory.

Kolata, Gina (1986) "Anthropologists Suggest Cannibalism is a Myth," *Science* 232 (June 20): 1497–500.

Komparu, Kunio (1983) *The Noh Theater*, New York: Weatherhill; Tokyo, Kyoto: Tankosha.

Konner, Melvin (1982) *The Tangled Wing*, New York: Holt, Rinehart & Winston.

Kris, Ernst (1964) *Psychoanalytic Explorations in Art*, New York: Schocken Books.

Kumiega, Jennifer (1985) *The Theatre of Grotowski*, London: Methuen.

La Barre, Weston (1954) *The Human Animal*, Chicago: University of Chicago Press.

(1972) *The Ghost Dance*, New York: Dell.

Labov, William (1972) "Rules for Ritual Insults," in David Sudnow (ed.) *Studies in Social Interaction*, New York: The Free Press.

Laing, R. D. (1960) *The Divided Self*, Chicago: Quadrangle Books.

(1962) *The Self and Others*, New York: Pantheon.

(1969) *The Politics of the Family*, New York: Pantheon.

Laing, R. E. and Esterson, A. (1964) *Sanity, Madness, and the Family*, New York: Basic Books.

Langer, Susanne (1953) *Feeling and Form*, New York: Scribner's.

Langton, Basil (1973) "Journey to Ka Mountain," *TDR, The Drama Review* 17 (2): 48–57.

Lannoy, Richard (1971) *The Speaking Tree*, London: Oxford University Press.

Law, Alma (1979) "The Theater on Chekhov Street," *TDR, The Drama Review* 23 (4): 27–30.

Layton, Robert (1986) *Uluru, An Aboriginal History of Ayers Rock*, Canberra: Autralian Institute of Aboriginal Studies.

Lea, Henry Charles (1967) "The Wager Battle," in Paul Bohannan (ed.) *Law and Warfare*, Garden City: Natural History Press.

Leach, Edmund (ed.) (1967) *The Structural Study of Myth and Totemism*, London: Tavistock.

Leslie, Charles (ed.) (1960) *Anthropology of Folk Religion*, New York: Vintage.

Lessing, Doris (1981) *Shikasta*, New York: Vintage.

Lévi-Strauss, Claude (1963) *Structural Anthropology*, New York: Basic Books.

(1966) *The Savage Mind*, Chicago: University of Chicago Press.

(1969a) *The Elementary Structures of Kinship*, Boston: Beacon Press.

(1969b) *The Raw and the Cooked*, New York: Harper & Row.

(1972) *From Honey to Ashes*, New York: Harper & Row.

Lewin, Tamar (1984) "Ex-Stewardesses vs United," *New York Times*, February 21: D1, D15.

Lewis, I. M. (1971) *Ecstatic Religion*, London: Penguin.

Lex, Barbara (1979) "The Neurobiology of Ritual Trance," in Eugene G. d'Aquili, Charles D. Laughlin, and John McManus, *The Spectrum of Ritual*, New York: Columbia University Press.

Linden, Eugene (1976) *Apes, Men, and Language*, New York: Penguin.

Loizos, Caroline (1969) "Play Behaviour in Higher Primates: A Review," in Desmond Morris (ed.) *Primate Ethology*, Garden City: Anchor Books.

Lommel, Andreas (1967) *Shamanism: The Beginnings of Art*, New York: McGraw-Hill.

Lorenz, Konrad (1959) "The Role of Aggression in Group Formation," in

B. Schaffner (ed.) *Transactions of the Conference on Group Processes of 1957*, New York: The Josiah Macy Jr Foundation.

(1961) *King Solomon's Ring*, New York: T. Y. Crowell.

(1965) *Evolution and Modification of Behavior*, Chicago: University of Chicago Press.

(1967) *On Aggression*, New York: Bantam Books.

Lowen, A. (1967) *The Betrayal of the Body*, New York: Macmillan.

Lowie, R. H. (1936) *The Crow Indians*, New York: Holt Rinehart.

(1948) *Primitive Religion*, New York: Liveright.

McCoy, Philip (1965) "King Lear and Game Theory," unpublished MS.

McNamara, Brooks, Rojo, Jerry, and Schechner, Richard (1975) *Theaters, Spaces, Environments: Eighteen Projects*, New York: Drama Books Specialists.

Malina, Judith and Beck, Julian (1969) "An Interview with the Becks: Containment is the Enemy," *TDR, The Drama Review* 13 (3): 24–44.

Marcus, George E. and Fischer, Michael M. J. (1986) *Anthropology as Cultural Critique*, Chicago: University of Chicago Press.

Marinis, Marco de (1987) "Dramaturgy of the Spectator, An Unlikely Association," *TDR, The Drama Review* 31 (2): 100–14.

Marshack, Alexander (1972) *The Roots of Civilization*, New York: McGraw-Hill.

Mauss, Marcel (1925) "Essai sur le don: Forme et raison de l'échange dans les sociétés archaïques," *Annales sociologiques* 1: 30–186.

Mead, Margaret (1970) "Presenting: The Very Recent Past," *New York Times Sunday Magazine*, March 15: 29–32.

Montano, Linda (1981) *Art in Everyday Life*, Los Angeles: Astro Artz.

Murray, Gilbert (1912a) *The Four Stages of Greek Religion*, Oxford: Oxford University Press.

(1912b) "Excursus on the Ritual Forms Preserved in Greek Tragedy," in Jane Ellen Harrison, *Themis: A Study of the Social Origins of Greek Religion*, Cambridge: Cambridge University Press.

(1925) *The Five Stages of Greek Religion*, Oxford: Oxford University Press.

(1961) "Foreword," to *Thespis* by Theodor H. Gaster, Garden City: Doubleday Anchor.

Nearman, Mark J. (1982) "Kakyo Zeami's Fundamental Principles of Acting," *Monumenta Nipponica* 37 (3): 333–74.

Nicoll, Allardyce (1963) *Masks, Mimes, and Miracles*, New York: Cooper Square.

Osinski, Zbigniew (1986) *Grotowski and His Laboratory*, New York: PAJ Publications.

Partridge, Eric (1966) *Origins: A Short Etymological Dictionary of Modern English*, London: Routledge and Kegan Paul.

Pavis, Patrice (1982) *Languages of the Stage*, New York: Performing Arts Journal Publications.

Performance Group, The (1970) *Dionysus in 69*, ed. R. Schechner, New York: Farrar, Straus & Giroux.

Pfeiffer, John E. (1982) *The Creative Explosion*, New York: Harper & Row.

Piaget, Jean (1962) *Play, Dreams, and Imitation in Childhood*, New York: W. W. Norton.

Pickard-Cambridge, A. W. (1962) *Dithyramb, Tragedy, and Comedy*, 2nd edn, revised by T. B. L. Webster, Oxford: Oxford University Press.

Plato (1945) *The Republic of Plato*, trans. Francis MacDonald Cornford, New York: Oxford University Press.

Rainer, Yvonne (1974) *Work 1961–73*, New York: New York University Press.

Rappaport, Roy A. (1968) *Pigs for the Ancestors*, New Haven: Yale University Press.

Read, Kenneth E. (1965) *The High Valley*, New York: Scribner's.

Reiss, Alvin H. (1968) "Who Builds Theatres and Why," *TDR, The Drama Review* 12 (3): 75–92.

Reynolds, Vernon and Reynolds, Frances (1965) "Chimpanzees of the Budongo Forest," in Irven deVore (ed.) *Primate Behavior: Field Studies of Monkeys and Apes*, New York: Holt, Rinehart & Winston, 368–424.

Roheim, Geza (1969) *The Eternal Ones of the Dream*, New York: International Universities Press.

Rosenberg, Harold (1965) *The Tradition of the New*, New York: McGraw-Hill.

Rothenberg, Jerome (1968) *Technicians of the Sacred*, Garden City: Doubleday. Revised edition (1985), Berkeley: University of California Press.

Rothenberg, Jerome and Rothenberg, Diane (1983) *Symposium of the Whole*, Berkeley: University of California Press.

Ruesch, Jurgen and Bateson, Gregory (1951) *Communication*, New York: W. W. Norton.

Schaller, George B. (1963) *The Mountain Gorilla*, Chicago: University of Chicago Press.

Schechner, Richard (1967) "Public Events for the Radical Theatre," *The Village Voice*, September 7.

(1969) *Public Domain*, Indianapolis: Bobbs-Merrill.

(1973) *Environmental Theater*, New York: Hawthorn.

(1982) *The End of Humanism*, New York: Performing Arts Journal Press.

(1985) *Between Theater and Anthropology*, Philadelphia: University of Pennsylvania Press.

(1986a) "Victor Turner's Last Adventure," preface to Victor Turner, *The Anthropology of Performance*, New York: Performing Arts Journal Press.

(1986b) "Wrestling Against Time: The Performance Aspects of *Agni*," *Journal of Asian Studies* 45 (2): 359–64.

(1987a) "A 'Vedic Ritual' in Quotation Marks," *Journal of Asian Studies* 46 (2): 108–10.

(1987b) "The Future of Ritual," *Journal of Ritual Studies* 1 (1): 5–34.

Scheflen, Albert E. (1973) *How Behavior Means*, New York: Gordon & Breach.

Schlemmer, Oskar, Moholy-Nagy, Laszlo, and Molnar, F. (1961) *The Theatre of the Bauhaus*, Middletown: Wesleyan University Press.

Schneider, Rebecca (1997) *The Explicit Body in Performance*, London: Routledge.

Shipley, Joseph T. (1984) *Origins of English Words: A Discursive Dictionary of Indo-European Roots*, Baltimore: Johns Hopkins University Press.

Shirokogoroff, S. M. (1935) *Psychomental Complex of the Tungus*, London: Kegan, Paul, Trench, Trubner.

Shubik, Martin (ed.) (1964) *Game Theory and Related Approaches to Social Behavior*, New York: John Wiley.

Smith, A. C. H. (1972) *Orghast at Persepolis*, New York: Viking.

Smith, Michael (1967) "Theatre Journal: 'Victims of Duty,' " *The Village Voice*, May 11: 24, 28.

Sokal, Robert R. (1974) "Classification: Purpose, Principles, Progress, Prospects," *Science*, September 27: 1115–23.

Somma, Robert (1969) "Rock Theatricality," *TDR, The Drama Review* 14 (1): 128–38.

Spariosu, Mihai (1989) *Dionysus Reborn*, Ithaca, NY: Cornell University Press.

Spencer, B. and Gillen, F. J. (1968) *The Native Tribes of Central Australia*, New York: Dover.

Staal, Frits (1987) "Professor Schechner's Passion for Goats," *Journal of Asian Studies* 45 (2): 105–8.

Stebbins, Genevieve (1902) *Delsarte System of Expression*, repr. 1977, New York: Dance Horizons.

Svoboda, Josef (1966) "Lanterna Magika," *TDR, The Drama Review* 11 (1): 141–9.

TDR, The Drama Review (1964) Special issues on "Stanislavsky in America," 9 (1) and (2).

(1972) Section on "The New Dance," 16(3): 115–50.

(1975) Section on "Postmodern Dance," 19(1): 3–52.

(1985) Special issue on "Processional Performance," ed. Brooks McNamara and Barbara Kirshenblatt-Gimblett, 29(3).

Tinbergen, N. (1965) *Social Behaviour in Animals*, London: Scientific Book Club.

Trilling, Ossia (1973) "Robert Wilson's 'Ka Mountain,'" *TDR, The Drama Review* 17 (2): 33–47.

Turnbull, Colin (1962) *The Forest People*, Garden City: Doubleday.

(1985) "Processional Ritual Among the Mbuti Pygmies," *TDR, The Drama Review* 29 (3): 6–17.

(1990) "Liminality: A Synthesis of Subjective and Objective Experience," in Richard Schechner and Willa Appel (eds), *By Means of Performance*, Cambridge: Cambridge University Press.

Turner, Frederick (1985) *Natural Classicism*, New York: Paragon House.

Turner, Victor (1969) *The Ritual Process*, Chicago: Aldine.

(1974) *Dramas, Fields, and Metaphors*, Ithaca: Cornell University Press.

(1982) *From Ritual to Theater*, New York: Performing Arts Journal Press.

(1983) "Body, Brain, and Culture," *Zygon* 18(3): 221–45.

(1985) *On the Edge of the Bush*, Tucson: University of Arizona Press.

(1986) *The Anthropology of Performance*, New York: Performing Arts Journal Press.

Turner, Victor W. and Bruner, Edward M. (eds) (1986) *The Anthropology of Experience*, Urbana: University of Illinois Press.

Ucko, Peter J. and Rosenfeld, Andrée (1967) *Paleolithic Cave Art*, New York: McGraw-Hill.

Van Gennep, Arnold (1908) *The Rites of Passage*, repr. 1960, Chicago: University of Chicago Press.

Vatsyayan, Kapila (1996) *Bharata: The Natyasastra*, New Delhi: Sahitya Akademi.

Ward, R. Gerard and Lea, David A. M. (eds) (1970) *An Atlas of Papua and New Guinea*, Glasgow: Collins, Longman.

Williams, F. E. (1940) *The Drama of the Orokolo*, Oxford University Press.

Winnicott, D. W. (1971) *Playing and Reality*, London: Tavistock.

Zarrilli, Phillip (1984) *The Kathakali Complex*, New Delhi: Abhinav Publications.

(1986) "The Aftermath: When Peter Brook Came to India," *TDR, The Drama Review* 30(1): 92–100.

(1990) "What Does It Mean to 'Become the Character': Power, Presence, and Transcendence in Asian In-Body Disciplines of Practice," in Richard Schechner and Willa Appel, (eds) *By Means of Performance*, Cambridge: Cambridge University Press, 131–48.

Index

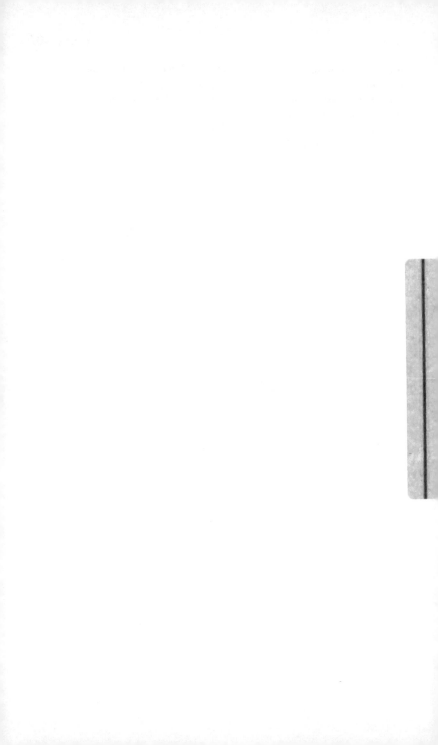